The Fatal Friendship

The Fatal Friendship

Marie Antoinette,
Count Fersen
& the Flight to Varennes

Stanley Loomis

DAVIS–POYNTER

First published in Great Britain by Davis-Poynter Limited
Broadwick House Broadwick Street London WIV 2AII

Copyright © 1972 by Stanley Loomis

ISBN 0 7067 0047 3

Printed in Great Britain by Compton Printing Ltd

For

JOAN LINDSLEY MOSER
RUDOLPH MOSER

who were killed at Aarsele near Ghent, Belgium
on October 2, 1971
In ever loving memory.

"And all is well tho' faith and form
Be sunder'd in the night of fear."

Contents

Illustrations following pages 102 *and* 230

The Fatal Friendship

PART I

Versailles

In the winter of 1774 Paris was at the meridian of the brilliance that made it known throughout Europe as the City of Light. Circumstances had momentarily combined to give the French capital a distinction of tone unique to its time and place. The Seven Years' War that had bankrupted the treasury was over and forgotten. The intimations of approaching disaster that were to cast their shadow over the subsequent decade were not yet apparent. It was a city and a society that lived off its capital like an imperious woman of great beauty, great breeding, and impeccable taste but of reduced income. Three, perhaps four generations separated France from the source of its wealth when Louis XIV brought his court out of the confinement of the feudal world into the open vistas of Versailles. At a time when the rest of Europe was trying to emerge from the Middle Ages and scrape up enough money to build imitations of Versailles, France was indulging a profligate second generation. The pompous rigidity of the Baroque was cast aside for the delicious line of the Rococo. And by 1774 the Rococo too had been sent to the attic to be replaced by the neo-Classic style.

In Paris style was everything. Its influence reached beyond clothes or decoration. Conversation and manner of thought were as markedly Parisian as the furniture of the celebrated cabinetmakers of the day. There was a lightness, a skepticism, an interplay of irony and audacity that made the conversation of the famous *salons* as difficult a manuever as juggling with greased balls. The hard, precise chatter heard at the *salons* of Madame du Deffand or Geoffrin was considered the principal attraction of Paris and by many it was believed to be an art of its own.

Like certain wines that are best tasted on their native soil it was a product that did not travel. The petty autocrats of Europe's hinterlands would in any case have been reluctant to import the heady sedition of the *philosophes* into their rural principalities. So by the middle of the eighteenth century it had become the custom of the European nobility to send their eldest sons or heirs to Paris where it was hoped they might learn to converse in the French tongue and acquire a polish that would distinguish them from the hoydens of their homeland. They would usually stay in the city for some months and because they were young men of consequence they were generally sponsored by an ambassador or some relative who had *entrée* to those places where they could partake of the capital's celebrated pleasures.

Among their number in Paris during that winter of 1774 was a young Swedish nobleman named Hans-Axel von Fersen. Accompanied by the inevitable tutor, he had been sent abroad at the age of fifteen, some four years earlier, to do the Grand Tour of Europe. Like so many of his kind he had been marked by his father to be an officer and courtier in the service of his king and country; he had applied himself to military studies in Prussia, to history and the arts in Italy. Sessions of instruction with his tutor would occupy his mornings. Sightseeing and society would occupy his afternoons; pleasure and society his evenings. He had visited Brunswick, Lausanne, and Geneva (where he had paid the traditional call on Voltaire, who must have begun to have his fill of traveling noblemen). From Switzerland he had gone to Italy where, at the court of Turin, he had been received by the King of Sardinia, and at Modena by the regnant Prince. He had visited Florence, Rome, and Naples and in each he had paused to view the sights that are still on the list of today's conscientious tourist: in Naples, Vesuvius; at Pompeii, the excavations; in Florence, the works of art; and, in Rome, St. Peter's. And in each of these cities his credentials as the son of a Senator and Field Marshal of Sweden had put him in touch with the local prince and his circle of grandees.

Fersen was eighteen when in November of 1773 he finally reached the city with whose fortunes his life was destined to be fatally interbound. He was already endowed with a physical beauty that was to earn him the sobriquet *"le beau Fersen"* when he returned to his homeland. His dark and brooding appearance communicated a type of masculinity generally unfamiliar to the French. "He was formed to be the hero of a novel," observed a Parisian writer, "but not of a French novel." All who in later years were to recall Axel Fersen were to comment on his unusual reserve. For some people this reticence betrayed a personality that was without *esprit* and consequently not interesting; for others it bespoke "prudence" and "discretion" and was admirable.

4

He took lodgings at the Hôtel d'York on the rue de Colombier (now rue Jacob) and presented himself to the Swedish Ambassador, Count Creutz, whose responsibility it was to introduce such favored fellow countrymen to the French royal family and the principals of the Parisian scene. As Creutz reported to the King of Sweden a few months later, he found Fersen to be an unusually attractive young man. "No one could have been more correct or distinguished in his bearing. With his good looks and his charm he could not help but be a great success in society here."

Immediately after his arrival in Paris, Creutz took him to Versailles where he was presented to the aging Louis XV, to the dauphin and the dauphine, and even, indeed, to Madame du Barry. He seems to have made a favorable impression on the Minister of Foreign Affairs, the duc d'Aiguillon, who a few years earlier had brought down the all-powerful ministry of the duc de Choiseul. The duc d'Aiguillon at that moment was the most important man at court and the center of violent storms and furious intrigues. Through Aiguillon, Fersen was given *entrée* to some of the private receptions at Versailles. Among those were the dauphine's Monday evening balls. Marie Antoinette, then eighteen years old, had established the custom of receiving guests at a dance which was held in her apartments every Monday of the winter until Lent. Sponsored by Creutz and the duc d'Aiguillon, Fersen soon gained admittance to these receptions and, as events were shortly to indicate, he was noticed by the dauphine among the crowd of ambassadors, courtiers, and princes who flocked there to pay court to her.

Fersen kept a journal that survives today. This record is of considerable interest not only because it reveals some of the hidden mechanism of his character, but because it throws an unexpected flash of light onto the day-to-day life that was led by the pleasure-seeking visitors to the French capital. As his diary reveals, Axel Fersen had a methodical and meticulous mind. His entries are brief, bare statements of fact. He wastes no time on descriptive embroidery but notes all dates and hours with precision. One would be left with the impression of a dry and rather sterile intelligence were these entries not sometimes punctuated by a kind of sigh or suppressed lament that betrays a hidden strain of melancholia. "I was not destined to be happy like other men," he writes in one such characteristic passage. "Life will always deny me both luck and happiness." This tendency to gloom was to increase with the passing of time when he became caught in events that seemed to substantiate his forebodings.

He was at heart a *solitaire,* one of those individuals whose nature does not permit him to confide his inner thoughts or feelings to others. For him serious matters were always to be taken seriously and he never acquired that tone of persiflage and flippancy that characterized Parisian conversation. But this was a deficiency that in no way compromised his reception in the world to which the Swedish Ambassador introduced him. His Journal makes record of all his social outings during that winter of 1774. His days were filled with a round of dinners, card parties, supper parties, visits, and all the other distractions of the day. One need only cast a glance at his daily notations, hastily scribbled down, to pick up the tempo of life in eighteenth-century Paris.

On November 27, for instance, only a few days after his arrival, he notes that he went to Versailles at eleven o'clock; he had dinner ("dinner" in those days meant lunch, while "supper," usually held at a late hour of the evening, meant what today is generally called "dinner") with the comte de Cort, was presented to the marquise de Durfort, then went to the Opéra, afterward went to a reception given by the comte de Noailles, then went on to another given by the duc d'Aiguillon, and finally at a late hour returned to Paris. A few days later he dined with the Swedish Ambassador, paid a call with him on Madame du Deffand, then on to a reception given by Madame de Beauvau and afterwards went on to a gambling party given by the Sardinian Ambassadress.

In between the dinner parties at Versailles and the gambling and supper parties of Paris there were visits to the Opéra and the theater and the pleasure ground of Vauxhall. One of the famous amusements of Paris were its Opéra balls. They were held every Saturday at the Opéra and they were open to anyone who could afford the admission. Because many guests, especially the women, wore masks at these dances it was possible without compromise or embarrassment to meet members of the opposite sex whom one might not meet in the ordinary course of life and to indulge in some innocent and sometimes not so innocent flirtation. The ever-present possibility of "adventure" lent an air of expectancy to the Opéra balls.

Accompanied by his tutor and a friend, Fersen went to one of them in the early part of January and there he had one of these little adventures that he records in his diary. His description communicates perfectly the tone of the Opéra balls:

6

"I supped with Baron Ahlfeldt, a Dane who is *attaché* at the Embassy, then at midnight went to the Opéra ball with Bolemany. I met a very pretty *masque* who said to me in a low voice that she was sorry I wasn't her husband so that she could sleep with me. I told her that that shouldn't stop her. I tried to persuade her but she ran away. Another woman that Plomenfeldt was chasing wasn't so difficult. She sat down in a hallway and we had a long conversation with her. She wore only a light veil over her face which made it easier to kiss her as much as we liked and she seemed to do it very well. We thought she was a singer from the Comédie Italienne who sings very prettily, Mademoiselle Biliou, but she insisted that she wasn't. However I believe that she was and I continue to believe it. She was still very pretty when we left the ball at three o'clock."

Two weeks later, on January 30, he went again to the Opéra ball and again he met with an adventure. Life's most momentous happenings are sometimes introduced by events that at the time of their happening appear to be without significance. Fersen could not have imagined that his little adventure of this night was the prelude to a larger adventure which was to change the course of his life.

When he arrived at the ball toward one in the morning he noticed that there was a more than usually large crowd of people present. The respectable older folk kept to their boxes where, as was their habit, they watched the scene with an intensity of interest they rarely accorded any performer on the stage. On this particular night the halls were so thronged as to be impassable. An undercurrent of excitement could be sensed in the crowd. Fersen had been there perhaps half an hour when a heavily masked young woman approached him and engaged him in conversation. In his Journal he states simply that "she talked to me for a long time." One is left to surmise that this may have been for five or ten minutes. At a discreet distance three or four other masks hovered about the unknown woman, but Fersen continued his conversation with her without any suspicion of her identity. All at once he noticed that a great crowd had closed in about them in various attitudes of deference, excitement, and curiosity. Suddenly his masked acquaintance seemed to take alarm and withdrew toward a box. Before departing, however, she lowered her mask. It was then he discovered that his chance acquaintance of the evening was Marie Antoinette.

The days of Louis XIV when men's fortunes rose or fell according to the inclination of the sovereign's head were long past in the France of 1774. All the same the young Swedish visitor to Paris had been accorded an attention that must have made him the object of interested scrutiny and discussion by the public assembled at the Opéra that evening. It was not in Fersen's nature to confide his passing emotions to his diary, but one may believe that when he left the ball at three that morning (this detail, characteristically, he does record) he was in a state of some exhilaration. His response to the dauphine's interest is reflected elsewhere in his Journal for he states that henceforth he attended her Monday afternoon receptions until Lent. "For me," he wrote, "the Carnival season passed very quietly for I was unable to go to most of the private balls which were given in people's houses but went instead to all the receptions given by Madame la Dauphine." He records no further notice by the dauphine at any of these.

With Lent the festivities at Versailles came to their end. In Paris they continued discreetly behind the closed doors of the great palaces on the rue de Grenelle and the rue de l'Université where five or six couples would gather to laugh and dance until dawn. At one of these dances Fersen met with a more serious adventure than any he speaks of at the Opéra. According to reports sent back to Sweden by his father's friends in the French capital he was extended something more than the hospitality of her house by a certain marquise de Blacas and this distraction appears to have occupied his attention until he finally left Paris on May 12.

There are no entries in his Journal during the whole of April and there are only a few sketchy fragments about the amusements of May. He notes that on the second of that month he visited Madame Geoffrin, dined with the composer Grétry, and visited the marquise de "B". On the third he left for Crosnes where the marquise de "B" had one of those country properties near Paris that were then much in vogue. He stayed at Crosnes for a week and then returned to Paris to pack his luggage and make his farewells. Just before his departure there occurred an event of some historical interest which he carefully noted in his diary, but without comment: "The King, Louis XV, died today, May 10, at ten in the evening."

His acquaintance of the Opéra ball had become Queen of France.

Few figures in history have been more persistently misunderstood than Marie Antoinette. In the course of the nineteenth century her name became affixed to one of those ready stereotypes that are easily comprehended by children, and are convenient for people who are disposed to draw quick and satisfying moral conclusions out of events. No number of words, no amount of facts are likely now to detach the two. She is condemned to dance forever down a flower-strewn path over the necks of a starved and groaning populace, condemned forever to make the remark she never made, "Why don't they eat cake?"

The most revealing insight into both her behavior and her fate is to be found in the disparity between the position occupied by Marie Antoinette, the Queen of France, and the temperament of Marie Antoinette, the woman. This division between the public personage and the private person, always significant in the lives of those who play a role in history, was, in the instance of Marie Antoinette, fatal. At the very beginning of her life, as at the very end, her individuality was at critical variance with the position into which she was born.

She was not five years of age when this Austrian Archduchess was marked by her mother and her mother's chancellor, Count Kaunitz, to be the flesh and blood surety of a treaty that was detested everywhere, but most especially in France. This treaty, the Franco-Austrian Alliance of 1755, had been signed the year of Marie Antoinette's birth. In the diplomatic history of Europe it is correctly considered to be one of the most important events of the eighteenth century for it upset, violently and decisively, the age-old balance of power in Europe. The Seven Years' War was its direct outcome, and that debacle led to the loss of French power in the New World, the consequent alliance of France with the American Republic, and the ruin of French pre-eminence in the council chambers of Europe.

For centuries Austria and France, the dominant powers of Europe, had been enemies. Their emnity was founded on natural causes for, in the disposal of territorial power on the European continent, the aggrandizement of one necessarily meant the diminishment of the other. The cornerstone of Louis XIV's foreign policy, as it had been the cornerstone of Richelieu's, was the reduction of Austria. But behind these natural causes of "reasons of state" (to introduce the expression of the time that was used by statesmen to justify everything, and on which Marie Antoinette was to be sacrificed) there lay an instinctive antipathy between the Gallic and the Teutonic temperaments that corresponded to the incompatibility of cats and dogs. The courts at Schönbrunn and Versailles reflected these differences.

At Schönbrunn, Maria Theresa ruled a court that was almost Spartan in its simplicity. She kept etiquette and parade subservient to palace economies and "reasons of state." This far-from-benevolent despot did not suffer spoiled or intriguing courtiers. Immorality in the streets of Vienna was dealt with as summarily as at court. Although it was a dull and dowdy court, the Empress was a sovereign of immense distinction.

The French, who had once been ruled by Louis XIV, were well aware of Maria Theresa's imposing dignity and resented it. They took comfort in the impressive appurtenances of majesty that surrounded their monarch at Versailles. This attitude was not confined to the nobility of the French court. It was encountered by visiting foreigners everywhere among the humbler people of Paris who, with a mixture of polite curiosity and patronizing disdain, would ask them if their ruler lived in as magnificent surroundings as the King of France. It was an attitude that particularly irritated visiting Englishmen. It was to be borne by Marie Antoinette from the moment of her arrival at Versailles.

The French court, extravagant, licentious, glittering with the ceremonial of some Byzantine exarch, was in every way the opposite of its Viennese rival. But Louis XV, whatever his merits, was not a sovereign worthy of the crown he had inherited. Overcome by inertia and self-indulgence, he had long since removed himself from any enthusiastic participation in the ritual of which he was the purpose and justification. The celebrants of the rite continued to go through all the steps and genuflections prescribed by tradition, but they worshipped before an empty altar. By the year 1755, the year of Marie Antoinette's birth, the King had relinquished the reins of effective power to his mistress and her favorites. The tone of that profligate, stylish society was set by Madame de Pompadour.

Madame de Pompadour had been dead ten years when Marie Antoinette arrived as a bride in France, but it was the marquise who laid the cornerstone on which the Archduchess' fate was to be constructed. Without Madame de Pompadour there would have been no Marie Antoinette in French history, for Madame de Pompadour was, in effect, the author of the Franco-Austrian Alliance.

The marquise was a woman of taste, intelligence, and charm

who was born to be exactly what she became, the mistress of an absolute ruler, a clever woman in charge of all the costly entertainments needed to keep a capricious lover from growing bored. She was not formed to be a statesman for she was quite incapable of the farsighted and dispassionate view of affairs that is demanded of statesmen. What she saw she saw very clearly, but her range of vision was short. Like most women and many men she permitted her feelings to affect her judgment. She advocated the alliance with Austria because she saw in that *rapprochement* a means of avenging herself on Frederick the Great. The Prussian King had made a mockery of her modest origins and of her equivocal position at the French court; he named the bitches of his kennel after her and all Europe had laughed at her humiliation.

She suffocated from a rage to which there seemed no possibility of relief. Then in the summer of 1755 the Austrian Ambassador approached her with the Empress' greetings and a proposal that France and Austria forget their ancient rivalry and join together against the Prussian ogre. It was a masterful move on the part of Maria Theresa to make her initial overtures to the mistress. But while Madame de Pompadour's hatred of Frederick was founded on little more than female spite, Maria Theresa's was founded on very concrete causes. Frederick had already seized Silesia from Austria and it was learned in Vienna that he was preparing to seize more Habsburg land. Austria thus had much to gain by having France as an ally in the approaching conflict. France, on the other hand, stood to gain little no matter what the outcome of Austria's war with Prussia. Such realistic considerations, however, were not in Madame de Pompadour's style. Overjoyed by the opportunity of doing Frederick an ill turn and intoxicated by the prospect of herself working side by side with Maria Theresa the mistress of the French King drew France into an alliance that was ruinous. At the end of the Seven Years' War, when the extent of the disaster became apparent, the name of Pompadour was execrated everywhere and the treaty with Austria abhorred.

It is at times a weakness in the French character to blame other countries for the calamities that periodically strike France. In the middle of the Reign of Terror Robespierre was repeatedly to warn his countrymen against "foreigners creeping around in disguise amongst us." The nationality of these enemies will vary according to historical circumstance. From the middle until the end of the eighteenth century they were Austrian. It is not possible to understand

Marie Antoinette's situation in France without an appreciation of this fact. She arrived at a court where she was already hated by a large and powerful faction led by the duc d'Aiguillon. Yet by another faction, that of the duc de Choiseul who was the heir to Madame de Pompadour's authority, she was welcomed as a potential ally in the bitter fratricidal war that raged between these two opposing parties. Enmeshed even before her arrival in France in intrigues of the most venomous description, the future Queen of France was totally unprepared to deal with the perils that surrounded her.

Neither by temperament nor by training was it given Marie Antoinette, the individual, to comprehend the subtle, malignant nature of warfare as it was waged at the French court. It is noted by all who have ever written about her that she arrived in France without the rudiments of a proper education and that observation is correct. It was not, however, expected of the marriageable princesses of that day that they be able to compose verse in the Latin tongue or cap the wit of a Madame du Deffand. It was not because she was illiterate that this famous deficiency in her education was dangerous; it was rather because she was undrilled in the disciplines of work and in coherent thinking, which are the first fruits of a supervised education. And the Archduchess Marie Antoinette had exactly that nature which most urgently stands in need of such training. She had inherited none of her mother's plodding, thorough, duty-ridden character. Her father, Francis of Lorraine, died when she was six. From him she inherited—as did all Maria Theresa's children—the dominant strain in her character: a happy but fickle disposition reminiscent of the sparkling white wines of Francis' country. These qualities, given the suitable circumstances—just as that wine given the suitable meal—may be charming, but they do not lend themselves to positions of responsibility and power or to circumstances of crisis and danger.

As one examines the records of her youth and reads the few surviving descriptions of Marie Antoinette, the child, one is suddenly struck by an unexpected recognition. Down to every apparent detail she is unmistakably the familiar, too high-spirited, slightly tomboyish girl who has been the affectionate despair of untold generations of parents. Right down to the love of dogs and donkeys and the bad marks at school the figure we glimpse romping through her mother's Tyrolean garden at Schönbrunn is the perfect prototype of all her kind. It may be significant that the child princes and princesses of

Versailles, powdered, corseted, and posed in their embroidered robes of state, leave us with no such sense of community.

In the immemorial tradition her teachers declared that she could get much better grades if she only tried, that she was intelligent but not working. "She is more intelligent than is generally supposed," her French tutor the abbé de Vermond, reported to Paris. "Unfortunately up to the age of twelve she was not trained to concentrate in any way. A little laziness and a great deal of frivolity make it still more difficult for me to teach her . . . her judgement is always sound, but I cannot get her to go to the bottom of a subject on her own initiative, although I know her to be capable of doing so. I now realize that she will only learn so long as she is amused." Then the tutor went on to add in a phrase all too familiar to modern parents: "She wouldn't make these mistakes if only she would make herself pay attention to what she is doing."

These faults of character that might have made her a charming sovereign in some small Italian or German state were in France to contribute directly to her destruction. As dauphine and then Queen of the wealthiest and most powerful monarchy in Europe she was permitted without restraint to indulge her propensity to laziness and frivolity in precisely those circumstances where she should have been most circumspect. For it was in appearance only that she was above the law. In effective fact she was more answerable to the regulations of her environment than the meanest subject of the land. Because she was imprudent with all the reckless imprudence of headstrong youth and without appreciation of hidden danger, she did not recognize this. Lured down the path of pleasure by the passing whims and caprices of an undisciplined, childish nature she was soon to find herself lost in a land where ambush lay on every side. Neither Maria Theresa nor French observers in Vienna seem to have been unduly anxious about the Archduchess' flighty or "frivolous" personality for it was supposed that maturity and the birth of children would soon stabilize her.

A natural deportment that in its time was conceded to be without equal in Europe further distracted people's attention from the girl's deficiency of education. Although Marie Antoinette could not finish a consecutive sentence in her lesson book, she took to her instruction in dancing and deportment like a duck to water. There was an inborn sense of rhythm and a love of music in her Austrian nature. She rapidly and readily became the mistress of those movements of the feet, the hands, and the body that constituted what was then called "carriage." From the moment of her first instruction up to the moment she mounted the steps of the scaffold she was incomparably royal. Even the hypercritical French conceded her this superiority. All who in afteryears were to remember her as they had known her at Versailles were to make note of the extraordinary beauty and distinction of her walk.

"She had two ways of walking," recalled her page, the comte de Tilly. "One was firm, a little hurried and always noble. The other was indolent, half-swaying, one might say caressing . . ." This gliding, swift, half-undulating step was unique to Marie Antoinette. In the words of the artist Vigée-Lebrun, "It stamped her as Sovereign in the midst of all her court."

It is interesting to have the testimony of so many courtiers corroborated by one who was a stranger to the high life of Versailles. One of the more obscure deputies to the Estates-General in 1789 who had never before seen the Queen made particular note of her famous "walk." "Her way of walking is peculiar to her. One cannot distinguish her steps; she glides with an incomparable grace. She holds her head much more proudly when she thinks that she is alone as she did the day when we watched her."

She was not beautiful. Even at so young an age as fourteen the pendulous lower lip that characterized the House of Austria (as the mighty nose characterized that of France) marred the regularity of her features. In time this defect was to become more pronounced and during the Revolution whenever a caricaturist wished to give an unfavorable picture of her he had only to take her likeness in profile. The hanging lower lip could readily be interpreted as an expression of scorn or contempt while the high carriage of the head appeared as haughtiness. In his famous "sketch" of Marie Antoinette on her way to her execution the artist David seized on the lip with devastating effect. Rarely have the imperfections of a woman's face been turned with more cruel purpose against her.

But regularity of feature does not always constitute attraction in a woman's person and Marie Antoinette, despite the lower lip and despite a tendency to heaviness in later years, appears to have been an attractive woman in the full meaning of the word. Sénac de Meilhan, whose observations are accurate and dependable, says of her that "she had more sparkle than beauty. There was nothing remarkable about her features taken singly but in their *ensemble* there was the greatest attraction. The word "charming" is the exact word to describe the final effect of this *ensemble.* Her movements were of an extraordinary grace and nobility, calling to mind the words of Vergil, *"incessu partuit Dea."* The author of this description goes on to touch upon another deficiency of character that was to provoke criticism at Versailles and for which posterity, too, has reproached her. She lacked *esprit,* the rapid, nimble footsteps of the intellect so greatly admired by the French from which comes wit or at least the appearance of it. "Her *esprit* was without brilliance and she had no pretentions on this score. But she had another quality that seemed to come to her intuitively. Somehow she always knew the exact phrase that should be used in every circumstance. These always came from her heart rather than her mind."

With a complexion of extraordinary transparency (a feature that was highly prized in those days—it was said admiringly of Charlotte Corday that you could follow the course of a glass of wine down her throat so delicate was her skin) with her porcelain-blue eyes through which every expression passed without dissimulation, with her golden hair and above all with the fresh and wholesome vitality of her youth, she was, in the words of the French Ambassador to Vienna, "a delicious little morsel." In an age when most European princesses were pock-marked, hunchbacked, or had spines bent in the form of a U or an S, the Empress had good reason to be satisfied with the "morsel" she was sending off to the nuptial couch of France.

The marriage bed was of course central to all the Empress' calculations. It was there that the Alliance would really be promulgated and from that coupling would come the bond in flesh that would tie Habsburg indissolubly to Bourbon. A few months before Marie Antoinette's marriage, in February of 1770, the court doctors informed Maria Theresa that her daughter had become a woman. The Empress had Marie Antoinette's bed set up beside her own and here in the Imperial Bedroom and in homely terms she instructed the bride-to-be in all the obligations of a wife.

Maria Theresa was an ample-bodied woman of big and open appetite. Rutting with the fulsome rut of good, German livestock she had been brought to bed of sixteen children. The refinements of sexuality, the sadistic interplay of cold *esprit* with hot lust that lent to French union its interesting, feline character were foreign to her nature and experience. She communicated to her daughter the rudiments of earthy natural fact. In the end all her instruction returned to two points. First, a woman must submit to her husband's needs and second, children must be the fruit of all marriage. On the day of Marie Antoinette's departure for France her mother sent her a note of farewell which contained the summation of this advice. "A woman," she wrote, "must be submissive in everything her husband desires and she should have no other preoccupation than to please him. The only true happiness in this world is a happy marriage. If I may say so, all depends on the woman, who must be gentle and obliging . . ." The words would have had old Louis XV and his circle of raddled *débauchés* rolling on the floor with laughter.

Maria Theresa was either monumentally ignorant or incredibly naïve. Perhaps she was a bit of both and so deliberately closed her eyes to certain rumors about the dauphin that reached her from Paris. Her Ambassador to France, Mercy d'Argenteau, with his customary discretion hinted at what others more openly surmised. "Nature," he reported, "seems to have withheld all her favors from the dauphin."

The Empress probably attributed these whispers to Prussian malice and discounted them as lies. For she knew that Frederick's embassy in Paris had been ordered to use slander and invent gossip as a means of discrediting the approaching union. "It goes without saying," concluded one such directive, "that you must be extremely cautious with your insinuations and drop them skillfully so that no one will suspect from where they come."

But Maria Theresa was a ruler who never had difficulty reconciling her conscience as a woman with her obligations as an empress. She had too long coveted the French crown for her daughter and had worked too hard to win that prize to relinquish it for the sake of any vague maternal scruples. *Alii bella gerunt; tu felix Austria nube*: "Other nations war; you, happy Austria, marry." The Habsburg motto once again served.

And so, on April 21, 1770, Marie Antoinette was sent to France, one more in the long, historic procession of princesses of her House who had been sent abroad to give heirs of the Habsburg blood to Europe. She was fourteen and a half years of age.

Among the elements that combined to form the inauspicious design of Marie Antoinette's life the character of the French royal family, as it was in 1770, must be considered one of the most important. With the exception of Louis XV's, her destiny was to be fatally interbound with theirs. They were all to play a part in the disaster for which she was marked. And they were all there to greet her at the edge of the forest of Compiègne when on May 14 she made her official arrival in France and was presented to the King.

Behind a façade that commanded the envy and adulation of Europe the Bourbons, like France itself, were in a dilapidated state. So splendid was the front of the edifice, so brilliantly polished its surface, that the rot which silently ate at the foundations was visible only to a few keen-sighted observers. But behind the gilded railings that protected them from the common gaze, behind the ritual that was designed to keep them at arm's length from the great lords and ladies of their court, the House of Bourbon was a house divided against itself, rent by spite, jealousy, ambition, and all the passions of ordinary humankind.

At the head of his family was Louis XV, who in the last portrait of him painted by Drouais gazes at posterity with the weary, sarcastic eye of a man who has seen all things. He had four more years to live and in many ways they were to be the happiest of his life. In the year preceding Marie Antoinette's arrival at Versailles he had formed the last of his many illicit attachments and openly received Madame du Barry at his court as official mistress. She was a woman of amiable disposition who brought to Louis' private life a tranquillity he had never known before. But her appointment had unleashed storms of a violence that in any other place but Versailles would pass belief. Among the grandees of the French court every small private event, every personal grievance, had its political extension. The gravest matters of state, matters of critical international import, were so closely connected with the mean and petty passions of that gossip-ridden, venomous society that they were inseparable. The advent of Madame du Barry had, inevitably, consequences of immense significance to the court, to France, and to Europe and these in their turn were to be consequences of significance to the fourteen-year-old bride who arrived among her new relatives on that mild May day of 1770.

Reduced to its simplest structure—for these intrigues had almost endless ramifications and interlocking considerations—the new mistress was being used by a faction headed by the duc d'Aiguillon—Fersen's future friend—to destroy the King's all-powerful, high-handed minister the duc de Choiseul who was the heir, so to speak, of the vanished Pompadour. Choiseul, a man of bold resource, a born gambler, and ruthless opponent in intrigue, was prepared to use any weapon in the struggle to hold his position. Among these weapons was Marie Antoinette. If the Pompadour had been the author of the Austrian Alliance the duc de Choiseul with a prescience and a clear-sighted appreciation of his own interests that in no way conflicted with his reputation as the Great Statesman of Europe, had advocated, supported, and advanced the marriage between the heir-apparent to the French throne and the Austrian Archduchess. Whatever his reasons as statesman for the marriage, his reasons as a political opportunist were evident. The young dauphin hated him. (This enmity was a legacy from the dauphin's father: at Versailles these animosities were bequeathed like heirlooms. The ghosts of dead intriguers were active everywhere.) And Choiseul with characteristic boldness returned the dauphin's sentiment, sneering openly at the future King's awkward manner and ungainly carriage. He knew well that after the old King's death his enemies would fall on him unless he had protection in high places. It was with this eventuality in mind that he had arranged the dauphin's marriage with the Archduchess. A pliable princess indebted to him for her grand marriage, a young wife who had gained ascendancy over a weak husband would be a high card in his game. He had always used women with skill and he planned to use Marie Antoinette much as he had used Madame de Pompadour: as a shield in his incessant battle to retain power.

On the morning of the bride's arrival at Compiègne his stock had risen a bit for he had been accorded the honor of escorting the dauphine's carriage into the presence of the King. He flaunted this little triumph before his adversaries with a great deal of show. But the Aiguillon party were soon to trump him with a brilliant little success of their own. That evening the King gave a great reception in honor of the dauphine. Conspicuous among the members of the royal family and great lords of France who were present at this affair was the comtesse du Barry. Her public presence on so unsuitable an occasion evoked a gasp of astonishment and left no further doubt in anyone's mind about her hold over their sovereign.

The sixty-year-old King surveyed these skirmishes with tired eyes that momentarily lighted when he examined the "delicious little morsel." In his later years he had developed a discriminating palate for young flesh and he studied the budding charms of his grandson's bride with the appreciation of a connoisseur.

The King's long-suffering wife, known vaguely to history as "good Queen Maria Lescynska," had died two years earlier in the holocaust of death that had struck at the French ruling house between 1765 and 1768. Dead also was his heir and only son as well as his son's eldest son. It was through a series of untimely deaths therefore that Marie Antoinette's *fiancé* suddenly found himself heir to the French throne. This boy who had successively lost his older brother and his father soon afterward lost his mother. Louis XV's daughter-in-law was a princess of the Saxon house and a hereditary enemy of Austria. Had she lived she would never have permitted her son to marry Marie Antoinette. Her sudden death was among the first of the innumerable small "accidents" that one by one contributed to the final design.

Of the old King's surviving children three remained at Versailles. Their names were Sophie, Victoire, and Adélaïde, but to the court they were known collectively as "Mesdames." Sophie and Victoire were ineffectual old maids, the first too timid to speak, the second too plump and too absorbed in her love of food to have much initiative for troublemaking. By themselves they would not have been a factor of any significance at the court. Their elder sister Adélaïde, however, was something else again and under the energetic leadership of this spinster the three sisters became a force to reckon with. Arrogant, ambitious for power, full of spite and disaffection, Madame Adélaïde stirred up an ever-bubbling brew of mischief in the vast apartments she shared with her sisters on the ground floor of the palace.

Pride of race and hatred of Choiseul made her an implacable enemy of Marie Antoinette's long before she had even laid eyes on her. She viewed all that pertained to Austria with the contempt of an invested descendant of Louis XIV. Since the death of her sister-in-law, Madame Adélaïde had taken first rank among the women of the royal family. And now another woman, and an Austrian at that, was to supplant her. The circumstance filled her with rage which only prudence and plans of revenge enabled her to dissimulate. She loathed Choiseul and would have done much to achieve his downfall, but she hated even more the ignoble party that had formed around her father's latest strumpet. She had therefore cooked up an ingenious little scheme with which she planned to injure them all. She intended to ingratiate herself with the naïve dauphine, and egg her on against the du Barry. In this way Madame Adélaïde would be able to inflict an injury on the mistress for which the dauphine would be blamed. The King would then turn against Marie Antoinette and the Austrian Alliance would be weakened if not indeed broken.

Her plot was to succeed only too well. Prompted by Madame Adélaïde, Marie Antoinette was to take an intense dislike to Madame du Barry and, encouraged by the three aunts, refuse to speak to her. The King became angry and the Alliance was seriously imperiled, as Madame Adélaïde had hoped. This took place at the very moment when Maria Theresa was planning to pluck the first fruits of her daughter's marriage. The Partition of Poland was at hand and it was essential for Austria that France remain neutral during this rape. Louis went so far as to hint that France would not remain neutral if Maria Theresa's daughter persisted in her obstinate attitude toward those, as he phrased it, "who comprise my inner circle." Pressure from very high places had to be applied to the dauphine before she finally sacrificed her pride to the demands of state and spoke to Madame du Barry.

This intrigue cooked up by Madame Adélaïde typifies perfectly the innumerable similar intrigues in which Marie Antoinette was to become enmeshed. Usually trivial in origin, these palace squabbles invariably became momentous in their effect since the State itself would in one way or another ultimately become involved in them. Invariably, too, Marie Antoinette would be used by others who were more skillful in intrigue than herself to advance causes or score off enemies. A blind and childish obstinacy would keep her attached to these causes even after she had perceived their futility or danger.

After Marie Antoinette had acknowledged the presence of Madame du Barry, Madame Adélaïde retired disgruntled from the field of battle. As usual Marie Antoinette recognized too late the malicious motives behind her "friend's" advice. She no longer opened her heart to Madame Adélaïde, who became from that moment an open enemy. In her aunts' *salon* was formed the first of the palace cabals against her. It was not among the fishwives of the Paris streets where the epithet *l'autrichienne,* thrown at Marie Antoinette on her way to the guillotine, was coined. That word was invented by Madame Adélaïde and was first used with all its venomous intent in the gilded apartments of Mesdames at Versailles.

The King's late son had left five children. Two of these, the comte de Provence—known at court as "Monsieur"—and the comte d'Artois, were to play prominent and unfortunate parts in Marie Antoinette's life.

The comte de Provence was within a week the same age as his sister-in-law Marie Antoinette, but no community of friendship was ever to unite them. From the moment of his earliest consciousness Provence had jealously resented his older brother's approaching inheritance of a crown that he coveted for himself. With the passing of time this resentment was to increase rather than to diminish and as the Revolution approached he became one of the most assiduous of the palace intriguers who undermined his brother's authority and fomented revolt.

Monsieur, even at so early a date as 1770, was already half-incapacitated by the corpulence that in time was almost to immobilize him. But an alert and energetic intelligence dwelt within that fat, sluggish body. He was the "intellectual" of the family and his especial delight was Latin. The polished verse that he composed in the classic tongue was greatly admired by the little circle of *gens de lettres* that he gathered about him once or twice a week. Studious, retiring, always prudent, he was, in fact, a ruthless and crafty intriguer. Across his brother's decapitated body, across the blood-filled chasm of the French Revolution, the Empire, and the Napoleonic Wars he was at last to ascend the throne he had so long coveted and as Louis XVIII become one of France's least known but most capable kings.

Monsieur played no role in the frolics of his sister-in-law's circle at Trianon. In later years he was to recall his disapproval of her "too free manners that exposed her to censure." He expressed his disapproval by remaining apart from the noise and glitter of her private court and he ordered his wife to do the same. The latter was a princess of Piedmont to whom he had been wed in the year following his brother's marriage to Marie Antoinette. The malicious tongues of Versailles were seldom in harmony, but all were in accord about the comtesse de Provence. She is described as being of a surly, irascible disposition, red-necked and scrawny. It is recorded that her chest was "hairier than a man's"—a singularity that did not want for admirers. A certain Madame de Gourbillon who was known to have unusual tastes soon became her inseparable companion. Monsieur saw his wife as infrequently as was compatible with appearances.

The youngest of the dauphin's brothers, the comte d'Artois, was a prince of a very different description. He had escaped the fat that was the affliction of his brothers and sisters and was the only member of his immediate family to be favored with the physical graces that were admired by the French as being "royal." A likeness of him taken in his fifteenth or sixteenth year shows a pretty little oval face, not unlike that of Madame du Barry in riding clothes as painted by Drouais. He was vain of his well-shaped calves, his slender waist, and his lissom *tenu*. He dueled, danced, shot, and flirted with lacy grace and was as swift with his tongue in the *salon* as he was nimble with his rapier on the dueling field. Beneath these shallow accomplishments he was a fool and a vapid fop who was promiscuous with women and reckless in his pursuit of pleasure.

Marie Antoinette could hardly have picked a more harmful *confident* than the comte d'Artois, but a certain superficial affinity of taste brought them together in the heavy atmosphere of the old court and together they set about forming a circle of the young and mindless to offset the influence of those whom they called "the old fogeys." He encouraged her in follies toward which she was already too disposed and escorted her down the primrose path that led to the sweet futilities of Trianon. Since his company was tantamount to compromise it was not long before the gossip of Paris became the rumor of Europe and it was said that the comte d'Artois was her lover. In truth, she had never liked him and finally saw him for what he was, but the recognition came, as usual, too late. Artois was incapable of serious intrigue, but the harm that he did her was no less serious than that done by his brother Provence.

There were two sisters in the family. The eldest of these, Clotilde, married a prince of Piedmont soon after Marie Antoinette's arrival in France and played no role in her life. The younger, Élisabeth, was still in the nursery in 1770. Circumstances were one day to bring them very close but not at Versailles. And then there was her husband, the dauphin, soon to become Louis XVI.

Marie Antoinette had been sent the usual formal portraits of her *fiancé*. One of them, of the dauphin in ceremonial dress, had given her great satisfaction and the report went back to France that "she had mused before it for a long time." Maria Theresa, familiar with the trickery behind these royal portraits, interrupted her daughter's reverie with the reminder that there was no such thing as love in marriage. "Domestic happiness consists in mutual trust and kindness," she informed her. But her mother's words had no more meaning for the young princess of 1770 than they would for any fourteen-year-old girl today. She continued to fondle the portrait and several times was found by a lady-in-waiting gazing at it "with a tender expression" as she made her way across France to the appointed meeting at Compiègne.

It must have been with a sinking heart that she finally saw the man to whom she was to be bound for life. In the carriage that bore the King, the dauphin, and herself to the château de Compiègne it was noticed by the courtiers that while engaged in lively conversation with the King, she cast a number of furtive, inquisitive glances at her future husband. It was further observed that the bridegroom evinced not the slightest curiosity about her but stared into space with leaden indifference as though he were not a participant in the scene.

In truth the poor dauphin of France lacked every external favor that was expected to grace the person of a king or to awaken the sensibilities of a young bride. Burly and broad-shouldered, he had a gait that was more that of a plowman than a prince. His heavy features prefigured the fat that in a few years' time was to engulf him. He was nearsighted and this affliction lent a further awkwardness to his unprepossessing appearance. At a court where it was considered *de bon ton* that the feet of the courtier should never leave the floor but that he should glide gracefully forward as though on skates, the dauphin's rolling gait was a scandal. He was, furthermore, one of those persons who are hopelessly untidy. Surrounded though he was by valets, chamberlains, and attendants of every kind, his buttons would pop at unsuitable moments, his hands would always be dirty, and his hair powder was scattered all over his clothes. "He seems to have been brought up in the woods," the Neapolitan Ambassador reported.

The open contempt with which this Prince of the Blood, the heir to the French Crown, was treated by a nobility that was supposed to respect and serve him may be considered among the more notable auguries of the French Revolution. When a high-ranking minister such as Choiseul was able to write that "this prince is a half-wit and it is to be feared that his imbecility and the ridicule it will invite may in the natural course of events produce a decay of authority that will deprive the King's descendants of the Throne," there was indeed reason to fear for the throne of France. It does not seem to have occurred to Choiseul that in flaunting his contempt for the dauphin he himself was leading the procession of those who were inducing "a decay of authority."

The dauphin's unfortunate appearance happened in fact to conceal a number of virtues that in almost any other place and at almost any other time might have made him the very model of a good king. Among these qualities, notably lacking in some of his ancestors, was a deep and genuine love of the people over whom he was called to rule. In the most turbulent storms of his ill-fated reign that affection was never to leave him and in a real sense it may be said that, caught in a conflict that could only be resolved by bloodshed, he sacrificed his crown and his life to what he believed to be the best interest of his people. Had it been given to him to rule France and the French people in the immediacy and proximity that he was called upon to govern his disaffected and ungovernable nobility, history might have had a different story to relate of his reign.

Tradition unfortunately imprisoned him in the narrow enclave of Fontainebleau, Compiègne, Marly, and Versailles and rarely was he ever able to break out of this prison to meet his real subjects with whom he had so much more in common than with the birds-of-paradise of his court. The thick fingers that were a subject of derision to Choiseul happened in fact to be extremely capable at the manual labor that was his chosen recreation. He was a fine locksmith (some of his work remains today to testify to his competence at the forge) and he was by all reports a skilled plasterer and stonemason. Whenever there was construction at the palace the dauphin would be found at the scene and often up in the scaffolding itself, discussing the fine points of the work with the workmen. With men of the soil and artisans he was able to talk in a free manner that never came to him easily among the dukes and duchesses of his court.

Nor was he lacking in intellectual credentials. The loneliness of an unhappy childhood, the isolation imposed on him by his position, had driven him at an early age to the companionship of books. Reading, especially in history and geography, was always to be for him a happy distraction from affairs of state and at the end of his life reading was to become his principal solace. Louis XVI was, in fact, one of the best-read men of his day, but this was not evident in his conversation. He was incapable of the rapid chatter which was fashionable in Paris. He was the sort of reader who takes careful notes as he goes along even though his memory of facts and figures may be excellent. His conversation reflected this plodding, methodical, and thorough manner of reading. Imagination and aesthetic sensibility were lacking in his nature but these are qualities less needed in a monarch than the simplicity and kindness that were so large a component of Louis' character.

Unfortunately his many virtues were not suited to the society over which he was born to preside and in the political arena where circumstances were to force this man of gentle nature to do battle they were almost entirely negated by a deep-seated timidity and a ruinous lack of self-confidence that today would be called an inferiority complex. Endowed with post-Freudian insights, we may examine, with a compassion and understanding that was not accorded him by the men and women of his time, the sexual origin of these faults of character that were to have so disastrous an effect on his reign.

In many royal courts of an earlier century it had been the courtiers' privilege not merely to escort the bridal pair to the nuptial couch, but to remain in the room and witness the consummation of their union. Indeed, among the Gonzagas of Mantua it is recorded that at one such "scene" a priest was called upon to insert his hand between the couple to verify full intromission. Such robust customs were no longer in vogue at the court of France at the time of Marie Antoinette's marriage, but their purpose, apart from entertaining the spectators, was practical. It was in this manner that the legitimacy of the future heir was symbolically verified. In the same tradition of things the Queen was expected to give birth to her children in public, not merely before the court but in front of various delegations of fishwives, artisans, and workers from Paris. This custom remained in France until the Revolution.

In the evening that followed their wedding the dauphin and Marie Antoinette were escorted to their bed by a throng of chattering courtiers. The bedchamber was so filled with people that the newly married couple could scarcely go through the prescribed ritual. The dauphine was obliged to undress before them, then the ranking married woman of the court, in this case the duchesse de Chartres, passed her her bedclothes. The dauphin in his turn was divested of his clothing. The King handed him the requisite nightgarb. The Archbishop of Rheims blessed the bed with aspersions of Holy Water and the royal couple climbed in. The bedcurtains were lowered and then were suddenly raised again—a symbolic vestige of the earlier

25

custom when the union would have been witnessed. Everyone in the room made a deep reverence before the bed and then, led by the King, they all filed out. The curtains were lowered again. They closed over a tragedy that was to have consequences not only for the young couple but for the Crown and for France herself.

In the enfevered atmosphere of Versailles where the most insignificant steps of personages such as the dauphin and the dauphine acquired political implications anything that took place behind those curtains could not be concealed for long from the prying eyes of the court. Dawn had scarcely broken when it became known to everyone that nothing, in fact, had taken place there. The dauphin's sluggishness was attributed to fatigue induced by the celebrations of the preceding day. As time passed, however, and as the days turned into weeks it became apparent that something was seriously amiss in the bedchamber of the heir to the throne of France. And so, inevitably the "situation" became fraught with every imaginable implication for a wide variety of people.

Among those most immediately concerned was Maria Theresa's Ambassador to France, the comte de Mercy d'Argenteau. This "old fox" (as in later years Madame Élisabeth was to call him) was the very model of the eighteenth-century diplomat. He was supple, discreet, unscrupulous, and his powdered countenance was a mask of imperturbability. His principal task as the Empress' Ambassador at Versailles was to keep an eye on the Archduchess and to send off an almost daily report about her conduct to the Empress. As one of his earliest letters to Maria Theresa reveals, he wasted no time getting to work on this assignment. He began by bribing Marie Antoinette's servants to spy on her. "I have made sure of three people in the lower ranks of Mme. the Archduchess' service," he reported. "These are one of her women and two garçons de chambre who give me an exact report of everything that goes on around her . . . so that there is not a single hour in the day of which I am not in a position to give an account about what Mme. the Archduchess may have said, done, or heard . . ."

It was typical of the large strain of naïveté in Marie Antoinette's character that she should ever have given her trust to this slippery diplomat whose only real loyalty was to Austria. Without forethought, without hesitation Marie Antoinette would bubblingly confide to him some thought or some mildly reprehensible bit of information about her personal life. Off to Vienna would go Mercy's report of the conversation and then a few days later Marie Antoinette would receive another of her mother's scolding letters. She could never understand how her mother came to hear of it and she would confess her mystification to Mercy, who with much knitting of the brows would affect to be as perplexed as herself. Although he was to remain in Marie Antoinette's intimacy long after the Empress' death and to see her daily and twice daily for a period of more than twenty years, Mercy had little loyalty toward her as a person. It was as a daughter of Maria Theresa and as a pawn in Austria's unceasing political game that he extended what appeared to her to be his fealty. When she ceased to be a pawn, when she had lost her crown and could be of no further service to Austria, he abandoned her to her fate. Like so many others whom she had so foolishly thought of as friends, Mercy left France when the Revolution began in earnest. He heard the news of her execution with the equanimity of an eighteenth-century rationalist and the *sang-froid* of an experienced man of state.

The dauphin's impotence was a matter of grave concern to Austria. In the first place, so long as the Archduchess' marriage remained unconsummated it was liable to annulment with ecclesiastical sanction. The French Bourbons had been known to send back their brides. At such a juncture it did not significantly matter whose "fault" it might be, although the enemies of the Austrian Alliance hastened to attribute the failure to Marie Antoinette's "insufficient ardour" while Mercy scurried about gathering evidence that the trouble began with the dauphin. In effective fact the marriage could at any moment be declared null and void and that fact gave satisfaction to a number of parties at Versailles, foremost among whom were the Prussians and the other dynastic enemies of Austria.

Because the succession remained in danger until an heir was given France by one of Louis XV's grandsons, certain intriguers concocted a plan that gave Mercy further cause for anxiety. These schemers wanted Louis XV to remarry and sire an heir of his own. The enemies of the du Barry joined this group, among whom were to be found a number of diplomats whose sovereigns had princesses eligible for the honor. Of these men the Spanish Ambassador, the comte d'Aranda, was the busiest. He too had planted spies among the domestics of the dauphine's bedchamber.

In Mercy's first report of the situation to the Empress, within four days after the couple had been put to bed, he hazarded a medical explanation. "The dauphin's development is late probably because his constitution has been weakened by a sudden and too rapid growth." And for a short while the Empress contented herself with her envoy's diagnosis. "You are both so young," she wrote. "As far as your health is concerned it is all for the best. You will both gain strength."

To Mercy she wrote: "I am preaching patience to my daughter and I assure her that she will not lose by it." The Empress might better have preached some patience to herself, for in less than two months her correspondence began to take on undertones of hysteria. "Be prodigal of your caresses," she advised Marie Antoinette seven weeks later. "You must be prodigal of your caresses." The report had reached her that the dauphin who had now turned sixteen had discussed "the problem" with his wife and made her the statement that "I am not ignorant of what is involved in the state of matrimony . . . the time limit I set myself has been reached. You will find that at Compiègne I shall live with you in the fullest intimacy." The whole court of France seems to have overheard this conversation and everyone was prepared for the momentous event when on the appointed day they arrived at Compiègne.

Again nothing happened and the bride with some asperity informed her husband that she too was "well aware of what was involved in the state of Holy Matrimony." Once again the dauphin promised to demonstrate his affection. He even set a date, October 10, when the court would be at Fontainebleau. He believed that the forest air would have an "invigorating" effect on him. Once more the court sat back and waited; once more failure was announced. Maria Theresa reached the end of her rope. "If a girl as pretty as the dauphine cannot arouse the dauphin," she declared, "then all remedies are useless."

On the Empress' urging the dauphin finally submitted to medical examination. It was discovered that he had a physical impediment that prevented him from the full accomplishment of the sexual act. The clinical name of his condition was phimosis, "a constriction about the orifice of the prepuce which makes it impossible to bare the glans." The Spanish Ambassador, whose interest in the matter seems to have taken him into territory well beyond the call of duty, sent off a report to Madrid which explains to us today as clearly as presumably it did to the King of Spain the exact nature of the dauphin's infirmity. "It is said that the foreskin is so tight that it does not pull back when the member is introduced and so causes a sharp pain which prevents

His Majesty from giving the necessary impulsion to the act. Others say that the foreskin is so tight that it prevents the head or point of the member from emerging and so His Majesty's erections cannot attain the requisite degree of elasticity." One wonders if the King and Queen of Spain followed these and subsequent details with the same intensity of interest as their envoy.

The French physicians were of the opinion that exercise and a fortifying diet would cure the malady and their advice corresponded with the dauphin's preferences. The alternative, which was surgery, terrified him. The fortifying diet did in fact have a stimulating effect, but it in no way removed the impediment to the consummation of either his desires or his wife's. And so in the intimacy of the dauphine's bedchamber began a cruel drama. According to most observers there was no longer any question of the young man's affection for his wife. His visits to her bed grew more frequent and he even had a small private stairs built to connect his apartments on the ground floor with hers. Night after night he would come to her bed and arouse in her appetites that he was unable to satisfy. Then after inflicting on her body what one contemporary writer calls "moments of nightmare" whose only effective result were a few stains on the bedlinen that the spies of the Spanish Ambassador would examine the next morning, he would depart. Pitifully the two ignorant children appear to have believed that these episodes would somehow result in pregnancy.

"Spots have been found on Their Highnesses bedlinen," announced the Spanish Ambassador, "that show that the act has taken place. But most people attribute them only to the outward ejaculations of the dauphin who, it appears, has still not succeeded in penetrating . . ."

This situation which the diplomats and courtiers of that day only saw in political terms that were immediately applicable to their particular schemes must be viewed today against the wider background of historical disaster. For there is not the slightest question that from the derangements of personality that were the inevitable consequence of the dauphin's impotence there sprang many of the weaknesses that historians most frequently criticize in the character of Louis XVI. The deadly timidity, the immobilizing lack of self-confidence, and the resulting inability to come to a firm decision were the most conspicuous of the monarch's faults. One need not be read in Freudian psychology to appreciate the origin of these deficiencies.

For the Queen her husband's insufficiency is perhaps largest among the numerous pieces of misfortune that form the story of her life. There can be no understanding of her character as it has passed into history without some grasp of this cruel accident that for years deprived her of the balance that her particular temperament most urgently craved: children.

Here once again her situation as Queen of France came into the worst possible conflict with her private personality. In some other court at some other time custom would have forced her to submit resignedly to a situation beyond her control. The possibility of finding solace in pleasure or amusement would not have presented itself. But at the dissolute, extravagant court of eighteenth-century France pleasure proposed itself everywhere not merely as a distraction from private sorrow, but as a way of life. And so this girl who was more formed by nature to be a mother than a Queen turned to pleasure to fill up the emptiness of her life.

At any other court at any other time the impotence of a regnant prince would not have lessened that prince's effective authority over his consort. The tradition of most European countries and the custom of earlier times would have discouraged the ascendancy of a woman over a man on almost any pretext. But France of the eighteenth century was a civilization whose most conspicuous characteristic was the emergence of women as a dominant factor in the upper strata of society. This was made manifest to Europe not merely by the rise of Madame de Pompadour, who wielded the scepter in matters of state, but by the supremacy of a Madame du Deffand and a Madame Geoffrin in the milieu of intellectual endeavor. It was notorious, too, that in most of the stylish households of the day the wife had extorted some sort of an agreement from her husband allowing her the freedom that tradition in principal denied her. Innumerable married women of the court openly kept lovers. Their husbands looked the other way and felt free to indulge themselves in their particular weaknesses. Given the social conditions in which they were made and given the cold, rational temperament of the signatories, such agreements were eminently sensible and a perfect expression of the hardheaded common sense of the French.

Those women who with their charm and intelligence dominated eighteenth-century France were not, in fact, ordinary women. They were a race apart, they were Frenchwomen with all the dispassion, the irony, the intuitive sense of measure and moderation of their breed. For them there was an inborn protection against the excesses or imprudence that so favored a position might have excited in women of some other race. They knew to an inch exactly how far they might go without appearing to violate the decencies.

Marie Antoinette, unfortunately, was of a different character and nothing could have been more ruinous for her—as ultimately it was for Louis XVI too—than the psychological ransom with which her husband now indemnified her for his shortcomings. Everything speaks of a deep though hidden strain of sensitivity in this outwardly stolid man and there can be no doubt at all that he felt his wife's unhappiness acutely. And so he gave her her way in the myriad small issues of daily life. The small issues by inevitable progression became larger issues and it was not long before she dominated him. Dominated him not through love or infatuation as the Pompadour and her successor had dominated Louis XV, but through remorse and guilt, a hold from which it is always more difficult to break. The intriguers of the court, the Choiseul party and all the others who had hoped that the dauphine would gain an ascendancy over the dauphin, were successful in a way they had not foreseen. Maria Theresa saw what was happening, recognized all its potentiality of disaster, and was appalled.

"I must admit quite frankly that I do not wish my daughter to have a decisive influence in affairs of state," she wrote Mercy shortly before Marie Antoinette's accession as Queen. "I know too well her childishness, her frivolity, her dislike of concentration. I fear for her success in governing a Kingdom as dilapidated as France is at the moment." In penning these sentiments the Empress deceived herself to the extent that she always deceived herself whenever interests of state were in question. On those occasions when Austria had something to ask of France she was perfectly glad that her daughter had a "decisive influence" in affairs and she never hesitated to use it. From this was to be born the most serious of the charges for which her daughter was to stand accused before the Revolutionary Tribunal.

It was soon apparent that the Empress' apprehensions were all too well founded. The child-Queen to whom so much power had been given was ignorant of statecraft, was bored by politics, and had not the slightest ambition to appoint cabinets or to run ministries. After the meddling in affairs of state by a Madame de Maintenon or a Pompadour one might suppose that here, at last, was one deficiency that might have spoken to her credit, but it was Marie Antoinette's misfortune that even her good qualities, negative though some of them may have been, were to act against her. Instead of experienced politicians, men such as Choiseul or Mercy, having any effective influence over her, a new breed of sychophant now made its appearance at Versailles, men as empty-headed as herself and women of a simpering sentimental disposition whose company the Queen preferred because they placed no strain on her own indolent intellect. It was through these people that the path to power lay during the reign of Louis XVI and it was to the Queen's favorites, not to the Queen herself, that the strugglers after position, the ministers and intriguers, had to turn. The favorites would then in their turn bring pressure upon the Queen, who would go to her husband with the request. More often than not she would be ignorant of its real source and oblivious of its political content. She would see in it only a means of pleasing a friend and perhaps of demonstrating her hold over the King. It goes without saying that such intrigues, so lightly entered into, were at times to have very serious consequences. The downfall of the Turgot ministry, the earliest and perhaps the most serious of Louis XVI's blunders, was the result of one such intrigue into which Marie Antoinette had been drawn for purposes of petty social vengeance.

Before the tribunal of history, ignorance can rarely be an admissible plea for one in the station of responsibility of Marie Antoinette. Most historians have passed harsh sentence on her for the role she played in French affairs during the critical early years of her husband's reign. Yet when one thinks of the long barren years of her youth at a hostile court, of her thwarted hopes as a woman as well as a mother, and of the humiliations that she endured with good humor and even dignity during those years, it is difficult to withhold all compassion.

And these humiliations were by no means confined to the privacy of her bedchamber. All too frequently she was obliged to hide her shame in the publicity of the Galerie des Glaces. On one such occasion her sister-in-law, the comtesse d'Artois, gave birth to a male heir that finally secured the succession for the descendancy of Louis XV. The comtesse d'Artois was a few years younger than Marie Antoinette and, like her sister the comtesse de Provence, of a disagreeable disposition. But it was she who gave birth to the much desired heir to the throne and that birth, after the custom of Versailles, took place in public. Marie Antoinette was, of course, present and in a letter to her mother she refers quite openly to the conflicting emotions with which she viewed this *accouchement* that in the normal course of events should have been hers. She was able to stifle her tears while in the comtesse's bedchamber. But on her way back to her apartments she was met by a band of *poissardes*—Paris fishwives —who were always present at these royal births. The women began to yell at her, "Why don't you give us an heir?" Her barrenness was a topic among them of licentious humor and they followed her to the very door of her rooms calling out obscenities and insults. Her composure abandoned her entirely and when the door was closed behind her she wept.

Her longing for children became morbid and a further symptom in the general pathology of her thwarted instincts. She would order her carriage stopped at the sight of a pretty child by the roadside, step out, pick it up and cover it with kisses and tears. She even legally adopted one such infant, bringing it home with her to keep as a sort of human pet that she could feed and fondle whenever the impulse seized her. The children of her friends were always to exercise the greatest fascination for her even after she had had children of her own. They would be brought to meet her, be given toys of every kind, be watched over with a solicitous concern that would often lead to pensions or lucrative appointments in the government. With her own children, when she finally bore them, she was to be a loving and responsible mother, full of Austrian good sense and not at all inclined to view with a tolerant eye weaknesses that might have reminded her of her own. Her attitude toward them, ironically, became very much like her mother's attitude toward herself.

It was seven years before Louis XVI submitted to the surgery which removed the impediment to his becoming a husband to his high-strung wife. The birth of her children was to effect an almost total change of character in Marie Antoinette, but the change came too late. By then certain attitudes between husband and wife had become fixed and certain habits of behavior too ingrained to be easily broken. Worst of all was the damage done her reputation during those seven years of emptiness when she sought solace in the amusements of the society she gathered around her. That damage was irreparable because Marie Antoinette was one of those naïve persons who believe that their innate decency is sufficient protection against the injury of slander and are therefore more or less indifferent to appearances. But in such a society as that of the French court of the eighteenth century appearances were, in fact, all that mattered. The etiquette and manners of Versailles had been evolved as a screen behind which real corruption and real vice might be practiced without attracting censure. In one of his books, de la Morlière describes a ball during the reign of Louis XV in terms that communicate perfectly the hypocrisy, the cynicism, and decay that lay behind the *maquillage* of the court's fine manners:

"The ball was almost over. The candles had shortened, the musicians were either drunk or asleep and no longer played their instruments. The crowd had dispersed, everyone was unmasked, rouge or powder flowed down the painted faces and exposed livid, flaccid, blotched patches of skin which offered the eye the disgusting spectacle of dilapidated stylishness."

It was against this style of things that Marie Antoinette, in her imprudent pursuit of happiness, rebelled. Her influence on the tastes of the expiring *ancien régime* was to prove as powerful as Rousseau's. She too tried to sweep away "the disgusting spectacle of dilapidated stylishness" and introduce a fresh and simple manner in which sentimentality—and self-deceit—was to replace hypocrisy. Her attitude first shocked then outraged the old court. And what was a scandal among the elect of Versailles soon became a matter of outraged gossip among the respectable middle class of Paris. In due time these rumors made their way to the provinces where the provincial nobility, traditional enemies of the court, heard them, pursed their lips, and handed them on to their farmers and their farmers' wives.

By the time that she was brought to bed of an heir to the French throne and the conditions that were at the root of her instability had been eliminated, her reputation was soiled throughout France. It was from this material, all of it in its essence untrue, that Fouquier-Tinville was to cut most of the charges that twenty years later were to bring her neck under the blade of the guillotine.

The ups and downs of hope along with the social chatter that went with them made Marie Antoinette's situation the more difficult to bear. Toward the end of 1773, after three years of marriage, another flurry of hope caused Mercy to write Vienna and the Spanish Ambassador to communicate with Madrid. Someone saw the dauphin kissing his wife in public. There were reports that his visits to her bed, the source to her of so much unseen anguish, had significantly increased in frequency. And so the gossip went abroad that the dauphine would soon become pregnant. "One may hope every day for this longed-for event," announced Mercy.

At Marly the dauphin was heard to ask his wife, "Do you really love me?" And the dauphine was heard to reply, "Yes, you cannot doubt it. I love you sincerely and I respect you even more."

Then, as Mercy described, "He began to caress the Archduchess tenderly and told her that he would continue with his diet and hoped that when they returned to Versailles all would go well."

But when they returned to Versailles all did not, of course, go well. There was another disappointment to be shared with the public. "By the most incredible misfortune," wrote Mercy, "our hopes instead of increasing now seem to have become still more remote." This happened in mid-December and with it something radical finally seems to have taken place in Marie Antoinette's character. For her it seems to have been one of those moments of crisis when deep in the heart certain irreversible changes occur. She was in her nineteenth year and in four months' time was to become Queen of France. On January 30, accompanied by her husband and her brothers-in-law, she went into Paris to taste for the first time the forbidden fruit of the city's delights. She had heard much talk about the masked balls at the Opéra and she was determined to have a glimpse at the spectacle for herself.

What she saw seems to have exceeded all expectation. On that very night she acquired a fatal taste for the Opéra balls, a distraction that in later years was to become the most angrily criticized of her amusements. As she moved about the crowded room swathed, as she fondly supposed, in anonymity, she caught sight of the young Swede who had been presented to her in November and whom she had noticed at several of her Monday evening receptions. For a royal personage such as Marie Antoinette one of the principal attractions of the Opéra balls was that behind a mask she could speak to whomever she wished without having to go through introductions or other tedious formalities. At Versailles, surrounded by equerries and ushers, it would have been difficult for Marie Antoinette to enter into private conversation with a foreigner such as Count Fersen who seemed to be so interesting. Behind her mask she could talk to him without constraint, ply him with questions, and satisfy her curiosity about him without reserve. He, in his turn, not realizing who she was, could exchange words with her that the restraints of etiquette would not

elsewhere permit. She would thus be able to indulge in a little innocent *coquetterie*.

Nearly all contemporary descriptions of Marie Antoinette make
mention of the bantering, half-teasing manner which she would as-
sume with men she liked. This propensity to flirtation was another
indiscretion that was to do her great harm, because in eighteenth-
century Paris there was no such thing as "innocent" flirtation. In
France all outward congress between the sexes was regulated by rigid
convention. Although a man of rank might be practicing the whole
repertory of sadic vice with a woman of the same *milieu* and although
that fact might be known to everyone in the room, convention forbade him even to touch the back of the chair on which she was seated
when in the presence of other people. No appearance of sexuality was
tolerated in this aristocracy, which was one of the most dissolute that
the world has ever seen. "It requires the greatest habitude to discover
the smallest connection between the sexes here," Horace Walpole reported on one of his visits to Paris.

Ignoring this convention as she ignored so many others in
France, Marie Antoinette went up to the Swede whom she spotted
in the crowd and began to talk to him. Her pleasure in the conversation was no doubt enhanced by the fact that he did not realize
with whom he was speaking. When the fawning crowd began to
betray her identity, she lowered her mask. One may suppose that she
took some amusement at his surprise as she withdrew to the seclusion
of a *loge*.

Mercy reports that on the following week she went again to the
Opéra ball and that "she drew on herself all the applause and admiration with which the public hastens to do homage to her, both
because of her choice of people to whom she spoke and the things
she said to them." But Fersen seems not to have been present when
Marie Antoinette made her second appearance at the Opéra ball, for
in his Journal, where his attendance at such social events was always
meticulously noted, he makes no mention of being there.

Yet sometime between their first encounter at the masked ball
and the time of his departure from France three months later he
and Marie Antoinette formed the first frail bonds of the friendship
that was to carry them beyond the happy dream that was Trianon
into the historical reality that was the night at Varennes, then darkness, prison, and disaster. She became Queen of France in May of
1774 at the exact moment when he left Paris. She was not to see

him again until the autumn of 1778, after more than four years' absence. But when he returned she recognized him. Her little exclamation of pleasure when he was formally presented to her and the royal family for the second time communicates exactly the character of the friendship they had formed during his first visit to France.

"But it's an old acquaintance!" she declared when she saw him. And her words give us the evidence that is not elsewhere recorded that they must have met and talked on other occasions after that first brief meeting at the masked ball.

When Axel Fersen returned to Sweden at the end of his Grand Tour it was his father's intention that he should settle down to a place of importance in the affairs of his homeland. For generations the Fersen family had served Sweden with honor. It was expected that young Axel, educated now in the ways of the civilized world, should follow in the steps of his father, and become an officer and nobleman of Sweden. He was nineteen. It was time for his apprenticeship to begin. In a few years' time he would be expected to marry a woman of wealth who would give him heirs. He would then train his own son for the position in the world that this son, in his turn, would occupy. And so, it was assumed by the generation of Senator Fersen, would the immemorial cycle go on.

Almost from the moment of his return to Sweden, Axel found himself in silent resistance to these traditional ambitions imposed on him by his father. In later years the conflict with his father was to become open and bitter as he tried to break away from the narrow confines of Sweden and the old Count's world. Everywhere within Europe's noble families a similar struggle between generations was being waged as the new ideas from Paris were brought back to the provincial cities and ancestral châteaux by young noblemen such as Fersen who had been sent abroad for their education. The stagnant air of the feudal world stirred expectantly when in the writing of Jean-Jacques Rousseau the first intimations of Romanticism appeared and the hero in revolt against his society presented himself. Everywhere in Europe the old ways of life were being questioned, everywhere the old and venerable institutions of feudalism had started to crumble.

In Sweden itself there had occurred a momentous upheaval a few years before Fersen's return there. In 1772 the young King, Gustavus III, overthrew the Swedish Parliament and declared himself to be the absolute ruler of his country. It was an event that exemplifies perfectly the mistake that may be made by confusing today's political vocabulary and concepts with those of another century. Gustavus' *coup d'état*, despite the sound of it in today's ears, represented a step out of the darkness of the Middle Ages into the clear air of the Enlightenment. The Swedish Parliament or Riksdag was, in fact, the bastion of an entrenched, reactionary, and ignorant nobility whose hatred of the King and whose continual battles with the Crown had nothing at all to do with any concern for the democratic aspiration of the Swedish people. These were rather expressions of the nobility's determination that their prerogatives and privileges should never be threatened by a strong monarch. The heir to the Swedish Crown was in a sense "kidnapped" by the Riksdag and educated by tutors appointed by that parliament. When he became King he was held in thrall, a powerless prisoner of his aristocracy, behind the walls of the royal castle.

By the time of the accession of Gustavus III in 1772 the Riksdag, which was rent by its own inner quarrels, had brought Sweden to a condition close to anarchy and collapse. This was exactly what her two neighbors, Russia and Prussia, wished and had always encouraged. By bribery, by threats, by frequent rattlings of the sword, Frederick the Great and Catherine of Russia made it clear that they would tolerate no changes in the Constitution that kept Sweden weak. By furthering the same sort of anarchy in Poland that they fostered in Sweden, Catherine and Frederick had found the pretext they needed to occupy that unfortunate country and to take large slices of its territory for themselves. Having subjected Poland to partition, these two Enlightened Despots now turned covetous eyes toward Sweden, where everything was propitious for another profitable partition. It was at this moment that Gustavus III, with the *panache* and speed that was to characterize all his moves, overthrew the Riksdag by armed force. Before dissolving the assembly he read to them the new Constitution that he had prepared. It was a model of eighteenth-century lucidity and idealized theory. Although it imposed a strong monarchy on Sweden, that monarchy, by the King's own desire, was kept well within the limits of constitutional restraint. The Riksdag retained the ultimate authority to declare war and to pass on such measures as the King put before it. No proposed measure could become law without approval of the Riksdag. The appointment of ministers, however, became the King's exclusive prerogative and the control of the army, the navy, and foreign affairs passed into his hands.

The success or failure of such strong monarchies in the end depends on the character of the monarch. In the case of Gustavus III, Sweden was fortunate, for he was a remarkable man and one of the most capable of the Enlightened Despots who were the bridge in Europe between Feudalism and the French Revolution. For the first ten years of his rule Sweden prospered and enjoyed all the benefits of a kindly paternalism. The medieval guilds were abolished and free trade established. Currency was stabilized and taxes on the peasantry lowered: the exact reforms which in France poor Louis XVI hoped to effect but could not because, unlike Gustavus, he was never able to break from the stranglehold of France's medieval *parlements*. When Gustavus instituted a program of public education, when he guaranteed the freedom of the press and broke the hold of the harsh Lutheran oligarchy on public worship, Voltaire himself saluted the King of Sweden, who was the youngest and the last of his disciples.

Gustavus III was twenty-six years of age when he seized power and everything appeared to qualify him for the position he had by force assumed. He was young, intelligent, full of grace, charm, and vitality. His mother, Louisa Ulrica, who was the sister of Frederick the Great, had raised him on a diet of Voltaire and the Encyclopaedists. This forceful woman dreamed incessantly of the great day when her son would overthrow the odious Riksdag. It was in preparation for that hour that she had instilled in him a veneration for the civilization of France.

The authoritarian attitude of Louis XIV modified by the lucid, rational prescription of Voltaire exercised an irresistible spell over the Enlightened Despots of the eighteenth century. French, not Swedish, was Gustavus' first language and until the Revolution Paris was for him the Athens of the world. It was in Paris, indeed, while he was "shining like a Northern Star" at the *salon* of Madame Geoffrin that he learned of his father's death and of his accession to the throne of Sweden. He was to visit Paris again as King of Sweden and to be feted by Marie Antoinette at Trianon.

To the Queen of France he swore oaths of undying devotion that were heard all over Europe, but that fealty was not taken until the Revolution had made Marie Antoinette its prisoner and her end had been forecast. He had not been an admirer of the lightheaded Queen of Trianon; the Queen of Sorrow was more to his liking and with the advent of misfortune he was to play an important role in the various projects designed by Fersen to effect her escape from France. Gustavus' assassination in 1792 was one of the most momentous of the many fatalities that entered into the design of her doom.

After Gustavus' *coup d'état* the Swedish court took on a French tone. The formality and style of Versailles were introduced to the snowbound cities of the Scandinavian peninsula with effects that in French eyes were sometimes ridiculous, for French measure and French laughter were not really in the Swedish character. In the King himself there were strange conflicts that combined oddly with his Gallic pretensions. An excessive, almost frenzied frivolity would be followed by long, dark periods of introspection. In a moment he would pass from glacial reserve to wild and exalted demonstrations of affection. There was an instability in his character that in future circumstances was to suggest the presence of insanity.

He who loved masquerades, architecture, and dancing had been forced by his Parliament to marry a princess of Denmark who considered the theater sinful, who dressed without style and was of a sweet submissive nature. His mother shared his dislike of his wife. Within the confines of the royal palace mother and son joined forces to make life miserable for the Queen who had been fobbed off on them by the Riksdag. Gustavus and his wife lived in separate quarters of the palace. He rarely spoke to her and rarely saw her. The court took its tone from the King and despised the neglected Queen, who spent most of her life in the solitude of her rooms, weeping and praying.

Gustavus III had a discriminating eye for beautiful women and in later years his too public admiration of their charms was to win him a reputation as quite a lady-killer and to cause the Lutheran lips of his middle-class subjects to tighten with disapproval. But among those who traveled in the inner circles of Gustavus' society it was said that the King's appreciation of women was more aesthetic than sensual and that he did not, in fact—like many lady-killers—care for them in the full meaning of the word.

His appreciation of handsome men was of an equally ambiguous character. No *mignons* ever brought scandal upon his court. The favors and affection he gave a Creutz, a Taube, a Staël-Holstein, and certain young officers of his army was at all times restrained by an awareness of his position. His admiration for the virtues of masculinity that he saw in the person of his favorites appears to have corresponded in its innocence to the chaste kisses that Marie Antoinette showered on her beloved comtesse de Polignac.

With these proclivities it is no wonder that the King was pleased when he caught sight of young Count Fersen who had at last returned to Sweden after completing his education abroad. His ambassador's enthusiastic reports from Paris were not belied by the man with his reserved good manners and his unhappy air. Fersen was invited to join the palace frolics. The King had a passion for dressing up, for theatricals, for masquerades of every kind, and it was expected of his nobility that they join him in all these diversions. Staid old Swedish dowagers were compelled to mount the boards with the giddy young folk of Stockholm society. Stern patriarchs, many of them accustomed to command on the field of battle, were obliged to don blue satin knee-breeches, hold a beribboned shepherd's crook, and make believe they were peasants in palace *divertissements* with such titles as *Le temple de Cythère* and *Le château enchanté*.

Axel Fersen was soon at the center of these gatherings whose purpose was to amuse the temperamental King. It was a life that he found boring. In his letters of this time he does not attempt to hide his dissatisfaction with this existence to which he felt he was forever condemned. He was made a captain of dragoons, but the position was more decorative than functional and the life of an army officer in the Stockholm of that day was as dull and artificial as the life of a courtier.

When the harsh, dark Swedish winter finally came to its end the King would repair to one of his residences outside Stockholm and the high-ranking nobility such as Fersen's family would go to their farms or estates in the country. Then would begin the strange white nights of the North that engendered an atmosphere propitious to the practice of witchcraft. The seeds of the French Enlightenment never really took firm root in Sweden, any more than they did in Russia or in Germany. In the hothouse air of the royal palace a few plants might be forced but they were spindly of stalk and of unhealthy flower. Beyond the fragile glass of the conservatory howled the winds of a ruder climate than that of the Île-de-France. In the countryside the old, necessary customs of the race continued untouched by the newfangled theories of French philosophy. Beneath the polished surface of the court itself the old practices still prevailed. Conversation at the palace might be in French about Diderot, but at home there were yellowed parchments on demonology and it was these that were consulted in times of need or emergency. Behind the murder of Gustavus in 1792, which in far-off France was to seal the fate of Marie Antoinette and Louis XVI, lie hidden paths that lead the assiduous historian to the witches' coven and the ageless craft of sorcery.

Fersen would often stay with his family at one of their country properties during the summer lapses when the court was dispersed. In a letter to his sister Sophie he described the *ennui* of one such visit, characteristic of them all. Everyone would keep to their rooms until dinner, then they would assemble and exchange conversation. After the meal his mother and father would settle down to a game of piquet and Axel would retire to his room to practice the flute or to read. On this particular visit a continual rain prevented any excursions out of doors. "You know our amusements and you know that they aren't exactly what you could call lively," he adds petulantly.

His sister Sophie's company was Axel's greatest pleasure. During his four-year stay in Sweden he formed a deep and enduring friendship with her that was to comfort them in the years to come. In 1776 she was seventeen, vivacious and pretty. The King's younger brother, the Duke Frederick of Sweden, fell in love with her and wanted to marry. Despite the odd and violent character of this Prince, Sophie had been strongly attracted to him. But Senator Fersen, one of the leaders of the Riksdag, looked on the royal family with a suspicion that the ritual of respect could barely conceal. He refused his permission and Sophie, by her father's wish, was married to a man named Piper with whom she was unhappy. While married to Piper she formed a lifelong attachment with one of the King's favorites, Baron de Taube. Taube was a close friend, too, of her brother Axel, who not only gave his blessing to his sister's illicit union, but joined it so to speak. Between these three there were to be no hidden thoughts, no secrets. They lived together in harmony and mutual love until Taube's death, when Fersen and his sister were drawn still closer together by veneration of their departed friend. Gustavus looked on this *ménage à trois* with complaisance and indeed at times was so intimately involved in it that it became something of a *ménage à quatre*.

Axel had another sister, Hedda, and a younger brother, but he was never to be on terms of intimacy with them. Between his brother Fabian and himself a sense of rivalry was to arise when it became apparent to their father that Axel, heir to the family name and fortune, was a disappointment. Senator Fersen then turned to Fabian for advice and comfort, which this younger son was not reluctant to give. Sophie was always to take Axel's part in the family rows that were to erupt in the approaching years.

In 1777, soon after Sophie's marriage to Piper, Senator Fersen decided that the time had come for Axel to marry. He was twenty-two yet oddly unsettled. The senior Fersen attributed his son's restlessness to his need for a wife and the responsibility of a family. But considerations that had nothing to do with his son's happiness lay behind the Senator's proposal. Once again as in every generation, it had come time to regild the family arms. Once again the coffers, emptied by the expenses of court life and the maintenance of the family châteaux, had to be refilled. It was not only a wife that Count Fersen wanted for his son: it was a rich wife.

In such countries as Sweden and among such families as Fersen's it was the custom for the daughters of the house to find their husbands at home, taking suitable spouses among the second sons of the local grandees. But the eldest son or heir would go abroad to seek a better endowed consort than he was likely to find in his homeland. For Swedes the pickings were often fruitful in such cities as London or Paris, where there were to be found heiresses whose middle-class or Protestant origins made them ineligible for an alliance with the historic names of France or England. A Fersen or his equivalent would come along bearing his pedigree, proffering the promise of a fine position in Sweden, and as often as not the heiress or her father would be persuaded to accept. The most spectacular marriage of the century was to be made by another Swede, Fersen's contemporary, Baron de Staël-Holstein, who landed the daughter of Jacques Necker, the richest banker in Europe.

As it happened Axel had such a *partie* in mind when his father broached the subject of marriage. She was the only child of an enormously rich man of affairs named Leijel. Swedish in origin, the family had left its native land some decades earlier and gone to England. They took the respectable fortune they had made in ironworks with them and changed their name to Leyell. In England they became directors of the Compagnie des Indes and the respectable fortune soon multiplied manyfold. Two uncles had died without issue and their legatee was the father of the girl whom it was proposed that Fersen marry. He had met her several times in his travels through Europe, in Berlin, in Dresden, in Paris and London. Accompanied by her parents, Mademoiselle Leyell, like himself, was doing the Grand Tour. She and Fersen had struck up an acquaintance that did not discourage hopes of matrimony. He found her "charming, talented, and sweet-tempered." Despite the girl's inferior birth, Senator Fersen encouraged an alliance with her. As Countess Fersen, invested with her rank at the Swedish court, the ironworks would soon be forgotten and only the revenues from the Compagnie des Indes remembered.

Axel's father promised to defray the expenses that his son would incur in laying siege to the prize. Axel was to remain in England for the four or five months that might be needed to conclude the courtship and then when the wedding contract had been notarized and the terms of the dowry settled, he would return to Sweden with his bride to lead the life that his pedigree and her money had designed for him. It does not seem to have crossed his mind nor his son's either that Mademoiselle Leyell, countess or not, might find the prospect of life in Stockholm something less than interesting and the Fersen family less impressive than it believed itself to be.

In the early part of April of 1778 Axel set forth on his second trip abroad, going this time to London. He took lodgings at 7 Suffolk Street and, after having been presented to George IV, he settled down to the courting of the Leyell heiress. Every day for two months he paid his respects to her and to her family. Discussions were delicately begun and the proposal finally made. At the end of June, Mademoiselle Leyell gave him her refusal with the reason that she did not wish to leave her parents. This must have been a pretext to spare his feelings because in a few years time she did leave her parents in order to marry Lord de la Warr. His *amour propre* in any case was badly wounded and he was afraid that his failure had disgraced him in the eyes of his father. A letter written to Sophie reveals his feelings:

"I am in despair at the thought that this will hurt our father but I did everything possible. I could console myself over the loss if I could be sure that my father can be persuaded that I did everything in my power to please him and win the girl's consent . . ."

Axel's concern over his father's feelings sprang as much from selfish motives as from filial respect. He did not want to return to Sweden. This is apparent in every line of the letter he wrote Sophie as it is in a letter he later wrote his father. But without his father's consent and an adequate allowance to go with it, it would have been impossible for him to remain abroad. So he tried to pacify the old Count by proposing various enterprises that he, Axel, might undertake abroad while waiting for the gossip about his failure to die down in Sweden. A position at the embassy in Paris was first suggested but the only suitable post there had been given to young Staël-Holstein who, with Gustavus' encouragement, was now hot on the trail of the Necker millions.

Then a military career was suggested. By training in actual combat Fersen might become a field marshal like his father. "I only want to be able to walk in your footsteps, dear father," he wrote. "To be useful to my country and to serve it as you have served it is all I desire . . ." In those days going to war was a traditional expedient for men of Fersen's kind when they had suffered a disappointment in their affairs of the heart. The consolation was a convenient one for they rarely had to look very far to find a war in which to fight. There were, in fact, three wars available at the time of Axel's letter to his father. War had broken out between England and France over France's treaty of alliance with the American colonies. War raged between England and her colonies on the American continent and there was a war between Prussia and Austria over the Bavarian Succession. After a consideration of these choices Axel decided to offer his services to Frederick the Great, whose armies were the best trained in Europe.

To win his father's permission Axel even fanned the ashes of hopes that anyone else would have pronounced dead. After all, the young woman had admitted to him that she loved him: "I mustn't entirely abandon the project therefore. Let us allow matters to take their course. If she loves me I can always pick up where I left off and I am certain that four or five or even six years will be time enough to start thinking seriously about the matter. Papa Leyell is old and he's sick. When he dies the objections from his side will die with him. All the money would then come to me directly . . ."

These hopes with which Fersen soothed his own wounds appear to have softened the Field Marshal for he gave his consent to Axel's plan to remain abroad for a time. Fersen immediately left London and went to Paris, where he awaited the outcome of his application to serve in the army of Frederick the Great.

He could not have picked a more agreeable city in which to forget his sorrows. Under the new reign Paris had become a more frantic capital of *mondaine* pleasure than it had been four years earlier at the time of his first visit there. But however seductive the delights of the city, he intended his stay there to be an interlude. It is important to realize that he arrived there with his decision to join an army already made. It has been stated too often by novelists and even by responsible biographers that when he left France at the end of the following year to fight in the American war he did so because he had fallen in love with Marie Antoinette and she with him and he wished to absent himself from romantic difficulties that were insoluble. The truth is that he had made up his mind to take that step well before he and the Queen had formed the friendship that was to be the central happening of his life.

From Axel's letters to his sister and from the entries in his Journal that were written at this time one receives the impression of a man who is at loose ends, who has momentarily lost his way or is stifled by the insufficiency of the world into which fate has placed him. In Fersen's life, as in Marie Antoinette's, the hidden spring is a discrepancy between the person and the circumstances into which he was born. The day had come to its end in Europe for Fersen and those of his kind whose purposes were interbound with the social conditions of feudalism. No longer needed as leaders of their race and vassals in the harsh, primary struggle against the oppression of a king or the depredations of some rival lord, they had been given in exchange the soft, safe life of courtiers. For many of them it was not enough. It is this that one so strongly feels in Axel Fersen's situation when he returned to Paris after his matrimonial defeat in London. With all his resources, his courage, his physical beauty there was no place for him in the world of 1778. That is why when, in August of that year, he returned to France he came in search of challenge and was prepared for adventure.

Fersen was to stay in Paris for more than a year and a half on his second visit there. As he wrote his father, he had been flattered by Marie Antoinette's welcoming words, "It's an old acquaintance!" when the Swedish Ambassador presented him to the royal family for the second time. But despite the warmth of this unexpected greeting he did not return to Versailles for some weeks. One day Marie

Antoinette asked the Swedish Ambassador why Count Fersen never came to her Sunday afternoon receptions. The words were repeated to Axel and thereafter he appeared at these affairs assiduously.

Not long afterward he was singled out for another attention. As an officer in the Swedish army Fersen had letters of introduction to some of the important commanders in the French army. He decided to do a tour of inspection of the Army of the North, stationed in Normandy. He was accompanied by a Swedish friend, Curt de Stedingk, who held a commission in the French army. To make the tour in proper style they donned the new Swedish uniform that had been designed by Gustavus III. It consisted of a "blue doublet over which was a white tunic, tight-fitting chamois breeches and a black shako topped by a blue and yellow plume." It was the first time it had been worn in France and it caused a small sensation. Thus attired, the two Swedes presented themselves at the *salon* of one of Paris' hostesses, Madame de Boufflers, who pronounced it to be very "snappy" (*leste*). Through Madame de Boufflers news of the Swedish uniform reached Versailles. When Fersen returned from his trip in Normandy a message was given him that the Queen would like to see the famous uniform. He was asked to present himself not at her *lever*, but in the private apartments.

Several reports remain of this meeting and they all agree that Marie Antoinette examined the uniform with close attention and in doing so left no doubt among the observers that she was pleased with what she saw. "All Versailles can only talk of a certain Count Fersen who came to court wearing the Swedish national outfit which the Queen examined very carefully," reported one witness, the future Bishop Lindholm.

The comte de St. Priest, a diplomat and Minister of the King's Household, wrote in his memoirs that "Count Fersen of Swedish nationality finally conquered the Sovereign's heart. He was specially noticed by her in 1779 when, having come to France to serve, he appeared at Versailles in the new Swedish uniform. The Queen saw him and was struck by his beauty. And at that time he was indeed a remarkable figure. Tall, slender, perfectly formed, with fine eyes, a colorless but animated complexion, he was made to catch the eye of a woman who sought rather than feared exciting impressions. Her equerry who gave her his hand told me that he felt in the movement of the princess' hand a keen emotion at first sight . . ."

It was not long before Axel was invited to join the group of favored friends with whom Marie Antoinette had surrounded herself at Trianon. Of all the Queen's follies during this period of her life the establishment of the *coterie* known as "the Queen's circle" was the most injudicious. The members of this exclusive little court within a court had it in common that they were young and as shallowminded and affectedly free from care as their sovereign. The capital of their toy kingdom was the little château of Trianon that Louis had given Marie Antoinette soon after the death of the old King. This enchanted, artificial land, not France, was to be Marie Antoinette's real realm for all too many years.

Simplicity was the style at Trianon, where, surrounded by bowers of roses and skillfully planted meadows of wildflowers, amid English lawns, slow-moving streams, and a miniature wood, the delights of country life *à la Rousseau* were enjoyed. Its little *hameau* was indeed the expression in beam and plaster of the pastoral fantasy that Rousseau had conjured forth in words. For Marie Antoinette, Trianon became a kind of eternal summerland where none could ever grow old. All serious—and therefore boring—topics were banished from this enclave. Laughter, singing, flirtation, and children's games such as blindman's buff and hide-and-seek were alone permitted.

It goes without saying that those not accorded an *entrée* into this paradise—ninety-nine percent of the court, including the King— viewed it with bitter resentment. "A great court," her mother warned her, "must be accessible to all people." And some of those who romped on the lawns of Trianon were far from being the innocent children Marie Antoinette believed them to be. One or two of them were, in fact, very bad numbers whose influence on her was nefarious.

Her brother-in-law the comte d'Artois was a member in good standing of the inner circle. In 1775, soon after she had become Queen of France, he introduced her to horse racing, just then brought over from England to France, and for a short time she became an impassioned addict of that particular diversion. Surrounded by her chattering friends she would be seen at the racetrack in the Bois de Boulogne behaving in an unreserved manner that the conservative Parisians considered highly improper for a Queen of France. In 1778, the year Fersen returned to Paris, everyone was discussing one of Artois' typical exploits. He had bet Marie Antoinette that during the court's eight-week stay at Fontainebleau he could cause a house to be built. Nine hundred men worked night and day and the building, Bagatelle, was finished in time for him to win his bet. But to complete it on schedule the Swiss Guard had been ordered to impound any load of stone or plaster that might come along the high-road to Paris. The owners were indemnified, but it was a piece of arrogance that outraged public opinion. The King was known to dislike his brother's highhanded behavior and everyone wondered why he tolerated such a frivolous abuse of royal prerogative. The Queen was blamed in the end. "It is generally believed," Mercy reported to the Empress, "that the King would never have tolerated the comte d'Artois' flightiness without the protection given him by the Queen."

For all his weaknesses, Artois was the least dangerous of Marie Antoinette's friends. His royal rank put him on an easier footing with her and he did not try to hide his faults. Some of her other associates were obliged to be more circumspect and she did not discover until too late that they were not friends at all but selfish and ambitious courtiers no different, except in their costumes and their affectedly simple manners, from the painted sycophants of the old court.

One of the worst was the duc de Lauzun. "Among the giddy people whom the Queen allows too free an access there is one who is very dangerous through his turbulence and all sorts of bad qualities: it is the duc de Lauzun." In making this report to the Empress, Mercy spoke elliptically. It was known to everyone except perhaps Marie Antoinette that Lauzun had the sexual appetite of a satyr. The eighteenth century viewed these matters indulgently. The Revolutionary Tribunal did not. Like all dedicated revolutionaries the authorities of Robespierre's Reign of Virtue were puritanical and the charge of promiscuity, too, was prominent among the accusations that brought Marie Antoinette's head under the axe.

The truth was exactly the opposite. It was precisely because of a strain of prudishness that Marie Antoinette turned Lauzun into one of her most implacable enemies. One day behind closed doors, where she had inadvisedly received him, Lauzun made open proposals to her. She grew impatient and then, as the man pressed his suit more ardently, indignant. There was a scene of some sort whose outlines have been blurred by conflicting reports, but its conclusion remains clear. She flung open the door and in angry tone said, "You may leave, Monsieur!"

Lauzun thereafter joined the ranks of his fellow *débauché* the duc d'Orléans and became a mortal enemy both of the Queen and of the monarchy. He was to fight as an officer in the Revolutionary army but during the Reign of Terror he was recalled to Paris and guillotined a few months after Marie Antoinette.

There was the comte de Vaudreuil, a moody young man who was subject to violent outbursts of temper. He belonged to the "liberal" element of the court and loved to tell people of his dream of the Golden Age of equality that lay ahead. Declaring himself to be a "man of nature" he made a show of his dislike of the artificiality of court life. "True feeling is so rare at Versailles that I stop to watch a dog gnawing at a bone in the street when I return from there," he once declared. Nonetheless, all that he owned he owed to that court he so despised. He was the lover of Marie Antoinette's friend Madame de Polignac and from this connection there flowed a stream of favors, pensions, and appointments for which he was never reluctant to ask.

There was Valentin Esterházy, a Hungarian officer of wild appearance. Marie Antoinette paid his gambling debts and secured a regiment for him. When this regiment was posted to Montmédy, a dull frontier town, Esterházy complained. Marie Antoinette went to the Minister of War and demanded a better garrison for him, and the affairs of a busy ministry were momentarily halted while a more lively post was found for this officer of no particular merit.

The baron de Besenval was another of the Queen's dangerous associates. Swiss of origin, he was at fifty the oldest member of the little circle, but an iron constitution and an irrepressible gaiety of spirit caused those who knew him to forget his years. He was a witty man and he had the gift of tailoring his wit to suit the childish tastes of Marie Antoinette. Imitations, faces, a joke now and then, and all the other little money tricks that never failed to send her into gales of laughter were at his disposal. The Queen could hardly bear to be separated from him and would buy away one of his pouts or a fit of sulking at almost any price. He had great influence over her and this influence, as he unashamedly reveals in his memoirs, he put to use in a spirit of idle mischief. He enjoyed pulling the strings of power as others might enjoy a game of whist. He would goad the Queen into asking for this appointment or that dismissal and was incessantly at work behind the scenes encouraging her girlish animosities, inciting her to show off her authority. He was directly responsible for the dismissal of the duc d'Aiguillon because, as he declared, Aiguillon had been behind the fall of Choiseul and "it suited my personal feelings to punish him for it." Through his favor with the Queen, Besenval was to secure other dismissals for which history has condemned her. He was deeply implicated in the very serious matter of Turgot's downfall.

The reigning sovereign of the Trianon *coterie* was not, in fact, Marie Antoinette but her friend the famous comtesse de Polignac, a woman who was to do irreparable harm to Marie Antoinette's reputation and to the French Crown in its final years.

Even as dauphine, Marie Antoinette had shown a weakness for what the French call the *amitié amoureuse*, the titillating friendship often between persons of the same sex that is not quite sexual but partakes of myriad stifled longings. The *amitié amoureuse* between women was one of the characteristic expressions of late eighteenth-century civilization. A woman might have a lover, but if she were a creature of any sensibility she would certainly have a lady friend with whom to exchange sighs and kisses. Hand-holding, tear-mingling, sudden embraces, and the fondling of one another's breasts were among the innocent delights that two such intimates would share.

Marie Antoinette's first such friend had been the princesse de Lamballe, a young widow whom she had impulsively befriended with the ardor of one starved for affection. Madame de Lamballe was appointed Superintendent of the Queen's Household and loaded with lucrative favors. The princesse had all the qualities requisite to a tender friendship. She had them—unfortunately for herself—in overabundance. She was too good, too devoted, too sentimental, too cloyingly sweet. In the fast-stepping world of horse racing, high-stake gambling, and fashionable dress in which Marie Antoinette's friends moved the Queen began to crave something with a little more bite.

She finally found it when the court was at Fontainebleau in the autumn of 1775. At a concert there one evening her attention was caught by a beautiful woman whom she had never seen before. Upon inquiry she learned that the woman's name was the comtesse Jules de Polignac, that she was twenty-six years of age, although of still girlish appearance, and the mother of two children. When Marie Antoinette approached her and asked her why she had not seen her before the young woman had a disarming answer. She replied that she and her husband were too poor to afford the expense of many visits to the court and that they lived in the country. The Queen, whose dislike of courtiers and their pretensions was notorious, was charmed by the modesty of this reply. In the days that followed their acquaint-

51

ance ripened into warm friendship. When the moment of parting finally came and the penniless comtesse prepared to return to her château the Queen implored her to stay, offering her her protection. But Madame de Polignac was not so easily caught as a vapid Lamballe. In her case the deportment of a sweet and wide-eyed *ingénue* never conflicted with the psychological acumen of a clever and experienced woman of the world. She burst into tears.

"I feel the moment approaching when I would be unable to leave the Queen," she declared. "Let us forestall such sorrow and let Your Majesty permit me to leave now."

The Queen began to weep with her. The two friends fell sobbing into one another's arms and began to "mingle their tears"—the moment of consummation in the *amitié amoureuse*. Unfortunately, at exactly this moment the comte d'Artois happened into the room and with a significant clearing of the throat said, "Oh, I didn't mean to interrupt you!" He hurried off and passed the story around the court that he had caught his sister-in-law and her friend in a compromising position. Inevitably Artois' malicious gossip made its way from the court to the streets and in a few years' time obscenities of every kind were to be printed concerning Marie Antoinette's partiality for the comtesse de Polignac. Marie Antoinette was quite aware of this gossip. "Both tastes are attributed to me here," she wrote her mother cheerfully. "For women and for lovers."

Madame de Polignac stayed. From that moment until the day, fourteen years later, when the Bastille was stormed and a number of placards appeared in the streets of Paris offering a reward for the head of "the Polignac woman," the Polignac clan was to hold its prey in an unyielding grip. Their insatiable greed for annuities and appointments was to cost the treasury sums reminiscent of the grand days of the Pompadour. The favorite's husband, the comte Jules, was made the Queen's First Equerry—over the head of a hereditary incumbent, the comte de Tessé, who thus became an enemy of Marie Antoinette. The expenses connected with that department of the Queen's household soon doubled and then tripled as Polignac systematically lined his pockets with loot from this office. In a few years he was to be given the brevet of duc and his wife granted the prized right of the *tabouret*, while Madame de Polignac was eventually to be appointed Governess of the Children of France with all the emoluments that went with that position.

Far more serious than such financial deprivations was the influence of the Polignac clan on affairs of state. The comtesse Jules was herself a lazy woman. All who knew her were to speak of her strange, almost pathological lassitude. She was as indifferent as Marie Antoinette to politics. But she was the ready instrument of relatives and friends more enterprising than herself. The real power in the Polignac family was her husband's unmarried sister, known at court as the comtesse Diane. According to most observers, it was this able and intelligent woman who maneuvered behind the scenes, manipulated the strings, and turned her sister-in-law's favor to profitable account. In her capable hands the so-called "Queen's circle" became a powerful political party that had to be taken into serious account by the King's ministers.

It was to these people that Maurepas turned in his intrigues to overthrow the Turgot ministry. Mercy leaves no doubt of this in one of his reports to the Empress. "I have discovered," he wrote, "that the comtesse de Polignac has been won over by the comte de Maurepas and is being guided by him. My proof of this has been well supported by certain remarks that the comtesse de Polignac dropped when trying to persuade the Queen that it would be to her best interest if she could persuade the King to appoint the comte de Maurepas his First Minister."

Wheedled by Madame de Polignac, incited by her friend Besenval, Marie Antoinette would all too often try to "persuade" the King to take this or that step in affairs of state. And all too often there were times when Louis would listen to his wife's tearful pleas and submit. It was by this path that the duc d'Aiguillon's enemies secured his downfall—a typical intrigue in which Marie Antoinette was the unknowing tool of others throughout. The wheels of the little world of Trianon were, in fact, so closely interlocked with the larger wheels of state at the palace that it is impossible to separate them. Anyone who would wish to understand the history of late eighteenth-century France must be as familiar with the small social chronicle of that time as with the weighty archives of more official history.

It was into this world that Axel Fersen stepped in the spring of 1779. He appeared there quietly: "without intrigue and without seeking notoriety," noted the Queen's page, the comte de Tilly. The Queen's *coterie* accepted his arrival in their midst without protest. The comte de St. Priest offers a reason for this unexpected passivity. "Madame de Polignac did not oppose her friend's preference. No doubt Vaudreuil and Besenval were behind this attitude because they felt that a lone foreigner who was not very enterprising would be less dangerous to them than would be some Frenchman surrounded by relatives who might win all the favors instead of themselves and perhaps end up as the head of a clique that would eclipse them all. The Queen was therefore encouraged to follow her inclination. She indulged it without much prudence."

It was not only at Trianon but at the masked dances at the Opéra in Paris where Marie Antoinette would meet Fersen. The two would often promenade about the room together. Fersen's friend Baron de Taube was in Paris that winter and in a letter to Gustavus III that was discovered in the Swedish Royal Archives in 1933 he confirms the fact that the Queen and Fersen were often seen together at the Opéra during the early months of 1779: "She often walked about with Count Fersen, even entered a box alone with him and remained there talking to him for a long time."

Inevitably these attentions came to the notice of French courtiers. "People spoke of meetings, of prolonged *têtes-à-têtes* at the Opéra balls, of looks exchanged in place of conversation at intimate parties at Trianon." It was reported that at one of these parties at Trianon the Queen, accompanying herself at the spinet, sang the aria from Piccinni's *Didon* that begins with the words:

> *Ah! Que je fus inspirée*
> *quand je vous reçûs dans ma cour*

As she sang she was seen to seek Count Fersen's eyes "with a troubled expression in her own." This bit of apparently idle gossip is partly confirmed in Fersen's Journal. Twenty-six years later across an abyss of grief and time he happened to hear *Didon* sung again at the Royal Opera House in Stockholm. His mind returned to Versailles. "How many memories," he wrote, "and how many painful regrets does this opera recall to my heart!"

When Marie Antoinette secured for him the brevet of Colonel in the Royal Deux-Ponts Regiment there was a murmur of resentment among the young Frenchmen in her entourage. It was as an officer of this regiment that Fersen made plans to go to America and fight in the Revolutionary War.

His application to serve in the Prussian army had been rejected. He decided therefore to join the French Expeditionary Force that was about to set sail and give aid to the Americans in their War of Independence. This project was much in the air at the period when he and Marie Antoinette were seen together at the Opéra. His impending departure on that adventure may well have imbued him with an aura of additional interest in Marie Antoinette's eyes. His orders to go to le Havre and await embarkment did not arrive until September but expectancy was everywhere in the air that spring. As early as April it was believed he might be called up. The effect on the Queen was visible. It was at this moment that Count Creutz wrote the confidential letter to Gustavus III that provides posterity with the most reliable evidence of Marie Antoinette's interest in Fersen at that time. Creutz was a dispassionate witness and had no reason to invent stories or exaggerate facts.

"I must inform Your Majesty in confidence that young Count Fersen has been so warmly received by the Queen that a number of people here have taken umbrage. I must admit that I cannot help believing that she has an inclination for him. I have seen signs that are too clear to be doubted. Young Count Fersen's behavior on this occasion was admirable in its modesty and reserve . . . By deciding to go to America he has avoided all danger, but assuredly this decision must have taken a strength of character beyond his years. During the last days the Queen has hardly been able to take her eyes from him. Whenever she looked at him her eyes would fill with tears. I beg Your Majesty not to let this information go beyond himself and Senator Fersen. When all the favorites heard that the Count was going to leave they were overjoyed. The duchesse de Fitz-James said to him, 'What, Monsieur! You are abandoning your conquest so easily?'

" 'If I had made one I should not abandon it,' he replied. 'I depart unfortunately without leaving the regrets of anyone behind me.'

"Your Majesty will allow that this answer shows a wisdom and a prudence far beyond his years."

Axel did not finally set sail until early May of 1780, nearly a year after Count Creutz wrote these words. The "inclination" of which he speaks thus had ample time to ripen and the "danger" which Fersen was planning to escape was not terminated so abruptly as the Ambassador's letter suggests. A year is a long exposure to that particular danger and one wonders how ripe the "inclination" may have become. We are without report. It must be remembered that those of the Queen's intimate circle who wrote their memoirs did so long after her execution when the frivolous *comédie* enacted on the lawns of Trianon could be seen as the prelude to a tragedy in the tradition of Euripides. Among Marie Antoinette's few close friends who had been circumstanced to observe her growing friendship with Axel Fersen the injunction that one should speak no ill of the dead would have had an unusually forceful application. In any case one of those startling silences that are sometimes louder than noise surrounds his name. And yet, one has the testimony of Creutz, of St. Priest, and indeed, obliquely, of Fersen himself.

One can only surmise. It seems likely that the "inclination" was enjoyed in the light spirit of Trianon and with all the sentimental appurtenances: "Stolen Moments," "Hidden Sighs," confidences shared with Madame de Polignac, tears welling up over songs at the spinet. But behind these cardboard trappings she may well have sensed the awakening of some genuine emotion. And behind the "lover" she may have glimpsed the presence of a devoted friend.

The lover in any case seems to have been a lover in appearance only and not even St. Priest, who kept a close eye on things at Trianon and who never minced words about what at a later time he declared to have been a full, physical relationship between Marie Antoinette and Fersen, believed that the inclination of 1779 was anything more than that. But the spark of a deeper understanding than the trivialities of Trianon admitted, the communication of a sympathy not visible to the supercilious eyes of a St. Priest or an Artois had been exchanged between them. When he set sail for America in May of 1780 she may for once have found herself an unwilling actress in the charade that custom now obliged her to play before her friends. For "The Departure of the Lover" was one of the most relished scenes in the charade of love and one may be sure that the *coterie* now flocked forward to applaud her performance in "Love's Regrets."

He was to be gone for three years.

As aide-de-camp to Rochambeau, commander of the first French Expeditionary Force sent to America, Fersen was to be brought into close touch with the American Revolution. His letters from America written to his father were edited and published in 1929 by F. V. Wrangel. They give a fresh and unexpected glimpse of the Revolutionary War through the eyes of a young foreigner and they are full of interest. He met Washington. ("He has the air of a hero; he is very cold and he speaks little, but he is polite and a gentleman.") He was to fight at Yorktown and be witness there to the birth of a new

56

world just as in Europe he was destined to see the extinction of the old. A first enthusiasm for the "natives" ("They are happy with the little necessaries of life that in other countries would only satisfy the lower class. Their clothing is plain but good and their customs have not been spoiled by European luxury.") gave way to more querulous opinions after a winter of inactivity at Newport: "Money is the first motive of all their actions. Everyone here is out for himself, none cares for the public good. They have been robbing us blind. I don't wish to say that there aren't decent people among them . . . but I speak of the nation as a whole and believe that it is more Dutch than English."

In America he found the adventure that he sought and he returned to Europe with many a tale that in his old age might have spellbound the young who gathered about his hearthside to hear him talk. On the merits of his American voyage alone Fersen might have achieved a certain small celebrity, but in Europe he was marked for more important adventures and so this three-year passage in his life must be considered an interlude, a moment of suspension that did not have significance in the larger prospect of his life.

He did not return to France until July of 1783. He found that many changes had taken place there during his absence.

The American Revolution that had provided the bored young noblemen of the French court with so exciting an excursion had, on the dull economic level of life, repercussions of the gravest sort. It is impossible to name a precise figure because France's initial support of the Americans was done through loans that were hidden behind the veil of a dummy trading company in order to prevent an overt rupture with England. The records of later loans and gifts are equally unreliable and one can only estimate the final cost of the naval and expeditionary forces sent to America by the French government. Statements about the cost of France's intervention in the American Revolution therefore vary considerably.

"It has cost France some 772 millions (*livres*) to make America independent," declares the author of the *Correspondance secrète*, "and France has received no advantages in exchange." The author of these words was a spy at the court of Louis XVI in the pay of a middle European sovereign or German prince. His reports were found some years ago in the archives of St. Petersburg and they have been used extensively by all who have ever written about the period. They are observant and well informed. In the matter of the cost of the American war the writer is probably quoting what was then the current opinion of people at court who were "in the know," perhaps that of men attached to the Ministry of Finance or the Foreign Ministry.

Seven hundred and seventy-two million livres would be a sum somewhat in excess of a billion and a half dollars of today's money. But such figures can never be really translated. It is only by comparison with other sums of the same currency that one is able to form an idea of how staggering an amount of money this represented in the France of Louis XVI. At the time of Turgot's appointment in 1775 the deficit was 135 million livres, a sum considered so serious that stringent economies were imposed on the Crown. Because of it the whole substructure of France's economic system was pronounced in danger and because of it Turgot's commendable reforms were presented to the *parlement*. The cost of the American war came to more than six times this sum.

The American Revolution broke the French treasury beyond repair and no expedient, no measure was to put the pieces together again. From that moment until the outbreak of the Revolution six years later the foremost problem of the French government was its insolvency. Ministry followed ministry, each trying, and each failing, to solve a problem that was insoluble. The Swiss minister Necker came and went and then came again. Necker's expedient to keep the French treasury afloat was to borrow abroad. Since foreign financiers were reluctant to extend money to a government in so precarious a financial condition Necker was obliged to overcome their hesitation with the offer of high rates of interest. The money appeared and the illusion of solvency was temporarily purchased. But from that moment a new factor, the cost of interest, was added to the country's financial problems. It began to accumulate at such a rate that it alone became a staggering expense. So carelessly managed were France's financial affairs that at one moment the government with one hand was borrowing abroad at high interest rates and with the other was lending to the Americans at low rates.

One of the Finance Ministers called in on the case at the last moment was Calonne, an intimate of the Polignac "party" but not of Marie Antoinette, who disliked him. Calonne, a notorious spendthrift himself, accepted his portfolio with a flippant remark that amused the court: "I would never have taken the job if my own finances had not been in a worse state than France's!" During his ministry Calonne was able to put his own affairs in order but he could do nothing for those of the government.

The Estates-General were finally convoked in order to submit the problem of the debt to the consideration of the nation, and as readers of French history know the Estates-General soon found that it had other matters than the national debt to discuss. So opened the first act of the French Revolution. The American Revolution may be considered its prelude.

But the American Revolution had repercussions in France on other levels than the economic. In England, for instance, Louis XVI's government had gained a determined enemy. The English henceforth were as ready and as eager as the Prussians to foment disturbance in that unstable realm. Even when it became evident that the Revolution in France presented a threat to the English Crown along with that of Louis XVI, England remained a tardy and unenthusiastic ally in the "cause of kings."

The young noblemen who, like Fersen, had gone to America to fight in the War of Independence set forth in search of excitement. Surfeited with life's luxuries, bored by leisure and the enervating sweetness of too extended a summer's afternoon, they longed for ruder weather and like Chateaubriand cried, "Arise, ye desired storms!" They returned to France with many ideas about the nature of government and they communicated these ideas to their friends who had stayed at home. Republicanism, constitutions, and the Social Contract became topics of conversation in the *salons* of the Faubourg St. Germain. As, under the weight of its insoluble problems, the old order began to crumble, the possibility of a new order based on American principles presented itself with ever-increasing allure to the *mondaine* society of Paris. The simplicity that Marie Antoinette had introduced at Trianon and which had been so bitterly criticized suddenly became popular. Furniture grew plain, rooms bare, gilding was reduced to a minimum, and many people ceased to powder their hair.

During Fersen's absence Marie Antoinette had become the most hated person in the land. There are times of national stress when *vox populi* requires a flesh-and-blood effigy on which to put the blame for its anger, apprehension, and disappointment. The pillory in its day answered a deep and instinctive human need. By 1784 Marie Antoinette for the mass of the French people had become exactly such an effigy. Natural as well as national disasters were declared to be her fault. Crop failures, the deficit, France's discredit abroad, the blame for everything was blindly, indiscriminately heaped on her shoulders. Within the family circle of France's *bonne bourgeoisie* her name was used to excuse every domestic quarrel or disturbance. Should a wife be less attentive to her husband's wishes than old French custom dictated, it was declared to be the fault of the "Austrian woman" who set so bad an example for decent French housewives.

A typical instance of such indiscriminate criticism took place in the spring of 1783. Paris was still buzzing over the matter when Fersen returned there in June. In tune with the new style Madame Vigée-Lebrun, Marie Antoinette's favorite artist, had painted the Queen not in customary formal court costume but dressed in a plain Creole blouse known as a *gaulle* that had become popular among her Trianon friends. The portrait was hung at the *salon* of that year and there was a terrible outcry when the public saw it. Marie Antoinette was accused of dressing like a chambermaid in order to humiliate France in the eyes of Europe. The same husbands and fathers who had angrily reproached her a few years earlier for setting an example of extravagance now declared that she was ruining the French clothing industry in order to favor her brother's weavers in the Austrian Netherlands. Marie Antoinette finally ordered the painting withdrawn.

This episode might be considered trifling, but it was characteristic of dozens of others that were reported and distorted all over France. Among simple country folk her name was not merely the symbol of extravagance and of foreign intriguing, but the embodiment of actual evil—a figure with whom disobedient children were threatened, a shadowy figure who filled their parents, too, with fear.

The English traveler Arthur Young was in Clermont in 1789 when the Revolution began. He suddenly found himself surrounded by a mob of angry villagers who accused him of being a foreign agent sent down to Clermont by Marie Antoinette in order to destroy their crops. "They declared I was an agent of the Queen who intended to blow up the whole town with a mine and send all who escaped to the galleys. The care that must have been taken to render

60

the character of that princess detested among the people is incredible; and there seems everywhere to be no absurdities too gross, nor circumstances too impossible for their faith."

Marie Antoinette was well aware of this malevolence. The author of the *Correspondance secrète* reports that after an official visit into Paris in 1785 the enmity of the populace was so palpable that she turned to a friend with the question, "But what have I done to make them hate me so?" The author goes on to say that it was not the French people who were to blame for this hatred. "The evil," he states, "comes from another direction. Clandestine writings, calumny and dirty songs that have been disseminated *from the court* have completely changed French good nature. Never have there been so many lampoons! These verses, these songs and satires have been circulated everywhere and they have done inestimable harm . . ."

A sampling of this torrent of abuse may be read today at the Bibliothèque Nationale in Paris where most of it has been consigned to the private rooms of the library known as *l'enfer* because it is considered unfit reading for the general public. But it is not the obscene drawings nor the lewd texts that cause the present-day reader to recoil as though he had touched a hot wire. It is the hatred which is of such intensity that one momentarily feels oneself in the presence of infernal forces. As one leafs through the pages of these really appalling lampoons one might suppose they were penned during the fever pitch of the Terror. They were not. The larger part of them, as the author of the *Correspondance secrète* points out, came from the court. It is not the clandestine presses of a Marat or an Hébert where one must look to find their source but to the *antichambres* of Versailles where powerful noblemen such as the duc d'Aiguillon and the duc d'Orléans sharpened their swords for a vengeance that was to be without limits. The hand of the King's own brother, the comte de Provence, is known to have added further poison to this brew. And behind these open enemies there moved the unseen ones such as the agents of Frederick the Great employed by their government to resort to any means of defaming Austria in French eyes and so break the Alliance. It was through them, for instance, that the story was spread that Marie Antoinette had ordered cartloads of French gold shipped off to her relatives in Austria, a calumny that probably did her name more harm than any of the stories about the Sapphic embraces of Madame de Polignac and the orgies of Trianon.

The reports of the *Correspondance secrète* state that the Queen

61

appeared to be sunk in a deep sadness at about this time. More and more frequently she withdrew to Trianon, where she would stay in seclusion for periods of as long as a month. And so the void that she had already dug between herself and the French aristocracy grew wider. The vast palace that had once been the beating heart of the kingdom now appeared abandoned as courtiers by the drove ceased to pay homage to a monarchy that was no longer there. They continued to draw their honorary emoluments and to enjoy the privileges with which their condition endowed them, but they preferred to spend their time and money in their *hôtels particuliers* in Paris where they could criticize the government at their ease rather than in the half-empty caravanserai with its heavy atmosphere and *démodé* gilding that was Versailles. The Queen herself had been the first to leave.

Marie Antoinette's increasing predilection for the solitude of Trianon may in part be attributed to an event of great significance in her private life. In 1781 she finally gave birth to an heir to the French throne. Louis had been persuaded to undergo the necessary surgery by his brother-in-law, Joseph II of Austria. A daughter, Marie Thérèse, had been born in the winter of 1779 and the birth of this first child had wrought a noticeable change in Marie Antoinette's character. "The Queen," reported the Swedish Ambassador, "is behaving with much more restraint than before." With the arrival of the dauphin two years later Marie Antoinette's way of life changed completely. She withdrew more and more to the pastoral tranquillity of Trianon where she could play undisturbed with her children and be alone with her friends—of whom Madame de Polignac, now appointed Governess to the Children of France, remained the favorite. Once again the instincts of the woman came into conflict with the obligations of the Queen, for her children did not really belong to her. In the eyes of the court they were the Children of France and as such pawns of the state. As usual with Marie Antoinette the instincts of the woman prevailed.

The birth of the dauphin brought her an unexpected burst of popularity among the French people and she was enthusiastically applauded in the streets of Paris when she appeared at the Hôtel de Ville to celebrate the event. At court where many parties were hard put to conceal their chagrin the rejoicing was more restrained. The anti-Austrian faction, led by the Prussians, was particularly upset. From Potsdam, Frederick wrote his Ambassador to suggest that Louis, now that he was "cured," be induced to acquire "a taste for mistresses in order to keep the Queen out of the picture." Mercy was soon *au courant* of this intrigue but he never guessed its source. "There are wretches in this perverted whirlpool," he announced, "who are secretly scheming to introduce the King to libertinism. I know of more than one person who has dared speak to him about an actress at the Comédie Française."

And the comte de Provence, who had heretofore considered himself heir to the throne, wrote a curious letter to Gustavus III when Marie Antoinette's first pregnancy was officially announced. "You have heard," he confided, "of the change that has taken place in my fortunes . . . Throughout I have controlled myself outwardly and behaved in the same way as before without showing any joy which might have looked like hypocrisy and which indeed would have been because frankly, as you may imagine, I feel no joy at all over this. My inward feelings have been more difficult to conquer and they still rise up at times."

It is a pity that Marie Antoinette could not have had a glimpse of her brother-in-law's hidden thoughts for they might have prompted her to the circumspection that her mother's warnings did not. The comte de Provence was one of the sources of the rumor that Louis XVI was still impotent and that all Marie Antoinette's children were therefore illegitimate. The applause of the populace of Paris dimmed as that report made its slow and deadly way through France. Yet despite the obvious indiscretion, Marie Antoinette at Trianon continued to consort with men such as Vaudreuil, Esterházy, and Lauzun.

In the fall of 1780, only a few months after Fersen's departure for America, Marie Antoinette had received the last of her mother's admonitions: "I know how boring and empty the ritual of holding state can be, but in your country with such a volatile people the little inconveniences are nothing beside the disadvantages." A few days afterward the Empress was dead. It is related that she collapsed sobbing when she pronounced a last blessing on her favorite daughter, the Queen of France. Everything indeed suggests that Maria Theresa discerned the outlines of the disaster that lay ahead and at the end she may even have had some intimation that her daughter's doom was beyond the possibility of alteration by human hands but was bound up instead with the larger forces of destiny.

Between mother and daughter there had been an almost total disparity of taste and interest, but the Empress' strength of character, her experience, her maternal concern had been anchors of stability

63

to Marie Antoinette. Like many another rebellious child she learned too late how necessary to her the vanished parent had been. Nothing more decisively closes the "generation gap" than death. Marie Antoinette was prostrated by grief and she closeted herself alone for many days afterward. Henceforth she was to venerate her mother's memory and in the dark approaching years she tried to emulate the Empress' dignity. "I shall not be an unworthy daughter of Maria Theresa": the phrase is repeated in many of her letters written during the Revolution.

With the death of her mother and the birth of her children certain physical as well as psychological changes became apparent in Marie Antoinette. Every portrait of her taken after the birth of her second son in 1785 communicates the fullness of body and face of a woman of mature years. The outline of the child receded and was replaced by the ample shape of the Empress. The effervescent and impetuous Viennese who had so offended the French court was no more. But her reputation remained.

When his vessel landed at Brest in the summer of 1783 Axel went immediately to Versailles. It was observed by the court that during his three-year absence he too had greatly changed in appearance. *Le beau Fersen*, it was said at court, was no longer *beau*.

"He had been ill in America," records the comtesse de Boigne, "and he returned to Versailles aged by ten years, having lost the beauty of his face. This change is believed to have greatly touched the Queen. Whether or not this was the reason, those who knew her did not doubt that she now yielded to the passion of M. de Fersen. He indemnified her sacrifice by a boundless devotion and by an affection that was as deep as it was respectful and discreet. He breathed only for her and all his habits of life were calculated to compromise her as little as possible."

Madame de Boigne's connection with the court and its gossip was through an aunt who was one of Madame Adélaïde's ladies-in-waiting. Because of that source her information cannot be considered reliable. But posterity has been left with a more dependable clue to Fersen's relationship with the Queen than the memoirs of Madame de Boigne. In Axel's letters to his family in Sweden there may be found two or three revealing remarks.

In one such letter—written hardly a month after his return to France—he communicated a curious thought to his sister Sophie: "No matter how much pleasure I would have in seeing you again I cannot leave Paris without regret. You will find this very natural when I tell you the reason . . ." In a letter written to his father asking his financial support in order to stay in Paris, Axel again seems to refer to this mysterious matter. "Your consent," he writes, "is the only thing that could make me happy forever. There are a thousand reasons for this which I dare not put down on paper."

Then to Sophie he makes a still more arresting confidence. Mademoiselle Leyell, whom sporadically he still hoped to marry, had suddenly married an Englishman. The possibility of an alliance with the Necker heiress was presented to him, but it was clear that his friend Staël-Holstein was about to win that dowry so with no reluctance he withdrew his hat from the ring. "I have taken my stand," he wrote Sophie in summation. "I don't want to form any conjugal ties. Since I cannot belong to the person to whom I want to belong, to the only woman who really loves me, I don't want to belong to anybody."

The reader is at liberty to interpret these words as he chooses, but Fersen certainly seems to state that there was a woman in love with him whom circumstances had placed beyond the possibility of marriage. There are many people who believe that this woman was Marie Antoinette.

Behind the lines of Axel's letter to his father tensions were gathering. The son had returned to France determined to acquire for himself what was known in the French army as a "proprietary regiment." These regiments that were bought and sold like blocks of real estate were attached to the service of the King of France and were, in effect, mercenaries. Although such regiments brought an income to their owners they were the expensive hobby of well-circumstanced noblemen, equivalent roughly to the ownership today of a stable of race horses or a baseball team. A number of them were foreign in origin, manned and commanded by soldiers who were not French. During the Revolution the Crown was to rely more on some of these foreign regiments than on the French army because they were independent of French political passions. The best known of the foreign regiments was the famous Swiss, the last defenders of the King who were massacred by the Paris mob on August 10 of 1792, the day when Louis

XVI and Marie Antoinette were made prisoners of the Commune of Paris.

Another well-known foreign regiment was that of Sweden, the historic Royal Suédois that had fought in the wars of Louis XIV. It was on this prize that Axel finally fixed his sights. The stumbling block was money. Since he was without resources of his own he had to turn to his father and again solicit his support. Unfortunately his father was in a very bad temper with him at this moment because Axel, instead of returning to Sweden after his American adventure, had gone to Paris. He considered his son ungrateful, undependable, and extravagant. It was with cold words that he extinguished Axel's hopes of financial help.

"I would gladly consent to this plan of yours," he wrote, "if I didn't see one small impediment: neither you nor I have the necessary money. You say you need 100,000 livres to buy the regiment. You say that you can find the credit to buy it. Allowing that it brings you an income of 12,000 a year you would still have to subtract 5000 from this for the annual interest on the loan. That would leave you 7000 a year. Could you possibly live in Paris on this? No. You would need a minimum of 25,000. Do you have it? No. Where do you expect to get it? From me, I suppose. But I don't have it either.

"Since your adventure abroad you have cost me between 300 and 500 thousand livres, a sum of money that is far beyond my means and that would constitute the whole fortune of many families. I ask you to put your mind for a moment on your younger brother, who is about to go into the world and who has certain rights in the paternal house, and on your two sisters, who are in the same circumstances. Is it fair to them that their older brother who should be their support becomes instead their ruin?"

This brought an indignant retort from Axel, which in turn provoked another angry lecture from the old Count. But in the midst of this exchange Axel, true soldier, never lost sight of his objective: possession of the Royal Suédois. He turned to Gustavus for support and Gustavus, although he disapproved of Fersen's adventure on behalf of the insurrectional Americans (he forbade him to wear the Order of the Cincinnati at the Swedish court), was more lenient toward this erring son. To induce the retiring commander of the Royal Suédois to part with his regiment in favor of Fersen, he promised him the Order of the Seraphim. Gustavus then wrote Louis XVI a warm letter soliciting the patronage of the King of France for his protégé.

66

Gustavus' price for these favors was a promise from Fersen that once awarded the regiment he would not become an expatriate but would spend at least six months of the year in Sweden paying court to Gustavus.

It was Marie Antoinette who answered Gustavus' letter to Louis XVI and who henceforth engaged herself in securing the Royal Suédois for her friend. The Queen's intervention brought Fersen's plans to a successful conclusion and a few days after her letter to Gustavus ("Count Fersen through his fine character and good qualities has earned the respect and affection of all who know him . . .") Axel announced to Sophie that "the business is finally settled. I am now Colonel Proprietor of the Royal Suédois Regiment . . . but don't say anything about this to Father should the subject come up. There is still the matter of the 100,000 to arrange with him." And in his correspondence book, a ledger in which he kept a record of all the letters he wrote or received, he notes (on November 7) that "I wrote the Queen today to thank her for the regiment and to ask that Stedingk be appointed Colonel-Commander."

The Queen's intervention on Fersen's behalf put any financial apprehensions of the regiment's previous proprietor to rest. The slightest hint of her favor was all too notoriously a better security than any bond. But Fersen, in fact, had no intention of turning to her for help in this matter. Bearing the *fait accompli* of his commission with him he decided to go to Sweden and again try to persuade his father to advance him the money. His sister Sophie was on his side and had already started pacifying their father on his behalf. So, immediately after receiving his appointment, he set out for Sweden. Along the way he paused for a night or two at Strasbourg, where he met his young brother Fabian, who, accompanied by a tutor, was doing the Grand Tour just as Axel had done it six years before.

Scarcely had he left Strasbourg when a letter from Gustavus was delivered to him. Out of a blue sky the King had decided to do the Grand Tour himself. At that very moment he was at Rostock and he wanted Fersen to join his suite as Captain of his Guard. Thus did Axel find himself obliged to pay off the first installment of gratitude. Such royal wishes were orders. Instead of continuing his journey toward Sweden, Axel made his way into Germany where the Sovereign impatiently awaited his arrival.

In Sweden old Senator Fersen fumed with rage when the news of this junket reached him. "I find it very hard on Father," Fabian wrote his sister sanctimoniously, "that he should have to forego the pleasure of seeing Axel after all the trouble and worry Axel has given him."

Axel finally caught up with Gustavus at Nürnberg. The King was in bed when he arrived, but that did not dampen the monarch's welcome. He opened his arms wide, clasped the young officer to his breast and covered him with tears of joy and words of tenderness. "He received me not as a king, but as a loving and sensitive friend," Axel reported to his father. Fersen and the Baron de Taube were to be the two members of the suite closest to the King during the long months of his tour.

Gustavus traveled under the incognito of the "comte de Haga" but his whims were at all times those of a spoiled and capricious young autocrat. He planned to make a leisurely tour of Italy during the winter and in the late spring go to Paris. Serious business of state lay behind Gustavus' trip, although it was difficult for Fersen and others in the King's party to realize it. Earlier that year Catherine had declared war on Turkey. It was Gustavus' plan, while her armies were occupied in the south, to recover some of Sweden's former possessions in the North that had been taken by the insatiable Empress. To do this he needed an assurance of French neutrality and French financial assistance. It was important that Russia have no suspicion of the motives behind his trip. Therefore his preliminary tour of Italy and its pleasures. Therefore the dancing, the masquerades, and the buffoonery without end. Gustavus appears to have successfully concealed even from himself whatever serious purpose there may have been behind his travels.

Fersen was soon disgusted by the King's behavior, as his letters to his father reveal. "We (always his sarcastic euphemism for the King) have a general principal of disorder and irresolution. We change our mind twenty times a day and each whimsy is more bizarre than the other . . . Every day I am forced to witness new follies, new extravagances, new inanities. Baron Taube and I spend most of our time trying to prevent them and trying to repair the damage, but we cannot always do so."

The too-earnest Axel was overly critical. A kind of charming madness seems to have cast its spell over their travels in the South. Eighteenth-century Italy was hospitable to the eccentricity of princes. At Pisa, for instance, Gustavus paid a call on the Grand Duke of Tuscany (the brother of Marie Antoinette and the future Emperor

Leopold of Austria) but he arrived at the palace without announcing himself, with only Count Fersen in attendance. When a footman asked his name he refused to give it, simply stating that "we are two foreigners who would like to meet the Grand Duke. We will identify ourselves when we see him." They were made to wait half an hour in an antechamber, which annoyed Gustavus. Then three new footmen appeared and ushered them to another antechamber. Gustavus peevishly turned to one of them, "I insist on seeing the Grand Duke." The servant to whom he addressed these words suddenly burst into laughter. "But I am the Grand Duke!" he declared. The two sovereigns shared a hearty chuckle over this joke.

The Italian climate was also propitious to light amorous adventure. Fersen records several such affairs of the heart. There was one in Florence with an Englishwoman named Emily Cowper and another in Naples with Lady Elizabeth Foster, the daughter of the Duke of Bristol, unhappily married to John Thomas Foster. The latter affair threatened to take a serious turn and Axel quickly withdrew. In his correspondence book he notes that he wrote her a letter in which "I told her everything." The phrase is so heavily underlined in his own hand and with such emphasis that one wonders what secret he may have imparted. He and Elizabeth Foster were to remain close friends for many years afterward. After the execution of Marie Antoinette the principal topic of their correspondence was to be the dead Queen.

After his winter's wanderings through Italy the King of Sweden —still alias the comte de Haga—and his party finally arrived in Paris on June 7. The French capital was to be the culmination of the tour. It was here that Gustavus planned to accomplish the business that was the purpose of his trip. Obsessed by French manners, by French style, and by the rays of glory that for him still emanated from the French throne, he planned to enjoy himself to the full in the City of Light. He lodged at the Swedish Embassy in the rue de Bac. Baron de Staël-Holstein was now his ambassador to France. The appointment had been one of Necker's conditions to his daughter's marriage with Staël-Holstein. So enormous was the heiress' fortune that Gustavus acceded without a murmur to the banker's demands. Not only was Staël-Holstein made ambassador, the compact demanded that the appointment be irrevocable. He was to be ambassador for his lifetime. The day was not far off when Gustavus would bitterly regret this concession. Baron de Staël-Holstein, following the lead of his wife and father-in-law, became an open enemy of Louis XVI and Marie

Antoinette and consequently, in Gustavus' eyes, a dangerous revolutionary and untrustworthy emissary.

No clouds were yet visible in the soft French skies when the King of Sweden arrived there in June of 1784; at any rate they were not visible to Gustavus, who happily plunged into a whirlpool of social distractions. His harebrained behavior that had so irritated Fersen in Italy reached a fever pitch in Paris. "We have been swimming about in parties, entertainments, and pleasures of every kind," Fersen reported to his father after the arrival of the Swedish party in Paris. "We have to be doing something all the time and we are always in a hurry. This sort of giddiness is very much to the taste of Monsieur le comte de Haga. We have already been given an opera in our honor at Versailles. We've had a ball in full dress, not to mention innumerable dinners and suppers. We don't miss a thing and we'd rather give up drinking, eating, and sleeping than forego a single minute of the social show. It's now become a kind of fever or mania . . ."

The crowning moment of Gustavus' visit came on June 21 when Marie Antoinette gave a supper party in his honor at Trianon. The moment not only seems to have capped Gustavus' personal delirium, it seems, too, in its way to have been a kind of culmination of the eighteenth-century spirit of *divertissement*. The insubstantial beauty of the age seems summarized and its fragrance distilled as one examines the accounts and engravings of that evening.

The party began with a performance in the Queen's Theater at Trianon of Piccinni's *Le Dormeur éveillé*. The diminutive size of the house restricted the number of invitations to this event. After the opera, however, supper was served at various pavilions in the garden and the gates were opened to a more extensive list of guests, who were asked to dress only in white. The little lake and the grottoes of the Queen's garden were illuminated by torches and pots of colored fire. A small flotilla of boats ferried passengers back and forth across the sheet of water where stood the Temple de l'Amour. A contemporary engraving of such a *fête* in the glades of Trianon shows the guests lolling on the banks of the enchanted isle in various pastoral attitudes reminiscent of some canvas of Fragonard. It was not the Revolution that brought an end to this fantasy. The century of the steam and internal combustion engines was about to dawn and the appearance of the earth and the attitude of everyone on it was to be altered forever.

Gustavus returned to his cold and distant kingdom in a fever of excitement. Trianon had enchanted him. He arrived in Sweden, his head swimming with projects. Had these ambitions been confined to architecture or landscaping, all might still have been well with him. Unfortunately he had formed certain grandiose political aspirations, too. He celebrated these by preparing to declare war on Russia and Denmark. The Riksdag, at this violation of the Constitution, rose in protest. In a kingly rage he dissolved it. Certain of his nobles remained loyal to him. Some did not. Among those who did not was Senator Fersen, who now became an adversary of the King. Having launched Sweden on a war that promised to be ruinous, Gustavus went on a domestic rampage. He increased taxes, seized control of the tobacco and liquor industries and made them Crown monopolies. He then gaily embarked on a spending spree, enlarged and redecorated his palaces, and built his exquisite little pavilion of Haga. It still stands today, a perfect monument to his trip to France in 1784, for it was designed in the neo-Classic style which at that moment was the last thing in Parisian taste. The costume parties and the jousts at Drottningholm grew more lavish; the theatricals more fanciful and frequent.

Gustavus' glimpse of high life at Versailles had for him every unfortunate consequence. From that moment he ceased to be regarded as a brilliant and benevolent young King and became in the public eye a gilded ninny, a tyrant whose follies had suddenly turned to madness.

Fersen accompanied his sovereign back to Sweden. On its practical level the trip had been a success, for Gustavus returned with French assurances of neutrality in his proposed attack on Russia and the promise of French financial aid. For its part, the government of Louis XVI had made an investment in good will which was to prove of significance in a few years' time. After the reception at Trianon, Gustavus became a devoted and loyal defender of the French Crown and particularly of Marie Antoinette. The time was at hand when she and Louis XVI were to find that he was the only disinterested friend they had among the kings of Europe.

For Axel Fersen the visit had been a success too. Gustavus had gone personally to Marie Antoinette and asked her for what Axel was too reticent to ask himself: a pension of twenty thousand livres that would permit him to buy his regiment without having to go to his father for the money. This step in the end did nothing to appease his father's resentment. The senior Count merely looked for, and readily found, other causes for complaint. But for Axel it meant that the

Royal Suédois was now his, and henceforth he could consider himself a subject of France as well as of Sweden. However, fetters of gratitude now bound him even more closely to his Quixotic King. Until the Revolution he was forced to divide his time between Sweden and France.

In the course of his trip back to Sweden in Gustavus' party Axel inadvertently dropped a scrap of information that has been noted by some of Marie Antoinette's biographers. In the correspondence book where he listed all the letters he wrote or received there suddenly appears mention of a number of letters to a certain "Joséphine." His ledger indicates that a letter to "Joséphine" was posted almost every day all the way across Europe. From his laconic comments it emerges that much of this correspondence with "Joséphine" has to do with the purchase of a dog for her in Sweden. At Lüneburg, for example, he notes that he wrote her a letter on July 27 "asking her what the dog's name should be and if I should keep the matter a secret." After his return to Sweden we find him complaining to a M. de Boye of Stockholm, evidently the owner of the kennel, that "the dog has not yet been delivered" and he asks what must be done to have the business hurried. Then, a week later, he makes note of another letter to M. de Boye. "I asked him to send me a dog that wasn't too small, about the size of those belonging to Monsieur Pollett. I told him that it was for the Queen of France."

It is apparent that the "Joséphine" with whom he was in secret correspondence was none other than Marie Antoinette.

The French Revolution was not a single convulsive movement but a succession of at least three separate revolutions, each with its own significance and each the product of particular and distinct conditions.

The first of these revolutions was the revolt of the nobility against the King. From this rebellion all else was to follow in its natural course: the nobility in its turn was to be overthrown by the Republican middle class, or the Gironde, and the Gironde was to be overthrown by the Extremists or Jacobins. Within the Jacobin revolution a bitter struggle was to break loose between various factions that finally led to the supremacy of Robespierre's Committee of Public Safety.

It was with the first of these revolutions, the revolt of the nobility against the Crown, that Marie Antoinette's life is historically interbound for it was not the so-called "people" who opened the floodgates of the French Revolution. No more was it "the people" who destroyed Louis XVI and Marie Antoinette. The King and Queen were first undermined, then abandoned and, in effect, finally handed over to their executioners by their own nobility.

This enmity between the Throne and the nobility had its beginning in the conditions of feudal history. There had been a time in the mists of their medieval origin when the great lords of France and many of the petty ones too had ruled in semisovereign authority over their domains. The attrition of time and the needs of the central government (or Crown) gradually deprived them of their autonomy. Under Richelieu's steel hand they were finally made subservient to the Crown. A unified country as well as a well-filled treasury was Richelieu's legacy to Louis XIV. And Louis XIV used this inheritance to bring the nobility still closer to heel.

As every French schoolboy knows, Louis XIV built Versailles, where he tamed his captive nobles with follies and favors. The energy of this aristocracy was put to work running the great machine of etiquette, whose purpose was to affirm the supremacy of the King. In the *mystique* of royalty as well as that of religion, distance has always been a necessary component. The ceremonial invented by Louis XIV was designed to keep the nobility at arm's length from the monarch. For it was never his people whom Louis XIV wished to keep at bay. Louis XIV was always graciously disposed toward his people and was without the slightest fear of them. It was his nobility whom he disliked and it was to cow them that he had evolved the ritual that in a later generation was to prove so tiresome to Marie Antoinette and against which she so ill-advisedly was to rebel. In disparaging and diminishing the rite of etiquette the Queen with her own hand unknowingly removed one of the most important barricades that protected her from the predators who roamed the court. The various dukes, duchesses, and noble lords whose hereditary offices were abolished or were allowed to lapse into disuse became *désoeuvrés* and in their idleness they were no less angry than an unemployed proletariat. And with the diminishment of each step in the ritual went a corresponding diminishment of the distance that kept the Crown from the disrespectful scrutiny of a self-seeking and disaffected aristocracy.

For despite Richelieu and despite Louis XIV an invisible and ever-widening split between the Crown and the nobility lay just below the veneer of the French monarchy's polished surface. As the century wore on, this quarrel expressed itself in the institution known as the *parlements* and in a claim of the *parlements* to a prerogative that was fundamental in the whole decrepit structure of the *ancien régime* in France. This prerogative was the time-honored "right" of the *parlements* of France to register all royal edicts or laws after they had been promulgated by the Crown. The right to register laws implied the converse right to refuse to register them. In other words, should the King wish to effect this or that change in the structure of the kingdom—as he did during Turgot's ministry—the *parlements* insisted that the right to finally incorporate this change into effective law lay only with them.

To modern ears the *parlements'* claim might ring with the clarion call of a cause that should be supported by all liberally disposed men. Nothing more perfectly demonstrates the mistake of accepting such words and situations at their face value. The French *parlements* were, in fact, the last bastion of a hereditary caste that was reactionary, ignorant, and narrow-minded—analogous in spirit and in fact to the Riksdag that Gustavus III had dissolved. They were determined not merely to defend their feudal privileges, but indeed to extend them. It has been observed by Mr. Sanche de Gramont that from the sixteenth century until the French Revolution there was not a single enlightened measure they did not oppose, from the creation of the Académie Française to the ending of forced labor on the public roads. They opposed all tax reform because they were themselves tax-exempt. They opposed the abolition of serfdom because they were landlords. And most of the outrages against humanitarianism that in the popular mind have been attributed to the kings of France should instead be blamed on the *parlements*. It was the *parlement* of Toulouse, for example, that ordered the torture and execution of Jean Calas.

The political history of the final years of Louis XV's reign is the record of almost constant skirmishes between the *parlements* and the King. In the end Louis XV wielded the supreme power and ordered the disobedient *parlements* disbanded. Short of outright revolt there was nothing they could do but submit. But Louis XVI, persuaded that such was the public wish, ordered them recalled at the beginning of his reign. It was probably the worst political error he ever made. From the moment of their recall they truculently objected to nearly every royal proposal and they tried to block every reform such as those

74

submitted by Turgot. As Louis XVI's reign wore on they grew bolder and ever more defiant. The parliamentary leader d'Éprémesnil spoke openly of his ambition to "de-Bourbonize" France. These words, which make him sound like a precursor of Robespierre, had nothing to do with the Republican sentiments they might suggest for he was a fanatical supporter of the old *parlements*, a religious bigot and a sworn enemy of the Encyclopaedists. "He wanted to de-Bourbonize France," observed the Girondin Brissot, "but only so that the *parlement* could rule supreme."

In 1788, when it became apparent that France could no longer continue in the state of insolvency and debt where the American Revolution, a bureaucratic government, and a costly court had placed her, Louis' ministers turned to the Paris *parlement* for help. The magistrates refused to give their sanction to any reform of the tax structure or to any economies that might have saved the state from bankruptcy. The Crown's attempt through a *lit de justice* to enforce legislation was met with outright rebellion by the magistrates. The *parlements* were ordered disbanded but in the provinces they refused to disband. At Grenoble an armed mob came to the defense of the magistrates resisting arrest. Rioting and violence followed. The picture of the "people" coming to the support of these reactionary bigots is one of the more paradoxical spectacles of the French Revolution.

Rejected by the Notables, repulsed by the *parlements*, the Crown finally turned to the representatives of the whole nation, the Estates-General, for help with a problem that like so many political problems was beyond the possibility of solution.

The most significant fact about the *parlements* in the final days of the *ancien régime* is that their membership had come to include all branches of the nobility. A few years earlier there had been a split between the so-called "nobility of the Robe" and that "of the Sword." The magistrates who sat on the *parlements* were almost all of the Robe. Their nobility had been purchased or in one way or another was associated with legal negotiation or even, indeed, commerce. The nobility of the Sword were men whose honors derived from their forebears' fealty to the King. They looked down their noses at the nobility of the Robe both because of its money-tainted origin and because on a social level its members were considered dull, provincial, and dowdy.

During the last years of Louis XVI's reign, however, these two antagonistic groups came to an understanding and the composition of the *parlements* included a number of highly placed noblemen of

75

the Sword. A great liberal such as the duc de La Rochefoucauld found himself seated in the same council chamber as the reactionary d'Éprémesnil or the vengeful *débauché* the duc d'Orléans. What brought them together was a mutual hatred of the Crown. And in its personal expression much of this hatred owed itself to Marie Antoinette, who had trampled over the little enclaves of pride and power that were the hereditary prerogatives of these noblemen. The very existence of a Trianon with its overtones of exclusivity, an exclusivity reserved for Frenchmen of equivocal antecedent and for foreigners such as Esterházy, Besenval, and Fersen, enraged the *grands seigneurs* of the old nobility of the Sword. In the small but characteristic episode of the Queen's First Equerry the traditional rights of a Tessé were sacrificed to the grasping demands of a Polignac. The family of Tessé never forgot or forgave. And in one form or another that episode was repeated a hundred times.

Marie Antoinette's final estrangement from the French aristocracy came in 1785 with the devastating scandal of the Diamond Necklace. In certain of its elements this swindle remains today the "mystery of iniquity" that it was described as being by the memoirists of the time. The crucial fact that emerges from it is that although she was innocent of even the remotest complicity in the affair, the Queen's reputation had been so tarnished by slander that nearly everyone believed her in one way or another to be guilty. And responding not as a queen but as an indignant woman to a situation whose deeper implications were political, she caused the business to be dragged before a public tribunal, into the court of the *parlement* of Paris, of all places, where in her naïveté she supposed her innocence would be proclaimed to the kingdom and the guilt of the Cardinal de Rohan made manifest. The public confrontation was between the Queen of France and a Prince of the Church, a great nobleman of France whom she hated out of all proportion to his faults, whom she hated personally with all the intensity of a woman whose small world was the shallow society into which she was born. She perceived nothing of the sinister distances, suspected nothing of the menacing depths.

When the case came before the Paris *parlement* where her name was execrated the Cardinal was acquitted on every count and borne home in triumph to his palace in the Marais. From all over Paris crowds flocked to his door to applaud the dissipated fop who had shamed the Queen of France. In that moment of wild accolade for the Cardinal de Rohan, Marie Antoinette glimpsed at last the abyss that lay ahead. The Affair of the Necklace has been described, and rightly so, as the gateway to her tomb. The Rohans were among the greatest lords of France, allied directly with the powerful houses of Soubise and Guemenée and by marriage to every other proud and historic name of the kingdom. They looked henceforth with implacable hatred at the foreigner, the arrogant Austrian who had dared drag their name and their class into the mire.

With the opening of the Estates-General in May of 1789 the French monarchy came at last to its halt. The solemn procession of priests, nobles, and deputies that moved through the streets of Versailles has often been described. With its tapestries, its falconers, its mitered bishops and beplumed nobles it was, in fact, the funeral cortège of the Capetian monarchy. The splendor of the parade could not conceal the animosities with which the air was charged. The hostility between the Third Estate, about to declare itself the National Assembly, and the Nobility and Clergy was the most conspicuous of these. The party of the court was just as divided and the Princes of the Blood were at each other's throats. The duc d'Orléans was bent on no less than the murder of the Queen, the dethronement of Louis XVI, and the installation of himself as King of France.

Marie Antoinette was now barely on speaking terms with her old companion in pleasure, the comte d'Artois. In his eyes and in those of his party the Queen was no better than a revolutionary. He accused her of supporting the People against the Nobility. Afraid of losing their sinecures the Polignac clan, like many of the Trianon "circle," joined the followers of the comte d'Artois and became uncompromising defenders of the old order. Thus did Marie Antoinette's few remaining friends at court become her enemies, and enemies more wounding and dangerous because they had once been her friends.

The historians who have described the pageantry of that opening session of the Estates-General rarely pause to observe a detail in the parade that separates perfectly the tragedy of Marie Antoinette, the Queen of France, from that of Marie Antoinette, the woman. When the procession passed the royal stables on the Place d'Armes she glanced up toward the balustered roof. Her eldest son, the dauphin, had been brought there in a cot to see the show. He was dying.

For more than a year he had been sick with a disease of the spine that had had the curious effect of aging him far beyond his years. In a few years' time the ten-year-old boy became a bent and withered old man. Not only was his body thus affected, but his mind too. He spoke words that on the lips of one of his age were disconcerting. Shortly before his death he clipped a lock of his hair to give to a gentleman-in-waiting of whom he was fond. "Here, Monsieur," he said, "this is a lock of my hair. It is all that I can give you for I have nothing else at my disposal. But when I am dead you may present this pledge to my father and mother and in being reminded of me I hope they will remember you." He became convinced that the duchesse de Polignac was trying to poison him and would not permit her to come near him.

His parents brought him to Meudon away from the pandemonium at Versailles. He died there a month after the opening of the Estates-General. It is recorded that Marie Antoinette's grief was unrestrained and terrible to see. When the Sacrament had been administered she retired with her husband to an adjoining room where sobbing in anguish she fell to her knees and buried her head in her husband's lap.

In the midst of state business at Versailles no one had time to notice the mourning of the royal couple. Indeed a delegation from the Estates-General insisted on seeing the King an hour after his son's death. "Are there no fathers among you?" asked Louis. But in the end he gave them their way and they delivered to him the speech that they had prepared.

Marie Antoinette herself best communicated the atmosphere of confusion in which she lost her son in a letter she wrote a few weeks after the boy's death. "My darling little dauphin departed and no one seemed even to notice."

The duc de Normandie, the second son of Marie Antoinette, now became heir to the throne. It was this boy, then three years of age, who was to be the lost King, Louis XVII, the Prince who never ruled about whose name and person an impenetrable fog of mystery has fallen.

The opening chords of the French Revolution communicated the rapid tempo of the score that was to follow. Even in its first months names, dates, and events come flying in a confusing whirl that has made this one of the most difficult periods in history to follow in any logical or sequential order. All through the months of June while the Estates-General sat in conference at Versailles, while the King and Queen mourned the death of their young son—so infinitesimal an event in history but so enormous for them—the city of Paris was torn by rioting. At the Palais Royal where the so-called "Orléans Conspiracy" had its center, the garden of the duc d'Orléans' splendid palace, one of the most charming corners of tranquillity in today's Paris, was a seething hive of agitators, orators, prostitutes, deserters from the militia, vagabonds, and every manner of man or woman disposed to quarreling and violence. It was from here that the train of powder leading to the storming of the Bastille in July and to the assault on Versailles in October was ignited.

The taking of the Bastille was the signal at Versailles for the hurried departure of those who felt that their lives might be in danger at the hands of the Paris populace. Among the first to abandon the leaking ship were the Polignacs and the comte d'Artois. The duchesse put up some resistance when the Queen urged her to leave France. The King himself "ordered" her to depart. In the years preceding the Revolution a chill had fallen between Marie Antoinette and her friend. As she grew older the Queen found the rakish tone of the Polignacs' *salon* less and less to her taste. Political differences had also arisen between Marie Antoinette and the Polignac clan.

At the moment of parting, however, all such petty discord was forgotten and only the sweets of their fifteen years of friendship recalled. Marie Antoinette was close to collapse when the moment of separation finally arrived. So dangerous was the duchesse's position that she and her family had to flee the palace under the cloak of darkness. She left disguised as a chambermaid. As she entered her carriage a note from the Queen was handed her. "Farewell, dearest of friends. The word is dreadful. Farewell . . . I have only the strength to embrace you." With this there came a purse from the Queen filled with five hundred louis d'or to defray the expenses of their trip into exile. They were never to meet again.

The comte d'Artois and his wife left France on the same night and within the following weeks nearly all the Queen's intimate circle abandoned her. The duc de Coigny and Madame de Polignac's lover, the comte de Vaudreul, departed along with Marie Antoinette's confessor and old friend from Vienna, the abbé de Vermond. Of the men and women who comprised this first wave of the *emigration* nearly all belonged to the party of the conservative view, those who had looked with indignation on any suggestion of compromise with the Third Estate or—as it soon was called—the National Assembly. They had always in fact been enemies of the Crown and many of them now became personal enemies of Louis XVI and Marie Antoinette, attributing to them as much as to the revolutionaries of Paris the plight to which the régime had been brought. During the early days of the Estates-General some of these nobles openly proclaimed the necessity of "saving the Crown from the King."

Grief-stricken by the death of her son, Marie Antoinette would often go to Trianon for a few hours during the early autumn days of the first year of the Revolution. The little palace and its gardens had been open to the public long before the Revolution, but the gathering of the Estates-General at Versailles brought the sightseers out in droves. All the deputies wanted to see with their own eyes the famous pleasure dome whose name epitomized the license and extravagance of the monarchy. It is recorded that many of them refused to believe that Gabriel's austere pavilion was really the fabled Petit Trianon and they looked in vain for the room studded with diamonds and rubies of which rumor had told them.

She was at Trianon in the early afternoon of October 5. The sky that day was heavily overcast and a fine drizzle that threatened to become rain hung in the air. The place was silent and remote. No tourists were in the gardens. Some instinct must have prompted her to wander across the leaf-strewn paths of this place so intimately associated with her life as Queen of France. She went to her grotto and here she sat alone for some time watching the little cascade that fell like a silver thread down the sides of a fern-covered cliff. She had been sitting there for perhaps an hour when a page sent from the palace came hurrying to her. He informed her that a mob of women from Paris was marching on Versailles and that she should return to the palace at once.

Even more clearly than the storming of the Bastille the march on Versailles may be traced to the duc d'Orléans. Some months afterward the government made a thorough and dispassionate inquiry into the origins of that movement. Hundreds of persons of every walk of life made their depositions before the court of the Châtelet. These statements may be read today. Far from being the march of fishwives depicted by Carlyle and other nineteenth-century writers, the movement began, in the words of one witness to it, with "women who were powdered, *coiffées* and dressed in white with an air of gaiety about them." The *poissardes* had little if anything to do with the march on Versailles. Indeed, a few days later they visited the King and Queen to disassociate their name from the event.

The deposition of a certain "St. Firmin, bourgeois of Paris" is but one of many statements that gives us a glimpse of the real impetus behind the uprising. On the day of the march this witness came upon a washerwoman working on her boat on the Seine. He expressed surprise that she wasn't at Versailles. The woman replied with indignation: "You make a mistake in imagining that it's laundresses and women of our kind who have gone to Versailles. Someone certainly came to my boat and made the proposal to my companions and myself. It was a woman who offered us six francs to march, but that woman was no more a woman than you are. I recognized her distinctly as a nobleman living in the Palais Royal or near it whose valet I wash for."

More than four hundred witnesses stated that a number of the "women" on the march were in fact men disguised as women. The duc d'Aiguillon was recognized among them as were many of the supporters of the duc d'Orléans. Not a few witnesses insisted that Orléans himself had been present. These men did not, of course, comprise the bulk of the so-called mob. Nor, in the customary sense of the word, do they appear to have been its leaders. They were *agents provocateurs* who incited and encouraged a human mass all too readily brought to frenzy. The Paris mob has always been notoriously volatile. Inflamed by brandy, driven by hunger, and excited by every kind of exhortation, it was to be a formidable auxiliary indeed to the various political parties that succeeded one another during the French Revolution. But, as events were to show, this faceless mass that was as inaccessible to words of reason as it was to the voice of pity, was without the slightest loyalty to any party and was indifferent to the ideologies over which the political leaders of the Revolution quarreled. The "mob" that swept the Girondins into power swept them out with howls that were just as loud. They screamed imprecations at Robespierre on his way to the guillotine no less lustily than they had screamed them at Marie Antoinette. Danton was pelted by them with the same ferocity as was his enemy Hébert.

Hungry and lashed by a cold rain that began to fall as darkness approached, they poured into the town of Versailles by the thousands in the afternoon of October 5. Brandishing pitchforks, pikes, and knives they gathered along the avenue de Paris and filled the vast square in front of the palace gates. For the first time in living memory those gates had been closed. They were guarded by the Regiment de Flandres, one of the foreign regiments loyal to the King.

Within the palace consternation had broken out. As night fell the tattered remnants of the court nobility and other personnel of the palace drew together in the Galerie des Glaces. "We paced about the great hall, witness to all the splendor of the monarchy since Louis XIV, without exchanging a word," recalled the marquise de La Tour du Pin. The Queen stayed in her room with her sister-in-law Madame Élisabeth; the King, surrounded by his ministers, remained in his office, to which there came an unending procession of breathless messengers, agitated officials, and the officers of his household. During one of these conferences the possibility of flight, a recourse that in the next few years was to be considered with increasing urgency, presented itself. The comte de St. Priest suggested to Louis XVI that he and his family go to the château of Rambouillet beyond the reach of the Paris mob where, free from coercion, he could try to bring order back to his realm.

St. Priest's proposal was sensible and had Louis XVI acted on it the Revolution might well have taken a different turn. But in this moment of crisis as in all others that were to follow the King was unable to act with decision. Other ministers advised him to remain. The unhappy man could only pace the floor and murmur over and over again, "I don't want to compromise anyone." Precious time was thus lost so that when at last he did decide to leave it was too late. As the royal carriages lumbered from the stables toward the palace an angry crowd fell on them with the cry, "The King is trying to leave!" and cut the harnessing. Short of force, which he always refused to use, there was now no way for the King to leave Versailles.

The events of that night have been recounted many times: the increasing bad temper of the horde bivouacking outside the palace gates, the sudden fraternization with this crowd by the National Guard of Versailles who were supposed to defend the palace but who, in fact, did not, the belated arrival toward midnight of La Fayette with his militia from Paris who gave his assurance to the King and to the King's ministers that all was now well and under control. Lulled by La Fayette's words, the King dismissed his attendants and at one in the morning went to bed. The frightened women and courtiers who huddled together in the Galerie des Glaces were informed that the King and Queen had retired. So one by one they too went to their rooms. Doors were closed and for the last time the candles of the vast galerie were snuffed out by the palace ushers.

In her apartments in the West Wing of the palace Marie Antoinette dismissed her women and retired to bed. Two of her waiting women insisted on spending the night in the antechamber adjoining the Queen's bedroom. In doing so they saved her life, for toward five in the morning a gate that gave access to the terrace of the château, to the Cour Royale, and to the staircase leading to the Queen's rooms was furtively unlocked. The most savage element of the mob streamed into the palace and up the Escalier de la Reine. One of the three bodyguards who were posted at the doors opening into Marie Antoinette's suite of rooms managed to alert her women with the cry, "Save the Queen!"

There was no doubt of the invaders' intentions. In an anonymous note Marie Antoinette had been warned earlier in the evening that she would be murdered at six in the morning. As the crowd rushed up the stairs and with axes hacked its way through the doors and barricades that had been hurriedly put in its way it shrieked, "Death to the whore!" and "We'll take her head back to Paris!" Marie Antoinette had barely time to throw a wrapper over her shoulders and escape through a concealed door beside her bed that led to an interior passageway connecting her apartments with those of the King in the opposite wing of the palace. The precious minutes that permitted her to escape were purchased at the expense of the two guards who had closed the doors on the invaders. The enraged mob soon broke through this barrier and cut down the guards, whose heads they removed on the spot. Put on pikes, these two trophies like triumphal flags were to be borne at the head of the procession that later in the day was to take the King and the Queen to Paris.

Marie Antoinette's life was saved, but the monarchy that day went down the first of the steps that led it into the abyss. When the sun finally rose over that scene of turbulence the King, his ministers, and the Queen had no choice but to submit to the cry from the human sea surging before their gates: "To Paris! To Paris!" Having captured their prize—and having learned, perhaps with surprise, just how easy that conquest had been—the Paris populace and its leaders had no intention of relinquishing it. The Crown must be taken to Paris.

From the balcony overlooking the Cour Royale the King announced that he would accede to the wishes of his people. "My friends," he called out, "I will go to Paris with my wife and children. I confide all that I hold most dear to the love of my good subjects."

Shortly after one o'clock that afternoon the King, Queen, and their two children entered the coach that took them to Paris and

83

captivity. Nearly two thousand carriages bearing the debris of the French court followed. The palace of Louis XIV was then shuttered and closed. It was never to be inhabited again.

Among those in the procession that accompanied the royal family to Paris was Axel Fersen. "I was witness to it all," he wrote his father a few days later. "I returned to Paris in one of the carriages that followed the King. We were six and a half hours on the road. May God preserve me from ever again seeing so heartbreaking a spectacle as that of the last two days."

He had been at Valenciennes that spring with his regiment. He had been at Valenciennes when the Queen's son died and he was still there when the Bastille was taken. But toward the end of July, a few weeks after the fall of the Bastille, he decided to return to the capital, close his flat there, and spend the coming fall and winter at Versailles. On September 27, one week before the march of the women on Versailles, he wrote his sister Sophie that he was at last settled in that town and would be there for the winter.

So it happened that Fersen was with Marie Antoinette and Louis when they were conducted to their first place of captivity, the dilapidated palace of the Tuileries in the center of Paris. And so it happened that at the very moment when it seemed to Marie Antoinette that all had abandoned her, at the moment when she was bereft of the power to grant further favor, and when henceforth friendship with her could only bring compromise and danger, a devoted and disinterested friend appeared. Fersen was to be at her side during the twenty months of the royal family's first captivity in the Tuileries that preceded the flight to Varennes. Always discreet, always reserved, he seems to have entered and left that palace, bristling with spies, unnoticed. Apart from St. Priest, who states categorically that he was the lover of Marie Antoinette and that he was seen on several occasions leaving her bedroom at three in the morning, no chronicler of the time makes note of his presence near the Queen. Fersen's Journal of this period was soon afterward to be burned, so that we have no account from him of his activity during these days.

It is through his letters abroad to his sister Sophie or to Sophie's lover, Baron de Taube, and through those of a more official character to Gustavus III that we realize how intimately and crucially he was engaged with the affairs of the French Crown during the year 1790 and the spring of 1791. There is, as Balzac once observed, "official history," which is composed of what Balzac calls "official lies," and there is the history of the corridors and the back stairs where in the obscurity of places rarely visible to the ordinary eye events of moment have their real source. Balzac might have pointed to Fersen's situation vis-à-vis Marie Antoinette in the critical first year of the French Revolution as a perfect example of his pronouncement.

On the "official" level the Crown and the Assembly went through the steps that are mentioned in every history of the period. The minister Necker was recalled; the Feast of the Federation, the first anniversary of the fall of the Bastille, was celebrated in the Champs-de-Mars, where the King and Queen were applauded. It is the opinion of a number of respected French historians that if things had stopped at this point the best accomplishments of the Revolution would have been realized and France would have been spared the Terror and the dictatorships of Robespierre and Bonaparte.

In the eyes of most Parisians of that time the Revolution did indeed appear to be over in 1790. At the palace of the Tuileries the old etiquette was resumed. The rituals of the *lever* and the *coucher* continued as though the court were still at Versailles and only those intimately engaged in the ceremony, perhaps indeed only the King and Queen themselves, were aware of the crevasse that lay just below the surface of these impressive appearances.

Of the courtiers who remained to celebrate the rite one group was attached to the new order and were partisans of the Assembly, not of Louis XVI and certainly not of Marie Antoinette. They could not therefore be viewed by the King and Queen as potential allies in any crisis. Another group was blindly devoted to the monarchic principle and equally blinded to all political realities. They could not therefore be counted on for any practical advice or indeed for any effective support. The domestic staff of the palace, the battalions of *valets-de-chambre*, *valets-de-pied*, waiters, and serving women that kept the vast establishment running, was filled with spies not merely of the Assembly but of the various factions who hoped to overthrow the Assembly as well as the Crown. They could not *en bloc* be trusted but time was to reveal some unexpected exceptions to this assumption. Even then, working in the depths of the palace kitchens and therefore unknown to Marie Antoinette, there was a serving boy

85

named Turgy who would one day offer her and her children a devotion beyond the possibility of any reward.

The palace military personnel, the King's bodyguard, and the militia whose function it was to protect the person of the King and to defend the palace had been appointed by the Assembly and in consequence were answerable to the orders of La Fayette rather than to those of the King. This was in fact the most critical change of all for without an adequate guard to assure his personal safety the King was, in effect, at the mercy of any group who might choose to invade the palace. By threatening his life, or the lives of his family, any concession or agreement could be extorted from him.

October 5–6 haunted Louis and Marie Antoinette and the fear of another such assault, this time on the Tuileries, never left them for a moment during the winter of 1790. The rumor of projected invasions came constantly to their ears, for they too had their spies who kept them posted on the condition of things in the city.

It was with good reason that they were in a state of perpetual anxiety for Paris in almost all its districts was seething with potential violence. In the atmosphere of semi-anarchy and uncertainty which the dissolution of the central power had induced, politicians, demagogues, and agitators of almost every conviction had suddenly made their appearance. Many of these men viewed the Assembly with as much contempt as they viewed the Crown. In the quarter of the Cordeliers, Danton had become the acknowledged leader, while in the nearby rue de l'École de Médecine, Marat and his newspaper had become powers for the Assembly to reckon with. Marat and Danton loathed one another but they had it in common that they loathed La Fayette and his National Guard more. Indeed, their hatred of the General was almost as intense as Marie Antoinette's.

It is no wonder, then, in this climate of dissension and menace that Marie Antoinette should lean with gratitude and confidence on the one firm arm that was offered her. To Axel Fersen, the friend who had returned at a time when all others had left, she now accorded her absolute trust. The *politique* that was devised between them, the various plans and policies that were the outcome of their mutual confidence belong to that scene which Balzac calls the "back stairs of history."

Fersen's role in the hidden *politique* of the French Crown was made more consequential by the fact that during the winter of 1790 Louis suffered a nervous collapse. The storm that had broken over the King's head seems momentarily to have overwhelmed him. Confined in the Tuileries, where he could no longer go on the long exhausting hunts that his heavy constitution required, his physical health collapsed. For the moment at least Louis XVI was effectively *hors de combat* and the reins of government passed into the hands of Marie Antoinette, who in turn grew increasingly dependent on the advice of Count Fersen. Thus at last Marie Antoinette really did begin to run the affairs of the French Crown as she had been accused of doing during the insouciant Trianon years.

But it was not the lightheaded shepherdess of Trianon who now stepped forward to engage herself in the tasks of statecraft. As, under the pressures of the struggle, Louis' powers began to fail, Marie Antoinette's grew. A latent strength of character that had gone unneeded and unused during the years of prosperity began to emerge in the days of adversity. This profound change of personality is indeed the most remarkable happening in Marie Antoinette's life. The night of October 5–6 that first brought her into touch with the actuality of physical danger marks its beginning. Many who saw her at Versailles that night were to remember her composure and courage. "In the midst of that terrible clamor I saw the Queen calmly maintaining an air of inexpressible nobility and dignity." Another observer remarked that "although she can surely have entertained no illusions about her possible fate, she was far more concerned for those about her than for herself. She communicated courage to those who could not conceal their alarm."

Grief, too, lent her character a deeper dimension. After the death of her son one begins to discern the rudiments of wisdom in her letters. Not the literate wisdom of the *philosophes*, but of peasant women brought face to face with harsh and primal catastrophe.

In her efforts to save the French throne Marie Antoinette's decisions were not always those, unfortunately, that might have been made by an able or experienced statesman. Her range of vision was limited and an unquestioning attachment to conventional principles narrowed her outlook still further. When, for instance, Mirabeau suggested fomenting civil war as a means of weakening the Assembly, she was shocked. In so critical a situation as that of France in 1790, audacity, cynicism, and an ability to compromise were the qualities most needed in a politician. They were the very qualities in which Marie Antoinette was conspicuously deficient. Bold, unscrupulous moves such as those proposed by Mirabeau were entirely beyond her

87

comprehension. She tried to stamp out the fire with her feet or to pour water on it. She did not know, as so experienced a demagogue as Mirabeau knew, that one could fight fire with fire.

Hard work, devotion to duty, self-discipline, and all the dull virtues her mother had enjoined upon her came too late to save the Queen, but they were to serve the woman. Through suffering she learned their truth and by suffering she became a mature and admirable human being. The distance she had come in self-discovery is communicated in a casual phrase she penned in a letter at about this time. "It is through adversity," she wrote, "that we finally come to realize who we really are." From a once frivolous and shallow-minded leader of fashion that is a remarkable observation.

During the years 1789-91 there were changes in her appearance as well as her character. The dauphine of France once glimpsed "shining as the dawn" by Edmund Burke was no more. One need only compare the famous portrait by Vigée-Lebrun, beplumed and glittering, with an unfinished study of her by the artist Kucharski done during the winter of 1790-91 to see the extent of these changes. It is to the eyes of this portrait that one's attention is immediately drawn. They are the same eyes, oval with their high arched brows, that are to be found in Vigée-Lebrun's vapid sitter, but there is an expression in them of *hauteur* and perplexity (to which the artist has added a curious trace of distant amusement), of mingled suffering and stoicism that holds the viewer fascinated.

It is the face of a woman in her middle forties or older. Marie Antoinette was in fact thirty-five. Events appear to have aged her beyond her years. She herself stated that her hair began to whiten during the night of October 5-6. At first glance one would not suppose it to be the portrait of a woman who might still arouse the interest of men. That a young and amusing Queen scattering favors and lucrative pensions from her light fingers should attract a Lauzun or an Esterházy is not surprising. But this woman, the mother of two children, whose youth was gone, who had no further favors to grant, and whose remaining beauty was only the beauty of a fine carriage and of suffering nobly borne, was now in fact to secure the devotion of an extraordinary variety of men, ranging from opportunistic politicians to ardent revolutionaries.

Of these knights Axel Fersen was the first, the last, and the most entirely dedicated. He was indeed the only one among them whom Marie Antoinette really trusted and her trust in him was absolute.

It is at this moment in her life that the question that has perplexed so many of the Queen's biographers arises: what was the exact nature of the "friendship" between Fersen and Marie Antoinette? Were they, in the word of one biographer, "lovers," or were they, in the phrase of another, "bound by a pure love worthy of the troubadours or the knights of the Round Table?"

In 1878, eighty-five years after the death of Marie Antoinette, a book called *Le comte de Fersen et la Cour de France* was published in Paris. Its author was the great-nephew of Axel Fersen, one Baron de Klinckowström, and it made a sensation in the literary and historical circles of the day. For along with a quantity of papers that revealed the unsuspected extent of Fersen's diplomatic activities on behalf of the King and Queen of France, the book also contained over fifty personal letters between Axel Fersen and Marie Antoinette. It became evident that the friendship between the Queen of France and the Swedish officer, which heretofore had only been hinted at in various memoirs or rumored in insubstantial whispers that still echoed in certain circles of the diplomatic corps and the old aristocracy, was in fact far closer than anyone had supposed.

Unfortunately this correspondence of such historic interest was published with a number of critical excisions in its text. At nearly every point when the letters leave political matters and begin to take on an intimate or personal tone the words are deleted and replaced by dots. Whole sentences and even paragraphs were removed in this manner and always at the very moment when one feels oneself coming into touch with the real Marie Antoinette or the real Fersen. "How is your health?" she asks in one such letter. "I'll bet you're not taking care of yourself and you are wrong . . . (*excision of two lines*) . . . as for myself I am bearing up better than you'd suppose."

In his introduction to *Le comte de Fersen et la Cour de France*, Baron de Klinckowström declared that the excisions in his book corresponded to inked-out passages in the original letters and he submitted the explanation that they were probably blacked out by Fersen himself because Fersen showed many of these letters to Gustavus III and he did not want the King of Sweden to be offended by certain of Marie Antoinette's private political opinions. But if one examines the matter with any attention one soon suspects that it was not Fersen but Klinckowström himself who was the censor. The Baron indeed seems to have realized how unsatisfactory his explanation was. "I am sure," he states rather in the tone of a Victorian paterfamilias dismissing inquisitive children, "that all the friends of that noble martyr the Queen of France will find my explanation sufficient and one that will dispel all injudicious conjecture." Evidently there were certain passages in the uncensored letters that made Baron de Klinckowström believe that the "noble martyr" was the mistress of his great-uncle, and to prevent others from entertaining similar suspicions he deleted those passages. The name of Marie Antoinette, blackened by calumny during her lifetime, met almost as sorry a fate after her death. The legend of the "noble martyr" affixed itself to the poor woman. The Royalist party, the very party in fact that had most basely calumniated her when she was alive, now founded a kind of cult about her name. Her former enemy the comte de Provence, who at Versailles had spread some of the most poisonous of the libels about her, returned to France as Louis XVIII, and put his sister-in-law's apotheosis to use as a serviceable political implement. All the virtues of Victorian sainthood were hung on this plaster image. To suggest that Marie Antoinette might have committed adultery would in the year 1878 have been tantamount to supporting social disorder. And this appears to be the real explanation of the excisions in the letters published by Baron de Klinckowström.

But, one asks, why don't we examine the original letters? The published version of them may be lacerated by gaps and dots, but with modern methods of detection, with X-rays and chemicals, we should be able to see through the passages amateurishly inked out in the originals. Alas, the originals no longer exist, and for this Baron de Klinckowström must be condemned without reprieve. In a scene out of some Romantic novel the old Baron summoned a faithful retainer to his deathbed, caused a fire to be built, and one by one committed the letters of Marie Antoinette and Fersen to the flames. No doubt he died with his conscience at rest, certain that he carried with him to the grave the secret those letters might have revealed.

It did not apparently occur to him that the suppressed passages might henceforth lend themselves to any interpretation and in fact be summoned to the support of the very contention that he wished to discourage. His willful destruction of those letters is used as one of the persuasive arguments that the relationship between Marie Antoinette and Fersen was indeed illicit. It is obvious that Baron de Klinckowström at any rate believed so. In contemporary ears, more in tune with eighteenth-century attitudes than the Victorians, the phrases that seemed so suggestive to Klinckowström might have had a different sound. It happens indeed that one short letter was spared the fate of the others and this fragment, uncensored and unaltered, communicates what must have been the tone of all the others. It was written in cipher—which no doubt is why it was overlooked by Klinckowström—immediately after the return of the royal family from Varennes, when they had been brought back to the Tuileries under armed guard. In one penetrating flash we catch a glimpse of the real Marie Antoinette as she must have appeared to the man whom many believe to have been the great love of her life. It is a far different woman who penned these lines than the cardboard effigy that Baron de Klinckowström with his scissors and paste presented to posterity.

"I can only tell you that I love you," she begins, "and indeed I hardly have time for that . . . let me know to whom I should address the news I may write you for I cannot live without that. *Adieu,* most loved and most loving of men. I embrace you with all my heart."

This is hardly evidence that might constitute proof of adultery in a divorce court. The letter was discovered by M. Lucien Maury and when it was published in 1928 it seemed to be the final though inconclusive word about the subject. But in 1930 Professor Alma Söderhjelm of the University of Åbo in Finland published a book that, like Klinckowström's of some sixty years earlier, made a stir among the amateurs and specialists of eighteenth-century French history. Miss Söderhjelm had been given access to papers belonging to another branch of Fersen's family, the descendants of his sister Sophie Piper. She had also been allowed to examine the papers in the archives of the Klinckowström family, including Fersen's Journal. The fruit of her research was a book called *Fersen et Marie-Antoinette; correspondance et journal intime inédits du comte Axel de Fersen.*

It is an admirable work, well organized, thorough, and full of heretofore unpublished citations. A careful reading of it is indispensable to anyone interested in the public as well as the private life of Marie Antoinette. But it is flawed by Miss Söderhjelm's conviction that Fersen was indeed the lover of Marie Antoinette. All her material is bent to bring support to this conviction. In a chapter at the end of her book she manages, it is true, to make a gesture in the direction of impartiality and she leaves the question open. But in the body of her work she is far from impartial. Indeed, there are moments when she seems blind to the material she is editing.

One instance of this curious blindness must be mentioned here, not so much because it illustrates one of Miss Söderhjelm's editorial lapses, but because it evokes the ambiguity that has always surrounded the subject and continues to do so.

Fersen's *confidente*, it has often been noted, was his sister Sophie Piper. Sophie herself was involved in an unhappy love affair with Fersen's friend Baron de Taube. Exchanges of confidence, words of advice and comfort constitute the bulk of the letters between brother and sister during the year 1790. It was but natural that, having commiserated with his sister about her problems, Axel should touch upon some of his own. Thus it emerges that he was in love with a woman whom he describes as "very unhappy, but very courageous." He never mentions this woman by name—his very caution is suggestive—but it is clear that Sophie knows who she is. Aware, as we are, of Fersen's close contact with the royal family in the year 1790, and knowing as we do that the friendship between Fersen and the Queen was far more intimate than most of their contemporaries suspected, everything in Axel's elliptical references to her suggests that the mysterious woman was Marie Antoinette.

"I thank you very much," he writes Sophie on April 4 of 1790, "for all you have said about my friend (*amie*). Believe me, Sophie, she deserves all your feelings about her. She is the most perfect creature I know and her behavior has won everyone to her side. I hear nothing but praises of her everywhere. You may imagine how happy this makes me . . ."

On April 10 he again speaks of his friend. "I am beginning to be a bit happier for from time to time I see my friend freely *chez elle* and that consoles me a bit for the misfortunes that she is suffering. Poor woman, she is an angel in her courage, her sensitivity, and her behavior. No one ever knew how to love like her. She is infinitely moved by what you have said about her. She wept and asked me to tell you how touched she was . . ."

On May 7 he says of his friend that "when one is unhappy one is more readily affected. Poor woman, she deserved something better than this. Perhaps one day she will be rewarded . . . she is an angel and I try to console her as best I can. I owe it to her. She is so perfect for me."

Then, in a letter dated June 28, there occur two small phrases that seem to have gone unnoticed either by Alma Söderhjelm or by other writers who are persuaded that Fersen's unidentified *amie* was Marie Antoinette. "Things become worse here every day," he writes, "and God knows where all this will end. The King and Queen are very unhappy. The nobility and the clergy are destroyed and everywhere one meets people who have lost everything. She *too* is very unhappy. Poor woman, her courage is beyond anything, *I am writing you from her house* (chez elle) *in the country.* (Italics are mine.) I do not know when I shall rejoin my regiment; everything among the military is in such bad shape here it is no longer a pleasure to serve. The King and the royal family are at St. Cloud. They are far better off there than in Paris and are able to walk about freely as they like. There is no one but their attendants with them and *I have not been there . . ."*

Now unless Fersen is throwing up a smoke screen it is apparent from his remark that "she *too* is very unhappy" and from his statement that he has not been to see the royal family that the Queen and his friend cannot be the same person. It is, in fact, very possible that Fersen was throwing up a smoke screen. The interception of letters, including those sent by diplomatic courier, was commonplace at that time and the mail of a foreigner known to be on friendly terms with the King and Queen would be particularly liable to surveillance. By boldly stating that he had not been to St. Cloud to see the royal family he could have the satisfaction of putting the police on a false track should they happen to read the letter, while Sophie, in on the secret, would know that her brother's words were a ruse. But this is nothing more than speculation. As they stand, Fersen's written words present a very different possibility and Miss Söderhjelm makes no attempt to explain them, although most of her contention falls to the ground with them.

In truth, there was never a shortage of women in Axel Fersen's life and the nameless *amie* from whose country house he tells Sophie he is writing may well have been one of these. He was a curious man, Count Fersen, full of contradiction in his character and moved by odd, unexpected quirks. The *chevalier pur et sans reproche* was also a conceited lady-killer, vain of his appearance and proud of his conquests. The restrained and gravely courteous knight from the North made careful note in his Journal of the times when he had had sexual congress with his mistress Éléonore Sullivan. And whatever doubt there may be about his relationship with Marie Antoinette there is none whatsoever about the nature of his connection with Mrs. Sullivan—who could not, however, have been the *amie* of Fersen's letters.

Nor was Éléonore Sullivan the only woman in Fersen's life at this moment. On the day of the flight to Varennes the police went to his house on the rue Matignon and impounded his papers. Among these were found four very personal letters in the hand of a woman later identified as the comtesse de St. Priest, none other than the wife of the Minister of the King's Household who so unequivocally declares that Fersen was Marie Antoinette's lover. The St. Priest couple had fled Paris a few weeks before Varennes. Madame de St. Priest writes her former lover from London. Her letters crackle with the recriminations of a spiteful woman who has been discarded for another woman, in this case Madame Sullivan. They open an interesting perspective onto Fersen's private life.

"I've been seeing much of Madame de Canillac recently," she declares. "I don't know why but I'm sure she's been your mistress too. I remember your telling me that she had a lover nobody suspected and that he was English—but I am certain that he was a lovable Swede . . . I dined with the Prince of Wales the other night, my dear Count. He told me that when he knew you you were as good-looking as Lord Randon. But all the women in the room said that you had greatly altered and had become very ugly. After that charming overture nobody spoke of you any more . . . The Prince then told us that he had once seen Madame Sullivan do a dance with castanets with the Spanish Ambassador. He said that she looked so ridiculous he thought he'd split his sides laughing. He didn't exactly sing Madame Sullivan's praises. He thinks she looks like an apple vendor and he went on to tell us all sorts of unpleasant things about her. I felt sorry for you when I heard that your only rival was M. de Reignière. It seems a pity when a man is as young and handsome as you are . . ."

In another letter this malicious woman touches on the matter of Fersen's friendship with Marie Antoinette. Her words are very interesting, for they reveal beyond all doubt that Axel's attachment to the Queen was a matter of general knowledge in certain circles of the day.

"Everything that people are saying here about you appalls me," she writes. "My husband declares that you have done and are doing great harm to a certain person whom you are exposing to public contempt. He says that everyone who speaks to him about it expresses astonishment at your lack of concern for her reputation and he believes that you are damaging her in the eyes of those who might otherwise have been of some help to Her. As for me I see the matter

94

very differently. You could not prove your attachment to Her more effectively at this time than by remaining at her side and giving her every proof of your devotion. What others find ungentlemanly on your part I find sublime."

In that part of the comte de St. Priest's memoirs that touches on the year 1790—just before he and his wife emigrated to London—he declares that Fersen used to come and go from the château de St. Cloud at all hours of the day and night and on one occasion was nearly arrested by one of the palace guard at three in the morning. St. Priest claims that he went to the Queen and told her that Fersen's nocturnal visits to the château could endanger her. According to him, Marie Antoinette received his advice with indifference. "Tell him if you think it is necessary," she said. "For my part I do not care." And so Fersen's visits continued—visits that in his letter to Sophie he declares he never made.

Madame de St. Priest's charges were not addressed to posterity but to Fersen himself. Although she may have exaggerated the extent of the rumors it is obvious that she could not invent them out of whole cloth when addressing the very man who was their principal subject, since Fersen of all people would have been the first to know that there was a foundation of truth to them.

The question of whether or not Fersen was the Queen's lover has been a matter of controversy between Marie Antoinette's biographers ever since the publication of Klinckowström's bowdlerized edition of their letters. One school of writers, heirs to the Victorian point of view, insists that it was not in Marie Antoinette's character to take herself a lover, even so discreet and honorable a one as Axel Fersen. They point to her gratified maternal instincts, undoubtedly one of the strongest parts of her character, and declare that she would never have risked injuring herself in her children's eyes. They argue, too, that on this level at least she had too profound a regard for the propriety of the throne to debase it by an adulterous connection.

A second school of writers, the post-Freudian biographers of Marie Antoinette, insists that she was *par excellence* an ordinary woman and found the "fullfillment" for which she was starved in the arms of Count Fersen. Stefan Zweig's biography of Marie Antoinette is the leading example of this school. With considerable dramatic effect he paints for us the picture of the unhappy Queen brought to emotional maturity through the consummation of a noble passion. There seems to be no limit to his scorn for the bluenoses, the Victorians, and the prudes who have tried to hide the "real" Marie Antoinette, a woman who gave herself "totally" with all the courage of some liberated woman of the 1920s.

In truth Zweig and his school have arranged the facts to suit their own convictions, for there is not a scrap of evidence in any known papers surviving today that could be used to prove that Fersen was anything other than an ardent friend of the Queen. Now and again one hears rumors in France of letters hidden in the archives of some noble family or of diaries that would shed a revealing light on this question. Such reports can hardly be taken as anything more than gossip.

It is the personal opinion of this writer that Fersen was indeed the lover of Marie Antoinette, but that opinion is supported by nothing more substantial than various psychological considerations. When one looks at Fersen—"a burning soul within a shell of ice," as one woman of his acquaintance described him—whose affairs of the heart were legion, it is difficult to believe that for his part he did not find himself attached by a stronger bond than chivalry to this woman for whom he was prepared to give his life.

On Marie Antoinette's side the psychology becomes more complicated. One must divest oneself of the picture of the undeveloped child or woman of fashion that she had been at Trianon, whose interest in men was merely flirtatious. Everything in that period of her life suggests that she was fundamentally untouched by French gallantry of the Artois-Lauzun variety. Her propensity to the *amitié amoureuse* with women, her feverish, equivocal attachments to the princess de Lamballe and the duchesse de Polignac tend to confirm this speculation.

But the woman of 1790 was a very different person from the girl of 1780 who had been cheated of her maturity by an accident of fate. Motherhood, grief, and adversity had wrought those changes that she herself recognized, and in her awakening to self-knowledge one begins to discern the making of what Balzac called "a noble soul." It is women of this sort who in propitious circumstances are temperamentally most susceptible to the exaltation of an ardent love affair. And for Marie Antoinette the circumstances in 1790 were assuredly propitious. Abandoned by all whom she once believed to be her friends, surrounded by menace in a palace that every day became more undisguisedly a prison, the woman who for so many years had been in unhappy conflict with the Queen may well have delivered herself to the relief of love.

In the end, of course, it does not much matter whether she slept with Fersen or not. Neither Klinckowström nor the late Victorian and the post-Freudian biographers of Marie Antoinette can have foreseen a time when such matters would be viewed with indifference. But present-day attitudes permit one to consider the question without emotion and to observe dispassionately that nothing in history would have been altered by either possibility.

What matters is that beyond all doubt she loved him. Every scrap of writing that has been salvaged out of the shipwreck testifies to this and in the storm that was about to overwhelm them one is left, if one chooses, to surmise the rest.

During that summer of 1790 when Fersen was at Auteuil the royal family was spending its last uneasy *villégiature* at the nearby château de St. Cloud. It was here in conditions of greatest secrecy that there took place an event of political moment. Mirabeau, the celebrated Tribune of the Assembly, Mirabeau, the fiery leader of the Revolution went over to the Crown! The man who had been in the pay of the duc d'Orléans, who, uttering terrible threats from the rostrum of the Senate, once shook his fist in the direction of the palace, suddenly glimpsed in a flash of prophetic vision the catastrophe that lay ahead and recoiled.

It was the spectacle of October 6–7 at Versailles when he saw the King's person at the beck and call of a mob—whose leaders, as Mirabeau was well circumstanced to know, were in the pay of the duc d'Orléans—that filled him with consternation. On the following day he made his first overtures to Louis XVI. Unfortunately he made them through the comte de Provence, who had no particular wish to see his brother extricated from a predicament that might possibly bring him, Provence, the Crown. The comte de Provence did not therefore pass Mirabeau's urgent message on to Louis XVI. Valuable time was thus wasted while Mirabeau considered other means to communicate to Louis XVI and to Marie Antoinette his proposal to save the monarchy.

Mirabeau's plan was that Louis XVI and his family should leave

Paris and retire to some provincial city in the north, preferably in Brittany or Normandy, where the people were known to be loyal to the monarchy, but in any case *far from any foreign frontier,* since that move might suggest that the King was seeking foreign intervention in French affairs. They were to leave openly and even to announce their day of departure, offering as an explanation for this step the fact that the King needed to deliberate on the grave decisions that came before him in an atmosphere of tranquillity away from the pressures that were being put upon him by Paris' factions.

Mirabeau was something more than a political realist. He was a man who belonged to the race of the great Richelieu, of Talleyrand and Joseph Fouché. He not only saw clearly, he saw far and he saw deep. He knew well that Might, while it may not make Right, assuredly makes governments. He knew well that without power to enforce it the most admirable constitution is nothing but a scrap of parchment; and that it is not God who protects our person or our property, but the police. The harsh fact that force is the *ultima ratio* within the human ant-heap is often forgotten in that ceremony of innocence which is the most felicitous expression of a society such as that of eighteenth-century France. The assumption of a Voltaire that Reason for people other than oneself will prevail over the passions, the assumption of a Rousseau that the human spirit, other than one's own, is perfectible, can only be made in a climate of civilized disciplines in which manners, if not morals, have come to conceal the rude substructure of things. Mirabeau saw beyond the frame of established conditions that ordinary men accept as preordained and gazed with equanimity at these truths. And he saw that the French Crown, the stamp and seal of all authority in the kingdom and the personification of the government, was about to become the hostage of Paris and at the service of any demagogue who might threaten it, just as it might be commanded by the leader of any mob who might assemble enough of a crowd to frighten it. These things had not yet happened, but in the events of October 6–7 at Versailles Mirabeau glimpsed their potential. He also saw what few others remarked: that the National Assembly too had bowed that day before the demands of Orléans' paid horde and on that day the Assembly too had been brought to Paris.

It was thus bearing dire warnings and bold plans that Mirabeau tried again to put himself in touch with the King and Queen. At last in March of 1790, five months after his first overture, a friend and admirer of Mirabeau, who also happened to be a friend of the Queen, one le comte de La Marke, acted as intermediary between Mirabeau and the royal family, or rather between Mirabeau and Marie Antoinette, for it was the Queen with whom Mirabeau really wished to be in contact. Marie Antoinette seems to have fascinated him long before he met her. He attributed to her a political sagacity in which she was totally lacking and a strength of character that was of a different stripe than that which she did indeed possess.

"You do not know the Queen," he declared to his friend Étienne Dumont during that winter of waiting. "She has a prodigious strength of mind and the courage of a man."

"Then you have met her?" asked Dumont.

Mirabeau had to admit that he had not. But through La Marke he had been put in touch with her. Negotiations had been entered into and Mirabeau, whose services to any cause always came at a high fee, had been paid the first installment of his bribe. Still he had not yet met the Queen face to face. In the ensuing months that ambition began to obsess him. He oiled his secret memoirs to the Crown with flattery ("not knowing the soul or the thoughts of the daughter of Maria Theresa, not knowing that I could count on this august auxiliary"), he appealed over and again to La Marke and insisted that it was necessary for him to see the Queen.

Marie Antoinette in fact had no intention of seeing him. She looked on this renegade nobleman, atheist, and voluptuary with revulsion. "His whole existence is nothing but deceit, cunning, and lies," she confided to a friend, "and this together with the personal reasons I have always had for hating him and the prudence with which I must behave prevents me from seeing him." Her personal reasons sprang from a threatening denunciation that Mirabeau had made of her before the Estates-General when she was in mourning for her son.

Nothing demonstrates Marie Antoinette's total lack of political sense more than her attitude toward Mirabeau at this critical moment. The child may have matured into a woman but woman at heart she still remained. She was quite incapable of making a separation between her principles and the exigencies of political necessity. The daughter of Maria Theresa was now possessed of all her mother's high moral standards but had inherited none of the Empress' ability to compromise those standards when needs of state required. She indulged herself in the ultimate luxury, the one that must forever be denied those who are called into the political arena: she permitted her personal feelings about people to affect her attitude toward them. Offering Mirabeau his bribe as though with tongs, she read his memoranda and depended on his influence in the Assembly, but she refused to meet him. And so more time was wasted.

Then in June and July of 1790 a blow fell on another of the trunk roots of the *ancien régime* and this legislation, the Civil Constitution of the Clergy, caused Louis XVI at last to seriously consider flight from Paris. It profoundly affected the King and undoubtedly it was this that finally determined Marie Antoinette to grant Mirabeau the interview he solicited.

Louis XVI had always been a deeply religious man, attached in every fiber of his being to the law and liturgy of the Catholic Faith. The foundation of this strong belief probably lay in his unhappy childhood and the regard in which he held his father's memory. But unlike his father, Louis XVI was not a bigot. He was responsible for an extensive amelioration in the liberty of worship for non-Catholics in his kingdom and he even appointed several non-Catholics—Necker and Turgot—as his ministers. All the same, in matters of religious propriety he was a stickler and he looked on the flagrant immorality of the clergy that characterized his reign with disapproval, refusing on one occasion to recommend a certain prelate to the position of Archbishop of Paris because he was known to be an atheist.

The Civil Constitution of the Clergy, which followed upon the confiscation of the church's extensive tax-exempt properties, upset Louis XVI as no other act of the Assembly had done heretofore, for having nationalized church property, the Assembly now proposed nationalizing the Faith itself. All lines connecting the French church with Rome were to be severed and the administration of church affairs, the appointment of priests, prelates, and bishops, were to fall under the jurisdiction of the National Assembly. The proposal amounted to nothing less than apostasy and it placed the King in a cruel dilemma between his private conscience and political necessity, for the Assembly demanded his sanction to their decree. Louis XVI himself best described his intolerable position in a letter to Pius VI in which he implored the Pope to guide him.

"Should I refuse my sanction I will be the cause of a cruel persecution and will only augment the enemies of the Altar and the Throne. They will be given an excuse to revolt and will increase the woes that now afflict them. But if I do give my sanction what a terrible scandal in the eyes of the Faith!"

The Assembly made it clear that if necessary it would wrest his sanction from him by force. The growling crowds, by now all too familiar to the King, began again to gather about the palace gates. Nothing could better have illustrated Mirabeau's argument that the royal family should leave Paris. From that moment the King gave serious consideration to Mirabeau's proposal that he seek refuge in some provincial city where such sanctions could not be extorted from him.

In these circumstances Marie Antoinette finally agreed to meet Mirabeau. The step was doubly difficult for her because Mirabeau was among those in the Assembly who were hot supporters of the Civil Constitution of the Clergy. He viewed such issues entirely in their political light and so, paradoxically, it was as a secret defender of the monarchy that he advocated a piece of legislature that was so deeply repugnant to the King. His reasoning was that the measure was certain to be as odious to the larger portion of the French people as to the King and would prepare the ground for the civil war which he hoped to foment in order to recoup for the Crown its fast-vanishing sovereignty. Louis XVI and Marie Antoinette were to recoil in horror from Mirabeau's scheme when he finally revealed it to them.

The meeting between Marie Antoinette and Mirabeau took place on July 3 in the park at St. Cloud. The greatest precaution shrouded their encounter since Mirabeau's whole strength for the Crown lay in the fact that he was not known to be their agent. He spent the night of the second with his niece at Auteuil and early on the following morning—a Saturday, when not many people would be abroad before nine—he drove to nearby St. Cloud in a two-horse chaise driven by his nephew Victor du Saillant, who was disguised as a postilion. Mirabeau had been instructed to go to a small side gate of the park, which would be opened by "someone" at his signal. Before entering, however, Mirabeau gave his nephew a sealed letter saying that if he was not back in three quarters of an hour the letter was to be delivered to the commandant of the National Guard, the tocsin was to be rung, and the perfidy of the court announced to the people. The garden gate then opened and Mirabeau was conducted by an unknown escort (one wonders who this may have been; it was surely not a palace servant, for the Queen trusted them no more than she did most of the court) down a series of paths to a spot in the recesses of the park where Marie Antoinette awaited him.

It is from the comte de La Marke, who was a friend of both, that we have the most reliable account of this extraordinary meeting. Marie Antoinette later told La Marke that she almost fainted when she saw the leonine head and pock-marked face of the man whom she believed to have been among those who exhorted the mob to murder her on the night of October 6. Instinctively she recoiled and just as instinctively she quickly took command of herself and delivered a short speech of greeting that she had prepared earlier. Mirabeau made the requisite gesture of obeisance and the two then began to talk. It is not known of what they talked. He apparently accused himself of being the principal cause of her sufferings and begged her to believe in his repentance. She apparently accepted his apology with "an affability that charmed him." If they talked of political matters it was only in the most general sense. It is known that he warned her of the extreme danger in which the Crown stood and told her that the peril would only increase if the King did not act more firmly.

But the real purpose of this meeting was to take measure of one another: she in order to determine if he could really be trusted as an ally and he in order to plumb with his own eyes that strength of character upon which he counted in his various projects to save the monarchy. In their brief meeting she saw that he could indeed be trusted and realized moreover that he was an impressive convert to their cause, while he, for his part, was struck not so much by her strength as by another quality of character he had not looked to find: that remarkable dignity of bearing which partook in part of suffering nobly born and in part of an inborn grace of gesture and movement that had always been hers. It communicated in its *ensemble*—one must remember that she was then a woman of thirty-five—an air of inexpressible majesty. Mirabeau was overcome. The great orator of the Assembly, like many great orators, had a well-developed appreciation of the theater, as on his deathbed he was soon to demonstrate.

Both parties seem indeed to have been touched by a sense of the historical import of their meeting. Both in any case were deeply moved. When it came time for him to leave she made one of those impetuous, graceful gestures at which she so excelled. She suddenly extended him her hand. He took it and with tears in his eyes fell on his knees before her. "Madame," he declared, "the monarchy is saved!"

1. Maria Theresa (1717-1780), Queen of Hungary and Austrian Empress. Painting by Joseph Ducreux, Academy Gallery, Vienna.

2. Louis XV in dress of a Knight of
the Holy Ghost. Tapestry made
at the Gobelins, by Gozette, in
1771. Portrait painted by L. M.
Vanloo in 1760, Versailles.

3. Marie Antoinette.

4. *Marie Antoinette à la rose* by Vigée-Lebrun, painted in 1779. It was the first of the artist's celebrated portraits of Marie Antoinette. The Queen was then twenty-four years old.

5. The duc d'Orléans. THE BETTMANN ARCHIVE.

6. Count Axel Fersen. SWEDISH
PORTRAIT ARCHIVE, THE NATIONAL
MUSEUM, STOCKHOLM

7. Count Axel Fersen. Painting by Gustav Lundberg.
SWEDISH PORTRAIT ARCHIVE, THE NATIONAL MUSEUM,
STOCKHOLM.

8. Count Axel Fersen.
Painting by Peter Dreuillon,
1793. SWEDISH PORTRAIT
ARCHIVE, THE NATIONAL
MUSEUM, STOCKHOLM.

9. Louis XVI taking the coronation oath. After Moreau. THE BETTMANN ARCHIVE.

10. The duc d'Aiguillon.
THE BETTMANN ARCHIVE.

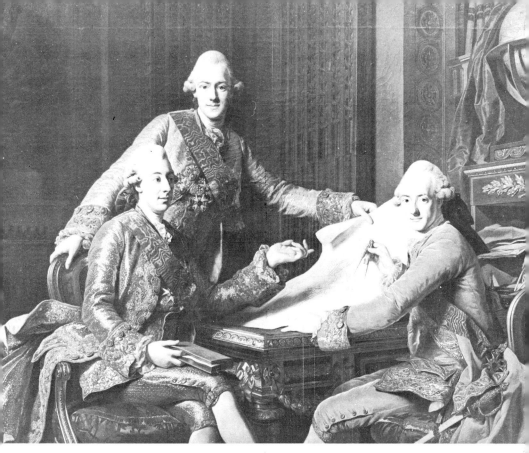

11. Gustavus III (with book) and his brothers Charles, the Duke of Söder-manland (left), and Frederick Adolf, Duke of Ostergötland (right). The Duke of Ostergötland proposed to Sophie Fersen. Painting by Roslin. Swedish Portrait Archive, National Museum, Stockholm. THE BETTMANN ARCHIVE.

12. "The hameau or farm of the Petit Trianon"

13. Portrait of Louis XVI. Painting by A. F. Callet, Versailles.

14. The comte d'Artois, brother of Louis XVI.

When he had been escorted back to his carriage he found Victor du Saillant uneasily awaiting his return; the three quarters of an hour were up. When the gate had closed behind him and the footsteps of his escort receded into the garden, he took his nephew's arm and in a low voice trembling with emotion said, "She is very great, Victor, she is very noble and very unfortunate, but I shall save her."

Unfortunately Mirabeau's plans to save them first startled then frightened the King and Queen. In August he revealed to them his plan to unleash a civil war. Marie Antoinette read the proposal with consternation. "How could Mirabeau or any other thinking being believe that the moment would ever come, especially at the present time, for us to provoke a civil war?" she wrote Mercy in distress.

Then in November with a great flailing of arms and hot words, he exhorted the Assembly to vote for the prosecution of priests who refused to take an oath to the Civil Constitution. A week later he sent the King one of his Letters of Advice that had the heading "On Ways to Make Good Use of the Civil Constitution." "No time," the King read, "could be more favorable than right now to unite all the malcontents behind the Crown and provoke resistance to the Assembly." Louis was shocked.

Mirabeau played his public part too well, roaring with the Jacobins whose president he became in November, advising the King—a very sound piece of advice—to introduce some of their members into his cabinet. It was in promoting this project that he made his celebrated remark that "a Jacobin who becomes a Minister is not always a Jacobin Minister." In the end the King and Queen lost confidence in his advice. They continued to pay him his substantial fees and, in the blind, groping way of the desperate, they continued to depend on him. But they lost faith in his judgment. They were temperamentally incapable of acting in the audacious manner that his proposals demanded.

In one matter, however, his advice still weighed. His proposal that the royal family leave Paris was considered and taken to heart. But by the time, in October, that the royal family finally decided to act on it, Mirabeau's original plan had gone through so many evolutions and modifications in their hands as to be almost unrecognizable. The crucial stipulations that the King and Queen were to retire *far from any foreign frontier* and that they were to leave Paris openly under the escort of the French army had been omitted. Mirabeau did not know about this second plan to which his own had been parent. It came into slow flower during the autumn and winter of 1790–91 in the inner recesses of the Tuileries.

Axel Fersen's was the hand behind this second plan that was to become the Flight to Varennes. It was probably Fersen who overrode Mirabeau's admonition about not seeking refuge near a foreign frontier. Mirabeau's advice undoubtedly had been good at the time he gave it. Fersen's undoubtedly had become correct in the spring of 1791, for by then it would have been out of the question for Louis XVI to leave Paris in the open. It was too late.

In concert with the King, the Queen, and Fersen two other men were involved in the making of these plans. The first of these was a gentleman of some sixty years, then living in Switzerland, the baron de Breteuil, a diplomat and former minister in whom the King had such confidence that he made him his representative or personal ambassador-at-large in Europe. The behavior of the *émigrés* in their various places of exile abroad had become increasingly compromising to Louis XVI and Marie Antoinette. Led by the comte d'Artois and the prince de Condé, they dreamed of a return to absolutism in France. In their eyes the King and Queen were as much their enemy as the National Assembly. They claimed that every order given them by the King had been extorted from him under duress and they set themselves up as a kind of government-in-exile, as though Louis XVI were already dead. It was the baron de Breteuil's job to communicate the King's real orders to them. He also acted as Louis' representative to the Powers of Europe, sounding out the possibility of intervention from some, gathering assurances of neutrality from others. In the plans for the flight from Paris, Breteuil played a difficult, delicate, and important role.

The other man was General Louis de Bouillé, in whose hands were placed all the logistics and military preparations that the project required. The marquis de Bouillé was then fifty-two years of age, an officer of the old school, a man of the greatest rectitude and honor. He had taken an oath to the Constitution because he was a believer in Constitutional Monarchy, but that in no way lessened his devotion to the King. Like many other Constitutional Monarchists of 1789 he had become alarmed by the summer of 1790. As Commander of the Forces in the East, Bouillé had observed with his own eyes the confusion that prevailed in the army. Some men were loyal to the King, some to the Assembly, and the larger portion uncertain. There had already been several mutinies within his command which

Bouillé had suppressed with a firm hand. In the factions' struggle to seize the toppled crown of power the support of the army and the National Guard was the decisive factor. General Bonaparte knew this well and it was his skillful use of the army and his rewards to competent men of the ranks, who were to become the peers of the Empire, which finally won him the supreme power.

Mirabeau told Louis XVI that Bouillé was the highest ranking officer on whom he could depend. Bouillé's men respected him and indeed in a kind of popularity contest that must have sent shudders down the spine of that general of the Old Régime, he had been elected by his men to retain command of his army. Mirabeau also knew, as did Bouillé, that in all rapports with the army speed was of essential importance, for it was no longer possible to know how long Bouillé's army would be dependable, nor was it indeed possible to know how long Bouillé himself would retain his command. The Assembly was beginning to appoint its own officers to such strategic commands as that which Bouillé held at Metz over the territory of Lorraine. It was Mirabeau's idea that Bouillé should be transferred toward the west to a command that would include Normandy and the château of Compiègne, one of the royal châteaux near Paris where Louis might set up his government. Mirabeau would use his influence in the Assembly to effect this important transfer.

But the King, the Queen, and Fersen had different plans and toward the end of October 1790, Bouillé was discreetly sounded out about the possibility of the King retiring within the area of his command, somewhere in the vicinity of the Belgian or Luxembourg frontiers, which were then extensions of the Austrian Empire. It was explained then, as it was to be explained for many years afterward, that in retiring toward a foreign frontier the King had no intention of soliciting foreign intervention in French affairs. The position, being near the Austrian frontier, gave Bouillé the great advantage of being able to move troops there long before the King's arrival without attracting the suspicions of the Assembly. In the event of a real *débâcle* the King, Queen, and their children could step over the border and find safety among the Austrians.

The marquis de Bouillé gave his wholehearted approval to their project. But he was a military man. With the eye of one experienced in the examining of strategies on maps he saw that their plan was fraught with many obstacles and difficulties. He offered his services without hesitation, but he warned the King that the execution of the scheme would not be easy. A code or cipher was then agreed upon and a secret line of communication was established between Bouillé's headquarters at Metz and the Tuileries in Paris. Fersen wrote most of the letters on behalf of the King.

The first decision concerned the exact place within Bouillé's command where the royal family should seek refuge. After a consideration of various alternatives the town of Montmédy was finally selected. This small community had a fortress that was easy to defend and difficult to attack. It was only sixty leagues from Paris on one hand and not many miles distant from the Luxembourg frontier on the other. Everything indicated Montmédy to be the place. The next matter for consideration was the route that the King and his family should take to reach Montmédy. This was a far more difficult decision and in December Bouillé sent his son to Paris to discuss it and other problems that had arisen. Young Bouillé describes the mission in his memoirs:

> The King and Queen were informed of my arrival in Paris but because it would have been too dangerous for me as well as for them to meet them in private it was arranged that the comte de Fersen should see me on their behalf and put me abreast of the situation both abroad and at home. I could then bring a report of this back to Metz. Their Majesties desired that henceforth I should treat with M. de Fersen, who was at their orders. It was thus at his house that my first discussion of the business took place. I took the greatest precautions not to be seen entering the home of a man known for his attachment to the palace. I arrived at night at a house set well back from the corner of the rue de Matignon and after we had made certain that we could not be overheard we entered into the matter . . .
>
> We discussed the various ways to reach Montmédy. The problem of leaving the Tuileries, all of whose issues were guarded with an extreme vigilance, seemed to me insoluble, but the comte de Fersen had carefully considered this difficult maneuver. He gave me enough details about the interior of the palace to see that there was a good possibility of getting the royal family out of it in secrecy.

At about the time that the marquis de Bouillé's son arrived in Paris for these consultations Fersen took the first active step in the material preparations for the King's flight. He ordered the carriage in which the royal family was to travel. To do this with discretion he went to a Swedish friend, one Baroness de Korff, whom he had known for many years in Paris. Madame de Korff, a woman in her middle forties, was the widow of a Russian diplomat and was one of the many foreigners who had elected to live in Paris during the pleasant last days of the eighteenth century. She lived with her two young children and a sister, Madame de Stegelman. She was not a member of the Queen's Trianon circle and indeed did not move in court society, but Fersen knew her to be a friend of the Crown. He also knew that like so many other foreigners in Paris at this moment, she was preparing to leave France. Her plans coincided perfectly with his own, because as a Russian and a Swedish national Madame de Korff was at liberty to leave when she chose. An order from her for a commodious carriage would not seem unusual. It was in her name therefore that Monsieur Louis, the finest carriage maker of his day, was ordered to construct a coach of the kind known then as a *berline*, a carriage large enough to accommodate six people inside and three on the box, with interior fittings of the most luxurious kind: "cushions to be covered with white taffeta, double curtains of taffeta and leather on all the windows, two cooking stoves of iron plate, two chamber pots of varnished leather . . ."

This was the famous carriage that so many writers declare to have been the principal cause of the failure of the Flight to Varennes. One historian in an ironic tone states that all that was lacking in it was a chapel and the royal musicians. The grandiose appearance of the carriage has been greatly exaggerated. Madame de Tourzel who traveled in it on the fatal trip as the children's governess afterward stated: "There was nothing extraordinary about it such as people have gone on repeating. It was a large *berline*, much like my own, but it was better made and it had a great number of conveniences in the inside."

All the same it was a mistake. Bouillé, who had recommended two light carriages, was troubled when he heard about it. The cumbersome vehicle required six horses to draw it and it could not move with the ease that Bouillé saw to be a vital consideration in the success of their plans. Furthermore, although it may have been plain on the outside ("wheels to be painted lemon yellow, the casing to be of dark green"), a carriage of this description lumbering along the highroad of a countryside in the midst of revolution was certain to attract attention.

The generous Madame de Korff made another contribution to the royal family. She gave them her passport, which covered herself, her two children, and her domestics. At the Ministry of Foreign Affairs she claimed she had lost the passport which she had given Fersen and so was able to secure another.

The carriage maker, Monsieur Louis, was mystified by the behavior of the man who placed the order: he kept pressing him to make haste, and even threatened to cancel the order if it wasn't finished by February 6. The coachmaker replied that it wasn't possible to finish it by that date, but he put more men to work, and by the end of the month it was finished. Then, after all this haste, no one came to claim it. For weeks it lay unused and undelivered in his *remise* and he thought it most peculiar.

The carriage was expensive but it was the least that had to be paid for. To avoid attracting the attention of the Finance Ministry, which was notoriously tight-fisted and at odds with the Ministry of War, Bouillé decided that the cost of the movement of troops at the frontier should be defrayed by Louis. This meant that money would be needed to pay for horses, to pay for their forage, for the movement of cannon and men. More money would be needed for unforeseen eventualities such as bribes, for the expenses of the trip itself, for postilions and horsemen at the various relays along the way. Bouillé estimated that at least a million francs would be required and his demands for the money became more insistent as the winter of 1791 progressed into spring.

Louis, like most kings, was without private resources. In the heyday of his reign his expenses had always been paid by the treasury. At the Tuileries the superintendent of his household was allocated such money as was considered necessary for his proper maintenance there. He was not expected to have any private expenses or to need cash. He did own some shares in a water company and these were discreetly sold and the proceeds deposited abroad. But this was all that he had. Marie Antoinette was in the same position. Her only possession was a quantity of jewels that had been part of her dowry. But it would have been difficult to sell these diamonds without attracting attention. For the first time in their lives the King and Queen needed money and they needed it desperately. One wonders if at this moment she may have recalled the lucrative pensions she had once so carelessly tossed to the Polignacs and their hangers-on who were now safely abroad in the entourage of her enemies the comte d'Artois and the prince de Condé.

To raise this money Fersen contributed all his own available cash and then had his friend Taube borrow abroad against his eventual inheritance. All he possessed in the world went into the fund, but it was not enough. So he went again to Madame de Korff and her sister, who contributed most of their own inheritance. Their "contribution," like Fersen's, was considered by all parties as a loan to which interest was attached. The poor women were, in fact, never to recover their money and their sorry plight in the final years of their lives is not least among the tragedies that belong to the epilogue.

Fersen next turned to two other friends. These were his mistress Éléonore Sullivan and Éléonore's lover, an Englishman named Quentin Crauford. This interesting pair was to be intimately associated with Fersen in the plans for the King's trip to Montmédy. Five years older than Axel, Éléonore Sullivan was thirty-nine years of age in 1791 and had led a very colorful life.

She had been born Eleonora Franchi and came of a family of Italian carpenters attached to a team of itinerant acrobats. By the age of fifteen she herself had danced and performed on a trapeze in the dusty piazzas of most of the cities of Italy. Acrobats and jugglers were very popular in eighteenth-century Italy and for a moment one seems to see some square in Lucca or Palermo and the young girl dressed as a Pierrot dancing there to a tambourine and flute. She was unusually beautiful, with enormous dark eyes and a lustrous warmth of skin. She married one of the troupe before she was sixteen. A few years afterward while dancing in Venice during the Carnival she attracted the notice of the regnant Duke of Württemberg, who fell passionately in love with her and installed her with every honor but marriage in his palace at Stuttgart. The Duke of Württemberg, who maintained a private *corps de ballet* of thirty beautiful girls, was one of the most profligate princes of that profligate age. She stayed with him for three years and had two children by him, a son who died when young and a daughter who in time was to become the comtesse d'Orsay and mother of the famous dandy of that name. The two children were brought up in the palace and the Duke of Württemberg provided them with a proper education. But she and her royal lover finally had a falling out and she was expelled from his harem.

She went back to her dancing and set out once more on her travels. These took her to Vienna, where Marie Antoinette's brother, the Emperor Joseph II, saw her and, like the Duke of Württemberg, fell in love. Their liaison was of brief duration, for Maria Theresa was still alive. The Empress' famous Chastity Commission paid the adventuress a visit and she was forced to leave Austria. Then she cast her lot with a French lover, one chevalier d'Aigremont, who persuaded her to go to Paris with him where he abandoned her. But women such as she do not go long without protection and in Paris she soon attracted another man, who became her second husband. His name was Sullivan. He was of Anglo-Irish birth, and his money came from the famous Eastern trading company, the Compagnie des Indes. As Mrs. Sullivan she returned with him to India, where he had decided to spend the rest of his days. It was in India, after several years' residence, that she met Mr. Quentin Crauford.

It may be surmised that by this time Éléonore Sullivan was something more than a beautiful or desirable woman. She had traveled far, had lived near thrones, had had many experiences and known many lovers. She appears to have been fascinating. Like his predecessors Crauford fell instantly and passionately in love with her. He persuaded her to leave Sullivan, return to Europe with him and do the honors of his household there.

It was a household of impressive substance. During his thirty-five years Crauford had done some traveling of his own. As the younger son of a noble Scottish family he had left home at eighteen and gone into the world to make his fortune. He too entered service with the Compagnie des Indes and had gone to India, where his ability so impressed his superiors that he was entrusted with a mission to Manila. The distances in that day between such places as England, India, and Manila were almost incredible. These were not trips of a few weeks or months, but of whole years. Crauford remained in Manila for three years, where he established the China Trade for the English colonies. This was the foundation of his fortune. When he returned to India he was a wealthy and important man. He continued to travel about India on various missions for the Compagnie des Indes, observed the customs of the Hindus, about whom in later years he was to write a history. But he was bored and wanted to return to Europe where he could enjoy his money in the manner of an English gentleman. It was in this frame of mind that he met

Éléonore Sullivan. He seems to have had no trouble persuading her to leave her husband and return with him to Europe.

They arrived there in 1780. For a few years they traveled about in great state, settling for a time in Rome, then Holland, Germany, and England. They collected furniture and paintings as they went along. Like so many other foreigners who had money and a taste for pleasure they finally settled in Paris. "One can make money any place," Crauford declared, "but there is only one place where you can really spend it and that is in Paris." In 1783 Crauford bought a house at 18 rue de Clichy, the Hôtel Rouillé d'Orfeuil, and filled it with the works of art that he had collected on his travels. And here he lived for eight years with Éléonore Sullivan. Their receptions came to enjoy a certain celebrity among the foreign colony and the racier members of the aristocracy. Talleyrand became a good friend, as did the duc de Lauzun and the future war minister, Narbonne.

Fersen met the Sullivans in April of 1789, just as the Revolution was beginning (*"dans le moment le plus intéressant de ma vie,"* as he was to recall long afterward). He was instantly smitten by Éléonore and seems almost immediately to have become her lover. Their attachment was to last for many years against a background of storm and disturbance. Crauford was to be long ignorant of the liaison between his mistress and Fersen. But thanks to the spiteful tongue of Madame de St. Priest the rest of Europe was not. She went through England, Germany, and Sweden spreading the news that Fersen was the lover of Éléonore Sullivan. Because this gossip was disseminated in the critical days that followed the *débâcle* at Varennes it was not without political reverberations and it was heard with interest by certain people in high places. Among others who heard it was Fersen's sister, and Sophie's words to him on the subject confirm the conjecture that the unidentified woman of whom Axel spoke so tenderly in his correspondence with Sophie was indeed Marie Antoinette. "I have not spoken to you about this (i.e., the gossip concerning Fersen and Mrs. Sullivan) or warned you about it out of respect for Her because She would be mortally wounded should this news reach her ear. Everybody is watching you and talking about you and you must think of Her and spare her this cruelest of blows."

It should be observed that in his letters to Sophie, Axel generally referred to Marie Antoinette as "Elle," using the capital letter. In his diary another distinction becomes apparent at the time of the

Flight to Varennes. He refers to Éléonore Sullivan as "el." or "elle," with the small letter. This seems to be almost consistent. There are many references to "el." in his Journal. The words *resté là* ("stayed there") underlined twice recur frequently in those places where he makes mention of visiting Mrs. Sullivan. Everything suggests that with this expression he referred to those occasions when he had had sexual intercourse with her.

There were frequent opportunities to do so, for Crauford was often away practicing his own infidelities—Madame de Korff's sister was one of his mistresses. He spent three months of every year in England. It was suspected by his French friends that Quentin Crauford was in the pay of the English. If this was true, as it well may have been, Fersen never doubted the attachment of Crauford and Mrs. Sullivan to the cause of Louis XVI and Marie Antoinette.

He now turned to them for help in preparing the King's escape. Crauford without hesitation contributed a substantial sum to the fund that Bouillé demanded. On the afternoon of the flight the *berline* came to rest in their stables on the rue de Clichy, where it was less likely to attract notice than in Fersen's stables. Crauford and Mrs. Sullivan were also convenient intermediaries for letters from abroad, for it had become risky to address any correspondence directly to Fersen. Night after night the three friends would gather in the rue de Clichy and discuss the project in all its details.

Despite urgent warnings from Bouillé that time was running out, Louis continued to procrastinate. Perhaps he hoped that the Pope would not condemn the Civil Constitution of the Clergy. Undoubtedly he hoped that there would be some unexpected improvement in the political situation. But by the spring of 1791 everything had, in fact, worsened and a series of incidents finally forced him into taking the step he so dreaded.

In February, Madame Adélaïde and Madame Victoire fled the country. The aunts sneaked out of their palace at Bellevue in the dead of night, leaving behind them the explanation that they wished to make a pilgrimage to Rome. They were arrested in Burgundy and might well have been sent back to Paris had not Mirabeau used his quick tongue on their behalf. He pointed out to the Assembly that it was ridiculous for serious senators to waste their time arguing over the fate of two old women. So the aunts continued on their way to Rome, where two years later they were to learn of the execution of their nephew and the Queen whom they had once so spitefully calumniated.

Mirabeau's skirmish in defense of the aunts was his last public performance. He died after a short illness on April 2, worn out by work and dissipation. He made his departure in a state of euphoria, calling for purple raiment and leaves of laurel to be put upon his brow. Talleyrand, who was at his bedside, made the dry comment that "Mirabeau seems to be dramatizing his death." Just before he died Mirabeau uttered the prophetic words, "I carry with me in my heart the death knell of the monarchy whose remaining scraps will become the prey of the factions after my death."

The gravity of their loss was immediately understood by those involved in the plans for flight. According to Fersen, Marie Antoinette wept bitterly at the news and cried out, "We have lost our last hope!" Fersen informed Taube that, "It is a terrible blow because he was on our side, was working for us and was just becoming useful. He would have been of the greatest help to them in the execution of their plan." In Brussels, where he was now living, Mercy declared: "Everything is going against us. There is no fighting against such bad luck."

And in these words the Ambassador provides the key to so much that henceforth was to happen: bad luck. Mirabeau's sudden death followed that of Joseph II and these were but the first in a series of untimely deaths that one by one were to extinguish hope.

Mirabeau's death forced the King to see that he must hurry. Bouillé, too, sent him a number of messages urging him to make haste. "There is going to be a rebellion among the troops," wrote the General, "and we shall soon lose even those who are faithful. It is certain that the officers are going to be forced to take a new oath and my situation is becoming more untenable every day . . . after the month of May everything will have become impossible."

A few weeks after Mirabeau's death, on Easter Monday, an incident took place that brought the King's indecision to an end. The Pope's condemnation of the Civil Constitution which Louis dreaded was announced before Easter. When he attended Mass at the Tuileries on Easter Day he did not take Communion, since he refused to accept the Sacrament from the hands of a juring priest. On the following morning he had planned to go to St. Cloud with his family for a few days' rest in the country. But the rumor had gone around that at St. Cloud he planned to receive the Sacrament from a non-juring priest. A great crowd began to gather before the gates of the Tuileries declaring angrily that they would not allow the King to go to St. Cloud. The royal carriages were called but the crowd wouldn't let the vehicles enter the courtyard. Marie Antoinette proposed that they leave by another carriage that was already in the Cour des Princes. They took their places in this and were preparing to depart when the National Guard on duty at the palace suddenly joined the crowd outside the gates and refused to let the carriage leave. By now the manifestation had assumed the proportion of a riot and La Fayette was summoned. But when he ordered his militia to open the gates and to force a way through the crowd for the carriage his men refused to obey him.

After two hours of waiting in the carriage, subject to all the now-familiar epithets and insults, the royal family returned to the palace. As she went up the steps the Queen turned to La Fayette, to the Mayor of Paris, and to the militia and in a loud voice said, "You'll have to admit now that we are not free." The incident did indeed effectively demonstrate that the King was not free and so provided him with a perfect and public justification for flight. La Fayette and the radical members of the Constitutional party along with the Jacobins were much annoyed by this ill-timed show of popular power. It was afterward discovered that the disturbance had, in fact, been fomented by the duc d'Orléans and it was recalled that along with cries for the dethronement of Louis XVI there had been a number of shouts, *"Vive le duc d'Orléans!"*

Two days later Marie Antoinette wrote Mercy that "The event which has just taken place confirms us in our plans. The palace guard surrounding us is the most threatening of all. Our lives are no longer safe . . . Our position is frightful and it is absolutely imperative that we put an end to it next month. The King now wishes it even more than I do."

Fersen then sent a note to Bouillé saying, "The King will be ready to leave sometime during the last fifteen days of May. He has decided to defer the business no longer for he realizes how pressing circumstances have become. The events of Monday have made him realize this more than ever." When he received this message Bouillé addressed himself to setting into movement all the military mechanics of the plan.

It was a simple plan but serviceable and apparently air-tight. It should have worked and even with the advantage of hindsight it is not possible to point to one particular place in it and declare that here lay the cause of its failure. It failed because of an extraordinary series of coincidences whose conjunction could not possibly have been foreseen by those who designed it. As with all schemes, whether they be great strategies on the field of battle or the small projects of workaday men, the invisible but decisive factor was luck. The real coachman of the carriage that brought the Bourbon monarchy to Varennes was Fate.

To understand the essentials of Bouillé's plan to rescue Louis XVI one must glance at a map of the route from Paris to Montmédy which the conspirators decided the King should take. After Louis and his family had left the Tuileries—the responsibility for this extremely difficult maneuver was Fersen's—they were to take the eastern road that led through the suburban village of Bondy, through the farming towns of Meaux and Montmirail to Châlons-sur-Marne, a community that lay some 175 kilometers from Paris. This lap of the trip, from Paris to Châlons, was well over half the distance to their goal at Montmédy and it was to be traveled without military escort both because Bouillé's command did not extend that far and because it would have been rash in the extreme to attract the notice of communities near Paris by the presence of an armed guard.

After Châlons, however, in the hamlet of Pont-Sommevesle, at the outer limit of Bouillé's command, the King was to be met by the first detachment of the escort with which Bouillé planned to protect him. This was to be a group of forty hussars under the command of the duc de Choiseul. Choiseul would know the reason why he was there, but his troops would not. It was to be explained to them that their services were needed to protect a shipment of gold that was being sent from Paris to the frontier to pay the army. After the King's carriage had passed they would fall in behind it and follow it to the next town, Sainte Menehould, where there would be another detachment of troops who would do the same. And so, with ever swelling ranks, was it to be at Clermont and then at Varennes until at last the King reached Montmédy, where he would don his dress uniform and award the marquis de Bouillé the *bâton* of a *maréchal de France*. The *bâton*, with misapplied foresight, was tucked away in the luggage rack of the carriage.

There had been a sharp difference of opinion between Fersen and Bouillé about this matter of troops. Fersen did not like the idea, for he saw that they would probably be useless if something went seriously wrong, while their presence might attract undue notice to the carriage and its occupants. "The best precaution," Fersen declared, "is to take none at all. Everything must depend on speed and secrecy. If you are not sure of your detachments it would be better not to have any at all until after Varennes, so as not to arouse notice in the countryside." And he repeated this admonition in other letters. *"Be very sure of your detachments or do not station any until after Varennes."*

But Bouillé was a soldier and he looked on the operation with the eye of a military tactician. He wished to close off the line of communication between Paris and the King's carriage after the King had passed. And in principle at least this was a proper precaution. Fersen finally acceded to it. But he did so with a kind of premonitory reluctance.

To actuate all the little wheels of the plan was no small task. Among other things the marquis de Bouillé had to approach the officers whom he intended to use and bring them into the confidence. This required a certain intuition in the judgment of human nature, for should he reveal the secret to someone who might betray them the whole enterprise would have misfired at its start. From the first the conspirators had decided to have as few people as possible in on the secret. Fersen had misgivings about the French propensity to chatter. "Above all," he wrote Taube, "don't confide in any of the French, even those who are the best intentioned. Their indiscretion is such that they will spoil everything. If they knew something they would not fail to tell about it right afterwards." Fersen did not even trust Gustavus III. It was only a month before the flight that Axel finally told him about the project. Gustavus immediately departed for Belgium so that he could be there in order to celebrate Louis XVI's escape from his ignominious captivity.

Despite these precautions half of Europe seems to have been in on the secret. As the hour of the royal family's departure approached it became the principal topic of conversation at the courts of the European powers. It was mentioned quite openly in the letters that went back and forth between Paris and the outside world. Madame de St. Priest, for example, wrote Fersen from London that "Madame de Korff tells me that you are planning to leave in ten days. Everything that people here are saying about it terrifies me for you." Important secrets of this sort that have become the subject of gossip among fashionable women have a way of spreading with the speed of fire. The police and the National Guard received a deluge of denunciations during the first weeks of June. In one instance La Fayette's aide-de-camp was informed that the Queen was planning to leave the Tuileries with her children through the apartments of the duc de Villequier to which she had a key. This was, in fact, so devastatingly accurate that one wonders who this informant may have been or by what means he came to learn such details of a plan supposedly known to only a few intimates of the King and Queen. On the very day of their flight, June 20, an article appeared in one of the leading newspapers that not only predicted the imminent departure of Louis XVI, but described in detail the role played by Fersen in the plot.

La Fayette doubled the guard around the palace and put the royal family under a more rigorous surveillance. From that moment haste should have been an imperative consideration.

But at that very moment the King was obliged to defer his departure because of the uncooperative behavior of Marie Antoinette's brother, Leopold II. The Austrian Emperor, who was supposed to move some fifteen thousand troops toward the Luxembourg frontier, now began to procrastinate. He declared that he was afraid of offending the English and offered a number of other explanations for his delay. In truth the Emperor was waiting to see what profit Austria might make out of the disturbances in France. As a private person he viewed his sister's plight with indifference; as Emperor he now began to make a number of secret moves in the age-old game of European politics. In the end Bouillé had to do without him. By spreading rumors and by sending exaggerated reports to Paris the General made it appear that there was a dangerous massing of Austrian troops on the frontier.

Fersen informed Bouillé that the King would be ready to depart on June 7 but at the last moment the day had to be changed because of an untrustworthy waiting woman among the dauphin's attendants. The date of June 12 was then set, but the waiting woman decided to stay on until the eighteenth and then until the morning of the twentieth. Bouillé's plans were altered in this manner three and then four times. These last-minute postponements were injudicious not merely because time could no longer be wasted, but because they imparted an atmosphere of uncertainty to the whole enterprise. How could anyone along the chain of command that stretched from Châlons to Montmédy be sure that the King was really on his way when he made his escape from the Tuileries? Bouillé was perturbed by all these changes of schedule.

He was far more perturbed by a last-minute decision of the King that the children's governess, Madame de Tourzel, should travel in the carriage with them. There were only six places in the *berline*, five of which were to be occupied by the royal family. Bouillé wanted the sixth to be taken by an able-bodied and resolute officer who might take command of things in the event of an emergency or some unforeseen breakdown in the plans. Fersen had, in fact, originally been scheduled to occupy that place but sometime in April Louis decided that he should not. The reason for that decision has never been explained. By some it has been attributed to the King's feeling that it should be a Frenchman, if anybody, who should escort him on his trip. Others have surmised that Louis XVI did not care to have his wife's lover conduct him to safety.

To replace Fersen in the carriage Bouillé proposed the marquis d'Agoust whom he knew to be devoted to the monarchy and endowed with all those qualities of character that enable certain people to successfully meet emergencies. But a few weeks before the scheduled departure Louis informed Bouillé that he wanted Madame de Tourzel to take the place of the marquis d'Agoust and Bouillé could not persuade him to change his mind. There is no more stubborn man than a weak man who has suddenly decided to show that he is strong.

In the aftermath of Varennes, in the storm of recrimination and accusation that followed the arrest of the King, Madame de Tourzel was much reproached for having taken the place in the carriage that should have been occupied by a responsible man of arms. And Madame de Tourzel was undoubtedly to blame to the extent that she insisted on her prerogative as Governess of the Children of France to be with her charges on all state occasions. Considerations of rank, etiquette, and precedence that had already proved the ruin of the French monarchy still very much obtained among the remnants of the nobility that remained at court. Revolution or no revolution there were those who insisted on being accorded the precise privileges that were their due. Among some of them, bickering about precedence was to occur at the very steps of the guillotine. But the fault in this case seems to have been more that of the King and Queen than of Madame de Tourzel. They did not want their children to be separated from their governess. Marie Antoinette and Louis realized that the final end of their adventure might well be exile and they could not face this eventuality without knowing that the kindly, trusted, and familiar governess would be with them.

This was not the first time nor was it to be the last that concern for their children caused Marie Antoinette and Louis to overlook considerations that their position as King and Queen should have imposed. It was because of the children that they were planning to leave Paris in one heavy carriage instead of two light vehicles. It seems that after the night of October 5 at Versailles they took an oath never to be separated from their children. In the matter of her young son and daughter the obligations of the Queen once more came into direct conflict with the emotions of the woman. Not only did she and her husband love their children, they loved them with a bourgeois solicitude in which reasons of state were excluded. "Truly if I could be happy," Marie Antoinette wrote the duchesse de Polignac after the latter had emigrated, "it would be through these two little creatures. *The chou d'amour* (her nickname for the dauphin) is charming and I love him madly. He loves me, too, in his way, without any ceremony . . . he is well and growing strong and does not get into tempers any more." Then again: "My only happiness now is my children and I have them with me as much as possible."

The boy was then seven years old and he appears to have been an interesting child. He was given to precocious remarks that delighted his parents and often charmed the revolutionaries or political leaders with whom he came into contact. Marie Antoinette herself wrote one of the most vivid remaining descriptions of him at the time he was handed over to the care of Madame de Tourzel. Her words to the governess merit quotation not only because they so clearly describe the dauphin but because they reveal a different Marie Antoinette than the Queen of Trianon:

Because of his rather delicate nerves he is frightened of noises to which he is not accustomed. For example, he is frightened of dogs. I have never forced him to see them because I believe that as he gains in reasoning power his fears will disappear. Like all strong and healthy children he is very thoughtless and can be violent in his anger. But when he is not carried away by his thoughtlessness he is good-natured and gentle. He knows how to control his temper and even conquer his impatience among people who are not familiar to him so as to appear gently and amiable.

119

He keeps his word faithfully once he has given it, but he is very indiscreet and easily repeats what he has heard and often without meaning to lie he adds things suggested by his own imagination. This is his greatest fault and it must be corrected . . .

My children have always been taught to have complete trust in me and when they have done wrong to tell me so themselves. I have accustomed them to accepting a yes or a no from me as being final, but I always give them a reason suited to their age so they will not think it a whim on my part.

At her trial those words, ". . . he easily repeats what he has heard and often without meaning to lie he adds things suggested by his own imagination," were to have a terrible application.

Her daughter, Marie Thérèse, was a less interesting personality. She was the only member of her family to survive the Revolution and it is with considerable anticipation that one turns to her recollections of the Flight to Varennes that she published some time afterward. Unfortunately she was only twelve at the time of Varennes and her account is written in a matter-of-fact, restrained style that throws no light into the darker corners of that event.

Along with Madame de Tourzel, the King, Queen, and their two children, one other person was to travel in the carriage. This was the King's younger sister, Élisabeth. She was then twenty-seven years of age and until the Revolution had kept to the wings of the stage. It would, in fact, have been better for everybody had Madame Élisabeth emigrated in 1790 or accompanied her aunts into exile in February, but she refused to leave her brother in his hour of tribulation when so many others had abandoned him. Now that the moment of flight had come Louis could hardly leave this helpless woman behind him to face the storm that would break after his departure. Madame Élisabeth was therefore included among the passengers in the *berline* and her lot henceforth cast with that of the King and Queen.

Despite a superficial softness of demeanor Élisabeth was a young lady of strong character and decided ideas who deplored the compromises her brother had made with the Revolution. She shared the reactionary views of her brother Artois and believed that strong measures should be taken to restore the *status quo* to the kingdom whether these led to violence or not. In the days of Versailles she had never been on terms of intimacy or of sympathy with the Queen. She belonged to the anti-Austrian faction and she disapproved of her sister-in-law's light life that rumor, via the aunts, reported to her. After Varennes the two women were to form a close friendship and in the intimacy of prison were to discover one another's better qualities.

During those first days of June when the hour of departure seemed imminent Marie Antoinette emptied her jewelry cases of their contents, which she wrapped in wool and packed away in a satchel that she planned to confide to the hands of her hairdresser Léonard—another individual who had been elected to play a role in the plan but who did not yet know it. The Queen viewed her jewelry as negotiable and saw in it a means to raise money abroad should money be needed, but undoubtedly, too, she viewed it as ornamental and her concern with her diamonds may be put in the same category of such ill-placed considerations as the marquis de Bouillé's *bâton de maréchal.*

Nothing attests more forcefully to such insouciant priorities on the eve of the French royal family's flight than the magnificent *nécessaire* or traveling case that Marie Antoinette ordered from Palma on the rue de Richelieu. This remarkable object, which is now in the Louvre, must surely be the last great work of art wrought by the artisans of the *ancien régime.* It is the size of a trunk and fitted with hundreds of articles, ranging from a manicure set to a complete tea service, all in silver or Sèvres porcelain. It was so heavy it couldn't be taken along for use on the Flight to Varennes but was sent ahead to await Marie Antoinette's arrival at Montmédy.

Despite such trivial considerations Marie Antoinette had a clear appreciation of the enormity of the step that she and the King had decided to take. In her letters to Mercy she spoke often of the unthinkable reckoning that would follow failure and Fersen echoed her apprehensions when he expressed his own in a letter to Bouillé: "One can only shudder at the thought of the horrors that would take place if they were stopped."

On June 13 Axel wrote Bouillé of the King's irrevocable decision to leave on June 20. "Their departure is now set with no further delay for the 20th at midnight. You can count on this date, for it will be too late to change things after that." On the following day he confirmed this announcement. "They will leave without fail on Monday the 20th at midnight," he stated. "They will be at Pont-Sommevesle on Tuesday at 2:30 at the latest. You can count on this absolutely."

There is an inflexible finality about Fersen's words, as though he were announcing the timetables of a twentieth-century airline.

And the wheels were once again put into motion, and the officers in charge of the detachment of troops at Pont-Sommevesle, that first critical outpost of Bouillé's command, were told to have their men there by noon of the twenty-first, in expectation of the King's arrival by two-thirty.

PART II

Varennes

ALL THROUGH THE DAY OF JUNE 20 THE RHYTHM OF PALACE LIFE continued as usual. The King worked in his study, where he received various deputies from the Assembly. To the officers of his household he gave his orders for the morrow. At eleven the Queen attended Mass. The dauphin went out to play in the garden. Madame Élisabeth —who had not yet been informed of the impending flight—spent the morning at her country property near Bellevue. She did not return until shortly before lunch when the King drew her aside and told her of the flight that was to take place that night.

Later that day Marie Antoinette took her children for a walk in the public gardens of the Chaussée d'Antin. In the course of their outing she drew her daughter aside and told her that something important was about to happen. "My mother told me that I should not be worried by anything I saw and she said that we wouldn't be separated for very long and would all be together again soon afterward." The children were scheduled to leave the Tuileries an hour or two before their parents and obviously the prospect of this separation upset Marie Antoinette. Far from soothing her, her mother's words filled the girl with foreboding. But she was an obedient child and she promised her mother that she would try to hide her agitation and say nothing to her women should they ask her any questions.

At one o'clock, just before lunch, Marie Antoinette sent for Léonard, her hairdresser, who occupied a room in the eaves of the palace. She received him informally in her *salon*. Marie Thérèse was on the floor playing a game with her brother when Léonard entered. The King was in an embrasure talking in a low voice to Madame Élisabeth; the Queen was leaning against a chimney piece. She asked him if she could depend on him. Léonard bowed low and swore to his devotion. Marie Antoinette replied that she had always been sure of this and said that this was why she was giving him an important mission. She then handed him a letter he was to deliver to the duc de Choiseul at his house in the rue d'Artois.

"You are to give it to no one but him and you must promise to obey him exactly as you would obey me, without asking any questions . . ."

Marie Antoinette told him no more than this. Léonard, flattered by her confidence, hurried off on the mysterious errand. Since he had been given no hint that he would be going on a long trip he brought neither a change of clothing nor any personal belongings with him. To reach the rue d'Artois he took one of the public cabs that were on call in the place du Petit Carrousel, not far from the palace gates.

Marie Antoinette's reticence with Léonard attested to her knowledge that he was not a man in whom interesting or important secrets might safely be entrusted. The hairdresser was a famous chatterbox and his role in a plan on which the fate of the French monarchy depended is one more of the imprudences one encounters everywhere in this story. Léonard had, in fact, already done enough damage to the Crown. For nearly fifteen years he and the famous *marchande des modes* Rose Bertin had reigned supreme over French fashion. It was Léonard who had invented the preposterous hairdos of the early reign of Louis XVI in which whole landscapes were depicted on cones of female hair that had been pulled up three and even four feet above the forehead. It was Léonard who later decreed that hair should come down. Like Rose Bertin he was haughty with women whom he felt "didn't belong," but who happened all too often to be wives of the Parlement nobility, of important men of state or, after 1790, of deputies to the National Assembly. The Queen, who extended him her protection, was blamed for these snubs.

Apart from being a gossip Léonard was a high-strung creature who was easily brought to the verge of hysterics. He wept under the stress of every passing emotion and in moments of crisis he would go to pieces. In short he was the last man who should have been chosen for any responsibility other than the dressing of women's hair. But that, in fact, seems to have been exactly Marie Antoinette's purpose in having him sent to Montmédy. Ostensibly he was to carry her jewels, which the duc de Choiseul would hand over to him at Pont-Sommevesle, but this commission could have been executed quite as competently by Choiseul as by Léonard. The truth seems to be that Marie Antoinette wanted her hair properly coiffed on that morning of glory at Montmédy when she appeared at the King's side and he awarded General de Bouillé the *bâton de maréchal*. Alas for the French monarchy, destiny had quite another role marked out for Monsieur Léonard. It was into the hands of this excitable flibbertigibbet that accident was to toss one of the most critical assignments in the whole enterprise.

At his house in the rue d'Artois the duc de Choiseul awaited the arrival of the hairdresser with impatience. It was nearly two o'clock in the afternoon and the schedule concerted with Fersen and Bouillé called for him to leave for Pont-Sommevesle some ten or twelve hours before the royal family made their exit from the Tuileries. As the last person to leave Paris before the King he was to ascertain that at the palace all was in readiness for the flight.

Choiseul was given responsibility for another important precaution. An outrider and saddle horse were to be stationed at the gates of the city. Should the King be stopped while leaving the Tuileries or the plan in some other way misfire, this messenger was to bring the news posthaste to the duc de Choiseul at Pont-Sommevesle who would then notify the other posts ahead of him of that fact. Those who were too deeply implicated in the affair to escape arrest, such as General de Bouillé or Choiseul himself, could then escape over the Luxembourg frontier. This was a time before the telegraph or even the semaphore had been invented. The frail line of communication that lay in Choiseul's hands was therefore of the utmost importance. Unfortunately it proved to be the very link in the chain that was to break.

The duc de Choiseul's deficiencies were less apparent than those of Léonard but he was not, in fact, a suitable man for the position of responsibility which he held. From the start Fersen had had misgivings about him. "If it is possible," he wrote Bouillé, "try not to send me the duc de Choiseul. No one could be more devoted, but he is a bungler and he's too young."

Choiseul was the nephew and heir of the famous minister who twenty years earlier had arranged the marriage of Louis and Marie Antoinette. He was very rich, very dashing, full of gallantry and dreams of glory. In short, he was a perfect specimen of his class and time. As an officer he was no more than an elegant dilettante and had had no experience with the rude actuality of armed combat. He was surprised and flattered by the importance of the role given him in the plan for the King's flight. When Léonard arrived at his house that afternoon of June 20 bearing the letter from Marie Antoinette, his head was full of exalted ideas. He could already picture himself at the head of his dragoons, prancing proudly behind the royal carriage, escorting the Capetian monarchy to fresh glories.

After reading the letter that Léonard gave him—it was Marie Antoinette's signal that at the palace all was ready for the evening's adventure and the order therefore for Choiseul to depart—Choiseul showed Léonard the last paragraph, which read, "I have ordered my hairdresser to obey you as he would obey myself and I repeat that order here." The duc then lit a candle and before Léonard's astonished eyes burned the letter. "And now," said Choiseul mysteriously, "follow me." A moment later the two men entered a light cabriolet and were on their way to the Porte St. Martin and the highroad to Metz. When he realized that he was being taken out of Paris, Léonard protested. "But I have an appointment with Madame de Laage this afternoon! What am I going to do? What's going to happen to Madame de Laage?"

When he saw that they had passed the posting stations at Claye and Meaux and were far out of Paris he had a *crise de nerfs* and began to weep. It was only many hours later, just before they arrived at Pont-Sommevesle, that Choiseul told him the truth. "Léonard," he announced, "the King, the Queen, their children, and Madame Élisabeth will be here this afternoon! They are going to Montmédy where they will be saved!"

"Oh, dear God, is it possible!" cried Léonard. And he burst into such floods of tears that Choiseul was hard put to calm him in time for their arrival at the posting inn at Pont-Sommevesle, where his distraught appearance might attract notice.

At about the time that Choiseul and Léonard passed the *relais de poste* at Claye, Fersen arrived at the Tuileries to make last-minute arrangements with the King and Queen. It was agreed between them that should something go wrong Fersen was to go to Brussels and act on their behalf with the European Powers. During this final interview Marie Antoinette's nerves gave way. "She wept a great deal," Fersen laconically wrote in his Journal. The King drew the Swede aside and said to him, "Monsieur de Fersen, whatever might happen I shall never forget all that you have done for me."

And it was no doubt at this moment that Louis handed Fersen a note that he was to present to Mercy in Brussels should their adventure end in failure. It was signed by both Louis and Marie Antoinette. In a moment of prevision they seem to have gazed beyond the possibility of arrest and seen the scaffold, for it was written in the tone of a bequest.

"We ask the comte de Mercy to remit all money of ours that he may have—approximately 1,500,000 livres—to the comte de Fersen. And we beg the comte de Fersen to accept it as the sweetest possible token of our gratitude and as an indemnity of all that he has lost."

Approximately half of this money was the King's, but the whole fortune of Madame de Korff and of Axel Fersen was tied up in the other half, which Mercy unfortunately handed over to the Habsburgs soon after the disaster at Varennes. It will be seen with what results Fersen finally solicited this legacy.

Axel left the palace soon after six o'clock and hurried to his house in the rue de Matignon. He had an active night ahead of him and from this moment he was busy everywhere behind the scenes. The *berline* in which the royal family was to travel to Montmédy was the first object of his attention. Far too imposing and cumbersome to be brought anywhere near the Tuileries, the coach was to be taken outside the gates of Paris and parked under the cloak of dark on the Metz road. Its passengers were to be taken from the palace to the *berline* in an ordinary hackney cab driven by Fersen disguised as a coachman. The logistics behind these movements, the conveying of the coach to the Metz road, the requisitioning of another carriage and the assembling of the necessary horses required the hands of more than one man. So, toward eight that evening, three other men were brought into the plot.

These three had been elected to play their various roles some weeks earlier, but it was decided that they should not be informed of that honor until the last moment. A few days before, they had been approached by a high officer of the King's Household and told that they might soon be going on a trip, that they should provide themselves with the livery and disguise of lackeys and that they should not whisper a word about these mysterious orders. But one of them did whisper about them to his mistress, who happened also to be the mistress of one of La Fayette's National Guard. This woman informed her republican lover, who in turn informed the police, who added the report to their files.

The three men were named Malden, Moustier, and Valory,

names that seem to evoke some story of historical adventure by Dumas. One's impression that this unlikely threesome might have stepped out of fiction is further enhanced by the description of them that emerges from the police investigation that followed Varennes. Moustier was so tall that people stopped to look at him in the streets. He had "squinty eyes, a pale complexion" and sported a ring of ill-kempt beard that fell below his collar. His eyesight was so bad he was barely able to see his hand in front of his face. Valory was so ignorant of local geography that he later admitted that he couldn't find his way from the Tuileries to the Palais Royal. All three had been members of the King's bodyguard that Louis had been persuaded to disband on the night of the storming of Versailles. They remained faithful royalists. Toward eight that evening, wearing a yellow livery they had bought in the secondhand market, they were introduced into the palace. When the King informed them of their assignment they were overcome by emotion. "Our fate is in your hands," Louis declared.

According to Moustier, when they heard these words the three men began to weep. "Our sobs were the pledge of the love and devotion that filled our hearts." Even the phlegmatic King must have been disconcerted by the spectacle of the sobbing officers to whom he had just committed his fate.

Ill-chosen though they may have been in their parts, these three had indispensable roles in Bouillé's plan. One of them—Valory—was to act as courier during the journey and, riding ahead of the coach, dash from one relay station to the next ordering fresh horses so that there would be no delay in harnessing. Another of them, installed on the box of the *berline,* was to act as coachman, while the third was to be an outrider who would keep an eye on the condition of things on the road both behind and ahead of the coach.

The King told Valory and Moustier that they were to join Fersen, who was waiting for them at that very moment on the quay close by the Pont Royal. Malden, however, was to remain in the King's apartment until the hour of flight, when he would be required to conduct Louis out of the palace to the place where Fersen's hackney cab would be waiting. The King gave these instructions hurriedly and told the two men that Fersen would explain their assignments to them in more detail. They left immediately afterward by the main staircase of the palace. Malden was then hidden in a closet, where he waited for the next four hours.

It was now nearly nine o'clock and time for the evening meal. Since the Revolution, Louis and Marie Antoinette had dispensed with the onerous ritual of dining in public and they usually took their meals together in Marie Antoinette's *salon*. It was a time of day when they could talk without undue fear of intrusion or of being overheard. Often on these occasions the comte and comtesse de Provence, who now lived at the Luxembourg Palace, would join them.

Although the comte d'Artois had left France upon the first blast of the storm, the comte de Provence, for a number of reasons, stayed on. His hands were in fact plunged deeply into the currents and crosscurrents of the Revolution, in which he glimpsed some hope of realizing his dream of succeeding his brother on the throne. In the opening days of the Revolution this intelligent prince had managed, at his elder brother's expense, to purchase himself quite a reputation as a "man of the people." But it did not take him long to sense certain changes in the political temperature that forecast stormier weather and he realized that in the *débâcle* about to overwhelm France he could play his game more advantageously in the safety of a self-imposed exile abroad. He and his wife—each in a separate carriage and each by a different route—were therefore planning to leave France on the same night as Louis and Marie Antoinette. Provence was well familiar with the details of his older brother's plans.

Although she had never much cared for Monsieur and characteristically had never troubled to hide her poor opinion of him, Marie Antoinette was choked with emotion as the moment of their separation approached. "Please don't say anything that might touch me," she whispered to him. "No one must see that I've been crying." The comte de Provence was more sanguine, and although he may have affected a tear or two he viewed the whole scene, as he viewed all scenes, with the dispassionate eye of self-interest. One may, in fact, wonder how deeply he may have been implicated in his brother's arrest at Varennes. Some of the rumors and reports that came to La Fayette's office a few days before the flight were inexplicably accurate. Still more inexplicable: La Fayette knew exactly in which direction to send his officers in pursuit of the royal family when the King's departure was discovered.

One can only observe that it was to the comte de Provence's advantage that Louis XVI and his family be arrested. The Assembly's pursuit of the King would distract everyone's attention from his own flight and then, once over the frontier, the effective power of the

French Crown would pass into his hands. He knew well that Louis XVI would cease to reign should he be arrested and returned to Paris. Perhaps Provence discerned some outline of the eventual end, the guillotine in the place de la Concorde and the young boy who stood between himself and the Crown (on whose legitimacy he had always cast doubt) dead or lost in the shadows of his prison. The comte de Provence too was one day to write an account of Varennes and it is in his own words that he tells us of his feelings when he learned of his brother's arrest: "After I dried my tears I reflected calmly on how I should begin the new career that opened before me."

Supper was finished early that night and they were sitting in the *salon* conversing in low voices when the clock struck ten. The Queen quickly rose, slipped through an adjoining room, and went upstairs to her daughter's bedroom. The stairway was at the end of a long, dark, and public corridor that was patrolled. It was a dangerous point in the evening's project and Marie Antoinette paused and looked carefully before she stepped out into the hall and furtively gained the stairs. She knocked softly on her daughter's door, but the princess' waiting woman, Madame Brunier, took alarm and didn't open until the Queen in an urgent whisper identified herself. Madame Brunier was told to dress her charge as quickly as possible and was then informed in a few words of the royal family's imminent evasion from the Tuileries. It was only then, to her astonishment, that Madame Brunier learned that she too was to be included in the journey. For incredible as it may seem, the King and Queen, with Fersen's approval, had decided that both Madame Brunier and Madame Neuville, the dauphin's waiting woman, should accompany them to Montmédy. The two women were to travel in a separate carriage, it is true, and to trot at a little distance ahead of the royal family's *berline,* but their presence in a hazardous escapade already encumbered by too many people almost passes belief. The domestic staff in attendance on the royal fugitives now included two maids, three equerries, a governess, and a hairdresser. With a second carriage added to it, the King's party took on the air of a small procession. The second carriage, if there was to be one at all, should have been occupied by two resourceful men of arms.

Leaving Madame Brunier to dress Marie Thérèse, Marie Antoinette went to her son's room. The dauphin had been asleep for more than an hour and his mother woke him gently. She whispered a few words into his ear and then as his eyes opened she told him he must get up, that "We are going on a trip, to a place where there will be lots of soldiers." The dauphin leaped from his bed and called for his sword. The Queen now informed Madame Neuville that she too would be going along on the trip. Their carriage was in fact already waiting for them by the river bank near the Pont Royal. They would be taken to Claye, the second *relais de poste* outside Paris, where they were to await the arrival of the rest of the party.

Both Mesdames Brunier and Neuville had husbands and families only a few yards away, but in the hurry of their departure they were unable to communicate with them. They seem to have accepted their assignments without complaint. Carrying with them only the necessaries for a night's trip, the two women made their way out of the palace to the quay where their carriage was waiting. A few moments later they were on their way to Claye.

Madame de Tourzel brought the children down to the Queen's *entresol*, where the dauphin was dressed in his disguise. He protested when he saw that he was to be dressed not as a soldier but as a little girl. His mother soothed him by telling him he was going to act in a play. His sister afterward recalled that he looked "charming" in his little frilled skirt.

It was quarter to eleven and *"le terrible quart d'heure,"* as Marie Antoinette called it, had now arrived. Their path of escape from the palace lay through an abandoned suite of rooms on the ground floor that opened onto the Cour des Princes, the courtyard of the Tuileries. This apartment had once been occupied by the First Gentleman of the Bedchamber, the duc de Villequier, who had emigrated. Locked, shuttered, and unfurnished, it had a door unguarded by La Fayette's sentinels that opened onto the courtyard. In the course of the winter Marie Antoinette had managed to secure a duplicate key to it. Access to this escapeway lay on the other side of the long public corridor that ran through the center of this wing of the palace. The corridor which was patrolled had to be crossed. It was one of the most hazardous points in the whole plan. Leading the way, Marie Antoinette paused for a long and cautious moment on the threshold of the hall and then, taking her daughter by the hand and followed by Madame de Tourzel, quickly crossed the corridor and entered the empty rooms of the duc de Villequier.

For reasons of ceremonial, to which the French are attached even in times of public disturbance or revolution, a portion of the central courtyard of the Tuileries Palace was reserved for the comings and goings of high-ranking government officials, officers attached to the King's Household, and others who were involved in the mechanics of palace ritual. This courtyard was known as the Cour des Princes and it was always filled with bustling functionaries, with carriages, cabs, and grooms. Although it might appear to be fraught with danger, the very bustle offered a kind of protection. Every evening toward eleven a long line of carriages would be drawn up close to the walls of the palace. They belonged to the officials who were involved in the ritual of the King's *coucher,* a ceremony that had not been interrupted by the Revolution. Fersen had noticed that anyone who wished to leave the palace unobserved might do so by walking in the shadows cast by these carriages against the palace wall.

It was quarter to eleven when Marie Antoinette and her little party reached the tall doors of glazed glass that opened from the duc de Villequier's apartments onto the Cour des Princes. The long summer's dusk had thickened into night, but the courtyard, lighted by torches and lanterns, was "as bright as day." Standing there in trepidation, the Queen suddenly saw a man's profile outlined against the other side of the glass. It was Fersen wearing the uniform of a coachman and a hat whose wide brim hid most of his face in shadow. Without a word he took the dauphin by the hand. Madame de Tourzel and Marie Thérèse followed them. And, most rashly, Marie Antoinette accompanied the group to the carriage. For the Queen this brief separation from her children was the most painful moment in the whole project and one that she had dreaded most. Against all the dictates of prudence she left the shelter of the building wearing neither a disguise nor a veil, and followed her children to their carriage, where there even seems to have been some hugs and kisses. Fersen, moving with dispatch, mounted the coachman's box, whipped up the horses, and turned out of the courtyard toward the river, where via a circuitous route he finally brought the vehicle to rest on the spot where the rue de Rivoli now crosses the rue de l'Échelle. In those days there was a small square known as the Place du Petit Carrousel at this corner. It was surrounded by a network of obscure streets and ill-lighted alleys that provided an ideal meeting place for the rest of the royal family who, in the next hour, would one by one leave the palace by foot and make their way there. Fersen parked the carriage and waited. The children went back to sleep.

Marie Antoinette retraced her steps to the *salon,* where she found the comte and comtesse de Provence in the midst of making their farewells. It was now nearly eleven and the hour had come for the King's *coucher*. Monsieur and his wife took their departure and the King immediately repaired to the state bedroom, where he went through the prescribed steps of the *coucher*. As usual La Fayette was present at this ceremony. He recalled afterward that although the King chatted away in his usual affable manner with the gentlemen of his household, he seemed strangely inattentive. His eye kept wandering to the windows and on several occasions La Fayette noticed him glancing up at the sky. Methodical in all things, Louis was one of those men who concern themselves about the daily weather and it is probable that when the General saw him looking out at the night he was trying to satisfy his mind about conditions that might be expected during his trip. They were propitious. The sky was overcast and the night was dark.

La Fayette lingered longer than usual that evening. He engaged the King in a discussion of the approaching Feast of Corpus Christi—the very day when Louis planned to celebrate his freedom by awarding General de Bouillé his *bâton*—and the King calmly gave him the orders he solicited. At last, after what seemed an interminable length of time, La Fayette came to the end of his conversation. The King then passed through the low wooden balustrade that symbolically separated the royal bed and its alcove from the rest of humanity. He fell to his knees, recited an orison, rose again and was divested of his outer clothing. He seated himself in an enormous *fauteuil* while two noblemen of the Household removed his shoes. The Usher-in-Attendance rapped the floor with his wand and cried out, "*Passez, Messieurs!*" All then bowed before the living symbol of France and filed from the room. The *coucher* was over.

The bed of state with its balustrade was for ceremonial use only. Louis' real bedroom was behind a little door that opened to one side of the bed of state. Here, assisted by his *valet de chambre,* the King hurriedly undressed and affected to retire for the night. The valet lowered the thick blue curtains around the bed and then left the room to prepare himself for bed. The valet slept on a cot that was set up every night in the King's bedroom. This was more a measure of surveillance than of any attention to Louis' needs, for the *valet de chambre* was also a guard. His few moments' absence gave Louis the opportunity he needed and no sooner was the man gone than the King slipped out of bed and left the room by a door that connected his bedroom with the dauphin's.

Madame Élisabeth had already left the palace. Time was running short and the King made haste. In the closet where he had been locked some four hours earlier the man Malden awaited his orders. Louis released him and with his help donned the disguise that Fersen had smuggled into the Tuileries. He was traveling as the Baroness de Korff's valet and wore an overcoat of bottle green, a brown waistcoat, and a brown wig on which was perched a hat. So confident was Louis in the efficacy of his disguise that, leaning on Malden's arm, he strolled out of the palace and across the courtyard without a qualm. At one point he even paused to adjust a shoe buckle that had become loose. He passed the gates of the Tuileries and walked by the sentinels stationed there without impediment. Five minutes later he was at the Place du Petit Carrousel, where, in the shadows, Fersen's hackney waited. The Swede was worried. It was now after midnight and the Queen, who should have been there before the King, had not yet appeared.

The possibility that Marie Antoinette might have been stopped filled the whole party with alarm. The King grew particularly agitated and as the minutes slipped by he suggested that someone go back and look for her. After more than half an hour of anguished waiting she finally loomed out of the dark and breathlessly described her misadventures. She had managed to leave her bedroom with the same ease as Louis and had clothed herself in a gray silk dress, a black shawl, and a large hat with a veil which she lowered over her face. But when she came to the long public corridor she found a sentinel standing almost directly in front of the door to the duc de Villequier's apartment. She drew back and had to wait nearly five minutes until he turned long enough for her to be able to dart across the hall. When she finally got out of the palace and crossed the Cour des Princes she had another fright. Just as she was going through the main gate La Fayette's carriage escorted by torchbearers passed her. Terrified, she had flattened herself against one of the gateposts. The General's carriage passed so close that she could touch its wheels. This experience so unnerved her that upon leaving the courtyard she took a wrong direction and instead of turning to the right as she should have done she went to the left and lost her way in the rabbit warren of unfamiliar streets that then covered this part of the city. It was more than half an hour before she finally found her way to the Place du Petit Carrousel and much precious time was lost. This was the first and perhaps most serious of the many small accidents that combined to cause the failure of the whole enterprise.

It was now quarter before one in the morning of the shortest night in the year and they were nearly an hour behind their schedule —a schedule, it will be remembered, that was firmly agreed upon with the duc de Choiseul. But Fersen, mounting the coachman's box, now did a foolish thing. Instead of going immediately to the Porte St. Martin, he made a long circuitous detour through the back streets of Paris to Crauford's house in the rue de Clichy in order to assure himself that the *berline* had left according to plan. Given the advantage of hindsight one can only shake one's head at this too meticulous thoroughness. More precious time was thus wasted and it was not until after one thirty that they finally passed the *barrière* at the Porte St. Martin and were at last beyond the city gates.

But here too they met with a mishap. Moustier, following orders, had concealed the *berline*. But he had hidden it so carefully that no one could now find it. The darkness of the night that should have been to their advantage acted against them and it was only after half an hour's search that Moustier and the coach were finally discovered far ahead on the Metz highroad drawn up to the edge of a culvert. Fersen quickly transferred the occupants of the hackney coach to the commodious *berline*. He then tipped the hackney into the culvert and, jumping onto the box of the *berline* beside Moustier, cried out, "Let's go and fast!" In less than an hour dawn would break and Paris begin to stir.

He forced the horses on at breakneck speed and they succeeded in reaching Bondy, the first relay post, in half an hour. At Bondy six fresh horses were waiting to be harnessed to the coach. Valory, who was in charge of arranging the relays, had also hired two fresh saddle horses at Bondy, one for himself and one for Malden, who henceforth would accompany the carriage as an outrider.

These *relais de poste*, or posting stations, were to be of considerable significance in the story of the royal family's flight from Paris and one must have some picture of them in order to understand the mechanics of that trip. Along so important an artery of traffic as the road from Paris to Metz they would be situated at intervals of ten or fifteen miles and here the traveler would pick up fresh horses to take him to the next relay station. The horses on hire would be accompanied by a postilion or two who would take charge of the animals belonging to his particular *relais*. When his horses had been fed and rested the postilion would escort them back, perhaps with another party of travelers, to their home posting station. It may be imagined that a certain amount of gossip was carried by these men from one

137

relais to the next. Life was dull in the little farm villages where the *relais de poste* were located and the smallest happening was an occasion for discussion. In the past year they had grown used to the sight of rich foreigners such as a Madame de Korff hurrying to the border. All the same, so important an equipage as the royal family's *berline* could not fail to attract notice. What made the King's party unusual was the number of horses that Valory had to hire at each relay—six for the coach, one each for himself and Malden, and then, after the posting station at Claye, three more for the carriage with the waiting women. The effect was similar to what might be expected today if a Rolls-Royce with chauffeur, footman, and uniformed maid were to stop for gasoline at some fueling station in the rural Middle West. Add to this an atmosphere of mystery imparted by drawn curtains concealing the passengers and one has an approximate idea of the sensation the King's carriage left in its wake.

At Bondy, Fersen left the party. It was a painful moment but there was no time to indulge in prolonged farewells. While the horses were being harnessed Axel approached the King and once again begged his permission to accompany him to Montmédy. The King, with words of gratitude, refused. It was the opinion of the marquis de Bouillé, expressed afterward in the exchange of recrimination that followed Varennes, that Fersen should have defied Louis' orders and gone along with the party. The Swede did indeed have misgivings when he saw the defenseless group setting out on their adventure: a King who was without decisive will, a Queen who had never before traveled on a public road in an ordinary conveyance, two children and three nursemaids. Should anything go wrong, should some unforeseen crisis arise, the fate of the whole party would be in the hands of Malden, Moustier, and Valory. Between Bondy and Pont-Sommevesle, a distance of 164 kilometers, there would be no one else. Fersen had his qualm but he quickly overcame it. It was a mistake that would haunt him all the rest of his days.

When the horses had been harnessed and the coach was ready to depart, he doffed his hat in the direction of the Queen and in a loud voice that could be heard by the postilions he said, "*Adieu,* Madame de Korff!" Marie Thérèse's recollection of his parting words differs significantly. "The Colonel," she wrote in her memoirs, "wished my father good night and then he flew away."

As the carriage rumbled off into the dawn Fersen mounted a fresh saddle horse and, taking a short cut, gained the northern road to Belgium. The night was, in fact, full of interesting parties hurrying toward the frontier. Traveling in a little two-horse gig, the comte de Provence, accompanied by his beloved comte d'Avaray, was on his way to safety. Traveling in another carriage, the comtesse de Provence, accompanied by her beloved Madame de Gourbillon, sped in another direction. Madame Sullivan and Crauford, too, fled to the Netherlands that night.

Nearly two hours behind schedule, the royal family lumbered off toward Claye. The iron wheels of the *berline* made such a clatter on the paving of the road that Louis stuck his head out of the window and asked Moustier to drive along the side of the road with two wheels off the paving. By the time they reached Claye, where Mesdames Brunier and Neuville had been waiting for nearly three hours, dawn had broken. Freshened by the night's dew, the countryside was lovely, but it was not until after Meaux that they were able to enjoy it. It was then they entered the valley of the Marne and knew they were safely away from Paris. The atmosphere in the coach suddenly became relaxed. It was time for breakfast and Fersen's provision was examined with interest and devoured with relish. "They ate," Moustier recalled, "without plates or forks, off pieces of bread the way hunters do."

Louis brought forth a copy of the letter to the Assembly that he had left behind him to be delivered to the President that morning. It was his justification for removing himself and his family from Paris. He enumerated the many concessions that had been extorted from him by violence or by the threat of it. And what, he then asked, had these sacrifices brought the nation? "All authority defied," he declared, "private property destroyed, the lives of private individuals everywhere endangered, and anarchy abroad in the kingdom." He pointed out to the Assembly that the person of the King was not free. He reminded them of what had happened at Easter when he had tried to go to St. Cloud. In summation he declared that the only hope for the nation lay in his removing himself to a part of the kingdom that was away from the political disputes of Paris.

Louis finished reading his letter in an expansive frame of mind. Their successful evasion from the Tuileries and the sense of freedom imparted by the countryside induced in him a new self-confidence. "Believe you me," he said to Marie Antoinette, "once my butt is back in the saddle I'm going to be a far different person than what you've seen before!"

Toward eight when they had passed the little farming hamlet of La Ferté-sous-Jouarre he took out his watch and chuckled, "I fancy that M. de La Fayette is rather embarrassed about now," he observed.

Strange as it may seem, neither he nor Marie Antoinette had ever seen anything of their realm beyond the enclave of Versailles, Marly, Fontainebleau, and Compiègne. They had been just as imprisoned by the dictates of etiquette and tradition as they had been by the armed guard of the Assembly. They had gone once to Rheims for Louis' coronation in 1774, and once, shortly before the Revolution, Louis had insisted, despite his ministers' opposition, on doing a tour of naval inspection in Normandy. That little trip had been one of the happiest passages in the unhappy monarch's life, for he had been acclaimed everywhere with a spontaneity of affection that informed him of the regard of his humbler subjects and touched him deeply. Away from the constraints of his court this awkward man of simple tastes became a different personality.

Now, wearing the disguise of a *valet de chambre*, the descendant of Saint Louis was able to view a corner of the realm he was about to lose with the eyes of an ordinary citizen. He had always been interested in geography and he had brought with him a map and a copy of the *Itinéraire complet du royaume de France*. With this material in hand he examined the countryside with interest and ticked off the name of each relay station as it was passed. After Meaux the road descended into the long, flat countryside of Champagne, whose monotony was broken by the chalky slopes on which the famous grapes of the province were cultivated. The road grew white and dusty. Bordered on either side by four parallel lines of trees, it seemed to stretch interminably and without a curve across the valley of the Marne, across Champagne, toward the east and the Argonne. Apart from an occasional farm wagon, it seemed deserted. The women lifted their veils, for there seemed to be no further need to hide their faces.

Somewhere along the road between La Ferté-sous-Jouarre and the *relais de poste* at Fromentières, the King caused the carriage to be stopped and, according to Moustier, "he got out and emptied his bladder and gave his family a chance to relieve themselves too." At Fromentières, which they reached somewhere toward noon, Louis behaved more rashly. He left the carriage and fell into conversation with some farmfolk who were gathered at the relay. In his loquacious and affable manner he had a talk with them about the harvest and chatted away with everyone at great length while fresh horses were being harnessed to the *berline*. Marie Antoinette was much upset by the imprudence while Moustier, standing in front of him in an attempt to conceal his face, had the greatest difficulty in persuading him to return to the shelter of the carriage.

"Oh, I wouldn't worry about it," Louis said blithefully. "I don't think any of these precautions are necessary any more. After all, we're out of danger now."

And indeed, although one knows how the journey was to end, it is difficult at this moment not to partake of the King's optimism. The most perilous part of the adventure, the escape from the Tuileries, had been successfully negotiated. They were now a good eight or nine hours from the capital. The possibility of pursuit, therefore, could cast only a faint shadow over Louis' sanguine temper. He knew his subjects well and he knew that there would be hours of excited discussion before anyone would set out after him. Toward eight his *valet de chambre* would discover the empty bed, the guards would be called, La Fayette would be sent for, there would be commotion and confusion. La Fayette would notify the Assembly and there would then be more confusion while the representatives debated what to do. And when at last horsemen were finally dispatched to overtake them, how would they know where to go? The road to Metz was but one of several possibilities. By the time they found the right trail, Louis and his party would be at Pont-Sommevesle within the jurisdiction of Bouillé's command and well behind the protective barrier of Choiseul's hussars.

Each time one reads an account of the Flight to Varennes one finds oneself hoping that this time they might somehow make it to safety. At Fromentières, some five hours away from Pont-Sommevesle, they were so close to success that it seems almost impossible that something could go wrong and that they should not reach their destination. One entertains this hope because in that carriage one suddenly sees them not as the French royal family but as unhappy, vulnerable, and familiar human beings.

Unfortunately they were not ordinary or familiar human beings. As the flesh-and-blood symbols of France they were both pawns and players in an epic struggle for power. One must pause at this moment and ask oneself what would have happened to France if they had succeeded in reaching the fortress at Montmédy? What course would the Revolution then have taken? Would France have been spared the Reign of Terror or the twenty years of war waged by Louis' successor,

Napoleon? It is impossible of course to answer such questions, but one can discern at least the outline of what might have happened had Louis XVI reached his goal.

Undoubtedly, just as Mirabeau had predicted and had desired, there would have been civil war. Marie Antoinette and Louis XVI might have called the struggle by some other name, but civil war, all the same, it would have been. And it was a civil war they would very probably have lost. For, as usual, they had acted too late. Mirabeau's project had been based upon his certainty of the army's obedience and his conviction that the provinces were both loyal to the Crown and resentful of Paris ascendancy over France. Mirabeau's estimate was undoubtedly accurate. Later events such as the uprisings in the Vendée and Normandy, the revolt of Lyon and the cities of the Midi, verify the justness of his appraisal. But six months had passed, Mirabeau was dead, and the situation everywhere had changed. A strong king, waving the banner of his cause with vigor, might still have rallied an enthusiastic and numerous army to his side but that king was not Louis XVI. He would have lost the battle, probably as much through the ineptness of his followers as through his own insufficient vitality. He and his family would then have escaped over the Austrian frontier, where they would have lived out their days on the niggardly dole of Marie Antoinette's relatives. In time, after Napoleon's downfall, the young dauphin might well have come to the throne as Louis XVII. The Revolution would probably have followed its predestined course with little change in its general chronology.

But what—and however "academic" the question, it should be considered—what would have happened had Louis XVI overcome his distaste for gunfire and succeeded, in his phrase, in "getting his butt back into the saddle"? Suppose he had returned to Paris at the head of his troops, and been restored to his sovereignty? What then would have been the course of the Revolution?

It must be remembered that while the French Revolution swept away the ramshackle structure of the *ancien régime* it also opened the path to power to Napoleon. The throne of the Emperor rose upon the ruins of that of Louis XVI. The palace of the Tuileries from which Louis XVI and his family fled in 1791 was in less than twelve years' time to become witness to the splendors of the Consulate. Those halls that in 1792 had been filled with recriminations against the King were in not too many years' time to resound with the hosannas of those come to pay homage to the Emperor. Unlike Louis XVI, Napoleon had few qualms about bloodshed. The army in the end is the base on which political power must be built and Bonaparte knew how to use and reward his army. The ducs, peers, and princes of his court were his officers, most of whom had risen from the ranks of the Republican army that had been the instrument of the overthrow of the *ancien régime*. The *gloire* of Imperial France was achieved by military conquest. It was booty that replenished the empty treasury that had been the ruin of Louis XVI. War was therefore the corner-stone on which the Empire was constructed.

When one considers the twenty years of carnage that lay ahead, when, through a haze of gunsmoke and fire one glimpses the battle-fields of Poland and Russia strewn with the countless dead, it is diffi-cult not to entertain some hope that Louis XVI might perhaps have succeeded with his plans and returned to his capital as the head of a Constitutional Monarchy. The abuses of the Old Order had been largely eliminated by 1791 and Louis XVI had no intention of restor-ing them. In breaking the hold upon the Crown of a parasitical and troublesome nobility the Assembly had achieved a goal that would greatly have appealed to Richelieu and indeed to Louis XIV for it was an old dream of the French kings to rid themselves of the *noblesse*. In his rose-tinted dreams, Louis XVI hoped to return to his capital as the crowned head of a monarchy tailored in the nineteenth-century *bourgeois* pattern. The Civil Constitution of the Clergy that was so odious to him would of course be revoked, but in the atmosphere of tranquillity that would be the gift of a moderate and benevolent representative body the French people would at last enjoy the fruits of freedom. According to Madame de Tourzel, as he described this dream to his fellow passengers "he enjoyed in advance the happiness that he hoped to bring France."

Unfortunate man! He could not see, as many still cannot see, that the French Revolution was something more than the outcome of a people's claim for liberty, prosperity, or even indeed happiness. The *ancien régime* was doomed because it had reached its term and no amount of reform could have saved it. It was as though some medieval town of rickety buildings and crooked narrow streets were brought face to face with the requirements of men driving automobiles. To make way for parking lots, for two-lane throughways and all the other necessities of modern living, demolition would not only be inevitable, it would be necessary. The *ancien régime* in France was comparable to such a medieval town. It could no longer accommodate the needs of men. The whole tottering structure was founded on the outmoded laws, traditions, and economy of feudalism.

Louis XVI's Constitutional Monarchy would have been provisional at best, for it could only have "modernized" the exterior appearance of things. But it was the substructure that was rotten and sooner or later, for one reason or another, the edifice would have fallen. It took Napoleon to hammer together an efficient military despotism built along up-to-date twentieth-century lines.

Leaving these imponderables, one returns to that coach lumbering across the dusty *champenois* plain with the conviction that the doom awaiting it at Varennes was interbound with those larger forces, far beyond the control of any individual, that condemned the whole *ancien régime*. Its passengers, who were not given to metaphysical speculation, saw none of this.

On the mundane level of more practical considerations, they should have had a few qualms about their schedule as they rolled into the posting station at Chaintrix. It was after two thirty and this was exactly the hour when they were expected at Pont-Sommevesle some thirty-five kilometers up the road on the other side of Châlons. They were well over two hours late. Instead of regaining the time that had been lost, they had lost more time. At no point do Valory, Moustier, and Malden appear to have spurred on the horses or forced the phlegmatic passengers to make haste. They seem to have been as insouciant about the matter as the King and Queen. Louis was cosseted in his undauntable optimism while Marie Antoinette seems to have been one of those people who are always late for appointments. At Chaintrix someone should have observed that at this very hour the duc de Choiseul was awaiting their arrival at Pont-Sommevesle, almost another three hours away. When one realizes that it was only by a matter of five or ten minutes that the royal family was arrested at Varennes, one begins to grow impatient with these easygoing travelers and their lackadaisical attendants.

And at Chaintrix the King was recognized. The son-in-law of the posting master had been to Paris the year before and had seen Louis at the *Fête de la Fédération*. When he informed his father-in-law of his suspicion, the *maître de poste*, a man named Lagny, graciously invited the passengers to do his house the honor of taking some refreshment. The afternoon was hot, the children were tired, and the manner of the man so respectful and cordial .that the princesses were unable to resist his proposal. Everyone got out of the carriage and a good half hour was spent enjoying the hospitality of the Lagny family. The women of that household were awestruck but amid a shower of reverential curtsies they accorded every attention to their august guests. The King and Queen were deeply touched by their welcome, which served to confirm Louis' opinion that outside Paris his subjects were all loyal and good. When it came time to leave, Marie Antoinette took two silver porringers from her traveling case and gave them to the *maître de poste* as a token of the royal family's gratitude. They are still owned today by his descendants.

Lagny would not permit such guests to be conducted to the next *relais* by any ordinary postilions. He insisted that his son-in-law mount the box and himself drive the horses from Chaintrix to Châlons. Someone at this point appears to have become aware of the now serious loss of time and the young man was told not to spare the horses. But he set off at so furious a speed that barely out of sight of the *relais* a wheel of the carriage flew off the road, the horses fell, and the harness broke. Another half hour's time was lost repairing the damage. Thus they did not arrive at Châlons until after 4:30.

Châlons was the last *relais* before they reached their *rendez-vous* with the duc de Choiseul's hussars at Pont-Sommevesle. It was the largest community along their route and was a thriving little city with all the municipal organization of Paris. There was a sizable post of National Guard and there was a local Jacobin Club. Among the populace there were the usual conflicting opinions about politics. It was the one stop about which everyone—Fersen, Bouillé, and the King himself—had expressed misgivings. For this reason, although Châlons was within the jurisdiction of Bouillé's command, it had been decided that Choiseul and his troops should be stationed at the next *relais* beyond it, at Pont-Sommevesle.

Despite a clear awareness of the hazards of Châlons, the King put his head out of the window at the bustling *relais de poste* and was immediately recognized by someone in the crowd, and probably by several people. "At Châlons," Marie Thérèse stated in her memoirs, "we were openly recognized. Many people praised heaven and wished their King godspeed." The postmaster at Châlons was informed of the identity of the party by the young man who had escorted the *berline* from Chaintrix. It is probable that his father-in-law told him to do so. The *maître de poste* at Chaintrix was a friend of the *maître de poste* at Châlons and the former knew that the latter could be trusted with so momentous a secret. In any case, the *maître de poste* at Châlons personally superintended the harnessing of the horses and tried to send the coach on its way as speedily as possible.

As he went about his work a man emerged from the crowd gathered in the yard of the *relais* and told him that the King and the royal family were in the carriage and that it was his patriotic duty to inform the municipality of the fact. The postmaster feigned disbelief and then declared that it was not for him to take responsibility in such a business.

But the mysterious individual, identified only as a "well-dressed *bourgeois*," was determined to secure the arrest of the King. He hurried to the office of the mayor, one Monsieur Charez, and told him that Louis XVI was at that very moment passing through Châlons on his way to the frontier. He urged the mayor to call out the militia and stop them, but the mayor did no such thing. Undoubtedly shaken by the news, he decided to temporize. Like the *maître de poste*, he took refuge in doubt. At last, when his visitor grew insistent, he turned his back on the matter with the words, "If you are sure of this then you should go out and announce the fact. But remember that if you do so you will be responsible for the consequences."

At this point the actors in the drama seem to take on the symbolic wraps of some morality play or fable. One has the nameless "well-dressed *bourgeois*," the anonymous bearer of a moral dilemma. One has Monsieur Charez, whose words are the age-old words of the safely uncommitted: the words of moral cowardice, in the ears of a religious or political bigot; the words of Mr. Prudent Everyman, in the ears of more tolerant observers of the human comedy. Throughout the Revolution, France was full of men of this stripe. It was on them Mirabeau had counted when he first outlined his proposal for flight. They will not support lost causes when to do so might endanger their lives or their property, but when the wind blows favorably they will gladly unfurl their sails and join the regatta. It is probable indeed that Louis had been recognized more times than anyone realized. At Viels-Maisons, a posting station before Chaintrix, the *maître de poste* definitely identified him but, being tight-lipped after the manner of his kind, he said nothing until it was safe to do so. Had Louis' project met with success, his return to Paris would have been followed by acclamation and his route strewn with flowers. Failure could only bring the reverse response.

Within the cocoon of their carriage Louis and Marie Antoinette were unaware of the turbulence they had left behind them at Châlons. The town was soon seething. Groups of voluble men gathered in the market place to discuss the event. Views were exchanged, hands flew and voices rose as opinions were volunteered and disputed. But it was not until eight that evening that the officials of the town finally gathered in an emergency session to consider measures.

Far from feeling any anxiety the King and Queen appear to have left the town reassured. The cordial welcome of Lagny at Chaintrix had been followed by further expressions of good will at Châlons. Louis' conviction that his people were loyal to him was bolstered by the furtive communications of regard that he received there. When the town gates were behind them and they were again on the open road Marie Antoinette could contain her joy no longer. "We are saved!" she cried.

And indeed, what danger could there possibly be now? Even had Châlons proved hostile, they were safely beyond it. And ahead, only an hour and a half away, lay Pont-Sommevesle where the duc de Choiseul and his troops were awaiting their arrival.

The road stretched ahead, silent and strangely empty, leading into the forest of the Argonne. They had traveled perhaps an hour, perhaps less, when a solitary horseman suddenly appeared behind them. The identity of this mysterious rider has never been established. Perhaps he was an emissary of the mayor of Châlons sent ahead to warn them. Perhaps he was the anonymous *"bourgeois"* of Châlons who, set upon their destruction, was hurrying ahead to alert the citizens of the Argonne. Whoever he may have been one has again the sense of witnessing a drama whose characters have a symbolic purpose. For like some personification of Fate the stranger drew close to the window of the coach and uttered the words, "Your plans have gone awry. You will be stopped!" And then he was gone, vanishing like a ghost into the air from which he appeared.

Whatever consternation this sinister harbinger may have aroused was soon quieted by the thought of the forty hussars awaiting them at Pont-Sommevesle. It occurred to no one that Choiseul and his troops might not, in fact, be there.

147

The duc de Choiseul had arrived at Pont-Sommevesle shortly before eleven that morning after an all night trip along the same road that Louis and his party were now traveling. He immediately retired to a room of the *relais* to refresh himself and don the uniform he planned to wear for the afternoon's event. The hussars had not yet arrived but his sergeant, a man named Aubriot, was there with the two fresh saddle horses that Choiseul had ordered a few days earlier. Aubriot had been given no hint of the reason behind this commission. When Choiseul emerged booted and spurred he drew the sergeant to a corner of the stables and in a low voice ("*M. de duc était aussi agité que moi,*" Aubriot recalled) told him the secret.

Aubriot, like everyone else in the story, was to write his memoirs and from this book as well as from Choiseul's we are able to catch a glimpse of the scene that morning at the *relais de poste* in the hamlet of Pont-Sommevesle. Aubriot's response to Choiseul's news imparts some sense of the almost mystical awe in which the French monarchy was still held. It is difficult for people today to comprehend this, but one encounters it everywhere along the forgotten passages of the past, in memoirs of such men as Sergeant Aubriot. Although we have seen the King and Queen of France as all too fallible human beings as they roll along the road toward Pont-Sommevesle, they were in fact invested with even more symbolic significance than Mr. Everyman of Châlons or the solitary rider.

"My whole body began to tremble," Aubriot recalled. "My legs gave way under the weight of my body. Sparks of fire began to flash through my veins. In short, the secret threw me into such a state of disorder that I was momentarily unable to answer M. le duc . . . When my senses were at last calm I swore with all my heart that I would defend my King and his august family and that I was ready to sacrifice myself for their sacred persons. Then M. le duc ordered me to have our horses ready for one thirty in the afternoon. That was the hour when the King's carriage was scheduled to arrive."

One thirty in the afternoon! The King at that moment was still many miles away, far on the other side of Chaintrix. But like children who can barely contain themselves in the expectation of some promised event, Choiseul and Aubriot put themselves in readiness well before a calm appraisal of the situation should have permitted. "We started to count the minutes," relates Aubriot, "and the nearer the hour approached when France was to be saved, the more our ardor grew impatient." How, on the highways of eighteenth-century France in a cumbersome coach drawn across a distance of more than 175 kilometers, could anyone possibly estimate a scheduled arrival within minutes? And in any case it was not at one thirty when the King was expected. It was at two thirty.

The hussars, led by a man named Goguelat who was in on the secret, arrived at noon and Aubriot arranged for them to be fed. He ordered an early lunch for himself, Choiseul, and Goguelat but the three men were in such a hurry to meet the King that they barely ate. By one thirty they were out on the road impatiently scanning the horizon for the distant cloud of dust that would inform them of the approach of the King's carriage. Their troops were ordered to saddle their horses and stand by in readiness to escort the "treasure" that was about to arrive. There was a great rattling of sabers and much flurry and flash as the hussars assembled in front of the *relais de poste*. And their presence was soon remarked by the local farmers who happened that day to be in the vicinity of the posting station. The news was quickly communicated to their neighbors and from field to field, from farmyard to farmyard, it was carried with the speed of wind.

The militia had never been popular in such rural communities as Pont-Sommevesle. They generally passed through on some punitive mission, requisitioning the produce of the peasants' land as they passed. Chickens would be eaten, eggs taken, and forage seized. To add to this injury, the troops were often foreign and attached in one way or another to the King's proprietary regiments. But in the eyes of the peasants of such places as Pont-Sommevesle anyone not of their own little community was considered a foreigner. Despite the newfangled administrative division of the country into *départements,* rural France continued to slumber in its old-world dream.

The new National Guard was one of the introductions of the Assembly that had met with the approval of these extremely conservative pockets of feudalism. Stationed in such communities as Châlons, the new guard was generally recruited from the peasants' own neighborhood and was "one of theirs." In any collision between the mounted militia attached to a command such as Bouillé's and the National Guard the peasantry everywhere could be counted on to support the National Guard. This was a pivotal consideration at this particular moment in the French Revolution. A few months earlier—at the time when Mirabeau had suggested flight—it would not have been so. A year or so later, when the dictatorial authority of Paris had made itself odious to much of the French countryside, it would not have been so. But at precisely this moment it was an invisible factor of considerable importance.

In ordinary circumstances the farmers of Pont-Sommevesle would probably have contented themselves with sullen stares and angry mutterings when they saw themselves suddenly and mysteriously invaded by a troop of hussars. But it so happened through another of those curious "accidents" that characterize the Flight to Varennes that for the peasantry of Pont-Sommevesle these were not ordinary circumstances. An absentee landowner, the duchesse d'Elboeuf, had been trying for months to collect her tithes from certain delinquent tenants in the neighborhood. There had been threats of force from her man of affairs and the whole community was in a rage about the business, determined to resist any armed extortion of money or produce. So when forty armed hussars appeared that morning in front of the *relais de poste* the farmers supposed that they had come to collect the duchesse d'Elboeuf's rents.

Choiseul was at first astonished and then alarmed as groups of angry farmers began to gather on the road. Brandishing muskets and pitchforks, they became increasingly menacing. An hour passed and then two, but the King's carriage did not appear. By three thirty or four o'clock in the afternoon hundreds of peasants had collected around the hussars and more kept flocking. In vain Choiseul explained that he was there with his troops to escort a treasure that was scheduled to pass through. "Your hussars may be shrewd," one of them replied, "but we're a lot shrewder."

The explanation about the treasure was, in fact, ill-chosen. One of the most persistent rumors about Marie Antoinette was that she would often ship French gold to her brother in Austria. This then, thought the peasants, was the reason for the hussars in Pont-Sommevesle! And next another rumor, a natural development of the first, went through the crowd. It was reported that the Queen herself was about to pass through on her way to Austria.

All the while Choiseul kept consulting his watch and nervously scanning the horizon. He was in a quandary. The King—if he was coming at all—was now nearly three hours late. Suppose he were to arrive in the midst of this tumult? His party was not armed. Would Choiseul's guard be able to protect them? What if the angry mob, which far outnumbered the hussars and which furthermore was armed, should suddenly rush in and attack his troops? The longer he waited for the King's carriage the greater the danger seemed to grow. By four thirty Choiseul was frantic. No such contingency had been foreseen when he, Fersen, and Bouillé had made their plans on paper.

In this young nobleman, born and bred to wear a sword, one again glimpses the weakened underpinnings of the old order. The sword was purely ornamental. He was not qualified either by temperament or training to be a soldier. The rude generals and marshals of the Empire, some of whom were then serving in Bouillé's ranks, would have handled the gathering of peasants with dispatch. Choiseul was unable to do so. And now he took fright. For only blinding fright can explain what he did. Summoning Léonard—whose nerves had long since broken down—he handed him a hurriedly scribbled note which he told the hairdresser to show to the leaders of the other detachments that were stationed up the road between Pont-Sommevesle and Varennes. The first of these was at Ste. Menehould—33 dragoons —and the next at Clermont—145 dragoons. Like Choiseul's detachment they were supposed to fall in behind the King's carriage when it passed and escort it to Montmédy. The execution of the whole plan depended on these movements. The note that Choiseul gave Léonard read: "There is no sign that the treasure will pass today. I am leaving to join M. de Bouillé. You will receive new orders tomorrow."

Bearing this message of devastating consequence, Léonard hopped into Choiseul's cabriolet and trotted off toward Ste. Menehould and Clermont to sow consternation and the seeds of disaster in his path.

Choiseul's act has been the subject of never-ending dispute between those who interest themselves in the minutiae of the Flight to Varennes. Some have seen dark and even sinister implications behind it and point it out as one more enigma among so many. Unreasoning fright seems to be the best explanation. And probably not so unreasoning. By communicating his own uncertainty, not to say panic, to his colleagues up the line, Choiseul may have hoped to apportion among them some of the responsibility for his defection. In any case, by four thirty in the afternoon, at about the time that the *berline* was leaving Châlons and Marie Antoinette had elatedly declared, "We are saved!" he decided to abandon his post.

Prompted by some lingering hope, he remained for an hour or so after Léonard's departure, but toward five thirty, after a last glimpse at the horizon, he took his men and departed. As though this were not enough, he departed by a road he thought was a short cut to Varennes and he headed into the trackless swamps of the Argonne forest. By nightfall he and his men were hopelessly lost. They did not emerge from the woods at Varennes until after the King's arrest.

As soon as Choiseul left, the angry farmfolk dispersed. Thus there was not a soul in sight when only half an hour later a cloud of dust far down the Châlons road announced the approach of Valory coming to arrange the relay.

Louis XVI was not in the habit of using exaggerated phrases. Therefore when he later recalled that "I felt as though the whole earth had fallen from under me" one may be sure that such indeed were his sentiments when he arrived at Pont-Sommevesle and discovered that there were no troops there to meet him. At the very place where he had thought to find safety he found a yawning abyss. Neither he nor Marie Antoinette could imagine what had happened to the duc de Choiseul, with whom they had been in touch only the day before. For reasons of prudence, neither Valory nor the King dared ask the postmaster if there had been any gathering of troops there during the afternoon. And Choiseul, who should have thought to station someone in the vicinity of the *relais* for the purpose of telling the King what had happened, had overlooked even this elementary measure.

It was with sinking hearts and oppressed by their first intimations of doom that the fugitives left Pont-Sommevesle and headed toward Ste. Menehould, the next town where troops were supposed to be stationed. This community was some thirty-five kilometers from Pont-Sommevesle, a trip of about two hours in that heavy coach. Valory hurried on the relay and this lap of the trip was addressed with more speed than the others. It is probable that the King and Queen hoped that they would encounter Choiseul and his troops somewhere along the way.

Louis XVI was a man of sanguine and optimistic temperament. His inability to apprehend disaster was at bottom parent to the cumulative disasters of his reign. As his coach lumbered along the road the shock he had received at Pont-Sommevesle diminished and he began to muster his spirits. The road, after all, was quiet. There was no evidence of pursuit. There was nothing to indicate the slightest danger or give reason for alarm. And ahead, only two hours away, was Ste. Menehould with Captain d'Andoins and his troop of thirty dragoons. Shaken though they had been by Choiseul's inexplicable defection, Louis and Marie Antoinette were certain that things would be in order at the next line of defense. On the box of the *berline*, Moustier exhorted the postilions to make speed.

In their preoccupation with the troops they hoped to find at Ste. Menehould, and the sanctuary they were certain awaited them there, they gave no heed to a fresh danger that in the past few hours should have presented itself. They looked ahead of them up the road toward Ste. Menehould. They did not look behind them in the direction of Paris. For it was nearly twelve hours since their disappearance had been reported to the Assembly and by now the hounds were in full pursuit of their quarry. Their coach at that moment has been compared to a vessel traveling in the illusory calm that is to be found in the eye of a hurricane. Both behind them and ahead wild storms were blowing to which they were oblivious.

Since nine that morning the tumult in Paris had been almost indescribable. The news of the King's disappearance reached the streets before it reached La Fayette. The General arrived at the Tuileries to find it surrounded by a tossing sea of angry humanity. They hissed him when he entered the palace.

The Assembly gathered in agitated session at nine. A formal announcement of the King's flight was made by Beauharnais, husband of the future Empress of the French, and further tumult was unleased. An order for the arrest of the King and his family was finally drafted. The exact wording of this instrument was a matter for extended debate. Louis' departure brought the Assembly to face with certain questions of constitutional law that it would have preferred not to answer. No one in the Assembly really wanted a Republic. A weak King who embodied the State was necessary to them because each party within the Assembly hoped to use him for its own particular purpose. A convenient fiction was therefore concocted. It was announced that the King had been "carried off by the enemies of the Revolution." The words "carried off" could be interpreted to mean that he had been swept away by bad advice.

But who was to sign this order preventing Louis XVI from continuing his route? (The word "arrest," too, had given place to a circumlocution.) For according to the provisional Constitution the King had to sign the Assembly's order. La Fayette finally solved the dilemma by signing the paper himself. This, as certain writers have justly observed, constituted a *coup d'état,* but at that moment even his enemies approved the General's audacity. The order was reproduced in six or seven copies and given to the fastest horsemen of La Fayette's guard. Each of these men now set forth on the various roads that the King might have taken. But it was discovered almost immediately by a man named Bayon that the trail led from the Porte St. Martin to the Metz highroad.

Bayon left the gates of Paris at noon, riding from the very start at almost incredible speed. And at every *relais de poste* where he stopped to pick up a fresh mount he was told of the great *berline* with its outriders and its carriage bearing two women that had passed some hours earlier. He knew with certainty that the passengers in that *berline* were the King and his family. Bent almost double in the saddle, he spurred his horse to ever wilder speeds. By six thirty that afternoon he was at Chaintrix where four hours earlier the King had paused for refreshment with the Lagny family. He had covered the distance in less than one half the time it had taken the King. At Chaintrix he collapsed. But before lying down or taking refreshment he handed the posting master a hastily scribbled note in which he announced the flight of the King. That note was to be taken as an order from the Assembly for anyone to stop the carriage and detain it until further orders arrived. Bayon told Lagny to deliver this message to the posting master at Châlons, who in his turn was to deliver it to the authorities at Ste. Menehould and beyond. One receives the impression that Bayon did not trust the Lagny family. They admitted to having received the passengers of the *berline* in their house earlier in the day but denied having recognized the royal family. They must have been thrown into a very agitated state of mind when Bayon, bearing his credentials from the National Assembly, staggered across their threshold that afternoon.

As he pursued the King, Bayon did not realize that he too was being pursued. For nearly five hours a man named Romeuf had been hot on his trail, riding at a speed as frantic as his own. Romeuf was a trusted officer of La Fayette, a man whose first loyalty should have been to the Assembly. But in the course of his tour of duty at the Tuileries he had come into close contact with the Queen and like many another person in those troubled times and in the still stormier times to come he was surprised to find a pleasing and amiable woman instead of the arrogant harpy that rumor reported her to be. He made a point of always addressing her with respect and this attention did not go unappreciated by Marie Antoinette. One of those strong understandings that are formed more on mutual silent regard than on any exchange of words gradually grew between them. Marie Antoinette trusted him and liked him. Romeuf knew this. So when he learned that Bayon, bearing La Fayette's order, was in pursuit of the King on the Metz road he himself leaped into the saddle and set forth in pursuit of Bayon. Ostensibly, like Bayon, he was an emissary of the National Assembly. In reality, he was determined to intercept Bayon and somehow delay him from delivering the fatal order that would secure the King's arrest. He rode an hour or so behind Bayon, but the latter's pause at the *relais de poste* at Chaintrix gave him a good advantage.

Ignorant of these storms that were now breaking on all sides of them, the royal family pressed onward toward Ste. Menehould. It was nearly eight when at last across the plain they glimpsed the church steeple of that town. The sun had set but the long midsummer's dusk had not yet fallen. They were thus able to see that the town appeared to be in a fever of excitement. At the posting station their carriage was quickly surrounded by a crowd whose temper seemed hostile. The King opened the window and looked about for the troops who were supposed to be there. He saw instead armed men wearing the uniform of the National Guard moving about the milling crowd.

Once again the fugitives asked themselves the terrible question: where were the troops?

Ste. Menehould like Châlons was a sizable community. Its beautiful *hôtel de ville* of eighteenth-century architecture and its posting station still stand and evoke today the generous proportions of the town as it was on that summer's evening of 1791 when Marie Antoinette and

Louis XVI passed through. Like all French towns of its kind it harbored an alert, nervous, and observant population. The smallest event did not go unnoticed by them. Any unusual movement of troops in their midst would have been certain to arouse their curiosity. One now begins to appreciate the sagacity of Fersen's advice to Bouillé: "If you are not sure of your detachments it would be better not to have any at all so as not to excite notice in the countryside."

All might possibly have been well had Bouillé limited the movement of troops through Ste. Menehould to the thirty dragoons that were to be stationed there under the command of Captain d'Andoins. But he made the mistake of having Choiseul's hussars spend the preceding night there. Led by baron de Goguelat, the hussars had gone on to Pont-Sommevesle early that morning, but they left behind them a long backwash of rumor and conjecture. The municipality itself had taken an interest in the matter and had sent a representative to Goguelat asking him the meaning of his "mission" in Ste. Menehould. Goguelat told them the story about the treasure and said that his troops would be moving on to Pont-Sommevesle early the next day in order to meet the shipment of bullion. Far from pacifying the town, Goguelat's explanation only aroused further curiosity. What treasure? Why, if there was a treasure to protect, were the troops only going to Pont-Sommevesle and not to Châlons? Why were there so many of them? When Goguelat departed that morning, the town was humming.

And inadvertently Goguelat had managed to stir up the beehive even further. He and his officers had put up at an inn called the Soleil d'Or across the street from the *relais de poste*. At Goguelat's expense—the money for this was taken from the fund Fersen had sent to Bouillé—the innkeeper also provisioned his men and horses. The innkeeper's name was Faillette. How was Goguelat to know that between Faillette and the town's *maître de poste*, a man named Drouet, there existed a bitter rivalry based on competing businesses? The posting master had only recently opened a little inn. When he saw this troop of foreign soldiers and their officers lodging at his competitor's hostelry he was furious. When in the morning Goguelat hired a pair of horses from the Soleil d'Or and not from the *maître de poste* Drouet flew over to the Soleil d'Or and had angry words with Faillette and his wife, who screamed back at him. Shaking his fist the *maître de poste* left, vowing vengeance.

On such small matters do the great happenings of history sometimes depend. Like the duchesse d'Elboeuf's tithes at Pont-Sommevesle, the fight between these two competing horse farmers was to have far-reaching consequences. For Drouet remained in a grim and vindictive temper all the rest of the day, and by the time the King's carriage arrived at his *relais* that evening he was well prepared to play his fatal role in the last act of the drama.

He was a personality worthy of notice, this Drouet whose name was about to be entered in the footnotes of French history. He was then twenty-eight years of age and after a tour of duty with the Condé regiment had returned to his home town of Ste. Menehould to succeed his mother as posting master. He was of solid peasant stock, tough-minded, able, and very shrewd in the small negotiations of life. One glimpses in him many of the characteristics that were to make for success in the world of the Industrial Age that was to arise upon the ashes of the *ancien régime*. Energetic, enterprising, and aggressive, he was formed to make his way in a competitive society. One cannot resist comparing him with the incompetent Choiseul and his kind whose sun was now setting, for it was Drouet as much as any single individual who hastened that day to its end.

Scarcely had Goguelat and his forty hussars left Ste. Menehould when d'Andoins and his thirty dragoons arrived. This was too much for the townsfolk. They went to the municipality and demanded arms. The magazines were opened and ammunition and weapons distributed. The local National Guard put itself on the alert. Captain d'Andoins was a man of stronger mettle than Choiseul. He had no intention of abandoning the post he had been ordered to keep. But as time passed and the hour scheduled for the King's arrival came and went, d'Andoins grew uneasy. Shortly after six o'clock he decided to investigate matters. He mounted his horse and set forth alone on the Châlons highroad. He had not gone any distance when a cloud of dust from down the road informed him of someone's approach. It was Léonard. In a state of breathless excitement he showed d'Andoins the note from Choiseul which announced that the "treasure" did not appear to be passing that day. Léonard then took it upon himself to tell d'Andoins that there had been a popular uprising at Pont-Sommevesle and that Choiseul and his men had been forced to flee. He advised d'Andoins to do the same. In his haste to get to the frontier Léonard barely alighted from his carriage. He took Choiseul's note back after d'Andoins had read it so that he might show it at the next post. A moment later he was gone.

D'Andoins returned to Ste. Menehould in a disturbed frame of mind. An ingrained respect for military orders spoke against a retreat such as Choiseul had made. So despite Choiseul's message he decided to remain at his post as he had been ordered to do, until either a courier appeared from Paris to announce that the flight had been canceled or until the King's carriage appeared. To pacify the townspeople he told his sergeant-at-arms that the men should dismount and unsaddle their horses. The dragoons drifted away in search of drink . . .

It was perhaps half an hour after the troops had dispersed that Valory galloped into the *relais de poste*. D'Andoins, when he realized that Valory was the King's outrider, approached him and in a low voice told him that the town was in an explosive state, that many of the citizens were armed and the National Guard had been called out. The two men could only talk for a moment, but during that moment it was decided that d'Andoins should not assemble his men until after the royal carriage had left Ste. Menehould. To do so earlier would risk having the carriage stopped by order of the municipality. D'Andoins and his dragoons would fall in behind it after it had left the town.

Fifteen minutes after this conversation the *berline* lumbered into the *relais*. It was clear to the crowd gathered in the courtyard of the posting station that if this were the carriage that the troops were supposed to protect it contained no treasure. It was occupied by human passengers and furthermore those passengers appeared to be persons of very high rank. When the coach passed by the Soleil d'Or one or two of the dragoons instinctively brought up their hand in a salute. In the recesses of the carriage one of the women was seen to acknowledge this attention with a graceful inclination of her head that according to those who witnessed it was both "regal and benevolent." Only the high and mighty of the world were trained in gestures such as that.

Trying to appear that he had nothing to do with the coach d'Andoins sidled up to it and out of the corner of his mouth muttered to Moustier who was outside on the box: "Hurry and leave! You are lost if you don't hurry!"

It was at this moment that the King put his head out of the window. According to some accounts he even opened the door. In any case, aware of the King's perplexity, d'Andoins made the mistake of speaking to him. In a low voice he said, "The plans have gone wrong. I am going to stay far away from you so as not to arouse suspicion." Those were his only words but they were enough to inform the bystanders that there was a connection between the passengers in the *berline* and the troops occupying their town.

The horses were harnessed and the coach about to move on when the *deus ex machina* of the drama now made his appearance. Drouet's story has become a favorite footnote in French history. It is related that he compared the effigy of the King on a coin—no doubt the coin given him by Valory in payment for the relay—with the face of the man in the carriage and so recognized Louis XVI. He then hurried to the municipality to give them the news, leaped onto a horse, and after a wild dash through the Argonne forest arrived at Varennes to rouse the town and cause the King to be arrested. *Vox populi* needs its heroes as well as its villains and Drouet was not reluctant to propose himself as the hero of this particular story.

The records of the municipalities of Ste. Menehould and Varennes tell a different tale. "Drouet has greatly distorted the facts," declared the town fathers of Varennes. And the account given in the civil registers of Ste. Menehould show that Drouet did not, as he later claimed, rush from his *relais*, alert the municipality, and cause the tocsin to be rung. The municipality, on the contrary, sent a representative to him to make inquiry about the mysterious travelers and Drouet declared that "If the King has a long aquiline nose, if he is shortsighted and has a blotchy complexion, then he did not doubt that it was the King in that carriage."

It seems certain that it was, in fact, the order written by Bayon at the posting station of Chaintrix that finally brought about the chase. Bayon's message reached Ste. Menehould at nine o'clock. It was shortly after nine that the municipality ordered Drouet and a man named Guillemin, the two best horsemen in town, to pursue and stop the *berline*. Long before then, however, the town fathers had caused Captain d'Andoins to be placed under arrest. His dragoons, drunk or disobedient, did nothing for him. Passively they laid down their arms and let themselves be led away to prison by the National Guard.

So it happened that at Ste. Menehould as at Pont-Sommevesle no armed troops fell in behind the carriage. And so, surrounded now by every danger, the French royal family lurched into the dusk toward the next two stops: Clermont and Varennes.

Léonard had preceded them at Clermont, where the leader of

that detachment, a Colonel Damas, like d'Andoins at Ste. Mene-hould, found himself confronted with an excited populace. After reading Léonard's message he too ordered his men to dismount and to lay down arms. Unlike d'Andoins, however, he did not permit them to disperse. When Valory and the *berline* finally appeared he could have assembled his men. But he did no such thing. When he saw that none of the other detachments were following the King's coach he made one of those rapid decisions that for men of arms will lead on to either fortune or disaster. Afraid should he call his men to arms that the townspeople might ring the tocsin and alert the countryside, he decided to let them stay as they were. He later ex-plained that he counted on the detachment at Varennes to protect the coach. He knew that beyond Varennes the massed forces of Bouillé's whole army lay waiting. And Varennes was now only four-teen kilometers away, a trip, at the most, of an hour and a half.

Marie Antoinette and Louis comforted themselves with the same reflection. For apart from the inexplicable defection of all the troops who were supposed to meet them, they still saw no reason for alarm. If they had traveled this far across so many hazards they felt that they could somehow traverse the last few miles without hindrance. Nightfall was now in their favor. Henceforth they would be traveling under cover of dark. The carriage lamps were already lighted when at a little distance beyond the posting station of Clermont they turned off the main route and took the road to Varennes. This turning in the road was another of the many crossroads in their adventure where a beneficent providence might have intervened on their behalf. The obvious route of the fugitive King would have been the highway to Metz. It would have occurred to no one that he might take the road to Varennes, an out-of-the-way little town in the woods of the Argonne.

The posting mistress of Clermont, one Madame Canistrot, her-self assumed that the party was on its way toward Metz, for it was only after the *berline* was well away from her *relais* that Moustier gave his instructions to the new postilions: "Route to Varennes!" It was unfortunate that Drouet's postilions, on their way back to Ste. Menehould, happened to have been within earshot. So it was that when these men met their employer between Ste. Menehould and Clermont on the first leg of his dash they were able to inform him that the coach had left the highway and taken the road to Varennes. And Drouet, not losing a moment, was able to stay hot on the trail.

The ten or fifteen minutes he might have lost on the Metz road would have been enough for the royal family to elude arrest at Varennes.

Instead of pursuing the carriage along the Varennes road, Drouet, who knew the countryside well, took a short cut through the forest of the Argonne. This path led along the top of a ridge that ran approximately parallel to the road taken by the carriage in the valley below. He surmised that the King's party might be under some sort of military escort and it was more to avoid being stopped by Bouillé's troops than it was to gain time that he took this dark trail through the woods. The forest of the Argonne has a strange quality; the malediction of history seems to hang over it. Since that famous night ride of Drouet to Varennes it has suffered invasion and battle almost without cease. It is with reason that Romantic writers of the last century were fascinated by the picture of the two horsemen bent over their saddles pounding through the night toward their *rendez-vous* with history. It was a scene, replete with owls and twisted tree stumps, that might have lent itself to some engraving by Doré.

Below in the ravine the *berline* moved slowly onward. Its passengers dozed. For them it had been a long and exhausting day, and a happy ending now seemed within sight.

Unlike the other communities of the valley the citizens of Varennes had not been upset by the unusual movement of troops through their town during the two preceding days. On the contrary, they had taken a certain pride in the matter. That very afternoon Monsieur Sauce, the town's procurator, had written a boastful letter about the troop movements to one of his friends. "Try to tell me now that we're not an important town!" he crowed. "Generals, aides-de-camp, colonels, that's who we've been having here. And you still think we're not a real capital?"

The two men in command of the Varennes detachment were the chevalier de Bouillé, son of the General, and the comte de Raigecourt. They were both young and like the duc de Choiseul sat well on a horse and knew how to give orders. Betweentimes, with much swirling of lace cuffs, there were amorous entanglements in the *salons* of Paris or various provincial garrisons. Like Choiseul they belonged to a caste that was doomed not because it was immoral but because it was incompetent.

These two officers had taken the precaution of stationing their troops at a far end of the town well away from the village streets. They kept themselves as little in evidence as was possible in a small and gossipy town. But once again accident managed to convert precaution into error. In the first place, Varennes was singular in that it had no *relais de poste*. It had been arranged therefore that eleven horses from Choiseul's private stables would be waiting for the King and his party, just before they entered what was known as the Upper Town of Varennes.

This distinction between the Upper and Lower towns at Varennes was to have a fatal importance. The town was divided by a river, the Aire, which passed through it. The Upper Town, where the King was due to arrive from Clermont, sat, as its name suggests, at the top of a steep slope. At the bottom of this slope lay the river with a bridge that one crossed to enter the so-called Lower Town and continue on one's way toward the east. The river presented a perfect natural defense, for by blocking the bridge one could effectively cut one side of the town from the other. Baron de Goguelat, who had passed through the town twenty-four hours earlier on his way to Pont-Sommevesle, saw this at once. He and the two young officers therefore made what they thought would be a little improvement in the original plan. They decided to move the horses needed for the King's relay away from the Upper Town, where they were supposed to be waiting, down to accommodations in the Lower Town on the other side of the river. In the event of any "trouble" in the Upper Town they could barricade the bridge and prevent the horses from being taken. Blithefully certain that he would be among the troops escorting the King's carriage into Varennes, Goguelat told young Bouillé and Raigecourt that he would send them a messenger as the party approached Varennes. They could then move the horses back to the Upper Town to the place of *rendez-vous,* where they were supposed to be. On the night of June 20 as they awaited this signal the two commanders of the Varennes detachment did not, of course, know that since the setting of the sun Goguelat, Choiseul, and all their troops had been floundering about the Argonne woods, hopelessly lost. So a commendable act of prudence became instead an act of almost incredible stupidity.

Along with the horses Raigecourt and the chevalier de Bouillé lodged themselves across the river in the town's principal hostelry, the Hôtel du Grand Monarque. An inn of the same name still stands today on the same spot but little else remains of the town of Varennes as it appeared on that June night of 1791. Nearly every stone of the old town has been razed in the bombardments of four different wars. The river Aire still transects the town and a bridge still crosses that river. Standing on the other side of the stream one can look back up the steep hill of the Upper Town down which Louis XVI's carriage had to pass to reach the bridge and safety.

Toward eight that evening Bouillé and Raigecourt left their lodgings at the Hôtel du Grand Monarque and went to the Upper Town to reconnoiter the road from Clermont. All was peaceful in Varennes that evening and although there was no sign of a courier on the Clermont road the two officers did not take alarm. They returned to their hotel in equable spirits and were standing in front of the doorway of the Grand Monarque taking a breath of air when toward nine thirty they heard the rattle of a carriage coming down the long slope of the Upper Town. They supposed at first that this was the messenger from Goguelat telling them to move the horses to the other side of the river. Alas, it was Léonard.

"Are you not the chevalier de Bouillé?" he asked. Bouillé did not deny his identity. Whereupon, without leaving his carriage, Léonard drenched him with a torrent of words.

"I have many things to tell you," he declared. "There are many important messages I've been asked to give you." In reality he had never been asked by anybody to deliver any messages to Varennes. Choiseul, expecting to reach Varennes himself, had limited his orders to Ste. Menehould and Clermont.

The village square seemed hardly the place to communicate such important messages, so Bouillé asked him to step into the inn, where they could talk without being overheard. As he was leaving the cabriolet Léonard noticed the horses intended for the King's relay.

"You must give me two of those horses at once!" he said imperiously, for he had been unable to get a relay at Varennes. When Bouillé managed to calm him he blurted forth the story of the uprising at Pont-Sommevesle, of the dangerous temper of the populace at Ste. Menehould and at Clermont. Between words he told them of his own role in the plot. "You don't have to hide anything from me," he stated. "I know everything. I have the Queen's diamonds with me . . . but now I'm afraid of being arrested. Everything has gone wrong. I need those horses and I must leave and I urge you to do the same if you don't want to be arrested."

Bouillé succeeded in procuring a fresh pair of horses for him from the stables of the inn and a moment later Léonard was off. He left, announcing his intention of reaching Luxembourg via Stenay, the village up the road where General de Bouillé and a full complement of troops were awaiting the King. Had he reached Stenay and informed the General of the confusion that had broken out among the detachments, he might have saved the day. For General de Bouillé could then have moved his militia into Varennes. Unfortunately, in this one circumstance where Léonard's tongue might have been of service, Fate decreed that he should lose his way and not reach General de Bouillé. After leaving Varennes he took a wrong turn in the road and headed not toward Stenay but Verdun.

Léonard left young Bouillé and Raigecourt in a state of consternation. The chevalier sent a message to his troops at the other end of the town to prepare to depart in a few hours. In the meantime the two officers decided that it would be wisest to await developments, to lie low and keep out of sight. They therefore retired to their room at the Grand Monarque, put out the candles and drew the shutters. It is probable that they went to sleep—although they afterward vehemently denied it—for they heard nothing of the commotion that broke out in the Upper Town at eleven thirty. It was only afterward when the tocsin began to clang and they heard the cry beneath their window "Aux armes! Aux armes!" that they realized that the King and Queen had arrived at Varennes and been arrested.

When it rolled into the Upper Town of Varennes at eleven o'clock, the berline was still a good twenty minutes ahead of Drouet. Had the horses been waiting at the entrance to the village the relay could have been made in less than ten minutes and in the remaining ten minutes the carriage could have crossed the sleeping village and attained the road to Stenay on the other side of the river. Beyond that bridge lay safety, for at that hour in the open country between Varennes and Stenay it would have been impossible to gather enough citizenry to stop the carriage. It is unlikely that Drouet would have attempted to pursue his quarry beyond that point, for he suspected that the countryside after Varennes would be swarming with General de Bouillé's troops. For Drouet it was Varennes or nothing. That explains the urgency of his dash through the Argonne woods.

In her memoirs Marie Thérèse recalled the jolt with which the carriage suddenly drew to a halt at the top of the road leading into Varennes. The dozing passengers were abruptly awakened and everyone looked around in bewilderment. They were at the spot where Raigecourt and the chevalier de Bouillé were supposed to be waiting with the eleven horses of the relay, but no one was there. Not even Valory, who had arrived at Varennes some fifteen minutes ahead of them, could be seen. Valory, in fact, had gone into the village hoping to find them there. Unfortunately it didn't occur to him to go across the river and inquire at the Hôtel du Grand Monarque, only five hundred meters away. While Valory was canvassing the deserted streets for some sign of the relay, Malden jumped from the box of the *berline* and began to look too. Louis, Marie Antoinette, and Madame Élisabeth then stepped onto the street and joined him in the search. The King rapped on the door of a shuttered house he thought might be the place of *rendez-vous*, but a sleepy voice answered his inquiry with the words, "I know nothing about it. Be on your way!"

After some ten minutes of futile wandering about in the dark, everyone returned to the carriage. Their hope now lay in persuading the postilions from Clermont to continue on to Stenay, or at least to take them to some farmhouse or hostelry where they might hire fresh horses. The postilions refused. They had been told by the posting mistress at Clermont that the horses would be needed for work in the fields early the next morning. Besides, the horses were too tired to go on to Stenay. No pleas, no offers of money, no imperious commands could induce them to change their mind. Everyone was so engrossed in the argument that they barely noticed two horsemen who galloped by them in great haste. They vanished down the street in the direction of the Lower Town and the river.

With an intuitive appreciation of the military side of the business Drouet and his companion decided first of all to block the bridge. Along their way they came on some late drinkers at the Bras d'Or, the town's other hostelry, and here they paused for a moment to pass the news and gather help. One of the men was sent to waken Sauce, the town's procurator and deputy mayor, and tell him that Louis XVI and his family were in Varennes and headed for the frontier. Drouet told the others to arm themselves in order to stop the carriage. He then hurried on to the bridge near which fate had decreed that there should be standing an enormous wagon filled with furniture that was to be moved on the following morning. The two men barricaded the bridge with these articles and returned to the Upper Town to set their trap. Not far from where the King's carriage had come to a halt an archway of medieval construction traversed the steep and narrow street down which the *berline* would have to pass to reach the river. Drouet posted himself and his men on the far side of this tunnel. Here they now waited, hidden in the angle that the masonry made with the street. They were armed.

During the time it had taken Drouet to go about his work Marie Antoinette had finally persuaded the postilions to take them as far as the Lower Town, where in front of the Grand Monarque Hotel they would have found the relay waiting for them. The carriage inched slowly forward and made its way down the decline that led through the vaulted passageway spanning the road. The cabriolet bearing the two waiting women passed through the tunnel and emerged on the other side. The *berline* followed. Its great size seemed to fill the whole width of the tunnel and it advanced at a snail's pace. It had not fully emerged from under the arch when the passengers heard the sharp word they had dreaded through all the past twenty-four hours. It was accompanied by a rattle of musketry: "Halt!"

In the dark they could discern a group of six or seven men, one of whom held a lantern. This was Sauce, the procurator. He approached, lifted the lantern to the passengers' faces and asked them where they were going.

"To Frankfurt," someone replied.

"In that case you have lost your way," observed Sauce. He asked to see their passport. It was handed him by a corpulent passenger who appeared to be valet to the party. From the back of the coach a woman's voice urged him to make haste.

Sauce took the passport and went into the Bras d'Or to examine it. It appeared to him to be in order, or at least so he declared to the men who gathered around him. It was issued to Baroness de Korff and her party and was signed by the King and countersigned by Montmorin, the Minister of Foreign Affairs. Sauce saw no reason to dispute the credentials of Madame de Korff and he announced that he was willing to let the party continue on its way. Most of the bystanders agreed with his decision.

At this point one cannot resist the supposition that Sauce knew or strongly suspected that the passengers in the *berline* were indeed the King and Queen, but like the mayor at Ste. Menehould he wanted the bomb out of his hands. How could he estimate the power of the various forces, "Royalist" or "Nationalist," that might come either to rescue or to capture these frail political tokens? He could only perceive the enormity of what had fallen out of the sky into his back yard. And he knew that in the France of 1791 a man could no longer be sure of where he stood. The victors of one moment might well become the vanquished of the next. Sauce decided to let the travelers continue on their way.

But Drouet now stepped forward and addressed Sauce with stern words. "I happen to know that the King and his family are in that coach," he declared. "They are on their way to a foreign country. If you let them continue you will open yourself to the charge of treason."

The procurator abruptly changed his mind. Accompanied by Drouet he returned to the *berline* and informed the passengers that they would have to get down since he could not visé their passports until after daybreak. The Baroness de Korff protested.

"But this is armed arrest!" she exclaimed indignantly. "Our papers are in order. We are in a great hurry to be on our way. You will be answerable for the consequences of this delay." The imperious tone of the Baroness did nothing to sweeten the temper of Drouet and his companions.

Sauce insisted politely that they leave the coach. He pointed out the darkness of the night, the uncertainty of the road, and—he laid stress on this phrase—"the emotions of the moment" that would be cleared away by morning. "The emotions of the moment" referred to the great crowd of people that had poured into the street from all corners of the town. The tocsin had begun to ring while Sauce was in the Bras d'Or examining the passport. Sauce's young children had raced into the street crying, "Fire! Fire!" People suddenly appeared from everywhere, many of them armed with pitchforks and other makeshift arms.

With the street made impassable by a swelling crowd of townspeople, with Sauce and his armed men at the door of the carriage pressing them to step down, the King and his family had no further choice. "We protested," recalled Madame de Tourzel, "but their instances were too strong to be resisted any further."

Sauce, who lived a few steps down the street, offered the accommodation of his house to the travelers. They could rest there for a few hours and then in the morning when he had viséed their pass-ports they could continue on their way. "I stalled for time," he wrote a friend a few days afterward. And that is exactly what he did in the following hours. He stalled for time until either an order should come from the Assembly or Bouillé's forces might arrive to deliver Louis and Marie Antoinette.

Monsieur Sauce was a grocer and candlemaker. His store, a single room of modest proportions, was on the ground floor of his house. Upstairs there were two bedrooms of equally modest size. The historian G. Lenôtre visited the place before it was demolished in the bombardments of the First World War and expressed astonishment that more than four people could possibly have squeezed into the miniscule bedroom where Louis, Marie Antoinette, and their children along with Madame Élisabeth, Madame de Tourzel, and the two waiting women came to the end of their journey. To reach this bedroom they had to pass through Sauce's shop, hung with candles and strings of sausages, and mount a narrow stairs at the back. They were preceded by Sauce and his wife and followed by a crowd of local officials and an improvised guard. Lenôtre has not been alone in observing that it was in such a setting, in this room above a rural grocery, that the Capetian monarchy, for whose kings had been built the most magnificent palaces on earth, reached its term.

The children were put to bed and fell asleep almost at once. Madame de Tourzel, her head sunk in her hands, sat beside them. Marie Antoinette installed herself in a little chair, where to some observers she appeared to be "frozen" and to others "extremely agitated." The King paced the room, talking to everyone who came and went. Outside, the tocsin continued to clang wildly: the crowd below their window swelled to an alarming size. Varennes' neighboring communities had been alerted by the sound of the bells and people poured in from far and wide to join the local populace. The street soon took on the appearance of a vast country fair. Stalls were set up to sell refreshments. Madame Sauce brought a bottle of wine and some glasses for her guests. She sent for a neighbor to help her with the food.

Through all this clamor the King and Queen still refused to admit to their identity. Since no one in the crowd had ever seen the royal family a man who had once lived at Versailles named Destez was sent for. He arrived a few minutes later and recognized Louis at once. He bent his knee and then pronounced the fatal words, "Oh, Sire!"

Victor Hugo, who was fascinated by the drama of Varennes, passes a stern judgment on Destez. "He approached the King in the manner of Judas," declares Hugo, "and he said, *'Bonjour, Sire!'* It was enough. They held the King. There were five people of royal blood in that carriage. With one word the scoundrel destroyed all five. His *'Bonjour, Sire'* meant the guillotine for Louis XVI, Marie Antoinette, and Madame Élisabeth. For the dauphin it spelled death in the Temple and for Marie Thérèse the extinction of her race and exile."

After Destez's recognition Louis dissimulated no further. "Very well then," he admitted with a sigh. "I am indeed your King." And with these words he opened his arms and embraced first Sauce and then Destez. He went about the room and took each of the municipal officers into his arms. The scene was very affecting and the King along with many of the witnesses to it began to weep. These were the sort of people Louis had always been able to touch; without affectation he always felt himself at ease with them. There is no reason to question the sincerity of the emotion that momentarily passed through the room. Such gestures were not, however, Marie Antoinette's specialty and she withdrew still further into herself at the spectacle of her husband weeping in the arms of a grocer.

With tears running down his cheeks, the monarch explained to everyone that he was not planning to leave France, that he was only on his way to Montmédy to escape "the knives and the bayonets" with which the factions of Paris threatened the lives of himself and his family. "I came to the provinces to find the peace and freedom that you enjoy," he declared. "If I had stayed in Paris I should have been murdered."

These words sent another wave of emotion through the room. One or two of the bystanders fell to their knees. Sauce and the municipal officers bowed and swore oaths of fealty. The grocer promised to give the King an escort of a hundred National Guard to conduct him to Montmédy in the morning. The qualification "in the morning" were the critical words in the offer. Sauce continued to play for time. He was certain that sometime before dawn the Assembly would manifest its wishes.

The King was equally certain that sometime before dawn Bouillé's troops would come to his rescue. Indeed, scarcely had Sauce proffered his promise when the clatter of hooves and the rattle of musketry were heard through the tumult in the street below. The sound announced the belated arrival of Choiseul, Goguelat, and their company of hussars. After hours in the Argonne woods they had finally found their way to Varennes. The clanging of the tocsin, the agitation of the town, the empty *berline* parked across the street from Sauce's *épicerie* told them what had happened. Choiseul first went in search of the chevalier de Bouillé's troops, who would make a respectable company if they were added to his own. But the bulk of them was nowhere to be found. They had either dispersed or were drunk. Their disappearance is another of the unexplained mysteries in the story of the Flight to Varennes. After this short unsuccessful search Choiseul and Goguelat returned to Sauce's shop, mounted the narrow stairs, and fell on their knees before the captive ruler. The King and Queen welcomed them with "much graciousness," Choiseul afterward recalled.

Despite the number of people in the little bedroom Choiseul managed to draw the King into a corner where in low voices the two men considered the situation. Slipping over any mention of his own dereliction at Pont-Sommevesle, Choiseul informed Louis that the chevalier de Bouillé's troops had abandoned their post at Varennes. Nonetheless he, Choiseul, had some forty-eight men at his disposal and he proposed an audacious escape by horseback. Louis, mounted on one horse, could carry the dauphin in his arms. The Queen and the other members of the party would each have a separate horse. By using their sabers and, if necessary, their muskets the hussars could force a way through the crowd. But, added Choiseul with a glance toward the street, there was not a moment to lose because the crowd below was growing by the minute.

Louis rejected the proposal without hesitation. To his horror of bloodshed was added a sound appreciation of the danger of such an escapade. "You have forty men," he observed, "but there are seven or eight hundred men in the street and many of them are armed. How can I be sure that the Queen, my children, or my sister might not be killed by a bullet in such an unequal battle?"

No, his only hope of escape was the arrival of General de Bouillé and his troops. By some means that has never been satisfactorily explained, Louis had apparently managed to communicate with the young Bouillé. For he now informed Choiseul that the chevalier had left Varennes soon after eleven thirty with orders to inform his father of the situation. It was only eight leagues to the General's headquarters, a distance that could be covered in two hours. The King calculated that it would take the General and his troops another three hours to reach Varennes. Bouillé should therefore reach Varennes by five o'clock in the morning. "And then," Louis declared, "we can leave here in safety without violence of any kind."

But in the hours that passed, it was not Bouillé's troops who arrived but the National Guard from all the villages and hamlets of the countryside. They arrived in their uniforms, bearing arms and drawing cannon. And in the congested streets of the town Choiseul's hussars began to partake of the wine and stronger spirits with which the guard was welcomed by the villagers. Many of them did not speak French and like most mercenaries they had only the vaguest notion of the political context in which their services were required. They were soon either too drunk to stand or were fraternizing amicably with the National Guard.

Then at five o'clock two men in a state near collapse staggered into the room. It was the very hour when Louis had calculated that Bouillé ought to arrive. But they were not emissaries of the General. They were Bayon and Romeuf, the couriers dispatched by the Assembly some eight hours earlier.

"Sire," cried Bayon, "you must return to Paris! Throats are being cut there. The lives of our women and children are threatened. In the interests of your people you must return to the capital at once."

In reality Paris was in no such state as Bayon described. Perhaps the King suspected this. In any case, he drew himself up and in a cold voice asked Bayon if he had orders to support his contention that the royal family should return to Paris.

"My companion has them," replied Bayon. He pointed to Romeuf, who, pale and embarrassed, now stepped forward and handed Louis the paper signed by La Fayette stating that the King was not to be permitted "to continue on his journey."

"You, Monsieur!" cried Marie Antoinette when she saw her friend hand the decree to the King. "I would never have believed it of you." The unhappy officer could not tell her that he had nearly killed himself trying to overtake Bayon on the road and prevent the Assembly's decree from being delivered. He lowered his eyes and murmured something about the citizens of Paris being massacred.

The order Romeuf handed Louis is one of the more significant documents of the French Revolution, for it represented a *coup d'état*, albeit clerical. The *Ultima ratio* of government is force and in that decree one is witness to the basis of all political power. Any close consideration of it gives rise to questions and statements about the nature of what Talleyrand was one day to call "legitimacy," which for the public tranquillity are best avoided. The Assembly's unspoken reply to Louis' protest that the decree was "unconstitutional" (as indeed it was) was the four thousand armed guard on the street below.

And that was a reply that the Assembly itself, to its sorrow, was to hear a year after the King's dethronement. For with the King gone the next line of battle in the struggle for power was to be between the Assembly and the Paris factions. Like Louis XVI the Assembly too was to be overthrown by force. Danton, who never minced words, phrased it succinctly: "The government belongs to us because we are the strongest."

But there was no time for speculation about the nature of power that night at Varennes. Louis read the Assembly's decree, recognized all its implications, and let it fall on the bed where his children were sleeping. "There is no longer a King in France," he declared.

Marie Antoinette snatched it from the bed and flung it onto the floor. "I will not have such a thing soil my children!" she cried. Sauce and some of the bystanders gasped at this sacrilege. Choiseul bent over and tactfully retrieved it.

The arrival of the decree from Paris and the conflict it brought about between the orders of the Assembly and the wishes of the King gave the crowd on the street a new cry around which to rally. People were no longer content with insisting passively that the royal family should be prevented from continuing on its way to Montmédy. A new and more active demand was now heard. "To Paris! He must go back to Paris!"

In the confusion that followed the reading of the Assembly's edict Romeuf managed to exchange a few words with Marie Antoinette. Like the King he saw that the only hope now lay in gaining time until Bouillé's troops should arrive and he promised her his help in this stratagem. Unfortunately his colleague Bayon was not long to perceive the same thing. Eager to share some of the laurels that were to be heaped by the grateful Nation on Drouet, Bayon later proclaimed himself to be singlehandedly responsible for the change of temper among the populace below. "I plan to prove to everybody," he later declared, "that I alone forced the King to return to Paris by inciting the people to cry out, 'He must leave! We insist that he leave!'"

And Choiseul, in his memoirs, confirms this statement. He recalled that Bayon kept going back and forth from the room where the

King and his family were confined to the street where he spread the report that Louis wouldn't leave because he was waiting for the arrival of General de Bouillé. "Bayon would then come back to the King," states Choiseul, "and deplore the terrible outcry on the street."

Bayon finally brought matters to a boil by informing people that if Bouillé should arrive before the King's departure they would all be massacred and the whole town of Varennes blown up. The rumor of this possibility swept through the streets like flame. The mob now grew frantic and the cry *"À Paris!"* more insistent. "We'll drag him out by the feet if we have to!" someone cried. And another voice was heard to say, "To Paris or we'll shoot them all!"

By six thirty there were more than ten thousand people in Varennes and it was obvious that Louis could temporize no longer. In a gesture of despair Marie Antoinette turned to Madame Sauce and asked her if she did not love her King. Pointing to her sleeping children the Queen implored her not to make them leave. But the peasant woman had a good common-sense retort to this appeal to her sentiments. "Your position is undoubtedly unpleasant, Madame," she replied, "and it is true that I love my King. But I happen to love my husband, too. He would be held to blame if you stayed, and I don't want them to chop off his head."

Madame Sauce lectured the King with some more French common sense. "After all," she told him, "the Nation pays you twenty-four millions. You'd think that would be worth keeping. Anybody who wanted to give that up would have to be pretty queer in the head."

This was more than even the patient Louis XVI could take and he is reported to have shot her a look of such scorn that she lowered her eyes.

One of the waiting women then affected a stomach ache and declared that she couldn't leave. Marie Antoinette said she wouldn't leave without her. A doctor was sent for and twenty minutes' respite was won by this ruse. Another fifteen minutes were gained by loitering over breakfast. But when seven o'clock had passed and there was still no sign of Bouillé everyone knew that the moment had come. Louis told Sauce that he was now ready to leave. The *berline* had already been harnessed and was waiting at the door. A few minutes later, in single file, the French royal family descended the narrow stairs they had mounted nine hours earlier. Just before leaving, Marie Antoinette called Choiseul aside. "Do you think Monsieur de Fersen is safe?" she whispered.

Choiseul replied that he was certain of this. With no further words the Queen followed her husband to the carriage. But among other questions that surely must have been on her mind at the moment was, what on earth had happened to General de Bouillé? Where were the troops that should have come to their rescue? In view of the total collapse of every simple military maneuver of the whole project, she may not have troubled to try to answer such a question. Her secret letters to Fersen written after the *débâcle* at Varennes reveal a very poor opinion of the French military ability. The experience of her years at Versailles had convinced her that the French were unable to organize themselves into any coherent or efficient body. She was certain that bickering and self-interest would always prevent them from becoming an effective military people. After the return from Varennes this conviction, unfortunately, was to become the foundation of her last desperate policy vis-à-vis the Assembly and the Powers of Europe.

One can only observe that Marie Antoinette was not the first or the last person to entertain this opinion, which in her case at least was legitimately formed within the confines of an intriguing court. From such a vista as hers she could not have conceived of the *esprit de corps* that was soon to weld the French people into an instrument of conquest that was to bring all Europe to its knees.

It may have been that Marie Antoinette dismissed Bouillé's defection as part and parcel of the whole ineptly executed operation. And the General's behavior was indeed inexplicable. Instead of moving his troops forward toward Varennes when the King did not arrive at Stenay on schedule, he moved them backward toward Montmédy. More than three hours passed before he received news of the King's arrest at Varennes. Another hour was spent trying to assemble his scattered troops. It was therefore reserved for General de Bouillé to administer Fate's final twist in this tale so replete with appointments missed by minutes and unforeseen coincidences. At the moment when the King and his family entered the carriage that was to take them back to Paris, Bouillé was less than half an hour away. It took time to gather the guard that was to escort the King's carriage back to Paris and the great vehicle could only move by slow inches through the vast crowd that choked the streets. Thus it happened that Bouillé, on the other side of the river, could see the procession that held the King its prisoner move slowly off toward Paris. There was a moment when he thought he still might come to the monarch's rescue, but the bridge was too heavily barricaded to be of use and the river too deep to be forded.

So poor had been the reconnoitering of his officers that no one realized that only two kilometers up the river there was another bridge that would have taken them to a road that intercepted the path of the imprisoned King and Queen. But even had Bouillé known of this short cut it is probable that he would have rejected any plan of rescue by force. When it was pointed out to him by his officers that more than ten thousand armed men and women surrounded the King's carriage and that some four thousand of them were National Guard he realized that any engagement would endanger the lives of Louis and his family.

Bouillé, "his features fallen apart in grief," reluctantly sounded the order for retreat and abandoned Louis XVI and Marie Antoinette to their fate. He headed at once toward the Luxembourg frontier. The battle was over and lost and he knew that from that moment his own life was in danger. He was the last of the Crown's loyal officers and with him departed the King's final hope of any military support from within his realm.

The Flight to Varennes has always fascinated French historians because many of the complex political conditions that comprised this phase of the Revolution are reflected in the various facets of the event. For those who are interested in the human component of history the story is no less fascinating, because for a short moment the direction of things seems to have passed from the control of parliaments, cabinets, and councils into the hands of individual men and women. One feels oneself momentarily in the presence of history reduced to its primary ingredient: the fallible human being. That explains the rash of recrimination and angry justification among many of the participants in the event. Each blamed the other for the disaster that befell the King and Queen. Fersen blamed Bouillé and Bouillé in his turn blamed the duc de Choiseul. Some declared that Fersen was at fault for not having accompanied the party beyond the outskirts of Paris. Others put the blame on the field officers, such as Damas at Clermont or d'Andoins at Ste. Menehould. In after years —for the dispute raged on long after Marie Antoinette and Louis were in their graves—Madame Campan joined the fray. As though speaking in the name of the dead Queen, she accused Goguelat, whom she detested, of a crucial negligence in the business. Goguelat answered with an indignant justification that was to become his particular account of the events at Varennes. He concluded his narrative with an apt and penetrating observation.

"If one considers the long chain of events that constitutes the destiny of men and of states," wrote Goguelat, "a chain whose entire combination will be altered by the removal or transposal of a single link, one finds oneself forced to go back to the first of all causes . . . by which I mean to Providence, whose powerful and mysterious hand casts down thrones or elevates empires as it chooses."

In the wrangling and accusation that followed Varennes one important voice was not heard. Louis XVI alone accused nobody. On the contrary, he tried to mitigate the remorse of those who felt they may have failed him. Nothing more eloquently testifies to the charity of this unfortunate monarch than the letter he wrote General de Bouillé a few weeks after his ignominious return to Paris. At a moment when Louis was beset by problems of the most terrible sort, he found time to think of Bouillé and of the doubts he was suffering.

"You must stop accusing yourself, Monsieur," Louis wrote him. "You risked everything for me and you did not succeed. Fate was against your plans and mine. Circumstances paralyzed my will and your courage and all our preparations were nullified. I do not reproach Providence. I realize that success depended on me. But one would have to be a monster to shed the blood of one's subjects by putting up resistance or igniting civil war. The thought of such possibilities broke my heart and all my resolutions melted away. Accept my thanks, Monsieur. I only wish it were in my power to give you some token of my gratitude . . ."

The return to Paris was a journey into horror that Marie Antoinette was to recall in shattered fragments through a distorting haze of heat and nightmare when she later recounted it to Fersen. The coach moved so slowly that they were four days on the road. A heat wave had fallen over the valley of the Marne. At every town and in each little hamlet throngs of infuriated people joined the procession and every cruelty short of death that humanity in mass can inflict upon the fallen or the wounded was visited on the prisoners. Like ferocious animals that have been put safely behind bars they were jeered at and tormented without pity. There was no escape from the crowd. If they closed the windows of the coach they stifled, if they opened them they were brought face to face with hordes of screaming people who pressed into the carriage. Louis and Marie Antoinette, who had once been the unwilling and inadequate living symbols of the Crown of France, now became the living symbols of all the grievances that anyone might have against the *ancien régime* in particular, and the bitterness of life in general.

At one point along the way a man was shot down and his head cut off because he tried to make a gesture of respect to the Queen. At another stop a man leaned into the carriage window and spat into the King's face. Louis said nothing, but it was noticed that his hand was trembling violently when he wiped away this token of his subjects' hatred. At Épernay, one of the towns where they paused to eat, the mob that assaulted the carriage became so menacing that they hesitated to leave the *berline*. A man bearing a gun was heard to say that he was going to shoot the Queen when she left the carriage. When, at last, they were forced to step down they could barely make their way through the surging crowd. Marie Antoinette's dress was ripped but she reached the inn alive. The man with the gun could not take aim because of the number of people. The town council of Épernay gave them a lecture while they ate. "That's what you get by traveling!" declared one of them. The remark was much savored by the bystanders. The return to the *berline* was just as hazardous. When Marie Antoinette hesitated a moment before setting forth into that raging sea of humanity a woman behind her gave her a shove and said, "Step pretty, little lady. They're going to give you lots worse when you get back to Paris."

The royal family were more concerned for the safety of their bodyguard, Valory, Moustier, and Malden, than for themselves. The King, the Queen, and Madame Élisabeth were inside the carriage, but the three bodyguards had been chained together and squeezed onto the coachman's bench outside the vehicle. They were thus exposed to the full fury of the populace and more than once had come close to being dragged from their perch and lynched. It was therefore with genuine joy that they welcomed the three deputies whom the Assembly sent from Paris to "protect" the King and his family. These men joined the party at the little village of Chêne-Fendu on the banks of the Marne on the second day of this *via dolorosa*. There were two more days to go. The Queen herself opened the carriage door for them. She and Madame Élisabeth were so overwrought they both spoke together.

"Gentlemen!" they cried, "for pity's sake, see that no harm comes to the people who accompanied us. Don't let them be hurt, we implore you!"

The presence of the deputies informed them that they were now prisoners of the government, but it also enabled them to relax and enjoy some of the advantages of prison: security and relief from all responsibility. Louis and Marie Antoinette were on friendly terms with one of these men, Latour-Maubourg. They did not know the other two. Someone, probably Latour-Maubourg, had the inspired idea of letting the two deputies who did not know the royal family ride in the carriage with them. There was room, and barely that, for only two more passengers in the *berline*.

One of these two deputies was the lawyer Pétion who was shortly to become one of the leaders of the party that has become known in history as the "Gironde." He was a representative of what then constituted the Extreme Left of the Assembly, an uncompromising republican and an avowed personal enemy of the King and Queen. No one has ever tried to make Pétion either a hero or a symbol of anything other than what he was: a fussy bureaucrat who happened to be ludicrously vain of his appearance.

The other was a man of very different stripe. His name was Barnave. He came from Grenoble of a family of poor and modest Protestants. It was among his class of people that Marie Antoinette's name was particularly disliked. There was no calumny spread by the Orléanist pamphleteers about the Queen that was not believed by the respectable Protestant community, which had many ancient grievances against the Bourbon monarchy. When he was in his twenties Barnave had been among the deputies elected to represent the dauphinois at the Estates-General in 1789. He was an eloquent speaker, full of fire and vision, and his eloquence expressed a kind of idealism that in times of social disturbance may sometimes be akin to poetry. He was, in short, the prototype of the Revolutionary of Romantic invention whose melancholy good looks seemed to reflect the ardor of his soul. He was thirty-one.

These were the men who now joined the royal family in the *berline* and who for two nights and two days were to travel with them in conditions of uncomfortable propinquity. There was hardly room for them in the coach. To make room for Barnave, Marie Antoinette had to take the dauphin on her lap. Madame Élisabeth took the girl on hers. Barnave installed himself between the King and Queen on the rear seat. Pétion sat between Madame Élisabeth and Madame de Tourzel on the seat facing them.

The conversation got off to a bad start when Pétion in an insinuating tone observed that people in Paris were saying that the royal family had been taken from the Tuileries in a hired hack driven by a Swede. He affected not to know the Swede's name and turned to Marie Antoinette for help.

"I am not in the habit of knowing the names of hired coachmen," the Queen replied haughtily. She lowered her veil and evinced her intention of having nothing further to say to the two deputies. Madame Élisabeth and the King were French in temperament and could not sustain this sort of silence for very long. They were soon chatting together in what Pétion described as "a most natural way." Pétion had no reluctance to join in. He afterward declared himself to have been astonished by the "pleasing simplicity and homely family affection" that prevailed between them. The King called Élisabeth *"ma soeur"* or "Babette" and the princess addressed her brother in the same familiar tone.

Barnave listened but like Marie Antoinette remained silent. It was the little boy who inadvertently broke the ice between them. The dauphin spotted the inscription on the brass buttons of Barnave's coat, *Vivre libre ou mourir,* and eager to show everybody how well he could read he spelled out the words and then in a hesitating voice pronounced them. Barnave was delighted and complimented the parents on their son's accomplishment. Although the slogan was not one that would ever open the way to Marie Antoinette's heart, the compliment was more than she could resist. She made a few observations about the education of children, one subject led to another, and in a few minutes she was drawn into the general conversation. She pulled up her veil and as the atmosphere grew less constrained she talked more and more freely. She even laughed once or twice.

Like Pétion, Barnave had been surprised by the familiar and unpretentious manner of the royal captives. The "tyrants" appeared, in fact, to be the same as the homespun *bourgeois* of his own milieu. And then, as the Queen began to talk, he grew aware of something else. She was an attractive woman who in no way resembled the popular picture of her. Instead of a licentious Messalina he found a solicitous mother. Instead of a domineering Catherine de Médicis he found a charming woman who bore her difficult position with a quiet dignity that was admirable.

Marie Antoinette was not long to realize that in this idealistic Revolutionary of stern principle she had made a conquest. And then in the strange propinquity of their journey together she too began to undergo an unexpected change of view. She had never before come into informal contact with any man of the Revolution. Mirabeau she had barely known and she despised him in any case because he sold himself for money. Barnave was something else. She was quick to perceive that he was a man of honor and integrity. These were qualities that she prized highly. Her own uncompromising attachment to black and white principles had in fact contributed substantially to her downfall. Tentatively at first, then more boldly, political views were brought forth and aired. The Queen listened, glimpsed, and for a moment or two may even have understood the attitude of a revolutionary. In her heart of hearts she could never sympathize with the ideas that Barnave presented to her, but she trusted the man and at some point during their trip back to Paris she saw a ray of hope in the monarch's apparently hopeless situation. With Barnave on their side . . .

They talked in low voices. Pétion declared afterward that he recalled no conversation between them. But Pétion was in fact absorbed in what he believed to be a Romantic "conquest" of his own. In a kind of comic counterpoint to the earnest exchange between Marie Antoinette and Barnave, Pétion was convinced that Madame Élisabeth, the virginal "Babette," had fallen passionately in love with him. In a passage of his memoirs that has made him the laughingstock of posterity Pétion described his delusion in memorable words. "Madame Élisabeth gazed at me with tender eyes," he recalled, "and with that air of languor that is imparted by misfortune. Our eyes met and there was a sort of intelligence and attraction between us. I stretched out my arm. The Princess touched it . . . I sensed a warmth rippling through her clothes and it seemed to me that her glances grew more tender. I noticed that her eyes had become moist. A note of volupté was now added to her melancholy. I may be wrong, but I think that if we had been alone, if by some magic everyone around us had been made to disappear she would have fallen into my arms and abandoned herself to the promptings of nature."

Poor, fat, innocent Élisabeth! She remained serenely ignorant of the agreeable hallucinations she was inspiring in her neighbor. Her only comment on the trip is to be found in a letter written to an *émigrée* friend soon after the return from Varennes. "You may think our journey with Barnave and Pétion was a torture for us, but it was no such thing, really. They were all right, you know, particularly Barnave, who is most intelligent and not at all ferocious as it is said." Like her brother the King she knew nothing of the game of coquetry or those who played it. She had lived at Versailles like a nun, protected by a cluster of pious and elderly waiting women.

It was not so with Marie Antoinette. The Queen had received her training in that particular game at the world's most celebrated school. Despite her fatigue, despite the thickening chin, the too ample bosom, and her thirty-six years she remained, and she knew it, a woman who could still arouse the desire of men and especially men of a chivalrous, idealistic, or serious bent such as Barnave or Fersen. In the years that followed her death there were a number of men of this character who were to verify that fact in their recollections.

In one of Barnave's temperament the "pale, shattered woman" who bore her sufferings with stoicism and dignity would probably have awakened more interest than the empty-headed flirt of Trianon who cast her laughing glance from behind the corner of a fan. In any case, before the end of their trip Barnave, who had been one of the most outspoken enemies of the Queen, Barnave, known to the streets of Paris as "The Tiger" because of the ferocity of his words about the King and Queen, had become another of Marie Antoinette's unexpected conquests. At Meaux, where they stopped for the night on the last lap of the trip before they entered Paris, she managed to see him alone. They strolled for a moment in the gardens of their billet and here, out of earshot of Pétion, Élisabeth, and the King, they were able to talk unconstrainedly. Nobody knows what was said, but it was at this moment that the first steps were taken toward that *entente* with Barnave's "party" of the Left that was to be the monarchy's final bastion of hope.

As the procession approached Paris on the following day the crowds that followed thickened and their attitude grew even more menacing. The women were particularly malevolent. Many of them howled for "the whore's head." Others called for her intestines to be distributed among them as cockades. At one point she lifted her son to the window, hoping to appease the screaming women, but someone yelled, "Take him away! Everyone knows the fat hog isn't his father!" The King's face froze into an expressionless mask and Marie Antoinette turned away to hide her tears. Alarmed by the fury of the mob, Barnave leaned out the window and called for the commander of the National Guard.

"I remind you, Captain," he said, "that you are responsible for the safety of the passengers in this carriage."

The dauphin now began to cry in terror. The boy had had a terrible dream the night before in which he saw himself lost in a dark wood, surrounded by wolves waiting to devour him. He had awakened screaming. Under the circumstances his dream is easily explicable, but it was destined to have a strange extension in reality, for two years later one of their party was in fact to be devoured by wolves. Proscribed by the faction of Marat that overthrew the Girondins, pursued by the police, Pétion was forced to seek refuge in the woods and there, dead of exhaustion and exposure, his body was found partially eaten by wolves.

With the exception of Madame de Tourzel and young Marie Thérèse every person in that carriage was marked for death by violence. Like Marie Antoinette, Louis, and Madame Élisabeth, Barnave too was to perish on the scaffold.

They entered Paris by the Champs-Élysées. The boulevard on both sides was lined by a surging sea of humanity, but no sound rose from this ominous mass. The Paris populace had been warned by the Assembly that "whoever insults the royal family will be beaten; whoever applauds them will be shot." The deathly silence of the city was broken by the slow steady beat of muffled drums. The funereal tone of the procession was further enhanced by the National Guard, who reversed their arms as though in mourning. The coach crossed the Place Louis XV—now the Place de la Concorde—and entered the garden of the Tuileries between the two stone horses of Coysevox that still rear back and paw the air today. From the nearby terrace of the Feuillants the duc d'Orléans watched with unconcealed satisfaction as the royal prisoners entered the palace.

When she had bathed and rested, when her immediate first comprehension of the magnitude of the catastrophe had been assimilated, Marie Antoinette sent for her lady-in-waiting Madame Campan, to whom she related many of the details we now know about that adventure. It was Madame Campan who first noted that during the course of the Queen's trip her golden hair had turned white as snow, "like that of a woman of seventy."

On the following day Marie Antoinette went to her desk and

began the correspondence in cipher and invisible ink that henceforth was to be the Crown's last contact with "the outer world." The first of these letters was a hurried note to Axel Fersen.

"I exist . . ." she wrote, "but how worried I've been about you and how I feel all that you must be suffering not to have heard from us! Will Providence allow this to reach you? You must not write me for that would endanger us. Above all, do not come back here on any pretext. They know that it was you who got us out of here and you would be lost if you were to appear. We are watched night and day. But you must not worry. Nothing will harm me. The Assembly wishes to treat us leniently. *Adieu* . . . I can write you no more . . ."

The dots in the concluding sentence represent more of those excisions made by Baron de Klinckowström. It is difficult to believe, as the Baron contended, that the deleted words were about politics.

PART III

Captivity

AFTER MAKING HIS *adieux* TO MARIE ANTOINETTE AND THE KING at the posting station at Bondy, Fersen took a cross-country road that joined the northern highway to the Belgian frontier. He rode all that day and all the following night and arrived at Mons at six o'clock in the morning of the twenty-first—at about the time that at Varennes in the upstairs room of the *épicier* Sauce, Marie Antoinette and Louis were making their last desperate play for time.

When he found himself safely over the frontier Fersen was elated, but he was characteristically cautious in expressing his relief. At the moment of his arrival he wrote his father a note that communicated these feelings. "The King and all his family safely left Paris on the 20th at midnight. I accompanied them as far as the first posting station. May God will that the rest of their journey be as fortunate. After I've seen Monsieur I will continue my route along the frontier and join the King at Montmédy—if he is so fortunate as to arrive there."

Monsieur, accompanied by the comte d'Avaray, had arrived at Mons before Fersen. The comtesse de Provence and her friend Madame de Gourbillon had traveled by another route to Namur. In the morning Fersen had a brief audience with Monsieur when he officially informed the prince of Louis' and Marie Antoinette's successful evasion from Paris. It was a statement for which all Europe had been waiting in anguished suspense. From Monsieur and other French refugees at Mons the news soon spread that Marie Antoinette and Louis had in fact safely reached their destination at Montmédy.

Immediately after his talk with the comte de Provence, Fersen left for Montmédy to join the King and Queen. He traveled southward just inside the Belgian frontier and arrived at Arlon, a few leagues from Montmédy in the evening of the twenty-third. At Arlon he ran into the marquis de Bouillé, who was still reeling from the disaster at Varennes. Bouillé told him the news but could give him no details about the *débâcle*. In his Journal Fersen made an unemotional note of this conversation. "Learned from Bouillé that the King was taken. No one yet knows the details. The detachments didn't do what they were supposed to do and the King wasn't firm . . ."

It was, in fact, the pivotal point in Fersen's life. He was to be haunted all his remaining days by the memory of that night. A letter to his father written in the first moment of shock reveals his state of mind more poignantly than the laconic words in his Journal. "All is lost, dearest Father, and I am in despair. Only imagine my grief and pity me . . ."

Louis XVI's parting words to him at the Tuileries had been that he was to "treat" with the European Powers on the Bourbons' behalf should anything go amiss in their attempt to reach Montmédy. It was with this commission in mind that Axel turned his steps back toward Brussels. From that moment all through the following year and a half his energies were to be dedicated to the single purpose of rescuing Louis XVI and Marie Antoinette. Along the way he stopped to inform Monsieur of the King's arrest at Varennes. One wonders if the comte de Provence was able to conceal his satisfaction from Fersen more satisfactorily than he did from Bouillé, who was to write a damning description of the Prince's response to the news. "There wasn't a trace of tears in those eyes as dry as his heart. All one could discern was their customary expression of falsity across which darted a few sparks of perfidious satisfaction." If Monsieur managed to hide his feelings from Axel he certainly made no effort to conceal his first thought. He charged Axel with the task of telling the King and Queen in Paris that he, Provence, should be given the unlimited powers of Regent. He even had the temerity to dictate the wording of this *plein pouvoir* in which he stripped his brother of sovereignty more thoroughly than had the National Assembly.

Monsieur did not trouble to wait for a reply from Paris. His orders to Fersen had only been a formality. Within a few weeks' time he set up his own government and his own court and presented himself as the legitimate executive power of France. He appointed his brother Artois Lieutenant General of this little realm and the prince de Condé was made chief of his armies. He accredited and received ambassadors and soon afterward established himself and his court at Coblenz in a palace given him by his uncle, the Elector of Trèves. This court-in-exile was to show itself a more intractable enemy of Marie Antoinette than the Jacobins of Paris.

Fersen's letter to Gustavus III announcing the arrest of the royal family was written in the same tone of anguish as the letter to his father. The King of Sweden was waiting impatiently at Aix-la-Chapelle for the announcement of Louis XVI's deliverance. The shock of the news of the French King's arrest seems to have unbalanced him. In a single moment Gustavus became an ultra-royalist and embraced the doctrine of absolute monarchy in its most extreme and purest form. His thinking carried him to the outer limits of cold, philosophic principle. The monarchy became everything in his eyes, the monarch nothing. "It's all one and the same to me," he wrote the Empress Catherine, "whether the King's name is Louis XVI, Louis XVII, or Charles X, so long as the monster that sits in the Manège (i.e., the National Assembly) has been brought to earth and its infamous principles stamped from the face of the earth forever."

Blinded though he appeared to be in his rage against the Revolution, Gustavus was, in fact, the only sovereign in Europe who saw the true significance of the storm that had blown up in France and he alone among them was prepared to sacrifice his narrow interests to the larger cause of kings. "The King and Queen of France may be in danger at this moment," he declared, "but their danger is nothing compared to that which the crowned heads of Europe face in this French Revolution."

In this spirit Gustavus now proposed an armed invasion of France. The army—of which he was to be the leader—was to consist of Swedish, Russian, Austrian, and Prussian troops, contributed to the common cause by their respective sovereigns. This force was to invade France through Normandy, march directly onto Paris and "throttle the Hydra in its lair." That in the event of such an invasion the King and Queen of France might be murdered by the populace of Paris did not trouble him at all. The monarchy, at least, would be saved.

Before Gustavus returned to Sweden he entrusted Fersen with the organization of this chimeric scheme. Crauford was to go to England to sound out Pitt and George III. Axel was to deal with the Austrians and the Prussians while Gustavus himself solicited the intervention of Catherine the Great. The sovereigns all echoed Gustavus' indignation and led Fersen to believe that they would be willing to contribute to the common cause. In reality none of them had any intention of coming to the help of the King and Queen of France. They promised, they prevaricated, and were soon deep in the impenetrable thickets of their own private schemes.

The only outspoken opponents to Gustavus' plan of an invasion were, paradoxically, the royal captives themselves. Marie Antoinette learned of the project with consternation and energetically opposed it, not only because of the obvious danger to herself and her family but also because she had certain secret plans of her own. Fersen learned with astonishment that she was planning to compose with the Assembly. "Do not worry about us," she had written him soon after the return from Varennes. "The leaders of the Assembly appear to want to treat us with leniency." And this announcement was followed some weeks later by a clear statement of her opposition to Gustavus' project.

"The King believes that open force would be of incalculable danger," she wrote, "not only for himself and his family but for all the French in the kingdom who are not supporters of the Revolution. Undoubtedly a foreign army could succeed in entering France, but the people are armed and in fleeing the invaders they would probably turn on those of their fellow citizens whom they regard with suspicion . . ." Then Marie Antoinette touched for the first time on the scheme that was to become the cornerstone of her private *politique* and which has been so persistently misunderstood. "The King wishes that the good will of his relatives should be demonstrated by a congress and by negotiation. Of course there should be an impressive force to support them, but always far enough behind the frontier so that it could not provoke crime or massacre."

This then is the genesis of Marie Antoinette's famous *appel à l'étranger* that so often has been interpreted as an appeal by her to the Powers of Europe to invade France and put down the Revolution. In reality her plans were precisely the opposite. She was terrified of armed invasion. In the words of Louis Madelin, "She dreamed in no way of a counter-Revolution brought to Paris in the band wagon of the foreigner but of a manifestation on the frontier by which means the Powers would show that they disapproved of the way the King was treated." Madelin dismisses her plan as "a woman's idea and perfectly childish."

Whatever its faults or possible merits, her scheme had the immediate effect of placing Fersen between two opposing policies: that of Gustavus, who wished to incite all of monarchical Europe into marching on Paris, and of Marie Antoinette, who looked on such a proposal with dread. Fersen thus found himself the trusted agent of two conflicting parties, a position that demanded the tact and *sangfroid* of an experienced diplomat. From one corner of his mouth he assured Gustavus that Marie Antoinette was not going to compromise the dignity of the throne, while from the other he tried to persuade Marie Antoinette that Gustavus was devoted to her cause and above all that the King of Sweden, despite his saber-rattling, was not in league with the comte de Provence, Artois, and the *émigrés.*

If Fersen in a sense deceived Marie Antoinette during that summer of 1791, Marie Antoinette for her part was playing a double game with him. For her call for an armed congress was but the by-product of another plan not yet known to either Fersen or Gustavus. And behind that plan lay the guiding hand of her acquaintance Barnave.

Through the intermediary of a trusted secretary, the chevalier de Jarjayes, Marie Antoinette had put herself in touch with Barnave soon after the return from Varennes. "Tell him," she said to Jarjayes, "that I was much struck by his character and the frankness I found in him during those two days we spent together. I should very much like him to tell us what we are to do in our present position . . . There is something to be done, I know. But what? In the course of our conversation he must have realized that I am of good faith. I believe that he wants to do good. So too do we, although people may say otherwise . . ."

Barnave was delighted when he received this message. But he did not reply at once. It was as a political figure that Marie Antoinette had approached him and Barnave was indeed a political figure. He belonged to an inner group of the Constitutional Monarchists known as the Triumvirs and he had two colleagues, a man named Adrien Duport and another named Théodore de Lameth. He showed them the Queen's letter. The two new men were less enthusiastic than Barnave. They did not think Marie Antoinette capable of "sustained thought" and they considered her "very frivolous." It is probable that he tried to correct their prejudice by telling them of his discovery that Marie Antoinette did not at all resemble the popular picture of her. He too had once thought her shallow and irresponsible. Then there came those two days when they had traveled together in the intimacy of danger. He had found instead a woman whose courage imparted an impression of high principles and steadfast character. Barnave may not have convinced his colleagues, but he finally obtained their cooperation in the secret and very dangerous correspondence that he now began with Marie Antoinette.

In his reply to her first letter he put his cards directly on the table.

He told her that there was now only one way left to save the Crown. The Constitution on which the Assembly had been working since the beginning of the Revolution was finished and about to be submitted to the King for his sanction. It was precisely to avoid being forced into sanctioning this charter that Louis had tried to separate himself from the Assembly and go to Montmédy. To save the throne and to spare France the horrors of civil war Barnave told Marie Antoinette that her husband would have to accept the Constitution, recognize that it embodied the wish of his people, and, once accepted, support it firmly and with "sincerity." In addition to this Louis was to try to secure the return of the *émigrés* and the princes. The Queen in the meanwhile was to write her brother the Emperor and solicit his recognition of the French Constitution. She was also to obtain from him a statement expressed in the clearest possible manner of his "friendly and peaceful intentions toward the French nation."

Now Marie Antoinette disliked the Constitution even more intensely than did the King. She disliked it not only because it reduced the monarch to a nullity lower than the King's ministers, but because she considered it unworkable. Nor was the Queen alone in this view. The Constitution was in fact a hodgepodge of contradictions and concessions held together by a glue of Rousseauesque philosophy. It was particularly hated by the revolutionaries. Camille Desmoulins said of it, "There has been such a confusion of plans and so many people have worked on it from so many different directions that it is a veritable Tower of Babel."

In her correspondence with Barnave, Marie Antoinette was frank enough to state most of her objections to the Constitution quite openly. She never tried to conceal from him her conviction that it was unworkable and she was probably unable to conceal from him her fear that the path down which he was leading her was the path to disaster, from which, should she wander too far, there might be no return. In any case, during the months of July and August, while promising Barnave that she and the King would "attach" themselves to the Constitution, "steadfastly and with sincerity," she was at work with Fersen on her alternative plan of an armed congress. Of this project Barnave was completely ignorant and her duplicity toward him is often pointed to as an example of her deceit and her attachment to Austria instead of France.

Under the dictation of Barnave, for instance, she wrote a letter to Leopold II in which she solicited her brother's support of the

French nation. She asked the Emperor to renounce all military projects against France and in effect to give his blessing to the Constitution about to be promulgated. The letter was duly dispatched to Vienna—via Mercy at Brussels—under Barnave's watchful eye. But scarcely had she finished penning it than Marie Antoinette wrote a second letter informing Mercy that the first had been extorted from her. "I felt I had to comply with the wishes of the party leaders here who gave me a draft of the letter," she informed him. "I would be very upset if my brother did not realize that in my position I am obliged to do and to write all that is asked of me. It is essential that my brother answer me in a circumspect letter that can be shown and that I can somehow use as a basis for negotiation here . . ."

She concluded this letter with her first admission to the outside world that she was secretly working with Barnave and his party. She then gave a private opinion of them that is not usually quoted by those who accuse her of betraying Barnave's trust. "Although they are tenacious in their opinions I have never seen anything but the greatest decency in them, a real strength of character and a genuine wish to restore order and in consequence the authority of the Crown."

She gave Axel no hint of her secret *entente* with Barnave. Her decision to accept the Constitution with apparent good will was still unknown to him. Marie Antoinette was therefore "duping" Fersen for Barnave in about the same degree that Fersen was duping Marie Antoinette for Gustavus III. And who in this complex tissue of conflicting aims and contradictory motives was not duping someone? Barnave, after all, was betraying the Assembly to the King, while the Assembly for its part was cheating the King. Leopold of Austria, whom the naïve Barnave supposed was at the beck and call of his sister's wishes, had no intention of helping the French royal family either by arms or even by moral support. The King of Prussia, while affecting to approve of the armed congress that Marie Antoinette solicited, was in reality delighted that the Franco-Austrian Alliance had at last been ruptured. Goltz, his ambassador in Paris who for twenty years had been one of the most energetic of Marie Antoinette's enemies, continued unabated to defame her name by calumny and evil report. At Coblenz the princes, who could barely conceal their elation over the failure of the Flight to Varennes, sent inflammatory threats to the Assembly full of hypocritical concern over their brother's fate.

Nor were the revolutionaries any purer in their behavior. Danton, successively in the pay of the Orléanists, the English, and the royal family, was now embarked on a still more dangerous double game. The Jacobin Club through its undercover agent Carra was at that very moment making overtures to the Duke of Brunswick in which they offered him the Crown of France—on certain terms. And the Duke of Brunswick, who in not many months' time was to lead the allied armies into France, listened, considered, and began to play his own double—and probably triple—game.

Beside these examples Marie Antoinette's game with Barnave seems like child's play. The explanation for the severity with which many French historians have condemned her may perhaps be found in a new note that at this point begins to make its appearance in her correspondence with Fersen. For it is no longer the Jacobins or the *émigrés* about whom she has sharp words. It is the French as a whole. "If you think that the French are capable of following an organized system you give them too much credit," she writes in one letter. Then, with more asperity, she declares that "the French are behaving atrociously."

In his Journals and his letters to Marie Antoinette and Sophie, Fersen delivers himself of far stronger opinions. "Vain, lightheaded coxcombs!" Gone were the days when the charming chatter of Madame du Deffand's *salon* commanded the adulation of Europe. "They are indiscreet to a fault and you can trust them with nothing." And as the Revolution advanced his tone grew shriller. "Wretches!" "Monsters!" "A cursed race!" But Axel Fersen was not married to the titular head of the French nation. Unlike Marie Antoinette he could express such opinions without being considered "unpatriotic." For, along with its other benefits, the French Revolution introduced to the world the concept of patriotism and introduced it furthermore via a people whose pride of race was already overweening. The innate superiority of the French had always been taken for granted by the French, but the innate superiority of France was a new notion that was not long in taking root there. The question of what exactly constituted France and who exactly was to administer it was another issue and was to become the subject of angry disagreement. The record of these disputes may, indeed, be called the political history of the French Revolution. It was Marie Antoinette's opinion that her husband incorporated the sovereignty of the French people. Others who succeeded Louis XVI were of the opinion that they did.

In any case, posterity's severe view of Marie Antoinette's "treachery" vis-à-vis Barnave probably owes itself in some part to outraged patriotic sentiment on the part of at least a certain school of French historians. She who for so many years had been rejected as "Austrian" by the French court and who because of the court's widely disseminated gossip had never really been accepted by her husband's people now began to express a few critical opinions about the French in general. And in the equation of patriotism her duplicity with Barnave appears to equal her duplicity with the whole French nation.

Over and again it is repeated that Marie Antoinette "used" Barnave and tried to make political capital out of his good faith. But rarely is it mentioned that Barnave was using her, too. Indeed he and his party were in as urgent a need of her support as she of theirs, for after the Flight to Varennes a party that stood far to the "left" of Barnave had appeared upon the political horizon. The Triumvirs, who only a year before seemed like extreme revolutionaries, had now become the party of conservation. And they believed that the only way to dam the torrent that threatened to sweep them away was to secure the Crown's firm support of the Constitution, or, in other words, of themselves. They also believed, and with undoubted sincerity, that this was the Crown's last chance to save itself. In short, they viewed the Constitution as a high-powered weapon in an approaching political battle. One does not question the sincerity of their conviction that their victory in that battle would have been for the benefit of France. But who, after all, in the sanguinary struggles that were about to rock France, did not believe this of themselves? Each party that entered the arena was well armored with that conviction.

Neither Marie Antoinette nor Barnave comprehended the power of the storm that had arisen around them. Neither therefore could perceive that the Constitution—for Barnave—or the Armed Congress—for Marie Antoinette—were but barricades of straw in a hurricane. In politics as in all phases of man's social existence there have always been problems to which there are no solutions. And there have been periods in man's history when the control of his destiny seems to have been torn from his hands by forces that are more powerful than reason, intelligence, or expediency. The French Revolution was one of those periods.

In summation of Marie Antoinette's *politique* during the months that followed Varennes it may be said that she never supported the Constitution with the "sincerity" that Barnave urged upon her. But neither did she actively undermine it as she has been accused of doing. Her policy was to accept, step aside and let the French people discover for themselves that the Constitution was unworkable. In a letter to Mercy she makes this perfectly clear. She informed him that all the King could do was to accept the Constitution, expressing as he did so the hope that it might bring peace to the kingdom and so give the French people the happiness they so deserved. "If we take this line we must stick to it," she concluded, "and above all we must avoid anything that could cause distrust. We must follow it to the last letter of the law. I promise you that this is the best way to disgust them with it."

But because she was afraid, despite their assurances, that the Constitutionalists would not be able to restore the liberty or authority of the King or be able to defend the lives of the royal family, she concerted with Fersen her secret alternate plan of a European congress. In truth both schemes, the one with Barnave and the one with Fersen, were irresolute, both were compromises and at bottom an expression of her particular temperament. Once again the woman and the Queen were at odds. One would not have seen a Catherine the Great quail before the possibility of a little armed action. The resolute Russian Empress, who had murdered her husband and imprisoned her son, would have mounted a steed and crushed any insurrection in her capital city with an iron fist. Marie Antoinette was not born to wear Catherine's mail. No more was she born to dissimulate with the skill of her mother. The guile for which she has been reproached was on the level of petty social intrigue among suburban clubwomen.

Buoyed one moment by Barnave's assurances that all would be well if only she and the King would support the Constitution, she was harassed at the next by the dire warnings of Gustavus, Mercy, and Fersen against any association with those whom they called the *enragés*. She had to appease both sides with all the little evasions and lies best known to women of her kind. Night after night she would bend over correspondence in which all those threads were brought together. Many letters were in code or invisible ink and she would often find herself faced with the task of deciphering or encoding long, critical messages. Her work was not made easier by the extreme surveillance under which the royal family had been placed after their return from Varennes. At night two sentries were posted before the open door of her bedroom and there was hardly a moment during the day when she was not under observation. One of the promised rewards for the King's acceptance of the Constitution was to be a relaxing of this vigilance. Barnave even promised her that they would be at liberty to "move about" once the King had accepted the Constitution.

The work tired her and there were times when she would have to force herself to keep her eyes from closing. Sometimes the strain would appear in her letters to Axel. *"Adieu,"* she wrote in one. "I am exhausted from writing. I've never done work such as this before and I'm always afraid of forgetting something or making some stupid mistake." And in another letter she declared with astonishment that "sometimes I barely recognize myself and I have to pause to realize that this person is really me . . ."

During those summer months of 1791 Marie Antoinette was without any news of Fersen. She wrote him a number of letters but she had no answer from him for nearly two months. It may be that Fersen's letters to her were intercepted. Or it may be simply that he didn't write any letters. Immediately after Varennes, Gustavus had ordered him to go to Vienna and try to secure the support of the Emperor and the King of Prussia in his project to save Louis XVI and Marie Antoinette by force. Since this commission was in opposition to Marie Antoinette's wishes, Fersen may have found it easier to resolve the conflict by not writing her.

Whatever the reason for his silence, Marie Antoinette was perplexed and hurt by it. In August she found a means of communicating with her old Trianon friend comte Valentin Esterházy, who had emigrated. She gave him her news and assured him of her enduring affection. "My heart is full of grief for I have no real friends here in whom I might confide my sorrows. I am glad that they are all safe and far away but to have no news of them is unbearable. Should you write HIM tell him that many miles and many countries can never separate hearts. I feel this truth more strongly every day."

The capital letters are in Marie Antoinette's hand and they leave no doubt that Esterházy knew well the identity of the unnamed man. In her letter she enclosed two small rings. "I am delighted," she wrote, "to find this opportunity to send you a little ring which I am sure will give you pleasure. In the past few days they've been selling like hot cakes here and they are very hard to come by. The one that is wrapped in paper is for HIM. Send it to HIM for me. It is exactly his size. I wore it for two days before wrapping it. Tell him it comes from me. I don't know where he is. It is dreadful to have no news of those one loves and not even to know where they are living . . ."

The ring that Marie Antoinette sent to Fersen was of gold and on its face it bore the inscription *Lâche qui les abandonne*. The Queen's parting words to Esterházy accord us a glimpse of her state of mind during the months of "house arrest" that preceded Louis' acceptance of the Constitution: "You must believe that we are doing what we do because we cannot do otherwise. I hope, despite what people are saying about me, that you know me well enough to believe in the nobility of my character and in my courage. They will never forsake me. My heart must know that this is the opinion of me held by my friends. As for the rest—I despise them too much to care what they may think."

Marie Antoinette did not hear from Axel until after Louis' acceptance of the Constitution in September. This event unleashed a storm of indignation through the governing circles of Europe and it was probably no accident that Fersen renewed his correspondence with her at exactly this moment. Gustavus was outraged by Louis' submission to the Assembly and for a moment it seemed that he might abandon the cause entirely. In St. Petersburg the Empress Catherine was as indignant as Gustavus. The "weakness" of Louis filled that warrior with scorn. "It must be very sad," she declared, "to find that your last hope is your rosary beads." This not very veiled hint that she planned to withdraw her support from the French monarchy upset Fersen and Gustavus. In truth the threat was just as empty as the promises it purported to revoke. She had never intended to give Louis or Marie Antoinette the smallest material support. She was in the advantageous situation of those who bargain for goods they don't intend to buy.

Worse and far more dangerous than the reaction of Catherine and Gustavus to Louis' sanction of the Constitution was that of the King's brothers. At Coblenz their outcry of indignation was followed by a barrage of abuse heaped upon the head of Marie Antoinette. The princes and the *émigrés* were in an even more advantageous position than the Empress Catherine. By the use of those public proclamations to which they were partial they were able to inflame Paris against their brother and sister-in-law wherever they chose to do so and always under the righteous guise of their cause. The popular mind associated Marie Antoinette with all the forces of reaction and the city of Paris was all too disposed to believe that she and her brother were in secret league against the French nation. Thus in a single public statement Monsieur could undo all Marie Antoinette's efforts to appear "sincere" in her support of the Constitution. Monsieur, when he learned that Louis was about to accept the Constitution, made just such a statement. He wrote his brother an open letter that he caused to be printed and distributed throughout France in which he stated that he knew that Louis had not accepted the Constitution of his own free will and that therefore he, Provence, felt himself free to act as he thought best—for the King's benefit. "Do not worry about your safety," he wrote. "We only live to be of help to you and we are working for you with ardor . . ."

Marie Antoinette's response to the Prince's expressions of hypocritical outrage over the King's sanction of the Constitution was an outburst of her own, which she confided to Fersen.

"We find ourselves in a different position since the sanction of the King," she wrote. "It would have been nobler to refuse but that would have been impossible in our present position . . . you will never know how much it has cost me to go through this yet that vile race of men who pretend they are attached to us and who have never done us anything but harm continue to vilify us . . . It is their behavior that has brought us to where we are."

Louis XVI himself wrote a letter to his elder brother imploring him to stop his agitating. This letter, unlike the comte de Provence's letters to Louis XVI, was not published publicly. It was intended for Monsieur's eyes alone and consequently it expresses Louis' private and real views about the Constitution and the matter of foreign intervention in French affairs. It is to be regretted that it has been so rarely cited by those who insist that Louis and Marie Antoinette were then hoping for a foreign invasion to restore them to their former power.

"France at this moment is on the verge of total collapse," wrote the King, "and her ruin will only be hastened if violent remedies are brought to bear upon the ills that overwhelm her. Union or force are the only two means to heal the division that now divides her. But the use of force can only come from foreign armies and that means having recourse to war. Can a king allow himself to carry war into his states? Is the remedy not worse than the disease? Such an idea must be abandoned at once and I must try the only other means left me—the union of my will with the principles of the Constitution. By opposing the Constitution I would have prevented the people from judging it. They would have noticed nothing but my opposition. But by my adopting these ideas and by following them in good faith the people will discover the cause of their troubles. A better order of things will be brought about by my acceptance. I wish to let you know the motive for my sanction so that your conduct will be in conformity with mine . . .

"I have been greatly grieved by the comte d'Artois going to the conference at Pillnitz without my consent. I can only point out that in acting independently of me he thwarts my plans . . . would you serve the fury of the sedition mongers here by having me accused of bringing war into my kingdom? You think you can outwit them by declaring that you are marching against my orders, but how can you persuade them of this when the declaration of the Emperor and the King of Prussia was occasioned at your request. *Will anyone ever believe that my brothers do not carry out my orders?* Thus you have shown me to the Nation as accepting the Constitution with one hand and soliciting foreign intervention with the other. What right man could respect such conduct and do you think to help me by depriving me of the esteem of all right-thinking people?"

The Conference at Pillnitz to which Louis alludes was a typical instance of the princes' treachery, but even Louis did not then realize quite how base this treachery was. The "declaration of the Emperor and the King of Prussia" to which he refers was in effective fact no more than a skillful forgery by his brothers. In August the comte d'Artois had gone to the Emperor and the King of Prussia at Pillnitz in Saxony and tried to persuade them to sign a statement expressing their intention of restoring the King of France to his former sovereignty by armed force. The Emperor and the King—whose distrust of one another was equal only to their mutual dislike of the comte d'Artois—did finally issue a short and noncommittal statement deploring the "disorders" in France, which they declared to be a matter that *should* be of common concern to all the sovereigns of Europe. They went on to say that they *hoped* that the other powers would agree to give such help as might be solicited of them. Should that be the case Their Majesties were resolved to use such force as they considered necessary to obtain the common good. The document was filled with subjunctives and slippery diplomatic phraseology. Reduced to its actual meaning it stated that the two sovereigns would only come to the help of the King and Queen of France if the other sovereigns of Europe joined them. And the Emperor Leopold knew very well that there was no possibility of this happening. That very week he had received secret assurances of England's neutrality and he knew that Spain would never join in such a league without England. It was in an equable humor therefore that he put his signature to the bland and meaningless declaration.

But the Emperor Leopold did not reckon with the resourceful intelligence of the comte de Provence, who saw at once that the Pillnitz Declaration as it stood was useless to him. Monsieur therefore had recourse to a clever trick. He drew up a long statement of his own which he described as an "interpretation" of the manifesto issued by the Emperor and the Prussian King. This "interpretation" converted the mild words of the original declaration into a bellicose statement full of threats against the French nation and the French people. It was this document that was printed and distributed throughout France and this document that was read before the outraged Assembly. It was seized upon at once by the radical enemies of the Constitutional party and held up as evidence of the Crown's bloodthirsty intentions and of the Queen's treasonable collusion with her brother. Marie Antoinette saw at last the depths of the Prince's treachery. "They have murdered us!" she cried when she had read the document. It is said that she then uttered the epithet "Cain!"

The King's acceptance of the Constitution did not bring about the public tranquillity that Barnave and his party had expected. For a few weeks Louis and even Marie Antoinette enjoyed an unexpected burst of popularity. There was even a moment when it seemed that the Constitution might work. The illusion was quickly dispelled.

Having completed their task of drafting a Constitution the deputies of the Assembly—called the Constituent—dissolved themselves and ordered elections to a new Assembly—called the Legislative. On a proposal of Robespierre those who had sat in the first Assembly were made ineligible for election to the second. The result of this maneuver was that Barnave along with the majority of the Constitutional party were put out of office and ceased from that moment to have any effective power in the government. In the new Assembly those of their party who remained found that they had become the party of conservatism while the places they once occupied on the left were taken by a new, far more radical representation. For the first time the face of the so-called *enragés* was seen in the senate.

Too late Barnave and his party realized that the monarchy could give them no support in the approaching struggle with their enemies among the factions. In the phrase of the historian Sorel, "Their last resource was a fortress whose ramparts they themselves had dismantled and whose garrison they themselves had dispersed." It was the Constitution they so ardently supported that was the cause of their ruin, not the duplicity of Marie Antoinette. For that charter stripped the King of all effective power except a veto that could not be backed by force. In vain did Barnave implore Louis to stand up against the agitators of the Left. But the King lacked both the power to do so and the will to exercise that power, even had it been accorded him.

Sometime in September, Fersen finally learned of Marie Antoinette's secret association with Barnave. It seems to have been a matter of general gossip in *émigré* society and was passed about with characteristic charity. "People here say that the Queen is sleeping with Barnave and is letting herself be led by him," Axel wrote in his Journal. This remark has been pointed to by many of the Queen's biographers as further evidence that Marie Antoinette and Fersen had themselves slept together, the argument being that Axel's matter-of-fact attitude and the absence of either surprise or indignation shows that he knew her to be capable of such a thing.

In truth, Fersen's response to this gossip was far from matter-of-fact. The angry and impolitic denunciation of the Constitutional party that suddenly bursts forth in his letters to Marie Antoinette show how stung he was. "Do not open your heart to these madmen," he warned her in one such letter. "They are all scoundrels who will never do anything for you."

Reading his words, one suspects that jealousy may have affected his political judgment. His lumping together of the extremists of the Jacobin Club with the Constitutionalists reveals so total an inability to discern critical political shadings that one can only suppose that he was momentarily blinded by personal passions. "You will never win over the *factieux*," he declared. "They are too deeply conscious of their wrongs ever to fear your vengeance while the nobility whom you have abandoned will no longer feel it owes you anything. You will debase yourself in the eyes of the Powers of Europe, who will accuse you of cowardice."

The nobility whom she had "abandoned"(!), the Powers of Europe, and Fersen himself (all of whom were safely behind the Austrian frontier) seem to have had only the vaguest comprehension of the fact that the knife was at Marie Antoinette's throat. The King accepted the Constitution because he could not do otherwise. Marie Antoinette's compact with Barnave was her last hope of saving the Crown—for her son if not for her husband. She and her family were prisoners under armed guard. Marie Antoinette rather tartly pointed this out to Fersen.

"Believe me," she wrote, "we would have fallen still lower than we are now if I had not taken this position as soon as I did. At least we'll gain time that way and time is what we need at this moment."

In this same letter there is a sentence that has often been quoted as an instance of her falsity vis-à-vis Barnave. "How happy I would be," she continued, "if one day I could prove to these scoundrels that I was not their dupe!" But in the context of her letter her word "scoundrels," *gueux*, clearly refers to the Constitutional party in general, of which the Triumvirs were a splinter group, rather than to Barnave and his two friends in particular. This is made clear when in the next paragraph of that same letter she informs Fersen, albeit elliptically, of her secret understanding with Barnave. It is obvious that she did not know that he had already heard of that fact. It is therefore apparent that it cannot be Barnave and his party whom she calls "scoundrels" a few lines earlier.

"I am holding for you the papers of a very curious correspondence for the happy day when we shall meet again. It is all the more curious because one must give due credit to the persons involved in it. No one in the world knows about this and if people speak of it at all it is so vaguely that it becomes one more of the thousand stupid rumors that are whispered every day."

So far as Barnave personally was concerned she retained her regard for him to the end. In any reference to him in her correspondence abroad she always made a point of saying, "credit must be given" or other words to that effect. On a political level she did not keep faith with him, but the nature of her bad faith has generally been distorted. She disliked the Constitution and she admitted as much to Barnave. But she induced Louis to accept it. And in all outward good faith it was accepted by both she and the King just as Barnave had asked. She intrigued against it abroad, it is true, by secretly soliciting her brother's support of an armed congress. But for his own political reasons her brother did not give her the support she requested and so, in effective fact, there was no foreign intrigue against the Constitution—there was only Marie Antoinette's inept attempt at one.

In conclusion it must be said that it was never Barnave whom she mistrusted—everything on the contrary indicates that she considered him completely trustworthy. It was his plan, rather, about which she had her misgivings. She disliked it and, more to the point, she did not think it would work.

Time soon proved her to have been right. For by December it was apparent that the Constitutionalists were in as much danger of annihilation as the Crown. It is interesting at this point to find Barnave urging the King to use force against his political adversaries. There had been a great outcry from Barnave's party when only a year earlier there had been some suggestion of the use of force against themselves. Force suddenly became respectable now that they were threatened. The Girondins, the party who finally overthrew the Constitutionalists by the use of mob violence, were themselves to be overthrown by that same instrument fourteen months later. In the context of these combats one might consider a quotation from the historian Pierre Gaxotte. Gaxotte here refers to the Girondins, but his words are just as applicable to the Constitutionalists: "They were satisfied with the power that they had won and they cherished the hopeful belief that they could emancipate themselves from the mob violence that had carried them to office . . . but they bristled with rage at the thought that those auxiliaries of yesterday were the masters of today. The law became sacred in their eyes now that it was they who made it. They said, as La Fayette had said before them, 'The revolution is now at an end. The revolution stops at the point where we now stand.'"

Realizing that the situation was rapidly worsening, Marie Antoinette expressed a desire to meet Barnave again face to face. This was dangerous and very difficult to arrange, but somehow she managed to see him alone at the Tuileries. She found that he still remained a friend. In a moment all his suspicions and his impatience with her political veerings vanished. He only saw the woman who was a Queen, not the Queen who was a politician. There can be no question at all of his infatuation with her.

It is believed that she saw him twice again. No one can know with certainty since a veil of secrecy was drawn over all such perilous meetings. In any case, it is known that at the end of January 1792, when the battle was definitely lost, he went to the Tuileries to bid her farewell. He planned to leave Paris and retire to his native Dauphiné away from the feverish atmosphere of the capital. His parting words to Marie Antoinette indicate that he glimpsed his fate.

"I am certain to pay with my head for the interest that your misfortunes have inspired in me and for the services I wished to render you. For my reward I ask to have the honor of kissing your hand."

And with tears in her eyes Marie Antoinette granted him the favor he requested. He was guillotined in October of 1793, only two weeks after herself.

With the decline of Barnave's party and the end of hope of any help from that quarter, Marie Antoinette turned again to her alternative plan of an armed congress. Axel Fersen, her emissary abroad, became the principal advocate of this project. His appeals on her behalf before the chancelleries of Europe were to bring him in touch with the three dominant Powers of the Continent. Like Dante conducted into the inner circles of Hell he was to wander far below the surface of things, deep into the rotting substructure of European dynastic politics.

The private fate of Marie Antoinette is so closely interbound with those politics that one must pause for a moment and glance at the courts of Prussia, Russia, and Austria as they were in that winter of 1792 when Count Fersen arrived among them bringing Marie Antoinette's appeal for help.

Frederick the Great of Prussia had died in 1786, three years before the gathering of the Estates-General in France. The emergence of Prussia as a European Power of the first order, probably the most significant happening of the eighteenth century prior to the French Revolution, owed itself almost entirely to the ability and vitality of that extraordinary ruler. With far more reason than Louis XIV, he could declare, *"L'état c'est moi."* The Prussian state was his creation as it was his private domain. There were no ministers of significance in his government and there was neither a nobility worthy of the name nor any *parlement* to which he was answerable. When he died there was not a single experienced or capable man to replace him. His heir was a nephew who came to the Prussian throne as Frederick William II and he was in every way unlike his predecessor.

Grossly fat, this "mountain of red German flesh" encased a singular personality. He was both pious and licentious, both ecstatic and sensual. Devoured at one moment by lust, he was tortured at the next by remorse and would cleanse the stain of an unbridled libertinage with the tears of religious fervor. In his contrition he had recourse to the panacea of the Mystics, of the Rosicrucians, and the Illuminati. Like so many heirs to the atheistic attitudes of the eighteenth century Frederick William replaced religion with superstition. The palace at Potsdam where Frederick the Great and Voltaire had once quaffed the dry, clear wine of Reason now swarmed with magicians, mediums, and wizards. The King of Prussia even turned to the spirits for their advice on political questions and Frederick the Great would on occasion be called back from his grave. It goes without saying that some among these practitioners of the Black Arts found a quick path to appointments of importance in the kingdom through the King's credulity.

Another path to power at that motley court was through the sensual appetites whose effect Frederick William tried to wash away with his retinue of sorcerers. The Prince was a glutton for women. His weakness had none of the light cynicism that had characterized the *volupté* of a Louis XV. The lash of contrition wielded by the blond vestals he courted drove him into a quagmire of perverse domesticity. He married his mistresses. Soon after his succession he divorced the Queen—who was amenable to the arrangement so long as the divorce was not ecclesiastical—and married a certain Madame Voss. In the eyes of the church of which he was titular head Frederick William thus became a bigamist. All the while he retained another mistress, one Dame Rietz, who was an intimate of the Rosicrucians. A few years after marrying Madame Voss he decided to marry Dame Rietz too. Court apologists lauded the King's "great tenderness of soul," contrasting it with the dry and heartless French way of managing these things. Frederick William kept Madame Voss as his mistress. But at the very moment when he was about to bring Dame Rietz to the altar a Mademoiselle Doenhof was presented at court and Frederick William was swept off his feet by her stern good looks. "She was more than blond," recalled an observer. "She was yellow." He married her instead. The pastor who blessed their union was the same who had blessed that with Mademoiselle Voss. Thus by 1790 the King of Prussia had three living wives. Dame Rietz, too, remained at court as his mistress. Two years later, in 1792, when in France the situation of Marie Antoinette and Louis XVI had reached its most critical point, he divorced Mademoiselle Doenhof and offered his hand to a Mademoiselle Bethmann.

Since all these women, whether wives or mistresses, had lovers of their own who also had ambitions to advance with the King, the court of Prussia by 1790 was a morass of contradictory political policies. The ship of state veered about crazily, steered first by one hand, then by another.

The King's First Minister, Hertzberg, who directed Prussian foreign affairs in the opening days of the Revolution in France, was a man of the old school, a Machiavellian and a believer in the aggrandizement of Prussia by any means. For him, Prussia's main purpose in France remained the destruction of the Austro-French Alliance and nothing was spared by him to achieve that end. Blackening the name of Marie Antoinette with the French people was his foremost weapon. Goltz, Frederick the Great's ambassador in Paris, went about his work with renewed vigor under Hertzberg's administration. Because the French Revolution meant the effective end of the Alliance it was acclaimed with joy at Potsdam. "The prestige of the French Crown is annihilated forever," Hertzberg informed Frederick William. "A condition now exists in that country which may be turned to the advantage of other governments." From Paris, Goltz sent the King another heartening announcement: "The fall of the Bastille and the total ruin of the Queen's reputation in France have greatly strengthened Your Majesty's position in Europe."

But the Flight to Varennes and the humiliations suffered by Louis XVI at the hands of his subjects caused the Prussian King to view the French Revolution in a different light. In the persons of Marie Antoinette and Louis XVI he saw the monarchic principle threatened. Furthermore, his circle of theosophs and ecstatic mistresses had begun to take offense at the "impiety" of the French Revolution. They had always hated Hertzberg and for years had conspired against him. In the French disturbance that the Minister had so energetically stirred up they now saw a means to effect his ruin. They presented Frederick William with a candidate of their own, a man named Lucchesini. Lucchesini told the King that there might be more profit for Prussia in fighting the Revolution than in aggravating it. Allied with her enemy Austria, Prussia could embark on a holy war against the godless French from which there might be some interesting territorial spoils. Austria would be permitted to have Alsace, but the price of

Prussia's complicity would be a province or two of Moravia, a chunk of Flanders, and, above all, Austrian compliance in another partition of Poland. Hertzberg fell and Lucchesini succeeded him. From that moment—it was exactly the moment when Fersen came begging for Frederick William's support of Marie Antoinette's armed congress—Prussia's foreign policy takes on a labyrinthine quality that makes it almost impossible to follow without a glance at those two other Powers, Austria and Russia, to whom the disturbances in France were of equal interest.

Like Frederick the Great, the Empress Catherine had once partaken of the light, intoxicating wine of French philosophy. Diderot and Voltaire had been her friends and when one reads the sparkling exchange of letters between her beloved *philosophes* and the Autocrat of all the Russias it is difficult to realize that it is the formidable Catherine who penned such charming and affectionate paragraphs. But the Empress drew a sharp line between the ruler and the woman of letters. Her gracious appearance of abdication in the presence of those whom she recognized to be her superiors in the republic of letters in no way affected the thinking of the woman of state. And in one of her letters to Diderot she said as much: "One might write some good books with your ideas but they would be useless for me in my daily work."

The woman of state was the most remarkable figure in that century of remarkable figures. Able, intelligent, and ruthless, all her powers were dedicated to the aggrandizement of Russia. During her reign she became infatuated with a grandiose scheme of conquest that she called *le projet grec*. She planned to expel the Turks from Europe, seize as much of the decaying Ottoman Empire as she could, and establish at Constantinople a new Byzantium over which her grandson Constantine would rule. Greece would become hers and Athens would be revived as a capital of Classic culture. "We will have the ancient Greek tragedies enacted by Grecian players in the theater of Dionysius at Athens," she wrote Voltaire. And the philosopher was ecstatic. "Peter the Great's plan of making Constantinople the capital of the Russian Empire will at last be realized," he replied. "It is not enough to humiliate the Turks . . . they must be routed forever."

Shortly before the beginning of the Revolution in France, Catherine finally took the first step toward realizing the *projet grec* and marched her armies into Turkish territory. In embarking on her crusade she had to have the complicity and support of Austria, whose territories also touched upon the Ottoman Empire and who too had certain ambitions in the east. Expediency alone brought the two powers together. They fought as allies against their common enemy the Turk, but when the war was won each planned to cheat the other out of his fair share of the spoils.

It was in the light of their ambitions in Turkey therefore that Russia and Austria first viewed the Revolution in France. And they were delighted. The collapse of the central power in Paris meant that France, crippled by internal problems, was now *hors de combat* in the arena of war and diplomacy. Henceforth they could continue their projects in the east without fear of interference from that quarter. "France has just fallen," crowed Joseph II when he learned of the fall of the Bastille, "and I doubt if she'll ever rise again."

In their gloating over the disturbances in France they forgot their jealous and obstreperous rival, Prussia. Taking advantage of Austria's preoccupation in Turkey, Hertzberg fanned the flames of revolt that smoldered everywhere within the Habsburg possessions. In Hungary his agents stirred up the nationalistic passions of the Magyars. In the Netherlands, promising Prussian aid to the Revolutionary party there, they finally brought the native populace to a state of open revolt. Thus in 1789 and 1790, at the exact time of the Revolution in France, another revolution, equally violent, broke out in Belgium. But it was a revolution of a different character than that of France, for the popular party in Belgium was that of the priests. And in the Belgian uprising the "patriots" were the ultra-conservative peasantry and laborers of Flemish ancestry who looked with loathing on the liberal-minded aristocrats whom Joseph II appointed to administrative positions in Brussels. Led by monks brandishing crucifixes, howling bands of revolutionaries ran through the streets of the capital tracking down atheistic noblemen known to be tainted by French philosophy. In March of 1790 there was a great pillage throughout the Austrian Netherlands. Only those houses with a picture of the Blessed Virgin painted on them were spared. The rest were sacked and their owners dragged into the streets where they were whipped and then murdered. "*Salus populi suprema lex esto!*" cried the Jesuit Feller. "The good of the people is the final law" . . . words that prefigure the public utterances of St. Just and Robespierre.

Joseph II had to abandon his war in Turkey in order to put down this uprising. It was, in fact, the deathblow of that Enlightened Despot, who had been so earnest a disciple of Voltaire and who, unlike Catherine, had tried to rule his empire in accordance with the precepts of the French philosophers. The Emperor was forced to suppress the revolt in Belgium by sanguinary means that were abhorrent to him.

Having incited revolt throughout Austria's possessions, Prussia turned her attention to those of Russia. The Poles were promised Prussia's support should they rise up against their Russian oppressors. Emboldened by this assurance and knowing that Catherine's armies were in faraway Turkey the patriots of Poland saw that the time was propitious to throw off the Russian yoke. In May of 1791 they ratified a Constitution that proclaimed their freedom from Russia.

Poland was something more than the principal jewel in the diadem of Catherine's conquests. It was the very cornerstone of her foreign policy, the geographic necessity that connected her empire with Europe. Beside Poland le projet grec was but a chimera. Poland is indeed the thread that leads the reader out of the labyrinth of intrigue and cross-purposes that constituted European politics at the time when Marie Antoinette began to send out her first distress signals.

Prussia was determined to have a share of the spoils should Russia occupy Poland. Austria on the other hand was determined that Prussia should have no share of Polish land unless she, Austria, received a due compensation. Catherine, for her part, was determined that neither country should have anything. In the First Partition of Poland she had had to share the loot with her two neighbors. But in the coming partition—for a partition was to be the outcome of the Polish revolt—she planned to seize as much of Poland as she could and to keep it all for herself. It was at this moment that with the simple guile of a child she saw how the Revolution in France could be turned to her advantage.

"I've been doing everything to push Vienna and Berlin into getting involved in French affairs," she confided to a friend. "I want them to become occupied with the troubles in that country so I can have my hands free. I have many plans that aren't yet finished and I want those two countries to be so busy in France that they won't bother me."

So, although she raved against the Revolution, Catherine's hidden tactic was to fan the conflagration to higher and hotter flames, hoping that Austria and Prussia would then take armed action against the French. She welcomed any news of the suffering and humiliation of Marie Antoinette and her children because she supposed that the Emperor Leopold would be moved by feelings of pity for his sister and intervene on her behalf. The Empress instructed her embassies to make political capital out of every new outrage inflicted on the French royal family. It is related that one day her ambassador to Vienna drew Count Kaunitz, the elder statesman of the Habsburgs, aside and depicted for him in all its doleful colors Marie Antoinette's anguish. "We have it in common," replied Kaunitz dryly, "that we've both heard all about it."

Austria was well aware of Russia's game ("The Empress," declared Kaunitz, "wants Austria and Prussia to be so busy in France that she can take Poland for herself") and had no intention of becoming Catherine's pawn. The Emperor Leopold had certain territorial ambitions of his own that, like his fellow sovereigns, he planned to advance by exploiting the French Revolution. Austria's objective was the exchange of her troublesome possession in the Netherlands for Bavaria. To achieve this end she was prepared either to march into Alsace, which she would hold as ransom, or else fling herself onto Poland and, demanding her fair share of the partition, force Prussia and Russia into recognizing her claim on Bavaria. Marie Antoinette's dream of an armed congress in no way corresponded with her brother's secret projects. A Constitutional Monarchy in France over which presided a Bourbon King whose wings had been well clipped was more in line with Austria's wishes. At a secret council of the Imperial government held in January of 1792—at the very moment when Axel Fersen was most urgently pleading for Austrian support of an armed congress—Kaunitz expressed Austria's real attitude toward any interference in French affairs: "To sacrifice our gold and our blood to give the Bourbons back their former power and to revive our formal rival would be an act of madness and one of the worst mistakes Austria could possibly make."

The Emperor Leopold was always polite to Fersen. He would affect to listen to him with interest and on occasion would make a vague promise or two, but his tactic was to wait and watch. His sister's predicament permitted him to prevaricate with facility. He read the letter she wrote him under Barnave's dictation and blandly interpreted it as the expression of her wishes. When Fersen confronted him with her real wishes Leopold replied he would make no contribution to an armed congress unless all the European Powers—i.e., Russia, Prussia, England, and Spain—were agreed to support it.

Such, roughly sketched, is the web of hidden motives and secret schemes into which Fersen wandered in the autumn of 1791. Count Fersen was a soldier, not a diplomatist, and he rarely saw beneath the surface of the situation in which he found himself. His judgment of people seems to have been as consistently inaccurate as his interpretation of their intentions. He was convinced, for instance, that Catherine the Great would contribute to the armed congress. Her wild denunciations of the Revolution ("France has brought a rotten, stinking abortion into the world . . .") and her apparently enthusiastic response to Marie Antoinette's project—merely an enthusiasm she wished communicated to Prussia and Austria—led him to believe that he could count on her.

He soon recognized the Emperor Leopold's falsity and very foolishly he put his trust in the King of Prussia instead. In the end he blamed the failure of everything on Austria alone and he did not hesitate to communicate this opinion to Marie Antoinette. He told the Queen that her brother was underhanded and a liar—"a real Italian." In truth, the Emperor was potentially a far more dependable ally than Frederick William. Leopold's moderate and rational attitude toward the Revolution in France might have served his sister's cause well had not an unforeseen and far more violent storm suddenly blown up in France.

During that winter of 1791–92 none of the sovereigns of Europe realized how desperate the situation of the French royal family had become. No one, not even Fersen, understood how close they now were to the end. In the security of their palaces in Brussels, Vienna, or Coblenz the diplomats who so busily spun their webs knew nothing of the menacing clouds that had gathered over the palace of the Tuileries. Despite the vigilance under which she and Louis had been placed, Marie Antoinette continued her correspondence with Axel. At his prompting she even wrote letters to Catherine of Russia and the King of Spain, entreating their support of her plan. And even as she wrote, just beyond the palace gates she could hear the rumble of the gathering thunder.

One reads those letters today and behind their lines one still can feel the fatigue that sometimes overcame her. Her courage would suddenly flag and she would see her cherished plan for what it really was, an insubstantial dream. Then in blind anguish she would cry out for her brother's help. "Persuade him," she wrote Mercy, "that we have no other hope but him, that our happiness, our very existence and that of my boy depend on him alone." She was certain that the son of Maria Theresa would answer this call of blood to blood and that somehow he would save her.

The line of communication that connected the Tuileries with Brussels had always been fragile. By the end of 1791 it had become hopelessly inadequate. Crauford and Éléonore returned to Paris in December, where they acted as messengers between Fersen and the Queen. Despite their part in the Flight to Varennes they had not fallen under the scrutiny of the police and Crauford came and went from the palace with considerable freedom. But there were messages that Crauford could not be trusted to communicate. There were many misunderstandings to be cleared up and many ideas to be clarified. There was even a new plan of flight proposed by Gustavus III in which Louis and Marie Antoinette, occupying separate carriages, would leave France by Normandy and the Channel Coast. So, in January, Fersen decided to go to Paris and talk to the King and Queen himself.

When she heard of this project Marie Antoinette begged him not to come for she knew that he faced certain death should he be caught. She pointed out to him the dangers that he would face in that city on the brink of another uprising; as Queen she even ordered him to stay in Brussels. But in the end she succumbed to his entreaties. She had not seen him for seven months and the call of friendship heard in that cold and friendless palace may have been too sweet to resist. In early February she sent him a note saying that conditions in Paris were favorable to his departure. A few days later, on February 11, accompanied only by an orderly named Reutersvard and bearing the falsified credentials of a Swedish diplomat *en passage* to Portugal, he set out for Paris.

It is thanks to his Journal that we know many of the details of Fersen's last visit to Paris and, because of another of those mysterious erasures, it is thanks too to this account of his trip that many writers have finally become convinced that Axel Fersen was indeed the lover of Marie Antoinette.

After a three days' journey he reached Paris at five thirty in the evening of February 13. He left his orderly and their carriage at the

Hôtel des Princes in the rue de Richelieu. From there he took a cab to the house of the baron de Goguelat not far away in the rue Pelletier. Goguelat, it will be remembered, had been one of the officers assigned to the detachment at Pont-Sommevesle at the time of the King's flight. After Varennes he had been arrested. His release had been one of the rewards promised the King for his acceptance of the Constitution. He returned to the service of the Queen in the capacity of secretary and although he, like the royal family itself, was under a close surveillance he was able to come and go from the Tuileries in freedom. Marie Antoinette therefore entrusted him with certain messages or commissions. On this particular evening he was supposed to conduct Fersen through the hedge of guards and other obstacles into the private apartments of the palace. The appointed hour of their meeting at Goguelat's house in the rue Pelletier had been six thirty. Fersen arrived there shortly before this hour and found to his dismay that Goguelat was not at home. Considerable importance appears to have been attached to the hour of their *rendez-vous*. Perhaps the guard was changed at the palace at about this time and it was therefore a propitious moment to enter the Tuileries unobserved. In any case, as the hour came and went Fersen, waiting on the street in front of Goguelat's house, grew uneasy.

A few minutes after seven Goguelat finally appeared. He explained that Fersen's letter announcing the exact day of his arrival had only reached the Queen that afternoon and he had been unable to leave the palace at so short a notice. The two men set out for the Tuileries.

"I went to her rooms by my usual route," Fersen records laconically. "Afraid of the National Guard. Her apartment very fine. Did not see the King . . ." And then comes the short erasure that has been the subject of so much dispute. Those who believe that Fersen was the Queen's lover insist that the inked-out words are *resté là*— "I stayed there." Others declare that no such interpretation can be justified. The passage has been photographed, examined under X-ray, and submitted to the inspection of experts, but the censored words still remain illegible. In truth, it seems probable that they do read *resté là*. The phrase is clearly composed of two words, of which the second seems to be less than three letters. In the first word one can discern the makings of an "r" and of a "t". Fersen wrote in a small hand. Given the general spacing of his letters there would be exactly room behind the erasure for the words *resté là*. It will be remembered

214

that this phrase occurs with frequency in Axel's Journal and that it refers, almost beyond doubt, to those occasions when he had had sexual intercourse with his mistress Éléonore Sullivan.

That he stayed at the Tuileries through the night of February 13-14 and very probably in the Queen's apartments is a certain fact, self-evident to both Fersen and any reader of his Journal. Therefore the phrase, "I stayed there," taken in its literal sense, can only be redundant. It is more likely that he intended the words—if indeed they are *resté là*—to have a different meaning. For once, in fact, biographers of romantic inclination seem to have a legitimate situation on which to exercise their talents. They have done so. The night of love between the woman from whom life had withheld happiness and the Swedish officer who loved her has been described on other pages. For Marie Antoinette's sake one can only hope that some part of it, at least, is true. "The night of love" was somewhat longer than a night. Axel did not see the King until six o'clock of the following evening. Thus, if we are to believe the evidence of his Journal, he spent nearly twenty-four hours sequestered in the apartments of Marie Antoinette.

When the King—wearing the *cordon rouge*—finally appeared, the first topic broached was that of flight. But Louis refused even to consider the possibility. The extreme guard under which the palace had been placed precluded any hope of escape, as Fersen himself soon admitted. But the real reason for Louis' refusal was that after Varennes he had promised the Assembly that he would never again try to leave Paris. "His scruples restrain him," Fersen noted, "because he is an honorable man."

In the course of their conversation Louis, Marie Antoinette, and Fersen discussed the political scene in France and Europe. Old hopes were discarded and new possibilities considered. Marie Antoinette informed Fersen—a curious piece of information that has either been overlooked or rejected by most historians—that her friends in the Constitutional party, Barnave, Lameth, and Duport, told her that the only hope left was the intervention of foreign troops. In other words, they urged her to follow the very course for which she has been so much reproached. Both she and the King still quailed before this alternative. "I know that people tax me with weakness and indecision," said Louis. "But no one has ever been in a position such as mine. I know now that I missed the moment . . . I should have left on July 14 (1789) and I wanted to, but Monsieur himself begged me not to leave. I missed the moment then and I have never found it since. I have been abandoned by everybody."

Louis' words recall those of Marie Antoinette uttered not long after: "Everyone, everyone has profited by our misfortunes."

The Queen then reminisced about Varennes. Axel learned many details of which he had previously been ignorant. They talked for more than three hours. Unfortunately Axel left no record of the bulk of their conversation. His discretion is much to be regretted, for the smallest fragment of that interview would certainly cast light into some of the darker corners of the history of the French Revolution. The fact, for example, that the Constitutionalists had urged the Queen to seek foreign intervention is of the utmost interest. One can only wonder what other information Fersen might have given us.

At nine thirty he took his departure. À 9:30 *je la quittai* he notes tersely in his Journal. But even this brief phrase opens doors of speculation. His use of the feminine gender makes its meaning unequivocal. *I left her.* Had the King departed before him or were his thoughts at this moment only for her? Painful indeed that moment must have been, for they both knew that these farewells were very probably their last. They were never, in fact, to meet again.

Before leaving, Fersen told her that he planned to go toward Orléans and Tours in the direction of the Spanish frontier to lend an appearance of "verisimilitude" to his journey. He later reported to Gustavus and Taube that he had done exactly that. In reality, as his Journal reveals, he did no such thing. From the Tuileries he went directly to Éléonore Sullivan's house in the rue de Clichy where he was taken to a maid's room under the eaves and there, unknown to Crauford, he spent a week enjoying the company of his mistress.

This light, illicit adventure enacted in a setting of danger and impending disaster was in perfect harmony with the incongruous spirit of the late eighteenth century. As one reads Fersen's account of his surreptitious interlude with Éléonore one might at first be reminded of some rollicking comedy of errors in the style of *opéra bouffe*. But it is rather Mozart's *Don Giovanni,* with its intimations of doom that lurk just below the surface of the minuet, that should be called to mind.

When Crauford was out Axel would leave his place of hiding and enjoy the comforts of the house. When Crauford returned, often late in the evening, Fersen would retire to his room in the attic. Crauford would then be served the left-overs of the supper that

Fersen had enjoyed with Éléonore. On the days when Crauford stayed home Fersen kept to his room and read novels. In his Journal he notes that he finished five of these. Éléonore or her maid would sneak upstairs and bring him food. It was explained to her servants that Axel was her illegitimate son by the Duke of Württemberg come to pay his mother a secret visit.

On February 21, after seven days of this *divertissement,* Axel wrote a letter that he had his orderly deliver to Crauford announcing his imminent return from Tours and Orléans. He then left the house by the back stairs, paused a moment, and re-entered by the front door. Crauford was completely fooled. "We played our parts well," Axel wrote, "and he believed us."

Once again one feels oneself confronted with an unpleasant side of Fersen's character, for with all due appreciation of the difference between eighteenth-century attitudes and those of our own time there is something repellent about his cold-blooded satisfaction over this piece of deceit. Crauford was to remain ignorant of the liaison between his mistress and his friend for some time to come. The rest of Europe was not. Only a few weeks earlier Sophie had heard rumors of it in Stockholm and she wrote her brother a reprimand: "I mention this, my dear Axel, for *Her* sake whom this gossip would hurt mortally. Think of her unhappiness and spare her this most terrible of griefs . . ."

Did the Queen suspect? In one of her letters to Axel she expressed concern when Crauford and Éléonore came to Paris in December because she knew how much their companionship meant to Axel in Brussels. A few comments of this nature are the only glimpse we have of Marie Antoinette's mind on the subject of Éléonore Sullivan. So far as Éléonore's attitude toward Marie Antoinette is concerned, she was a fervent worker in the Queen's cause. She was not, in any case, the sort of woman who might object to sharing the favors of a lover.

Fersen and his orderly left Paris at midnight. Two nights later, in bitter cold that reminded him of Sweden ("The wheels of our carriage squeaked against the snow"), he crossed the frontier.

Scarcely had he returned when a series of detonations blew into fragments the foundations on which he and the Queen had constructed their new plans. On March 1 the Emperor Leopold died without warning. Marie Antoinette had lost confidence in him and for some months Fersen had viewed him as an active enemy. But just before his death Leopold had come to an understanding with the Prussians—the first step toward any hope for an armed congress—while his moderate, levelheaded attitude toward the situation in France might have stood them well in the months to come. His successor was his twenty-four-year-old son, Francis, to whom Marie Antoinette was but another of many aunts. The Emperor Francis was to reign for forty-three years. He was to fight the Napoleonic Wars and in the Habsburg tradition (*Tu Felix Austria Nube . . .*) marry his daughter to Austria's enemy Bonaparte, whom in due time he would overthrow in order to re-establish a monarchy he had duped. He was, in Albert Sorel's words, to be the "imposing but impassable witness to vast catastrophes, one of those men who are carried by destiny beyond their talents, who 'represent' the history of their time, but who have not made it." One need only glance at the many portraits of him that still line the walls at Schönbrunn to realize that one would solicit his help in vain. Those pale cold eyes are as devoid of pity as they are of sensibility.

Her brother's death was a blow to Marie Antoinette and once more she wept bitter tears over an untimely loss. Like Mirabeau, like Joseph II, his death came at a bad time. So bad indeed that in Vienna the rumor was soon abroad that he had been poisoned by the Jacobins. But if there were celebrations in the streets of Paris, the delight of the *émigrés* at Coblenz was no less. Even Fersen in his letters to the Queen was hard put to hide his satisfaction.

Hardly had she dried her tears over Leopold's death when she and Fersen were struck by a far more devastating bolt. On March 16, Gustavus III, the Northern Star, was shot at a masked ball in Stockholm. The circumstances of his assassination well suited this boy-King who so intemperately loved masquerades and the theater. With little alteration Verdi was to use the story for one of his more improbable operas, *Un Ballo in Maschera*. But the truth was more melodramatic than the opera.

For some years the Swedish court had been divided by a sinister rivalry between the witches attached to the service of Gustavus who predicted a continuing glorious reign for him and the sorcerers of his younger brother, the Duke of Södermanland, who had other things to say. The cabalistic scenes taking place at the court of Frederick William of Prussia were as nothing beside those furtively enacted in the *cabinets particuliers* at Drottningholm. Sweden has a long historic tradition of witchcraft and it was perhaps inevitable that the brief moment of enlightenment introduced by Gustavus should be followed by a return to the older ways of the country. In any case, witchcraft as practiced in Stockholm had none of the overtones of buffoonery as in Potsdam. In Sweden they were experts.

Charles, Duke of Södermanland, like many younger brothers of kings, had long resented Gustavus' more brilliant position. He was a prince of shadowy personality whose instability of temperament was not unlike that of the King. In their blood there seems to have been a strong strain of madness. The Duke of Södermanland was ambitious for power but he was discreet. He joined the nobility in deploring his brother's extravagant behavior after Gustavus' return from France in 1784. Gustavus' views about the Revolution in France were another subject of difference between the brothers. In short, the Duke of Södermanland felt that he could run Sweden better than his brother. Gustavus had a son but the boy was a minor in 1792 and under Swedish dynastic law Södermanland, the boy's uncle, would become Regent during his minority. Effective power, power behind the throne, which is often sought by pensive or idealistic men, would thus pass to the Duke of Södermanland should Gustavus die.

The Duke Charles was a man of weak will. But behind him there was a wizard of the name Reuterholm who was an accomplished seer. In a series of strange prophecies—one of which, under a hypnotic trance, was made by Södermanland himself—Reuterholm informed the Duke that God intended him to play an important role in the coming regeneration of mankind.

At the beginning of the Revolution, Reuterholm hurried to Paris to be witness to the "new Deluge" that was to be the Judgment Day of tyrants and to cleanse the earth. At a séance there, held in the Swedish Embassy, a seer revealed that the Duke of Södermanland was "in possession of Truth itself" and that Reuterholm was to be his only instrument. The medium then made a strange prophecy concerning Gustavus, but according to Baron de Staël-Holstein, who was present, it was of such an ominous nature that "I don't dare trust it to my pen."

The threads that connected Paris with Stockholm in 1792 crisscross to form an interesting pattern. The Duchess of Södermanland, for instance, was another of Fersen's conquests. For years she had been in love with him. Her husband was perfectly aware of Fersen's liaison with the Duchess, but he kept his counsel. Events of later years suggest that beneath his impassive exterior he may have been devoured by a terrible rage.

Reuterholm, whom the Voices had appointed the Duke's "only instrument on Earth," was in close contact with all the movements in Paris. Through Staël-Holstein, Gustavus' ambassador, he was put in touch with many of the parties of the Revolution. Staël-Holstein, it will be remembered, had incurred the wrath of Gustavus III at the beginning of the Revolution and was never to regain his trust. Unfortunately, because of the wedding contract with the Necker family, the King was unable to recall him. After Varennes, when the pot in Paris began to boil in earnest, Gustavus and Staël-Holstein came into open conflict. The King sent his ambassador a number of curt letters in which he no longer bothered to conceal his dislike. Staël-Holstein consoled himself by spreading venomous stories about Fersen, whom he knew to be Gustavus' *confident*. ("Staël is saying horrors about me," Fersen wrote the Queen at this time.) By March of 1792 the chasm that divided Reuterholm and Staël-Holstein from Gustavus' party had grown deeper and wider. It is an odd fact that Staël-Holstein, although expressly forbidden by Gustavus to set foot on Swedish soil, arrived in Sweden on March 10 for reasons that have never been made clear. On March 16 Gustavus was shot.

The King's murder had been plotted among the officers of his army and his nobility. The King's predilection for masked balls was well known. Since masks offered a perfect concealment for his assassins it was decided to murder him at a ball. Gustavus was warned by several anonymous letters not to attend the ball. He ignored them.

When the King entered the ballroom he found himself surrounded by a group of dancers, all heavily masked. One of them approached him, put his hand on the King's shoulder and said, "*Bonjour, beau masque.*" It was the signal to the assassin—an officer named Anckarström—to shoot. The King fell but did not die at once. Only after two weeks of suffering did he finally expire. In his agony he saw visions and spoke of Plutarch. "I would speak to the people!" he cried out to his favorite, Armfelt. "Come then and like another Antony let us show the bloody garments of Caesar so that his enemies might be crushed." But in his last hour he spoke less exalted words. "The Jacobins in Paris will rejoice when they hear this news," he stated.

So came to its end the Enlightenment in Sweden.

Overcome by two such losses in less than a month, Marie Antoinette was momentarily stupefied. Fersen was in despair. There was a terrible moment when he suspected that his father might be among the accomplices in the King's murder, for the senior Count Fersen had long been one of Gustavus' most bitter critics. A letter from Taube finally relieved Axel of this apprehension. To the Queen, Fersen wrote: "You have lost in him a firm support and a good ally. I have lost a protector and friend. It is a very cruel loss."

Gustavus' death gave Fersen cause for another worry. Would his mandate as Swedish representative in Brussels be renewed by the Duke of Södermanland, now Regent? As Gustavus' agent at Brussels Fersen had occupied a quasi-official position, with all the remuneration and perquisites that went with it. Should the Regent decide to recognize the Assembly or for other reasons abolish Axel's post he would find himself without revenue or employment. But he assured Marie Antoinette that he was determined to remain at her service even though this should happen. By selling his furniture and moving to poorer accommodations he would be able to stay on in Brussels through the coming summer. "Nothing," he wrote, "could force me to abandon everything at this moment." At last, on April 17, the Regent renewed his appointment.

But by the time Fersen received this news another event had taken place beside which all earlier cataclysms were to pale. War was declared between France and the German powers. The hostilities were to last almost without interruption for twenty years and out of them were to come two dictatorships, the Reign of Terror, and at least three civil wars. The first to fall before the blast was the French royal family, who in less than four months' time were to be swept from the Tuileries and imprisoned in the Temple Tower.

In many books about the Revolution it seems to have been forgotten or overlooked that it was France, not Austria, who began the war—and began it furthermore for the most frivolous of motives. The origin of the war, as with all the momentous events of the Revolution, lay in the political disputes of Paris. In March the party of the Gironde had succeeded that of the Constitutionals. To make themselves indispensable to their country the Girondins were determined to embroil France in a war. No amount of rhetoric could conceal the stark fact, the despicable but all too familiar political tactic. "The French people need a war to consolidate them," Brissot proclaimed before the new Assembly. "They need a war to purge away the vices of despotism and the men who have corrupted them!"

Dulce et decorum est pro patria mori. The Girondins were idealists and it is one of the advantages of idealism that it can be summoned to the support of practically anything. Having urged the French to go to war, the Girondins made it clear that they had no intention of dragging France into a vulgar old-fashioned war of conquest. "We shall fight this war without any desire for territorial acquisition," proclaimed Condorcet. The Assembly greeted his announcement with a burst of applause in which the factional leaders did not join. Robespierre saw the political maneuver behind the Girondin's idealistic posturings and bitterly opposed the war. But when, in not many months' time, he had overthrown the Girondins and sent them to the scaffold, Robespierre, in his turn, became a ferocious advocate of the war. The war became the justification of the repressions of his Committee of Public Safety in May and June of 1794—at a moment, may it be said, when the war had ceased to be a menace to either French sovereignty or the Revolution.

The beginning of war, in short, changed everyone's view of the Revolution and everyone was now forced to make new plans. For Marie Antoinette the war came as a relief. She had carefully refused to solicit armed intervention and even had she done so the German powers would not have responded to her call for help. The Assembly itself had at last done the job for her and the Austrians and Prussians had had their hands forced. It could now only be a matter of a few weeks, a month or two at the most, before troops would arrive in Paris to deliver the French royal family from its captivity. In Marie Antoinette's mind there could be no doubt about who would win any war between the insubordinate and undisciplined French army and the well-drilled troops of the Emperor and the King of Prussia.

The Queen's estimate of the advantages of war soon proved as ill-founded as everyone else's, for first among the effects of the hostilities between Austria and France was a crystallizing of patriotic sentiment against herself. The epithet *l'autrichienne,* coined at Versailles and communicated in all its derogatory sense to the French people by the court nobility, now acquired sinister overtones. With the outbreak of war she became an "enemy alien" in a land caught up in a fever of patriotism. And from that moment she became liable to imprisonment or even death—all on the justifiable grounds of "the national interest." Old suspicions now hardened into open accusations. Stories about an "Austrian Committee" that sat in the Tuileries plotting French ruin circulated through the streets of Paris.

"From here I can see the windows of a palace where they are scheming ways to plunge us back into all the horrors of slavery . . ." So spoke the Girondin Vergniaud before the Assembly. He continued in words that referred unmistakably to Marie Antoinette: "Let those who live in that palace know that our Constitution grants inviolability only to the King. Let them know that the law will reach all who are guilty and that there is not a single head which once convicted can escape its sword!"

Although the Girondins could produce no real proof of the Queen's treasonable thoughts, their suspicions were of course well founded. She did indeed hope that the German armies would enter Paris as soon as possible. On March 30, on the eve of France's formal declaration of war, her treason went beyond mere thoughts and in a ciphered letter she revealed to Fersen the outline of French military plans she had overheard at a council. "They plan to attack through Savoy and the Liège country and hope to gain something this way because the two flanks cannot be protected. It is essential to take precautions on the Liège flank."

Her justification for this act of overt treason would have been that she in no way considered herself Queen of the France of 1792. She was fighting now for her life and the lives of her children against adversaries whom she regarded as insurrectionists, usurpers, and, indeed, brigands. She continued to make a distinction between the *factieux* and the mass of the French people, who were, she believed, in almost as much danger as herself. Somewhere in her mind she probably believed that she was fighting for them, too. But it was the woman and the mother who prayed in her heart for the swift arrival of her country's enemies.

Her sentence about the necessity of protecting the Liège flank constitutes Marie Antoinette's only known act of open treason, but it cannot be doubted that she would have revealed other French military plans had she but known about them and somehow been able to communicate them. After the outbreak of war the vigilance of the guards and spies surrounding her grew so rigorous that her correspondence with the outside world became increasingly sporadic. One of her most important contacts in Paris was broken when Crauford and Éléonore Sullivan returned to Brussels after the declaration of war. Crauford had a dependable housekeeper, one Madame Toscani, who had somehow managed to escape the notice of the police, and henceforth it was through Madame Toscani that the Queen's letters were passed on to Fersen. They were smuggled out of the palace in hat bands or hidden in the bottom of chocolate boxes. Most of them were written in invisible ink or cipher. When she wrote "in clear" she made believe she was the lady friend of a French exile whom she called "Rignon" whose business affairs she was managing. Behind this fiction she was able obliquely to relay certain messages or ideas. But from this moment her letters were necessarily shortened. The curtness of her phrases still communicates a sense of the tension under which they were written.

The royal family's safety now depended on the speed with which the German allies might manage to come to their rescue. In that city torn by angry factional dispute and threatened by foreign invasion their situation had become perilous indeed and every day was of critical importance because every day gave the factions time to muster their own forces and take countermeasures. One day the King and Queen learned that the Jacobins planned to take them to the south beyond the reach of the Austrians and imprison them. Then they heard that they were to be massacred.

Massacre had never been far from Marie Antoinette's thoughts since the return from Varennes. It was fear of massacre that had caused her to recoil from the radical projects of Gustavus III. That possibility had now become acutely real and Marie Antoinette was convinced that if the Allies did not arrive soon she and all her family would be murdered in their palace. On June 19 the King learned of plans to invade the Tuileries. So certain was Louis that the end had finally come that he sent an urgent summons to his confessor requesting the Sacrament. "I am through now with men," he wrote. "I must turn toward God. Great disasters are announced for the morrow. I shall have courage."

On the following day—the first anniversary of Varennes—a mob estimated by some to have been eight thousand and by others twenty thousand broke into the Tuileries. Drawing cannon, bearing pikes, axes, and firearms and exhorted by their leader, a man named Santerre, the invaders smashed their way through locked doors to the center of the palace, where they hoped to find the King. In the moment of confusion when the Tuileries gave way to the assault and the crowd poured in, Marie Antoinette and Louis had been separated. Accompanied by a handful of officials brave enough to remain at his side, the King went upstairs to the Oeil-de-Boeuf to meet those whom he believed to be his assassins. The Queen, persuaded that her presence at his side would only enrage the mob further, hurried to protect her children. Along with three or four of her women she sought refuge in a small concealed passage on the ground floor. Above their heads they could hear sounds of the tumult. Several times the wheels of the cannon crashed through the fragile wood of the inlaid floors with a terrifying effect for those huddled in the rooms below. They had been cowering there for more than an hour when a far more frightening sound was heard. A detachment of some fifty men and women left the main army of invaders and set out in search of Marie Antoinette. In her place of refuge she could hear the doors give way under the blows of their hatchets and then as they grew nearer she could hear them crying for her blood.

"They are going to kill me," she declared. She decided then to meet death at the King's side and most imprudently set out across a public corridor for the Oeil-de-Boeuf, where Louis was held fast by the crowd. She had only advanced a few steps when she was met by a man who refused to let her go any farther.

"Where are you going, Madame?"

"To the King. You must help me reach him, Monsieur. It is with me the people are angry. I am going to offer them their victim."

But the man would not allow her to pass. He told her that to reach the King she would have to make her way through the mob, which would mean certain death. Gently but very firmly he forced her to go with him to the Council Room, which had not yet been invaded, and here with the help of a few grenadiers whom he knew to be dependable he moved a heavy table into a corner of the room. Barricaded behind this table and protected by a handful of men Marie Antoinette and her children waited. It is probable that she did not know the name of the man who thus saved her life. But she was to remember his face and when, in a far more terrible hour, he was again to try to save her, she was to recognize him as a friend. He was the chevalier de Rougeville and his name should be remembered, for he was to be involved in the so-called Plot of the Carnation when, only a few weeks before her execution, a group of men tried to spirit her out of the Prison of the Conciergerie.

It was two hours before the invaders finally discovered the Queen. By then much of their ferocity had blown itself out and the Municipality of Paris had belatedly sent help to the palace. It was proposed that the Queen and her children be put on show. A kind of "barker" was stationed in front of the door leading into the Council Room and the crowd was urged to "come in and see the Queen and the dauphin." Santerre stationed himself next to the table and pointed out the exhibit to those who filed through the room. He also saw that order was maintained.

Witnesses to this scene describe Marie Antoinette as being deathly pale with red-rimmed eyes. But she held her head in that unbending posture that so many people found arrogant and once again her courage, along with that instinctive nobility of gesture that had so impressed Mirabeau and Barnave, held her in good stead. Many who came to insult or injure her left in a different frame of mind. Two different sources relate the story of one fury who shrieked at her, "You are a vile woman!"

"Have I ever done you any harm?" asked Marie Antoinette.

"No, but you are the cause of all the unhappiness of the French people."

"So you have been told, but you have been deceived," answered Marie Antoinette. "I am the wife of the King of France and the mother of the dauphin. I am French and will never again see the country of my birth. I was happy when you loved me."

"Yes," said the woman, "I can see now that I was wrong and that you are a good woman." She burst into tears.

Santerre pushed her away. "She's drunk," he explained.

It was not until after eight in the evening that the crowd finally dispersed, leaving the great rooms "in stupor and solitude." The palace was a wreck, the floors covered by a litter of broken furniture and shattered glass, the doors torn from their hinges or smashed. The King and Queen had survived, but they were under no illusions. It had been a very close shave. "Next time," said Marie Antoinette, "they will murder me and what will become of my children?"

"Next time" was the specter that haunted them after June 21. Marie Antoinette no longer dared sleep at night but would take short catnaps during the day when she knew that either the King or Madame Élisabeth was awake and keeping watch over her children. The thought of "next time" was in all her letters to Fersen and was central to what remained of her *politique*.

"I still exist," she wrote Axel a few days after the invasion of the Tuileries, "but it is by a miracle. It is no longer me they hate.

They want my husband's life and they don't hide it. He showed a strength that has saved matters for the moment but it can happen again at any hour. *Adieu.* Take care of yourself for our sakes . . ."

Then, writing under the guise of the lady friend of the *émigré* "Rignon," she sent out a distress signal to the European Powers. "Your friend is in the gravest danger. His disease is moving with terrifying speed. The doctors no longer recognize him. If you wish to see him again you must make haste. Tell his relatives of his dangerous condition."

As the month of July approached the calls from the sinking ship grew more urgent. "I can write you no more. Tell them to hurry with the help they've promised for our deliverance." In mid-July, Fersen received an even more desperate appeal. "Tell Monsieur de Mercy that the lives of the King and Queen are in the greatest peril and that the delay of so much as a day could cause incalculable harm . . . the band of murderers is growing by the hour."

It was in this atmosphere of urgency that the famous Brunswick Manifesto was conceived. By many historians that proclamation has been described as ill-judged, ill-timed, and a firebrand thrown into a powder keg. But one must remember that it was the direct outcome of Marie Antoinette's fear of massacre. When one has some picture of the situation of the royal family in July of 1792 one can better understand its origins. It was a desperate emergency measure because the King and Queen were convinced that the factions of Paris planned to murder them at the moment their "liberators" approached the city.

The Brunswick Manifesto has been pointed out as one more example of Marie Antoinette's total lack of political acumen, but she had in fact little to do with its wording. She suggested to Fersen that the Allies issue some sort of stern warning to the Paris factions threatening reprisals should the royal family be harmed. Axel did the rest. He was indeed the real author of the Brunswick Manifesto. In concert with a man named Limon, a renegade of the Orléanist faction—and an equivocal partner to say the least—who put Axel's ideas into supple French, Fersen drafted the Manifesto during the first weeks of July. It was finished before the twenty-third of that month and then presented to the Duke of Brunswick, commander of the Prussian and Austrian armies, for his signature. The Duke at first refused to lend his name to so inflammatory a proclamation. Among other threats, the one in Paragraph Five stating that "the inhabitants of towns, villages, and boroughs who may dare defend themselves against the troops of Their Imperial and Royal Majesties . . . will be punished at once with all the rigor of the laws of war and their houses burnt" introduced an interesting new concept of warfare. But the most impolitic paragraph in this highly impolitic document touched on the city of Paris and its inhabitants "without distinction." All members of the National Assembly, all members of the districts, the Municipality, and the National Guard were warned by Their Imperial and Royal Majesties that "they would be held personally responsible for anything that might happen, under peril of their heads and of military execution without hope of pardon." The members of the National Assembly, the Municipality, and districts who among themselves were at daggers drawn instantly cohered as a unit under this threat that condemned them all. Nothing more effectively induces an *esprit de corps* among quarreling men than a common danger. And the Austrians and Prussians who in reality had no intention of burning their fingers on the chestnuts of the King and Queen of France suddenly appeared in French eyes as the agents of Marie Antoinette and Louis XVI. When in the first week of August the contents of the Brunswick Manifesto became known in France a deep and unbridgeable gulf opened between the Tuileries and the rest of the nation. With the publication of the Brunswick Manifesto the dice were cast and only the speedy arrival of the troops who threatened to annihilate Paris could possibly save Louis XVI and Marie Antoinette.

But where, in fact, were those troops? France had declared war in mid-April. It was now the end of July and there was still no sign of any movement on the German frontier. There were no troops, and so far as Austria and Prussia were concerned there appeared to be no war. At Frankfurt the Holy Roman Empire was expiring in a blaze of pageantry. The lords and princes of Germany, their vassals and their guests were more interested in the coronation of Francis II— destined to be the last of the emperors to wear the crown of Charlemagne—than they were in the war. On July 14, when in Paris Louis XVI was going through the anguish of the celebration of the Feast of the Federation, Count Esterházy, Marie Antoinette's old friend of the Trianon days, gave a magnificent banquet and ball attended by the young Clément de Metternich, the future Queen Louise of Prussia, and Madame de Polignac. The troops who were supposed to be marching to the rescue of the French sovereigns were, in fact, on parade in Frankfurt. The spectacle of the well-drilled Prussian army put everyone in a sanguine temper.

Other reasons of a less frivolous kind contributed to Austria's desultory attitude toward the war. The Emperor and his ministers were afraid that Prussia might have come to a secret understanding with Russia on the matter of Poland. The Austrians were afraid that they were being pushed into a war in which they would be left holding the bag while Prussia and Russia would help themselves to Poland. Austria therefore decided to bide her time and make certain when the time came to march that Prussia had as many men and arms committed to the enterprise as herself.

It was not until the first of August that Brunswick finally gave his men orders to march. The Manifesto was promulgated on the same day. Fersen estimated that it would take eight days for the troops to reach the French frontier, and from there he foresaw a swift march on Paris. But his letters betray a profound apprehension. The Manifesto of which he was so proud suddenly frightened him. "The moment of crisis has finally come," he wrote Marie Antoinette on the day the Germans began their march, "and my soul shudders at the thought. May God protect you all. It is my only prayer." Rumors that the Jacobins planned to move the royal family out of Paris filled him with alarm and he advised Marie Antoinette to do everything possible to stay in Paris and await rescue. "Above all, try not to leave Paris. That is the essential point. Then it will be easy to get to you, which is the Duke of Brunswick's plan." Axel's anxiety on this score carried him to curious lengths. In one letter he advised her, should worse come to the worst, to run down to the cellar and hide. "There's a room in the basement underneath M. de Laporte's apartment that people don't know about. You could use that."

As the Allied armies marched into France they met little or no resistance. The French forces were routed at every encounter and retreated in a state of confusion. Fersen's initial anxiety suddenly turned into a transport of optimism. Nothing more forcefully attests to the man's inability to comprehend political realities than his letters to the Queen at this moment. Because of a few victories on the battle-field he supposed that the objective was as good as won. He was certain that it was only a question of a week or two before Brunswick entered Paris and delivered the royal family. To be sure, there was danger of civil disturbance in that volatile city, but the Manifesto would take care of that. His head was already busy with plans founded on the approaching liberation of the King and Queen. "The first thing you will need is money," he wrote Marie Antoinette. "How much do you have in London? You should arrange to have it made available the minute you are free . . . The Duke of Brunswick should be lodged at the palace when he arrives in Paris."

In another letter he went so far as to suggest a few cabinet appointments: "The War Ministry should be given to La Galisonnière, the Marine to du Moutier, Foreign Affairs to Bombelles . . . the Financial Council should be composed of six persons, Daniecourt, Fouache du Havre, and La Tour. I don't remember the others. Tell me as soon as you can what you think of this . . ."

A note of understandable impatience may be detected in Marie Antoinette's answer to this ill-timed bit of advice. She suddenly realized that Fersen had only the remotest picture of the condition of things in Paris. She informed him of the arrival there of the Marseillais, of the collapse of the National Guard, of riots in the Champs-Élysées. "In the midst of so many dangers it is difficult to put our attention on the choice of ministers," she wrote dryly. "If ever we find a moment's peace and quiet I will write you what I think about what you propose, but for the time being we must think about how to avoid daggers and try to struggle with the conspirators who surround a throne that is about to vanish. The factions no longer try to conceal their plan to massacre the royal family. They have only differed as to the means in the last two night meetings. I won't go into it all here. I will only add that if help does not come soon only Providence can save the King and his family."

By August 6, Paris was a caldron. When the news arrived there of the successive defeats of the French army and it was learned that Brunswick's troops were advancing unimpeded through France, political passions, already hot, rose to a boiling point. It was clear that if the Revolution and France were to be saved the government would need a firmer hand at the helm than that of the weak Girondin-dominated Assembly. Danton and his followers were determined at this moment of crisis to seize control of the state and bring the war to a successful conclusion. On the night of August 9–10, after those "secret preparations" to which Marie Antoinette makes reference in her letter to Fersen, this able and energetic leader summoned all the violent forces of Paris and with one blow of his massive fist smashed the Assembly, the Municipality of Paris, and the Throne. The *coup d'état* was total and the French Revolution from that moment took a

15. Marie Antoinette and her children. Portrait painted by Vigée-Lebrun.
THE BETTMANN ARCHIVE.

16. "I breathe only for you …a kiss, sweet angel!" Marie Antoinette and the duchesse de Polignac. An engraving used for the advertisement of a play called *The Destruction of the Aristocracy* given at Chantilly in 1789.
COLLECTION VIOLLET.

17. The assassination of Gustavus III. A nineteenth-century illustration that resembles Verdi's operatic version of the event more than it does the event itself. THE BETTMANN ARCHIVE.

18. Varennes: the capture of Louis XVI and his family. THE BETTMANN ARCHIVE.

19. Return of Louis XVI and his family to Paris after their arrest at Varennes. THE BETTMANN ARCHIVE.

20. Marie Antoinette, age thirty-five, as painted by Kucharski in 1791-92, soon after Varennes. This portrait was never finished. When the palace of the Tuileries was sacked in June of 1792 one of the invaders drove a pikeshaft through the canvas. The gash can still be seen in the lower left-hand corner. COLLECTION VIOLLET.

21. Louis XVI and his family are conducted to the Temple on August 13, 1792 (after a French print of the period). THE BETTMANN ARCHIVE.

22. The royal family at dinner in the King's room at the Temple Tower. A representative of the Municipality has just entered and is informing them that it is three o'clock and time, therefore, for the women to leave. The man putting the chicken on the table may be Turgy. COLLECTION VIOLLET.

23. The separation of Louis XVI from his family. A highly romanticized version. THE BETTMANN ARCHIVE.

24. Louis XVI at the time of the trial a few weeks before his death. Pastel portrait by Joseph Ducreux. THE BETTMANN ARCHIVE.

25. The Widow Capet at the Conciergerie, age thirty-seven. THE BETTMANN ARCHIVE.

26. The Queen leaving the court-
room after hearing her condemnation.
A nineteenth-century version. THE
BETTMANN ARCHIVE.

27. A photograph of the Queen's
cell at the Conciergerie as it appears today. The altar was added
in the nineteenth century and the
room enlarged to make place for
it. Nothing except a bit of the
floor is original. Even the window
has been enlarged and altered.
THE BETTMANN ARCHIVE.

28. Marie Antoinette seated on the plank of a tumbrel being led to her execution. This is the famous eyewitness sketch by David. COLLECTION VIOLLET.

different course. On the political level, Danton's seizure of the Municipality of Paris, known henceforth as the Commune, was the most important event of the evening, for the control of the Revolution now fell into the hands of the city of Paris. Danton explained the matter succinctly: "In times of Revolution power will always go to the strongest and we are now the strongest." The Commune, in other words, had ammunition and it commanded the populace of Paris.

The assault on the palace was of a more dramatic character and the attention of posterity is generally drawn to that spectacle. It took place in the early hours of August 10. All through that hot night the occupants of the Tuileries had heard the tocsin clanging its immemorial summons to arms. The bells of St. Germain l'Auxerrois behind the Louvre, those bells that two hundred years earlier had opened the massacre of St. Bartholomew's Night, sent out their call again. The moment Marie Antoinette had so long dreaded had come at last. The King did not undress that night. Fully clothed, he lay down from time to time and tried to nap. The Queen wandered from room to room. One hope remained and it was not a small one: the palace had arms and ammunition. The King's Swiss Guard, last of the proprietary regiments, was still loyal. It was possible that the National Guard on duty at the Tuileries could be exhorted to defend the palace—in the name of the Constitution if not of the King. With sufficient resolve, the Tuileries could very probably defend itself. Marie Antoinette therefore went about trying to instill others with her own determination to fight and, should fate so will it, to go down banners flying with the ship. It is the opinion of those who have examined the matter as a military operation that the Tuileries might have withstood the approaching assault if only the Paris militia had remained loyal. But Danton had caused their commandant to be murdered on the steps of the City Hall that night and the militia, from the moment of his death, took its orders from the leaders of the Insurrectionary Commune, who were appointed by Danton.

If only . . . At bottom those words constitute the whole story of Marie Antoinette's life. If only, too, the King had been able or willing to inspire those who would have defended him that night with some of his wife's courage the issue would have been different. But once again Louis refused to shed the blood of his subjects. At this critical moment—the last in which he would be confronted with that painful choice between violence and submission—he could not bring himself to act. He had long since "had done with men" and he

231

preferred now to abandon himself to the will of the God in whom he still believed.

So all through that night they waited for the first wave of the assault. At four Madame Élisabeth went to the Queen and, touching her gently on the shoulder, said, "Come, Sister. Let us watch the dawn break." The two women stood at a window overlooking the garden of the Tuileries and watched the sun rise in a red mid-August sky.

Less than two hundred miles away that same dawn broke over the Allied armies as they awoke and prepared to continue their slow march on Paris. In faraway Brussels, where Fersen, Mercy, and the Queen's other friends anxiously awaited news from the front, there was still no hint of the uprising in Paris, but Axel must have felt intimations of the disaster, for that very day he wrote Marie Antoinette in a far different tone than his earlier letters. All at once he wished that he had advised her to leave Paris. "I am profoundly worried about you. I haven't had a moment's peace and my only comfort is to have my anxiety shared by M. Crauford, who only thinks of you and of ways to help you . . . I very much regret that you are not out of Paris."

To the end and *in extremis* Axel persisted in his gallant lies. In truth, it was not Crauford who shared his anxiety. As the confidences of his Journal reveal, it was Éléonore Sullivan who was his support during those troubled hours, as she was to be in the months of anguish to come. The two were now inseparable and Axel scarcely troubled to hide the fact that it was in one another's arms that they assuaged their apprehensions.

This was Fersen's last letter to Marie Antoinette and she never received it. It survives as a copy made in Axel's hand. So far as is known, no other letters were ever exchanged between them, although through a third person Marie Antoinette was able to send him a few verbal messages.

At seven thirty in the morning, before even a shot had been fired, Louis decided to abandon the palace and to seek shelter with his family at the nearby Assembly. The King's well-known fear of bloodshed lay behind this decision, for he naïvely supposed that after he had left the Tuileries there would be no further reason to attack it. Louis' well-intentioned measures to avoid one ill only opened the door to evils far worse. He was later accused of abandoning those who comprised his household, the Swiss Guard, and the palace servants, and of delivering them unprotected to the massacre.

He and his family left the palace without ceremonial but quite openly. Accompanied by an armed guard, they went down the main stairway into the garden, which they crossed on foot to reach the Manège. It was here at the corner of the present rue de Rivoli and the rue de Castiglione that the Assembly sat in agitated session that morning. The royal family was greeted with an assurance from the President that they could count on the Assembly's protection. They were then escorted to a small box, not much bigger than a cupboard, behind the President's chair, which was normally occupied by the Assembly's stenographers. They were to be confined in this hot and airless room for nearly fifteen hours while they heard their fate being discussed by the deputies. Outside, from the direction of the garden, the sound of cannon and musket fire informed them of the assault on the Tuileries. Persuaded that further defense of the palace was unnecessary and that by laying down arms the Swiss might secure amnesty, Louis wrote them a hurried order to cease fire. It was the last order he was to sign as King of France. This interesting document may be examined today in the Musée Carnavalet in Paris. It was in actuality the death warrant of the Swiss Guard and many of the other occupants of the palace. Soon afterward the mob rushed in and a terrible slaughter began. The journalist Mercier has left an account of the appalling carnage. "To the servants in particular the horde showed no mercy. They, poor souls, had not thought of flying. Many indeed were imbued with Revolutionary doctrine and little dreamt that the rage of the populace would be turned against themselves. They remained calmly at their work in the midst of which the drunken mob surprised them . . . every man from the head chefs to the humblest scullion perished."

Louis and his family spent that night in a cell at the Convent of the Feuillants that adjoined the Manège. On the following day they were escorted back to the little stenographers' box at the Manège where they heard the Assembly dissolve itself and propose elections to a new body without a king to be called the National Convention. Impassively they listened to a long debate about their future residence. The Assembly proposed the Luxembourg, where, dethroned and stripped of all the regalia of his office, Louis could await the new government's decision about his fate, which even the most radical deputies of the Assembly supposed would be the banishment from France of himself, his family, and his descendants in perpetuity.

But the new masters of the Revolution, the men of Danton's

Insurrectionary Commune, now stepped forward and flexed their muscles. It was the men of the Commune who had stormed the palace and toppled the tyrant. They now demanded jurisdiction over their prize. This was the first of many coming struggles between the Paris Commune and the French National representation and its outcome prefigured all those that were to follow. The deputies glimpsed the knife and quailed. When the Commune's spokesman proposed sending the former royal family to the Temple they made only one attempt to save face. They affected to believe that the Commune meant the palace of the Temple and not its donjon. They then handed Louis and his family over to the authority of the city of Paris.

The Temple, which in the literature of the French Revolution is so inseparably identified with the captivity of Louis XVI and Marie Antoinette, no longer stands. It was razed in 1808 by order of the Emperor Napoleon, who wished so evocative a monument of his predecessor's suffering—a suffering that in the eyes of Napoleon's political enemies might readily be transformed into martyrdom—destroyed.

At the time of the Revolution it stood in the heart of the old quarter of Paris known as the Marais at no great distance from that other *monument historique,* also vanished, the Bastille. It had once been the residence of the Priors of the Knights Templar, words that evoke the medieval flavor of its origins, but in the enlightened years of the eighteenth century it had been occupied successively by the prince de Conti and the comte d'Artois. The palace was of seventeenth-century construction, commodious, austerely elegant, and furnished with all the attributes of what then constituted graceful living. But the Temple was a vast compound, and surrounding the palace there were a number of outbuildings and dependencies that belonged to an earlier time. Among these, far at the end of the gardens, was the donjon and keep. This building, one of the many vestiges of feudal times that were to be found in eighteenth-century Paris, was known as the Temple Tower. It was a square, turreted edifice, sixty feet high, of dark and forbidding appearance. Its interior was composed of four identical floors, each a hall whose ogival vaults were supported by a central stone shaft. The floors were connected by a narrow stairway that wound in the medieval manner through one of the towers. The walls of this donjon were ten feet thick.

Marie Antoinette already knew the Temple well, for in happier times the comte d'Artois had sometimes entertained her there at supper parties after the opera. It is related that at one of these receptions she glimpsed the Tower looming at the far end of the garden, shuddered, and implored her brother-in-law to tear it down. But her shudder was probably more that of the woman of fashion, the arbiter of the Petit Trianon, than of one endowed with second sight. Buildings of medieval origin such as the Temple Tower were looked upon with distaste by advocates of the neo-Classic mode. Fashion probably wrought more destruction on Gothic art in France than the Religious Wars and the Revolution combined.

When, as the light was beginning to fade, the French royal family arrived at the Temple that evening it never crossed their minds that their destination was to be the Tower rather than the palace. They were served an elaborate meal—in even its worst temper the Commune was never to stint on the food—in the Salle des Quatre Glaces, where the comte d'Artois used to receive the Queen. That the men who served this repast were in shirtsleeves or attired in "the dirtiest and most disgusting clothes" was only one reminder of their fallen state. Outside in the hot, fetid streets of the Marais, the Marseillais and the men and women of the Commune gathered from the far quarters of Paris to drink and celebrate.

The men of the Commune were not all without pity and among those who presided over the fallen family's supper table that night none could summon the courage to tell them that after the festivities they were to be taken to the Tower. Pétion, the mayor of Paris and compliant puppet of the Insurrectionary Commune—shortly to have his own throat cut by these new masters—could not find it in his heart to inform Louis of the fact, so in the middle of the supper he went to the Hôtel de Ville and suggested to the officials of the Commune that the palace rather than the keep should be the place of their prisoners' incarceration. But the Commune was adamant. To the Tower they must go.

So, at one o'clock in the morning, under armed guard, they were conducted across the garden to the donjon that they were only to leave to go to their trials and death. Even at this extreme moment they were accompanied by a handful of devoted friends and attendants, the last to remain of a retinue that once comprised a great court. With the Queen there was Madame de Tourzel, the princesse de Lamballe (who a few months before and in defiance of Marie Antoinette's orders had returned from a safe and comfortable exile abroad to be by her friend's side in time of need), and a Madame Augié. With the King there were his two valets, Hue and Chamilly, while another valet, Cléry, accompanied the dauphin. On the following day the *ci-devant* royal family was stripped of even this frail remnant of disinterested devotion and by order of the Commune their servitors were evicted from the Tower and placed under arrest. When she bade farewell to Madame de Lamballe, Marie Antoinette could no longer control her tears and the two friends embraced one another for a long time. The women were then taken to the prison of La Force. Two of the valets, Cléry and Hue, were soon released and allowed to return to the service of the King and dauphin at the Tower.

To do the "hard work" of the household the Commune appointed two domestics of its own. These were a man and a woman known as the Tison couple. They were an irascible, unhappy pair whom certain writers have called "abominable." The word is surely too strong. Through the haze of time and conflicting descriptions one seems to discern their true outline, which is not dissimilar to a certain kind of concierge or bureaucrat to be found in Paris today. They were disagreeable and inaccessible to the promptings of sentimentality or affection, but they were far from being the sadistic monsters some have declared them to have been. In addition to their domestic chores at the Temple they were employed by the Commune to spy on the prisoners. Indeed, they were ordered to submit a daily report of everything that passed at the Temple and to notice any happenings, however small or insignificant, that seemed unusual. Marie Antoinette disliked them on sight and knew at once that these were people whom she could never win by kindly words or noble gestures.

After the long months they had spent at the Tuileries under the constant menace of invasion the royal family at first found their confinement behind the walls of the Temple Tower something of a relief. Here, at least, they were safe from massacre. Their fate was now out of their hands and they took comfort in this sudden relief from all responsibility. The sounds of Paris rarely penetrated the thick walls of their prison. It was the Commune's tactic to keep them cut off from all communication with the outside world. Thus they were ignorant of events that were taking place in the city and they had no idea how near or far away the armies of the Duke of Brunswick might be.

They soon settled down to a daily routine tailored to their new circumstances. In the mornings, after he had dressed and said his prayers, Louis would instruct his son in Latin, history, and geography. The seven-year-old boy was unusually bright and he responded quickly to his father's supervision. Indeed, today one can still appreciate the improvement in his handwriting, for the Musée Carnavalet has kept several of his exercise books. When the lessons were finished Louis and the dauphin would join the rest of the family for dinner, a copious meal that ended toward three o'clock. Marie Antoinette and Madame Élisabeth occupied themselves with the education of the young Princess. Between times the ladies embroidered or read aloud to one another. After the noon meal Louis and Marie Antoinette would play backgammon. Were it not for the constant presence of armed guards in the room with them it would have been a placid and even pleasant existence for this family of essentially *bourgeois* inclination. But on September 3 they were given a terrible reminder that beyond their prison the tempest still howled.

Louis and Marie Antoinette had settled down to their after-dinner game of backgammon when they heard a great hubbub below their window. It was a sound they already knew well—that of the mob. All at once there was a piercing shriek and a moment later the valet Cléry, his eyes glazed with horror, rushed into the room and tried to close the curtains. He looked at the Queen but could not tell her what he had just seen—the head of the princesse de Lamballe at the end of a pike. He and the Tison couple were at lunch when this terrible object had been waved before their window. Madame Tison had shrieked and the crowd, crazed with the madness which feeds on blood, howled with joy, for in the Tison woman's scream of horror they thought they recognized the voice of the Queen.

As the cries below grew louder, the municipal guards, as ashen as Cléry, appeared in the room. One of them told Louis that the crowd had gathered because they had heard that he and his family had left the Tower. But another officer was more blunt-spoken and in the coarsest words told them what was afoot: "It is the head of the Lamballe which they have brought here to show you and to make you kiss. This is how the people takes its revenge on tyrants."

"Frozen with horror," Marie Antoinette heard his words, then fell to the floor unconscious. Her daughter was afterward to recall that this was the only moment when her mother's courage failed her. All through that night the Princess could hear her mother's sobs. The unhappy woman was more fortunate than she realized, for she was spared full knowledge of the circumstances of her friend's death. The details of the September Massacres never reached her ears.

The princesse de Lamballe was in fact only one of more than fifteen hundred men and women who were butchered by the hired murderers of the Paris Commune between September 2 and September 8. These appalling massacres, which conventionally and quite incorrectly are attributed to popular effervescence brought about by the advancing armies of the Duke of Brunswick, were in reality part of a coldly considered and carefully executed plan of the Paris Commune. "Popular effervescence" was the justification, not the reason, for the September Massacres. The registers of the Commune, examined and published in extract by Granier de Cassagnac, show that the assassins were hired by the Commune at twenty-four livres each and were recruited in large part from murderers and felons convicted under the old Commune who were released from prison by the new. Some days before the massacres the leaders of the Insurrectionary Commune dominated by Danton and Marat had drawn up a list of those whom they called "suspects": a number of priests who had not abjured and a great number of the private political enemies of the sectional leaders. These men and women were rounded up shortly before the massacres and put into prison to await a fate that had already been decreed. By this means Marat hoped to net a number of the Girondins, whom he loathed, but thanks to the intercession of Danton their names were stricken from the list of the proscribed.

The Commune's purpose behind these mass murders was to show to all France Paris' ascendancy over the Revolution and to intimidate the newly elected deputies from the provinces, soon to arrive in the capital city. The electoral returns from the countryside reflected a strong disposition to conservatism, but in Paris the Commune emerged triumphant. The September Massacres were its implement.

The massacres may have been planned in cold blood but they were executed with a savagery that places them beyond the pale of human understanding. Night and day for five days the slaughter continued and the prisons emptied. One by one the victims would be led from their cells to the courtyard of the prison, where, after the semblance of an interrogation or hearing, they were butchered like cattle. At night these scenes of horror were illuminated by torches.

During the day the victim soon to be murdered could see the corpses of those who had preceded him stacked like cordwood on the other side of the table where sat his "judges." The sounds that accompanied this carnage are said to have been indescribably terrible. The screams of the victims mingled with the howls of the butchers and the groans of the wounded and dying. The slaughter was indiscriminate. At the prison of Bicêtre, traditionally the prison of the poor of Paris, one hundred and seventy unfortunates, many of them beggars and the harmless castoffs of society, were put to the sword. Among their number were thirty-three boys between the ages of twelve and fourteen. The atrocities committed at Salpêtrière, another prison of the people, were worse. Here girls of ten were murdered. "If you knew the terrible details!" wrote Madame Roland about Salpêtrière. "Women brutally violated before being torn to pieces by these tigers . . . you know my enthusiasm for the Revolution; well now I am ashamed of it; it has been dishonored by this scum and it has become hideous to me." Madame Roland, who less than three months earlier had instigated the invasion of the Tuileries and who had never hesitated to avail herself of the services of the "scum" that suddenly filled her with such indignation, underwent a change of mind as soon as the tiger's breath brushed her own back.

Of the scenes enacted not far from the windows of the Temple Tower, Marie Antoinette and Louis XVI remained largely ignorant. The Queen never knew that her "dear heart" of the Trianon days had met a more terrible end than all the others, that she had been disemboweled, her heart devoured and her intestines trailed through the streets of Paris to the palace of her brother-in-law, the duc d'Orléans, who now styled himself Philippe-Égalité. But for Marie Antoinette the death of the princesse de Lamballe was another long step into the darkness and when, after that night of weeping, she arose on the following day she had aged by many years. Despite the efforts of the Commune to keep the prisoners incommunicado and out of touch with the happenings of the world, news still reached them within the Tower. The King's valet Cléry was able to come and go from the prison with a certain freedom, and through a series of movements of the fingers that they had agreed upon he conveyed the news without words. Another source of information was a kitchen boy, Turgy, who brought them their food every day. This man, who had once been employed in the kitchens of Versailles and the Tuileries, was to prove a remarkable friend. In the days when the court

239

had been at Versailles, Marie Antoinette could not have been expected to notice this obscure scullion, one of hundreds employed in the vast kitchens of the palace. But Turgy was at heart an ardent royalist and an admirer of the Queen. He followed the court when it moved to the Tuileries in October of 1789.

Turgy did not lodge at the palace and thus he escaped the massacre of the servants that took place there on August 10. When he arrived at the Tuileries that morning the battle had already begun. He turned from the smoking palace and accompanied by two fellow kitchen boys tried to make his way into the Convent of the Feuillants, where the King and Queen were temporarily lodged. In this he was unsuccessful, but when he learned that the royal family was to be incarcerated in the Temple he managed by a number of ruses to get himself appointed to the kitchen there. He told the commissioners of the Commune that he had been sent there by the Assembly with the approval of his section leaders. He then told his section leaders that the Commune had appointed him. In the confusion of the hour no one bothered to verify these credentials and soon it was taken for granted that Turgy and his two friends were officially employed at the Tower.

Sometime in early September he managed to indicate to the prisoners that he was their friend. It was Turgy's job to lay the table and serve them their meals. This was done under the close scrutiny of the municipal officers. Before every meal they would come to the serving room, where the dishes were prepared and tasted in front of them so that they might be sure nothing was concealed in them. Decanters and coffeepots were filled in their presence, and the table could not be set until it had been inspected above and below. Even the rolls were torn in half and the crumbs probed to make sure that no messages had been hidden within. Despite this vigilance Turgy was able to communicate with the royal family. At a turning in the stairway he would insert a message in the stopper of a decanter. Sometimes he would wrap his note in a piece of weighted paper and throw it into a pitcher of milk or almond water. There were times when out of earshot of the Tison couple and the guards he was able to murmur a few words to Madame Élisabeth and the Queen. Through these messages they finally established a system of signals whereby news of the outside world could be communicated more speedily. Many years afterward Turgy recalled a number of these that had been given to him in Madame Élisabeth's handwriting.

If the Austrians are successful on the Belgian frontier, place the second finger of the right hand on the right eye. If they are entering the country by the way of Lille or from the direction of Mayence, use the third finger as above.

Be sure to keep the finger stationary for a longer or shorter time according to the importance of the battle.

When they are within fifteen leagues of Paris follow the same order for the fingers but be careful to place them on the mouth. If the Powers should be concerning themselves with the royal family touch the hair with the fingers of the right hand. If the Convention should pay any attention to them use the left hand . . .

Clearly the royal family was far from abandoning hope and, as the drift of Turgy's signals indicates, that hope was based on the arrival of the Allied armies.

At first the news was heartening. Brunswick's men continued their advance toward Paris without resistance. One day a guard burst in with the news that Verdun had just fallen and, shaking his fist at them, told them that they would be murdered before the Germans reached Paris. From Verdun, Brunswick's armies marched into the country of the Argonne, where misfortune had already struck the Bourbons. Stenay, where in June of the previous year Louis had hoped to reach Bouillé's forces, was taken. Then on September 19 Brunswick reached Valmy, a few miles off the road that the royal family had taken to Varennes, near Ste. Menehould where Drouet had begun his celebrated ride in pursuit of the King. And here the last hopes of Louis XVI and Marie Antoinette were extinguished, for at Valmy the Allied armies were routed by the French.

It is with reason that Valmy has been labeled one of the decisive battles of history. Goethe, who was witness to the engagement, declared with the insight of a seer that "From this place and from this day forth begins a new era in the world's history and all who were here today can say they were present at its birth." Armed with little more than the principles of Liberty, Equality, and Fraternity the newborn army of the French Republic decisively defeated the drilled regiments of the Old World, a world of powdered wigs and snuffboxes in which the quarterings of nobility represented an officer's principal credentials.

But this battle of such historic import, from which in Goethe's eyes the modern world was born and which in Paris sealed the doom of Louis XVI, is also one of the most tantalizing mysteries in history. For in actuality there was no military engagement at Valmy. After a few rounds of bombardment the Duke of Brunswick without a word of explanation ordered a retreat. This extraordinary act has been attributed by some to bad weather and an outbreak of dysentery among the German troops. Others have declared that patriotism and a love of liberty imbued the Republican armies with an *esprit de corps* that suddenly permitted them to triumph over the invaders. Both explanations are insufficient. Dysentery and bad weather were old companions to these men, who had fought in the distant corners of Europe. They were fixed factors in eighteenth-century battle and it is very unlikely that at Valmy, so near Paris, they might have arrested the advance of Brunswick's troops. With all due credit to an enthusiasm for liberty, it seems odd that it had been of no help to the French armies at Longwy, Verdun, or any other battlefields along the line of the Prussian advance. In any case, since there was no true military engagement at Valmy there was no need for any particular valor on the part of the French.

The explanation of Valmy must be looked for elsewhere and for some years a strange conjecture has tantalized those who share Balzac's view of the back stairs of history. Since Marie Antoinette's end is so intimately interbound with the defeat of the Austrian and Prussian armies at Valmy, this conjecture must be touched upon. Examined in the light of the Queen's private fate, it is made the more interesting by the reappearance of a motif or theme that had once before entered into the pattern of her life. Diamonds, those jewels that played so fatal a role in her destruction, may perhaps be the explanation of the Allied defeat at Valmy.

The Duke of Brunswick was a curious man. Although he was a sovereign prince and endowed with a vast fortune that permitted him to indulge a notable inclination for luxurious living, he was a partisan of the new ideas in France and his court, like that of Frederick William of Prussia, swarmed with mediums and Illuminati. Certain of these men had brought him into contact with the factional leaders of Paris. In the inner circles of the Jacobin Club his name was regarded with respect—with so much respect indeed that Brunswick had been offered command of the French army—with the possibility of the French Crown as a reward—before he assumed command of the German armies. At the very moment he signed the inflammatory Manifesto that bears his name, the following singular paragraph appeared in one of Paris' revolutionary gazettes: "There is nothing more stupid than those who believe and who would like to make others believe that the Prussians intend the destruction of the Jacobins . . . If the Duke of Brunswick reaches Paris I would wager that his first act will be to visit the Jacobin Club and don the red cap of Liberty!"

Brunswick's closest contact with the extremists of Paris was an individual named Carra, a fervent Jacobin, a political adventurer and —the important fact in this story—an intimate friend of the man who in the *coup d'état* of August 10 had seized effective control of the Revolution—Danton. It was Danton who exhorted the French people to "audacity and still more audacity" in order to expel the invaders from French soil and it was Danton who announced that he would have recourse to any means whatsoever to bring the war to a successful conclusion. This statement was made at about the time that there took place one of the most sensational jewel robberies in all history.

The diamonds of the French Crown had always been a worthy complement to the outward magnificence of the Bourbon monarchy. In the course of three reigns this collection had come to include the largest and most splendid stones in the world, among them the famous "Regent," a diamond of 137 carats, the "Sancy," the "Tavernier," the "Dragon," and a stone known as the "Blue Diamond of the Golden Fleece," a particular favorite of Louis XIV that weighed 115 carats. These were but the more spectacular stones in a treasure trove that was the envy of every crowned head in Europe. At the time the monarchy was moved to Paris the crown jewels were inventoried and placed under lock and key in the royal warehouse in Paris. The inventory ran to many pages and listed such articles as Anne of Brittany's rubies, the diamond-studded sword of Francis I, and a great quantity of brooches, necklaces, and rings that had belonged to Marie Antoinette and the earlier queens of France. Their value in all was placed at more than twenty-five million of today's dollars—no mean sum for a country in bankruptcy and at war.

Between September 10 and September 16, in the course of four different raids, the French crown jewels were systematically stolen. The robberies were effected at night. The Garde-Meuble—or royal warehouse—was in the building on the Place de la Concorde that now houses the Ministry of the Marine. The complicity of the police —or of persons highly placed within the police—becomes more and more evident as one examines the details of this affair. The thieves simply lowered their haul in baskets over the colonnades of that façade of the building which faces the square. One evening they dined in the very room where they were packing up their loot.

On the night of September 14 the Blue Diamond of the Golden

Fleece was stolen. Three days later, on the seventeenth, the man Carra was sent by the Paris Commune to the line of battle, where Dumouriez, commander of the French forces, was about to meet Brunswick in combat. It so happened that Brunswick and Dumouriez were old friends, and under the flag of truce they had already met and had an exchange of sociabilities. The question that now presents itself is: did Carra and Brunswick also meet during the two days that preceded Valmy? And in the course of that meeting, as the price of a strategic retreat, did Carra offer Brunswick the Blue Diamond of the Golden Fleece which he had brought with him from Paris? The question appears preposterous only because one assumes that the great turning points of history must have causes proportionate to their gravity. But, in fact, it is far from impertinent. The Duke of Brunswick, it may be argued, was a very rich man, the owner of countless *châteaux*, the recipient of annual revenues that permitted him to indulge his every whim. What need had this man, whose palace doors were of malachite and ivory, to sell himself in so dangerous and despicable a negotiation? But that precisely is the point. There are objects beyond the reach of the richest men and these are exactly the objects that acquire a special luster in rich men's eyes, especially if that man happens to be a collector. The Duke of Brunswick was in fact a collector, and a collector furthermore of diamonds. The possibility that Brunswick may have acquired the celebrated Blue Diamond by the defeat at Valmy becomes something more than idle speculation when one knows that the Blue Diamond of the Golden Fleece that had so mysteriously disappeared from the French Garde-Meuble in 1792 was listed in the inventory of the Duke of Brunswick's collection when that prince died in 1806. Sometime between those two dates the Duke of Brunswick in secrecy had acquired the famous stone. That he probably acquired it at a date anterior to 1795 is suggested by the fact that it was minus a forty-carat chunk when it was discovered after the Duke's death. The missing piece was found to be among the jewels that his daughter Caroline had brought to England with her at the time of her marriage in 1795 to the future George IV. That piece is now known as the Hope Diamond.

Taken in their *ensemble*, these scattered bits of information form an impressive body of evidence, but they can never be construed as proof of Brunswick's venality. The Duke himself had the last and perhaps the most suggestive word about the whole matter. "No one," he declared, "will ever know the real reason for the defeat at Valmy."

Valmy was far more than a single battle lost. For the newborn French Republic it was the turning of that tide which "taken at the full leads on to fortune." The advance of Brunswick's army on Paris had been made at a leisurely and confident pace. Their retreat was more hurried. Driving the enemy off French soil, the armies of the Convention repossessed themselves of their historic bastions of Verdun, Longwy, and Mayence. By the first week of November the French began pouring over the borders of Belgium and the Austrian Lowlands, carrying the principles of the Revolution along with their cannon into the heart of Old Europe.

In Brussels, Fersen, Crauford, Madame Sullivan, and the comte de Mercy learned of Brunswick's capitulation with incredulity and consternation. It seemed to them inexplicable. "His astonishing behavior can only bring a terrible blame down on him!" cried the baron de Breteuil. "He is lower than the mud." Others echoed these sentiments in stronger words. The rumor spread among the *émigrés* that Brunswick had accepted a bribe of five million francs to lose the battle. Accusations and recriminations flew about like bullets. But the Duke of Brunswick and, strangely enough, the King of Prussia remained unperturbed by the shouting. Brunswick's attitude, allowing the possibility that he had the Blue Diamond tucked in his pocket, is understandable. But the King's indifference demands some explanation. Frederick William had been at Valmy in person, wearing his sword, his decorations, and his jewels. How could he have looked down on this ignominious defeat of his famous forces in so equable a frame of mind?

The reason is that Poland, not Valmy, was the principal preoccupation of Frederick William and his ministers. The march on Paris was little more than a feint in his eyes, a kind of flexing of the limbs preparatory to some real military engagement. In Paris there was no territory to be gained. Any aggrandizement of his kingdom would have to be realized afterward by bartering with the Austrians. Poland was another matter. Her borders fronted those of Prussia and her rich lands were of military as well as economic significance. The thought that Catherine might help herself to a slice of this pie was a source of constant worry to the King of Prussia and his ministers. Their anxiety proved well founded, for on the very day that Brunswick and his troops entered France, Catherine ordered her armies to march into Poland. The picture of the Russians working with a free hand in the territory that the Prussian King considered to be a geographic annex of Prussia cast a shadow over Brunswick's first victories in France.

The defeat at Valmy was therefore of no great consequence to Frederick William II. He had other plans for those troops engaged in the chimeric mission of trying to rescue the King and Queen of France. The minute the *débâcle* in France was finished he ordered his men into Poland, where they were told to take as much land as they could. What did it matter to the King of Prussia that Frenchmen by the thousands—soldiers of a republic that was the enemy of kings —streamed over the French frontier into Europe? It was Austrian territory they occupied. As the citadels of the Netherlands fell before the French onslaught, Frederick William could even congratulate himself on the happy turn of events. The Habsburgs would have their hands tied in the Netherlands when he joined the Empress Catherine in the plunder of Poland.

Few in Brussels had time to fathom the depths of Prussian treachery. The administrative capital of the Austrian Netherlands was thrown into a state approaching frenzy as word arrived there of the French advance. Fersen refused to believe that the Austrian army could be beaten on its own soil and the comte de Mercy was of the same opinion. On the afternoon of November 6 the weather was unusually fine and Axel, Éléonore Sullivan, and the Russian minister M. de Simolin took a little airing in the woods outside Brussels. All at once, coming from the direction of Mons, they heard the sound of far-off artillery fire. They had dinner that evening at Crauford's house. The comte de Mercy, who was among the guests, assured them that the sound they had heard was nothing more than the celebration of St. Charles's Day. In the middle of the meal a royal courier suddenly arrived requesting Mercy's presence at the palace. The diplomat was gone for more than an hour. When he returned his expression was veiled. He assured everyone that the sound of gunfire they had heard that afternoon was "only a little disturbance at one of the outposts."

In reality the Regent of the Netherlands—Marie Antoinette's sister, the Archduchess Maria Christina—had just informed Mercy of a crushing defeat of the Austrian army at Mons and of the imminent arrival of the French in Brussels. She advised him to pack his belongings and, like her and her husband, take flight as quickly as possible. She also advised him to keep the fact a secret in order to prevent panic in the city. It was not until the following day, therefore, that the news became generally known. The comte de Mercy was already en route to exile. Just before leaving he advised his friends to join him at Düsseldorf.

Fersen, Éléonore, Crauford, and M. de Simolin were not able to leave until the ninth. By then the city was in the throes of that panic which the Archduchess Maria Christina had foreseen. The French *émigrés,* most of whom had been proscribed by the Revolutionary government, were in a terrible state. Without funds, without influence in high places, they had to flee the city on foot and carry their few valuable possessions with them in bundles attached to the end of a pole, which they put over their shoulders. The roads leading out of Brussels were clogged with fleeing humanity: noblemen and farmers, the old and the young, the rich and the poor were all tossed together in this stream. It was a scene that prefigured countless others that were to occur during the next one hundred and eighty years in a Europe convulsed by war and conflicting creeds.

Crauford, Éléonore, and Simolin left in a carriage whose roof was piled high with luggage. Axel rode alongside on horseback. They went first to Louvain, then to Tongres, where they had to sleep on straw pallets on the floor of a stable. From Tongres they reached Maestricht, where more than eleven thousand other refugees had sought shelter. So began their wanderings throughout the provinces of Germany.

They had not left Brussels too soon. Led by Dumouriez, the French armies entered the city only a few days later. And with the fall of Brussels the whole of the Austrian Netherlands capitulated. There then ensued scenes of looting, rape, and bloodshed that were in the age-old tradition of military conquest. Those naïve Belgians who believed the high-flown mouthings of Vergniaud and his like in Paris and who saw in the arrival of the French a deliverance from Austrian tyranny were soon disappointed. They welcomed Dumouriez at the outskirts of the capital, gave him a Golden Key to the gates of their city, and saluted him as a hero. The General was genuinely touched by the warmth of their greeting and extended them his assurance that free elections would soon be held. He spoke of the abolition of feudalism and of the entrenched privileges that went with it.

But his promises, like those of Vergniaud, were as insubstantial as the air in which they were uttered. The "free elections" of which he spoke were held under the supervision of French administrators and according to rules laid down by the French. The words Liberty, Equality, and Fraternity, so freely tossed about the halls of the Convention in Paris, proved to have a variety of special meanings that depended upon the needs or the demands of the conquerors. It was announced, for example, that the government in Paris "would regard as its enemies all those who rejected freedom and equality." Those who complained, who resisted the confiscation of their property, or in some way made themselves unpopular with their new masters, were accused of "rejecting freedom and equality" and hauled off to a summary execution. The country soon groaned under the lash of a harsh military occupation.

In the baggage wagons of the conquerors came the civil administrators, the politicians, the Jacobin clerks, the spies of the factions, and, inevitably, the thieves. The country was systematically plundered by the administrators and clerks, the booty was inventoried, loaded onto carts, and sent back to Paris. The thieves robbed and looted for their own accounts. The most deplorable depredations took place in the churches, where, under the guise of a militant atheism, reliquaries and candelabra were melted down for their metal and crucifixes picked of their precious stones, then thrown aside. What was not stolen was destroyed. The articles may or may not have been "monuments to superstition," but they were works of art. Many of them had belonged to the treasury of the Dukes of Burgundy and they comprehended irreplaceable masterpieces of fourteenth- and fifteenth-century Flemish workmanship. It is said that a number of paintings by van der Weyden and the van Eycks, considered worthless by the looters, were wantonly destroyed. It is no wonder that the French "liberators" were soon hated by the local revolutionaries who had welcomed them, many of whom prayed for a speedy return of their former oppressors, the Habsburgs.

Among those who most heartily hated the French was their own leader, General Dumouriez. He was outraged by the behavior of the Jacobin emissaries who suddenly appeared in his camp and he was infuriated by the posturings of the politicians in Paris. When he learned that the Convention was considering the passage of a decree annexing Belgium to France, Dumouriez sullenly immured himself in the palace of the Prince-Bishops of Liège and began to plan a few moves of his own.

Despite the laurels he had brought his government, General

Dumouriez was in very bad standing with his superiors in Paris. In the eyes of the Jacobins he was one of the Girondins, with whom they had entered into mortal battle, and in consequence he was a man whom they were determined to overthrow and destroy. The War Ministry itself had in fact fallen to the extremists. The Minister of War, a man named Pache, was in the pay of Marat. In December, Dumouriez discovered that Pache was diverting arms and ammunition that should have gone to the army of occupation in Belgium to the Commune and to Marat's private army. They were the very weapons that were to be used in the coming spring to overthrow the Convention and arrest the Girondin deputies. But in that same December a far more startling piece of news reached his ears. He learned that the Convention was going to bring Louis XVI before its bar and try him for treason. The General's secret plans began to take a more definite shape . . .

On December 11, a few days before his trial, Louis had been separated from his family. For Marie Antoinette this was a fresh source of anguish. In the long weeks of their confinement in the Temple that ill-matched couple had finally come to know one another. In the awkward, unkingly man who had once been the object of amused derision to herself and her coterie of stylish friends she discovered qualities she had never appreciated. For his part, Louis came to know a wife who had always been remote to him and he saw the changes that time and sorrow had wrought in her. He had never doubted what he called her "maternal tenderness" and said as much in his Will. As in many unsatisfactory marriages, concern for their children had been the single tie that bound them. Now, in prison, after the terrible experiences they had shared for three years, they came to depend on one another's company. The moment of parting was made more painful because each in his heart appears to have foreseen the end.

The end was indeed a *fait accompli* even before the trial had begun. Louis XVI's execution was a political maneuver by the extremists of the Convention who wanted by that means to implicate their fellow deputies in a crime that in the eyes of Europe was heinous. For the Jacobins too regicide was a crime more awesome than mere murder. France may have declared itself a republic and the descendant of Saint Louis might now be called Louis Capet, but royalty had by no means lost its ultimate mystique. Louis' execution would bind the whole of the Convention in an association of blood guilt. The successes of the French army in Belgium made the moment propitious. "We shall throw the head of a king at Europe!" cried Danton. And his challenge had a bold and confident ring because Danton and his colleagues knew that Valmy had rendered Europe impotent.

Marie Antoinette was not to see her husband again until the night before his death, six weeks later. But every morning she would hear the heavy tread of his step as he left the Temple for the long hearings before the Convention and every evening she would hear him return, accompanied by his counsel, the officials of the Commune, and the ever-present armed guard. Sometimes Turgy or Cléry would be able to pass her a hurried word about the progress of the trial, sometimes she would hear the cry of a newspaper vendor who had been bribed by friends to station himself on the nearby rue de la Corderie and keep her informed of the more sensational developments. Of Louis' thoughts or comportment during this last station of his *via dolorosa* she knew nothing.

She did not know, for example, that on Christmas morning he called for pen and paper and wrote that remarkable document he called his Last Will and Testament. The weaknesses that in the public or political sphere had destroyed him became on the human level the attributes of the martyr and even the saint. Across nearly two centuries' time the pages of that paper are still aglow with a charity that remains profoundly moving. With reason, alas for himself, could Louis XVI say to his conscience that he had shed no man's blood, not even for that abstraction or symbol—and it is rarely difficult to commit murder in the name of a symbol or political ideal—once called the monarchy. In one paragraph he touched upon Marie Antoinette, who seems to have been much on his mind during the final weeks of his life: "I beg my wife to forgive all the pain which she may have suffered for me and the sorrows that I may have caused her during our union . . ." and then there comes a phrase that arrests the attention ". . . and she may feel sure that I hold nothing against her should she have anything with which to reproach herself." Men such as Louis XVI penning so momentous a document at so awesome a moment are not likely to use such phrases lightly. It is obvious that the King felt she did indeed have something with which to reproach herself. To what does he refer? To the days of frivolity? To the temper tantrums over favors not granted the Polignacs and their friends? To the follies of her youth out of which were confected the calumny that had helped bring him to the Temple Tower? Or do the words refer to some specific act known to the King and her- self, an act such as an adulterous liaison with Axel Fersen? The latter possibility has not gone unnoticed and it is mentioned here be- cause there are those who see in Louis' cryptic words his recognition of an arrangement that he felt might be the source of additional suffering to his wife after his death.

Marie Antoinette was apparently on Louis' mind to the end. Just before his execution he talked about her at length with his counsel. He regretted that the French people had never come to know her good qualities and that she had been exposed at too young an age to the pernicious influences of a court where there had been no older, responsible woman of his family to advise or help her. Over and again he recalled that she had been only fourteen when she arrived in France. "Poor woman!" he sighed. "She was promised a throne and it has ended like this." Of such conversations that took place only a few yards from them on a lower floor of the Temple, Marie Antoinette and her children knew nothing.

The records of the Municipality show that now the Queen's health began to fail. Always frugal at table, she lost all appetite and grew so thin that a dressmaker was sent to the Tower to take in her clothes. After January 1 she began to drink a medicinal soup that the doctors prescribed for her.

In the morning of January 20, through the cries of the news- paper vendor, she learned that Louis had been sentenced to death and that his execution was to take place within twenty-four hours. In an anguish of uncertainty, she spent that day trying to hide her sobs from her son. At eight in the evening the door of their room was flung open and they were informed that the condemned man had been granted permission to receive his family. Under guard they were escorted down the winding stair to Louis' floor. Even at so pri- vate a moment as this they were not allowed to be alone. The guards lurked in the shadows of the room and in a little embrasure of one of the flanking towers the King's confessor, an Irishman named the Abbé Edgeworth whom he had sent for to attend him in his last hours, read his breviary and tried not to listen. According to the Abbé Edgeworth in his recollections that were written some years later the Queen entered first, holding the dauphin's hand. She flung herself into her husband's arms. For more than ten minutes no one was able to speak coherently. Only the sound of their sobs and lamentations could be heard. Even Louis, stolid in most circumstances, joined in this chorus of woe. When they had exhausted their tears they began to talk calmly and in low voices. Louis told his wife about his trial.

It was then she learned that it was only by one vote that the King had been sentenced to death and that the vote of the King's cousin the duc d'Orléans, who sat among the extremists of the Convention, had been for death rather than banishment. The French Revolution had begun with the court nobility. It was but fitting that it should be a Prince of the Blood, a royal duke whom the heedless Marie Antoinette had once slighted in the halls of Versailles, who should strike the final blow.

Convulsed by sobs, the dauphin rushed to the officials of the Commune who were present and implored them to give him permission to go into the streets and beg "the people" for his father's life. Louis calmed the boy, took him on his knee and in a solemn scene made him promise never to seek to revenge for his death. "You must swear to me with your uplifted hand that you will fulfill this last wish of your father," said the King. And the dauphin repeated his oath.

At ten thirty Louis rose and, after more painful *adieux,* dismissed his family. He later told his confessor that he could endure no more. He needed time now to compose his spirit for the final ordeal. Although he promised Marie Antoinette that he would send for her in the morning he had no intention of doing so. Another such interview would be insupportable to them both, he declared. When he said good-bye that night Louis knew that it was forever.

In the room above, Marie Antoinette flung herself onto her bed without undressing. One wonders if among the scenes from the past that must have presented themselves to her during that long night she may have recalled the time in Madame de Polignac's apartments at Versailles when, stifling their giggles, she and her friend had moved the hands of the clock ahead an hour in order to be rid of "the poor man's" constraining company. Now in an access of grief she waited in vain for that last hour that the King had promised her. Seven o'clock passed and eight approached, but there came no summons. Below in the courtyard of the Temple and beyond in the distant streets she could hear the rattle of musketry and the rolling of drums that announced the gathering procession.

Oblivious to the world he was about to leave, Louis received Communion shortly after seven o'clock. The scene has been described many times and his *sang-froid* admired by royalists and revolutionaries alike. But there is one small vignette that is worthy of more attention than it usually receives. Louis was scheduled to depart at eight o'clock sharp. Certain delays in the religious ceremony and the King's slowness of movement caused the officials present to become anxious about the hour. Among the men who hurried Louis XVI on to his appointment with the executioner that morning and who did so with particular insensitivity, insistently addressing the doomed man as "Capet," was a fervent Jacobin of the name Cambacérès. Fifteen years later, under the Empire, this same Cambacérès, adorned in all the regalia of royalty, became Duke of Parma. As such he was heard to inform his old friends—many of whom, now nobles, had like himself once been revolutionaries—that "in private you may call me 'Monseigneur,' but in public I must be addressed as 'Your Highness.'"

Louis departed soon after eight. He walked from the Tower to the palace of the Temple. Abbé Edgeworth, who accompanied him, recalled that he turned several times and looked back at the prison where his wife and children still waited for him. In front of the palace he entered the carriage that took him to the place of execution on today's Place de la Concorde. His route lay along the *grands boulevards*, which, even in the cold mist of that winter dawn, were thronged with sightseers and lined with troops. It was a trip of more than two hours. Louis turned his face from the scene, never lifting his head from the breviary given him by the Abbé Edgeworth. He was therefore not aware of an attempt to rescue him that misfired along the way. More than three hundred men, all of them "of the people," were involved in this abortive plot, which had been engineered by an enigmatic adventurer named baron de Batz who some months later was to try to save the Queen, too.

The business was finished at ten thirty, at precisely the hour that the bureaucrats of the Convention had scheduled it. And, as the Convention wished, the vast square was choked with humanity. When the King's head fell there was a great cry of *Vive la République!* Souvenirs of the event were then auctioned from the platform of the scaffold: bits of the man's coat, his hat, pieces of cloth dipped in his blood. There were many who pressed forward to bid for these—some of whom may well have been secret royalists in search of relics. But the effect on Paris was not at all what the Convention had hoped. Nearly every eyewitness account speaks of the "stupor" that hung over Paris that day and of the "mournful air" (Prudhomme) one noticed in the streets. Many people stayed home behind shuttered windows; others "dared not meet one another's eye" (*Histoire de la Révolution par deux amis de la liberté*). An American witness, Gouverneur Morris, wrote Thomas Jefferson a report that confirms the description of French observers: "The late King of this country has been publically executed. He died in a manner becoming his dignity . . . the great mass of the Parisian citizens mourn'd the fate of their unhappy Prince. I have seen grief such as for the untimely death of a beloved parent. Everything (here) wears the appearance of solemnity which is awfully distressing."

Much of this "grief" undoubtedly came from a sense of the enormity of the step that France had taken and a general apprehension about its consequences. Louis himself expressed this foreboding the night before his execution. "I see the people delivered to anarchy," he told Cléry, "becoming the victim of all the factions. I see crimes following upon one another and insoluble dissensions rending France." To the end the unfortunate King was invested with a symbolic importance, and in his person fifteen centuries of French history and tradition were put to death. Even the radicals of the Convention were suddenly frightened by what they had done.

But in the eyes of many of his subjects Louis XVI was a man as well as a symbol, and he had always been genuinely liked. His simple ways, his coarse bonhomie, his natural kindliness were known to far more people than he realized and he was regarded by them with affection. It was his wife who was hated by that faceless entity called the public, never Louis. To the crime of regicide was therefore added the disquieting sense of a man having been unjustly put to death. It was in a thoughtful frame of mind that the people of Paris returned to their work that winter morning of 1793.

In the Temple Tower the King's family heard the stir that attended his departure. From afar they heard the muffled roll of drums that signaled the beginning of the march toward the scaffold. Shortly after ten, Turgy brought them their midday meal. The Queen tried to persuade her children to take food but they were unable to eat. Turgy was in the room when at ten thirty the distant sound of salvos told them that the deed was done. In the guardroom below there was a shout of *Vive la République!* Madame Élisabeth raised her eyes as though in prayer and said, "Monsters! Now they are happy." The dauphin began to cry and his sister screamed. But according to Turgy the Queen was unable to utter a word. For a long moment she stood motionless and silent, beyond even grief. Then she turned to her son. Louis XVI may have been dead, but the King of France was not. The throne may have fallen, but its living symbol remained. So within the walls of their prison the three women, led by Marie Antoinette, made the ritual obeisance before the seven-year-old boy who had become Louis XVII.

Fersen and his party reached Düsseldorf on December 20 where in a local gazette he learned of the King's trial. News in those days traveled slowly and it was often inaccurate. For over a month he supposed that the Queen too was on trial. "Oh, my friend," he wrote Taube, "how desperately I need the comfort of your companionship now. The news is appalling—I have been weeping without cease. Dear God, what a position for that poor family. My heart is broken."

On January 24 he wrote a letter to his sister Sophie in which he expressed his anguish unrestrainedly. Axel was still awaiting word of the Convention's vote when he penned these words. He did not know that Louis XVI had been dead for three days. "Tomorrow we will know the outcome of the voting, but I cannot hide my fear. Poor unhappy family, poor Queen. If I could save her by my blood it would be my soul's greatest happiness. I am feeling at this moment all that I might be expected to feel and all that I have ever felt. You may imagine then how terrible my state of mind is. Yes, dear Sophie, it is practically unbearable. *And I can do nothing for them!* The scum of the gutter, the dregs of humanity are dragging them to their death. The thought is unbearable to me. My happy days are over and henceforth I am condemned to eternal regrets and must finish my sad days in desolation. Their faces will haunt my memory forever. Why, oh God, did I ever know them and why didn't I die for them . . . ?"

Two days later he learned that the King had been put to death. And with this news came the report that the whole royal family had been massacred. In another outpouring of emotion he opened his heart to his sister. "I have lost everything in the world. Only you and Taube remain to me. You must not abandon me now. She who was once all my happiness, she who was my life (for I never ceased loving her nor could I have done so for an instant), she for whom I would gladly have given a thousand lives is no more. Oh, my God, I have reached the limit of all the grief I can bear . . . her face will be with me to the end of my days and I shall mourn her forever. Why, oh why didn't I die by her side—for her and for them—on June 20. It would have been better so than to have to drag out my days in sorrow and remorse . . ."

Varennes rose to haunt him in another letter he wrote Taube on the same day. "I have lived too long, my friend," he declared. "I would have been happier if I had died on June 20. Everything calls that day to mind."

Soon afterward he learned that Marie Antoinette had not perished with the King, but the news did little to relieve his agitation. Instead of grief he now suffered renewed pangs of apprehension. Louis' fate augured ill for the future of his widow at the hands of those whom Axel called "a nation of cannibals." "They are capable of anything," he cried, "and the thought of what she must be suffering tears me apart. Night and day I see her. In vain I try to hope, in vain do those with whom I live try to comfort me."

He was tortured, too, by the total absence of dependable news from Paris, for after Louis' death silence fell over the queen's prison. Of what was passing in the Temple Tower the outer world knew nothing.

On the day after the King's execution the Commune sent a dressmaker to Marie Antoinette who, at her request, fitted her with simple mourning. The *facture* still exists: black shoes, black stockings, and a black dress trimmed around the neck with white. From that moment Marie Antoinette acquires another personality and with the wearing of her weeds she entered into the third and last stage of her life. There had been the fashionable and vapid Queen depicted by Vigée-Lebrun. There had been the handsome and dignified woman of middle years painted by Kucharski. Now there appears the Widow Capet. It was by this name she was known to the Commune in their official reports to the government and it is by this name too that she is described by her biographers in the final months of her life. Kucharski was sent to the Temple to take her likeness again, so that, fittingly, this period of her life too had its "official portrait." Kucharski's painting has been reproduced in several versions but they all show a woman in whom the spark of life has nearly been extinguished. It is the face of one to whom suffering has imparted almost total indifference.

All verbal descriptions verify the impression communicated by Kucharski's portrait. "She was painfully thin," states an eyewitness, "and she wrapped herself in a mournful silence." She refused to go downstairs to take air in the garden, for she did not wish to pass the door of her husband's rooms. So she would spend long hours seated in a little chair covered in faded green damask knitting or daydreaming. Only her children and especially the boy could rouse her from this torpor. When they were with her, life would return to her empty eyes. She continued to instruct her son in his lessons and exacted from him an outward show of good manners to the Tison couple and the guards. The boy took his father's place at table and Marie Antoinette served him first. This was the only tribute she gave or was able to give to his position.

The woman's distress, her maternal solicitude, and her own un-failing gentle manners did not go unnoticed by her jailers, some of whom soon found themselves in silent sympathy with their prisoners. The Widow Capet had lost none of that power which had been the Queen's to touch men's hearts and arouse in some of them emotions akin to the devotion of the knights of legend. Among those who now succumbed to her charm was a guard—or "Commissioner of the Com-mune," as they were called—named Toulan. The story of this man, who was about to enter into an audacious and dangerous plot to save Marie Antoinette, is not without interest.

François-Adrian Toulan was thirty-two years of age when he found himself among those assigned to guard the royal family at the Temple Tower. He came from Toulouse and all the boisterous pas-sions attributed to the men of Gascony ran in his veins. He was full of flourish, sudden in his temper, and born for escapades. Four years before the beginning of the Revolution he had come to Paris with his wife and opened a bookstore. Like many other obscure men of that time the literature of the day filled him with a hatred of tyranny and a love of liberty. He embraced the Revolution with enthusiasm and there was no more ardent patriot in Paris on those occasions when the mob gathered to express its will. Undoubtedly he was among those who stormed the Tuileries on June 20. It is certain he led a battalion when the palace was assaulted on August 10. Because of his contribu-tion to the victory of the people on that day, the Commune appointed him one of its commissioners to guard the tyrant and his family at the Temple. Nothing could more forcefully attest to Toulan's revolutionary fervor than this appointment, for only the most ardent patriots were chosen for that position. Some of them, such as the defrocked priest Jacques Roux, were the personification of the sadistic psychopaths of royalist story. With his rough manners and wild appearance, Toulan seemed to the royal family to be one of the more frightening of their captors. Turgy, the pantry boy, later recalled that they dreaded the days when he would be on duty.

But the rude exterior of this man hid a heart accessible to pity—that same heart that had brought him to love liberty and fight for the happiness of the people. Toulan was not one of those people who love the abstract principles of liberty and justice more than the men and women who constitute humanity. At the Temple Tower in the persons of the former royal family he had before his eyes the spectacle of genuine suffering, and a suffering, furthermore, that was borne with patience and dignity. Within two or three weeks his hatred for the tyrants changed into admiration and pity. From indications left by Marie Antoinette we know that toward the end of September he gave the prisoners some overt sign of his sympathy—a furtive word of kindness or some other expression of good will. No doubt the King and Queen were at first suspicious, for the Temple swarmed with spies and false kindness was but one of the methods for enticing the prisoners into some confidence that might compromise them or their secret servitors, such as Turgy.

Toulan's overtures were soon backed by concrete gestures of regard. It was he who had the idea of having a newspaper vendor cry out the headlines near the Tower. During the King's trial, when Louis had been separated from his family, Toulan was able to carry messages between husband and wife. In his Will, Louis makes an unmistakable reference to these services. "I would like," wrote the King, "to express my gratitude to those who have shown me true and disinterested service. If on the one hand I have been deeply hurt by the ingratitude and disloyalty of people to whom I have given many favors, I have had on the other hand the consolation and comfort of the genuine attachment many people have shown me. I beg them to receive all my thanks. In the present condition of things now I am afraid of compromising them were I to speak more explicitly . . ."

One can only imagine the astonishment of the prisoners when they realized that this man in whom all the fury of the Revolution seemed personified was their friend.

A few days after the King's execution Toulan did Marie Antoinette a favor that brought him irretrievably into her camp. On the morning of his death Louis had given Cléry his wedding ring and his seal bearing the arms of France. He asked his valet to remit these to his wife. But immediately after the King's execution Cléry was put under arrest and held incommunicado. The ring and seal were taken from him and locked in a drawer in the guardroom. With his habitual audacity, Toulan went to the guardroom one night when there was no one on duty there, smashed the locked drawer and retrieved the two relics, which he then brought to Marie Antoinette. Since Toulan's outward manner toward the two prisoners was unchanged and his fulminations against "the Austrian" and her late consort were as loud as ever, he was beyond suspicion. The Commune finally decided that the robbery was without political overtones and had been committed by a common thief. The matter was soon forgotten.

Soon afterward Toulan took a more audacious step. He decided to help Marie Antoinette and her family escape from the Temple. The King's execution left little doubt among her friends about his widow's approaching fate. Toulan, who moved in the inner circle of the extremists of the Commune, was aware of their plans and knew he would have to act quickly. One day when the Tison couple were out of earshot he asked Marie Antoinette if she would be willing to attempt an escape from the Temple. She expressed doubt about the feasibility of any plan of rescue. The mere fact that there were four of them was enough to discourage any hope of success—and the Queen made it clear that she would not consider any plan of flight that did not include her children and Madame Élisabeth. Toulan assured her that even with four people his plan was workable. To put it into effect, however, he would need the help of another man. He then asked her if she had some trusted friend in Paris to whom he might turn.

As it happened, the Queen did have a friend whom she believed to be still in Paris. This man was the chevalier de Jarjayes, who had been her private secretary and intermediary in the correspondence with Barnave. Jarjayes was the husband of one of Marie Antoinette's former Women of the Bedchamber and the couple had stayed on in Paris after Varennes and after the overthrow of the monarchy on August 10. Before being taken to the Temple on that day Louis solicited a promise from Jarjayes that he would not leave Paris. Louis seems to have foreseen that one day there might be some service this loyal courtier could still render him or his family.

By means one can only surmise Jarjayes managed to elude arrest and was able to keep his promise to the King. He and his wife spent the day of January 21, the day of Louis' execution, in prayer and anguish. But after the King's death he considered himself absolved from his vow and he decided to emigrate. He was in the midst of preparations for his departure when on February 2—the date is of interest because it shows how rapidly Toulan had moved after Louis' execution—a man appeared at his door and asked to speak to him alone. It must have been with trepidation that the proscribed nobleman examined his mysterious visitor. Everything about him proclaimed him to be a revolutionary of the most violent party. But the face of the experienced courtier betrayed no emotion when, closing the door behind them, he asked him his business. It was then that Toulan identified himself as a guard at the Temple and a commissioner of the Commune. He declared that unwittingly he had done great harm to innocent people, that the spectacle of the Queen's suffering had wrought a change in his views and that he now wanted to make amends.

Jarjayes' response to these words was cautious. He suspected a trap and gave his visitor some evasive reply. But Toulan had foreseen this eventuality and took from his pocket a slip of paper that he handed Jarjayes. It was in the Queen's hand that Jarjayes knew so well: "You can trust this man who will speak to you on my behalf and who will give you this note," he read. "His feelings are well known to me and they have not altered for five months. Do not trust the wife of the man who serves us here. I trust neither her nor her husband."

That was all, but it was enough to convince Jarjayes of Toulan's sincerity. As he read Marie Antoinette's words his hand began to tremble and for a moment or two afterward he regarded his visitor in silent amazement. Then with no further restraint the two men began to talk. Toulan told the chevalier that there was no time to lose and that the Queen's life was in great danger. Every moment now counted.

Jarjayes promised to enter into any plan of rescue that was feasible, but he said that before doing so he would have to speak to the Queen. Was there some way he could enter the Temple and see Marie Antoinette? This, in fact, seemed an operation almost as difficult as the rescue itself. Apart from the guards there was the problem of the Tison couple. In communicating with Jarjayes the Queen's first thought had been to warn him against this untrustworthy pair. "*I trust neither her nor her husband . . .*" And in a second brief note she repeated this warning: "Be very careful not to be noticed by the woman who is locked up with us here."

But the resourceful Toulan soon hit upon a clever stratagem. It happened that there was a lamplighter who came to the Temple Tower every evening toward five. In the routine of his work this man would enter and leave the prisoners' rooms unnoticed by the guards or the Tisons. Since Jarjayes was more or less the lamplighter's height Toulan decided that he might be introduced into the Temple in his disguise. Toulan persuaded the lamplighter to lend himself to such a ruse in an inspired and simple way. Instead of bribing the man, which would be hazardous on every account, he appealed to his patriotic sentiments. He told him that he, Toulan, the ferocious revolutionary, had a friend who was as patriotic as himself and that this man wanted to enter the Temple Tower disguised as the lamplighter in order to see the Widow Capet in her humbled state. Never doubting Toulan's good faith and probably afraid of him, too, the lamplighter agreed to let this unknown person take his place one evening in his rounds of the Temple.

So it happened that on February 7 the chevalier de Jarjayes was able to penetrate the prison of Marie Antoinette. It was with considerable emotion that he saw the former Queen of France whom he had known in her youth and splendor at Versailles seated in a corner of that dark, ill-furnished room dressed in her widow's weeds. Her hair had gone white and her eyesight, never good, had begun to fail. But her command of the graceful gesture, her innate dignity, and that gentleness of manner that had won Toulan to her side were, even in the brief moment of their interview, still very much with her. There was, indeed, time for only the quickest exchange of words. Marie Antoinette told him that he could trust Toulan absolutely, that he should listen carefully to any plan of evasion that he might propose and work in concert with him. Instructions such as these given in such a setting had more force than a mere request or a royal command. They acquired all the solemn significance of an oath and Jarjayes left the Temple determined to give his life if necessary to rescue Marie Antoinette.

The plot that was now worked out between Jarjayes and Toulan is well documented and we can examine it today in most of its detail, both because Jarjayes lived to tell the tale and because he kept the few letters the Queen was able to send him. What is notable about the plot is that it promised every chance of success. It might very well have succeeded but for a single flaw—the fatal recurrent flaw that was fundamental to the whole pattern of Marie Antoinette's life.

The Temple Tower was not quite the impregnable fortress that it appeared to be. The guards there had come to look on their duty as an onerous chore. The initial excitement of seeing the royal family in person behind bars had passed. The boredom of routine had set in and with boredom came indifference and incompetence. The fact that Jarjayes was able to make his way into Marie Antoinette's room testifies to the general state of affairs in the prison. And Jarjayes was not the only one. It is on record that others, motivated more by curiosity than by any desire to help the Widow Capet, came and went from the Temple Tower at ease. After the King's execution the Convention, in the grip of a mortal battle between the Girondins and Marat's faction, momentarily forgot the prisoners and the Commune even decreased the number of sentinels allotted duty at the Tower. The moment was propitious for an attempt at rescue.

Toulan's plan required the complicity of Turgy—a complicity that was already assured—and that of one other municipal guard. The lamplighter's services would also be required again, but that presented no problem. Finding a guard willing to join the plot was more difficult. Several of these *commissaires* by a glance or a discreet word had managed to communicate their private sympathy with the prisoners, but between friendly gestures and an act of treason there lay a world of difference and the conspirators were hard put to decide which of these men might be safely approached. In the end the choice was left to Marie Antoinette, who was best able to judge the value of the various expressions of furtive commiseration that had been extended her. After hesitation she finally chose a man named Lepitre.

This Lepitre was a revolutionary of a very different character than Toulan. In the days of the *ancien régime* he had been a professor of Latin and a royalist. He embraced the new order more for reasons of expediency than of idealism. Shortly before the Revolution he had placed his life's savings in a small boarding school and it was to protect this investment that he had become so fervent a patriot. Pusillanimous and pedantic, he seems oddly placed among the rough, illiterate commissioners of the Commune, but like Toulan he had been in on all the riots and was as enthusiastic a patriot as the next man. In early December he had been made a guard at the Temple and the sight of the descendant of Saint Louis and the daughter of Maria Theresa in prison disturbed him.

One day after one of his colleagues had spoken in an offensive manner to the King, Lepitre in a low voice asked Louis if he could borrow his copy of Vergil.

"Then you read Latin?" asked the King in surprise.

"Yes, Sire," replied Lepitre. Whereupon he recited a line from the Aeneid, *"Non ego cum Danais Troianam excindere gentem . . . Aulide juravi,"* that meant, in effect, "I have not like the Revolutionaries sworn the destruction of royalty." It was a subtle and flattering manner of revealing his secret views to the monarch, who was himself an accomplished Latin scholar. The King communicated his appreciation with a glance. Various other furtive gestures of respect finally caused Marie Antoinette to decide that Lepitre could be trusted. But there was a more important reason to pick Lepitre as a fellow conspirator. He was head of the passport committee of the Commune and as such his services were indispensable, for no one could then hope to leave Paris without a passport signed and stamped by a member of that committee.

Toulan then took the step from which, once taken, there could be no return and revealed to his colleague the existence of a conspiracy to save Marie Antoinette and asked Lepitre if he would be willing to join it. Lepitre did not lack imagination and the word conspiracy called up a procession of exciting images in his mind. Intoxicated by the picture of himself personally saving the remnants of the French royal family and intoxicated, very probably, by a picture of the honors that in due time would be his reward for so audacious a rescue Lepitre accepted Toulan's proposal. Alas, it was only in his imagination that this man was ever able to play a hero's role. An instinctive and deep-seated prudence soon brought all his romantic impulses back to ground. When that night he began to consider the practical consequences of the plot he balked. He would have to leave France at the same time as the Queen; and to flee France not only meant leaving his wife but the school for which he had worked and stinted. He would be without resources. The imagination that in the morning had made him a hero began in the evening to present pictures of a different sort: arrest, prison, and his severed head in the wicker basket of the guillotine.

On the following day he told Toulan that he could not engage himself in the plot unless he were given enough money to indemnify him for the loss of the school and assure his wife of a sufficient support during his exile. He asked that $20,000 of this sum be paid him in advance. It was with consternation that Marie Antoinette learned of Lepitre's condition. Brave and gallant men do not enter projects of this kind with remuneration in mind. But after a consultation with Toulan she decided that whatever the risk or price they would have to keep Lepitre with them. They had already revealed too much to him and his position in the passport office made him necessary. "He is absolutely indispensable and we must have him," she wrote Jarjayes finally. In the same letter she told the chevalier that he could get the money from a deposit she had with the banker Laborde. But rather than bring another man into their plan Jarjayes decided to use the remnants of his own fortune and he paid Lepitre himself.

With Lepitre's cooperation now purchased, they were able to begin preparations for the evasion. It was to take place soon after nightfall in the first week of March. Considering the number of people who had to be spirited out of the Temple, it was a practical plan. Marie Antoinette and Madame Élisabeth in men's clothes would leave the Temple disguised as municipal officers. They would have tricolor scarves and identity cards which they would flash at the downstairs guards. "It was sufficient to show the cards from afar," Lepitre afterward recalled in his memoirs. "The sentinels never bothered to examine them." The little King would be taken out by Turgy in the bottom of a laundry basket. It was Turgy's custom to fill the basket with the prisoners' dirty linen and the guards were long familiar with the sight of him coming and going with this basket. They paid no attention to it. Marie Thérèse was to leave as the lamplighter's son. He often went his rounds accompanied by his children and their presence had become part of the evening routine at the Temple. On that particular day the lamplighter's place would be taken by a man named Ricard, a shadowy figure in the plot who appears to have been a close friend or relative of Toulan. The lamplighter would be persuaded to cede his place to Ricard by the same means used for Jarjayes.

Once they were out of the Temple they would enter three light carriages waiting for them on the rue de la Corderie. Varennes cast its shadow over the enterprise and Marie Antoinette refused to even consider Lepitre's suggestion that they all escape together in another *berline*. She and the young King accompanied by Jarjayes would go in one carriage, Marie Thérèse and Lepitre would travel in another, while Madame Élisabeth and Toulan would depart in the third. Relays had been arranged all the way to the coast where, in a cove not far from le Havre, a friend of Jarjayes had put a boat at their disposal.

There were many small details, too, that had been considered. The Tison couple, for example, were to be drugged with a narcotic put in the Spanish snuff to which they were partial. Toulan and Lepitre managed to get themselves assigned to guard duty in the prisoners' quarters by a simple ruse. There were normally two guards on duty there at night and one in the day. The commissioners would draw lots for their assignments. "Toulan," according to Lepitre, "would write *day* on all three slips of paper and make our colleague draw his lot. When the latter, being the first to open his paper, had read the word *day*, we threw our papers into the fire without looking at them and went off together to our post. He hardly ever came twice with the same man and this device was always successful."

Unfortunately Toulan and Lepitre took too free an advantage of this trick and the vigilant Tisons noted that these two were together with the prisoners more frequently than chance might explain. They noted, but for the moment they said nothing.

On each of these tours of duty the two men would enter the Tower with bits of clothing concealed on their persons—sometimes a hat, sometimes a man's shirt or trousers, which would then be concealed under the mattresses. The prisoners were to don their disguises shortly before seven in the evening and make their escape immediately afterward. Timing was the critical factor in the project. "Our arrangements were such that no one could have started to pursue us until five hours after our departure," continues Lepitre. "We had made the most precise calculations. In the first place, no one in the Tower ever went upstairs till nine o'clock in the evening when the table was laid and the supper served. The Queen was to ask that supper be served at half past nine that night. They would knock and be surprised that the door was not opened. They would go down to the Council Room and inform the other members of this curious circumstance who would go upstairs with them and knock anew. They would have to send for a locksmith to open the doors. This would take more time, for one of those doors was of iron. Once inside they would search the rooms, shake Tison and his wife and not succeed in rousing them. They would go down again to the Council Room to draw up a report and take it to the headquarters of the Commune who would lose more time in fruitless discussions. Messages would be sent to the police and to the mayor and the Convention asking what to do. All these things would take so much time that we would have a chance of escaping successfully. Our passports would have been in order for I was the President of the Passport Committee and would have drawn them up myself. For these reasons we would have no anxiety on our journey . . ."

It was in 1817 under the Bourbon Restoration that Lepitre wrote these words. But it was in 1793 in an atmosphere of danger that the plot was conceived and Lepitre omits any reference to the fact that, faced with the reality of the business, he became frightened. It was his pusillanimity that caused the plot to fail. Once given his bribe, he had entered into the planning of the business with enthusiasm. Indeed, it was under his roof that the conspirators met and designed their plans. His training in the discipline of the classics enabled him to note several weak points in the general blueprint and his suggestions were generally useful and bold. So long as things were limited to plotting and projects Lepitre was a great help. It was when it came time to act that he fell apart. His job was to secure the passports that were so essential a factor in the scheme. And confronted with the actuality of that assignment he quailed. Ironically it would not, at that particular moment, have been difficult to secure the passports. The Council of the Commune had recently decreed that such papers were to be issued freely, although "always with circumspection" on the part of the Passport Committee—of which Lepitre was President. But he could not bring himself to take the critical step. "I confess," he admitted in his memoirs, "that it was with trepidation that I saw the moment approach when the sacred charge which was mine would be confided to my hands." This was as close as he ever came to admitting that he was a coward.

Day after day he would arrive with an excuse or a pretext instead of the papers. Marie Antoinette grew frantic and gave him a lock of the King's hair to exhort him. Madame Élisabeth knitted him a bonnet. The two women cajoled and implored; Toulan and Jarjayes implored and threatened but Lepitre, always with a good excuse, always with a promise to deliver the passports in a day or two, continued to temporize. The date planned for the evasion came and went. The weeks slipped by and then, in the middle of March, Dumouriez, Commander in Chief of the army of the French Republic, shook his fist in the direction of the politicians in Paris and went over to the Prussians. His defection changed everything. The Convention was thrown into a panic. Nominally Dumouriez belonged to the party of the Girondins and the General's treason spelled their ruin. With the French armies in full retreat from Belgium, with Paris on the verge of civil war, with revolt on its hands in Brittany, Normandy, and the

266

Vendée the Convention declared the capital city to be in a state of emergency and closed its gates. The guards at the Tower were increased and no further passports were issued except after a close scrutiny of each applicant.

Hunger, too, was now abroad in the unhappy city. A bread shortage more terrible than any the irascible populace of Paris had ever suffered under the monarchy drove them wild. Not yet ready to turn on its new masters, the mob remembered the woman in the Temple Tower who for so many years had been the symbol of their grievances. Once again the cry, "Death to the Austrian!" was heard in the streets.

With grief Toulan and Jarjayes saw they had missed their chance and that there was no longer any hope of rescuing the royal family as a group. Intrepid and tenacious to the end, however, the two men quickly concocted a second plan in which one of the prisoners could be rescued. Since Marie Antoinette was the member of the family in the greatest immediate danger she was designated as the one who should be rescued. Knowing her reluctance to be separated from her children and foreseeing her refusal, Jarjayes and Toulan turned to Madame Élisabeth and begged her to persuade the Queen of the necessity of flight. Élisabeth approached her sister-in-law in the name of the children, who had already lost their father, and she managed in this manner to make Marie Antoinette see that in saving herself she would be doing her young son and daughter a far greater service than by staying with them in the Temple. The Queen succumbed to this argument and was within a few days of leaving when one night she looked down at her son sleeping in his cot.

"May God give him happiness," she said to Madame Élisabeth. It is from young Marie Thérèse who, unable to sleep, was listening to the words from behind her partition that we have this story, perhaps not recalled with perfect accuracy when she wrote it down some years later.

"He will be happy, Sister," replied Élisabeth.

"Youth is as short as pleasure," murmured Marie Antoinette. "Happiness soon comes to an end like everything else." She rose and paced the room. "And you, too, dear Sister, when will I ever see you again? No . . . it is impossible! It is impossible. I cannot leave."

And so she relinquished her last real hope of escape. The gesture was as noble as it was foolish, for she knew that in effect she was signing her death warrant. Her only regret was the disappointment of the two men who had already risked so much for her person. To Jarjayes she sent a short and moving letter. "We dreamed a beautiful dream," she wrote, "and that is all. But much has been gained because this occasion has given me a new proof of your total devotion to me. My trust in you is without limits and on all occasions you will find that I have courage and strength of character. But the interest of my son is the only guide I have and no matter how happy I might be to be out of here I would never consent to be separated from him. Be sure that I feel deeply all the motives that have attached you to my interest. I know well that such an opportunity will never come again, but were I to leave my children I could enjoy nothing in life."

Her refusal made Jarjayes' further presence in Paris unnecessary. It was only by unremitting vigilance that he had managed thus far to elude arrest. As intermediary between Barnave and Marie Antoinette he was the repository of too many dangerous secrets to be safe in Paris. After Marie Antoinette rejected his second offer to help her escape he prepared to depart. The Queen was understandably upset by the thought that she was soon to lose this last dependable connection with the outer world, but her first instinct was always to consider the safety of others before her own. "I believe that once you have decided to leave it is best you do so as soon as possible," she wrote him. "How happy I would be if we could soon be reunited. I can never be grateful enough for all you have done for us. *Adieu!* The word is cruel!"

But before he left she had one last service to ask of the brave man who had risked so much for her. There were the relics of Louis XVI that Toulan had recovered from the locked drawer. She wanted them to be taken out of France to safety and delivered to those whom she designated as the proper recipients. They were in a sense testamentary bequests, for they were the last material objects remaining to her and they were objects, as she well knew, of great historical value and immense symbolic significance. To the comte de Provence she gave the King's seal. In the last four years of her life Marie Antoinette had been called upon to perform acts of abnegation far beyond the capacity of most men. Among the most difficult of these surely must have been the relinquishing of her husband's seal, that of the Crown itself, to a man whom she knew to have conspired and intrigued without cease for the power these objects symbolized. The sacrifice cannot have been rendered easier by the fact that her son, the legitimate King of France, was with her in prison when she made it. She wrote Provence a brief but affectionate note that was to be delivered with the seal. "The impossibility in our present condition of giving you our news and the extremity of our unhappiness makes us feel even more painfully the cruel separation that divides us. May it not be long! Until we meet again then I embrace you and send you my love. You must know that it is given with all my heart."

To Artois went Louis' wedding ring with the inscription *M.A.A.A.* (Marie Antoinette Archiduchesse d'Autriche) *19 April 1770.* This legacy too was accompanied by a note. "Having found a means of sending to our brother one of the last tokens we have of the man we all cherish and mourn I thought you would be very pleased to have something that comes from him. Keep it as a sign of the tender friendship with which I embrace you."

However affectionate their tone, these *adieux* to her brothers were in a sense a royal obligation. They were written by Marie Antoinette who had been Queen of France, the Widow Capet who was, as she fully recognized, already a historical personage. She was determined to die fulfilling the obligations of her rank. No doubt it was this resolution that gave her the strength of character to deliver the seal of France to the comte de Provence.

But there was that other Marie Antoinette who was the woman and there was another farewell to be made. She had not heard from Fersen for more than eight months. The news that reached her from the outside world was of battles and politics, brought to her in bits and pieces by Turgy or Toulan. Of Axel she knew nothing. Jarjayes' departure gave her a chance to convey a final message to the man who had played so central a part in her private life and whom she loved. Somewhere concealed on her person or hidden in her room she had a signet ring that appears to have had some particular association with Axel Fersen: perhaps he had given it to her, perhaps together they had once admired it. In any case, she now took a piece of paper and on wax made an impression of its seal. This she included among the tokens that were to be smuggled out of France by Jarjayes.

"Toulan will give you the things that are to go to the princes," she wrote him. "The wax impress which I include here is something else again. I want you to take it to the person you know to have come from Brussels to see me last winter and you are to tell him when you give it to him *that its motto has never been more true . . .*"

The motto to which Marie Antoinette refers was inscribed in Italian above a dove bearing an olive branch and it read, *Tutto a te mi guida:* "Everything leads me to thee."

The hope of rescue that for Jarjayes, Toulan, and Marie Antoinette had been extinguished by Dumouriez's defection was revived by that same event among Marie Antoinette's friends abroad. When the General went over to the Germans he came into their camp with the intention of leading an army of Frenchmen on the capital and crushing the squabbling factions in the Convention who had undermined his forces in Belgium. He planned to restore order in France in the person of the young King and by a new Constitutional Monarchy.

Unfortunately he was unable to arouse much enthusiasm among his troops for this cause and the "army" he brought with him into the Prussian camp was negligible in size. He did, however, manage to abduct five high-ranking officials whom the Convention had sent to arrest him and these men, among them the Minister Beurnonville, became hostages of high value for the Allies. Although the General was unable to rally many French troops behind him, his treason had effects that were no less heartening for Fersen. The French army of occupation in the Netherlands, weakened by political intrigues in Paris, was now in a state of almost total disintegration. The Austrian army regathered its forces and was soon in full pursuit of the French. On February 24 the Allies re-entered Brussels in triumph and on March 18 Mercy announced the evacuation of Holland. By midsummer the Austrians were marching across the border onto French soil. In July the fortress of Valenciennes, Fersen's old garrison, was taken. Once again the road to Paris was open.

More than this, the whole of the Vendée and most of Normandy had risen against the repressive edicts of the Convention. France was on the verge of collapse. Fersen now experienced one of those waves of optimism to which he was periodically susceptible and which too often proved to have no foundation in reality. "I have heard on good authority," he wrote Taube, "that at this very moment they are heating the apartments of the royal family at Versailles." And a few weeks later in a mood of blind exaltation he informed his friend that, "I am delirious with joy and I consider the whole business finished. According to all reports there is nothing to fear for the royal family and I wouldn't be surprised if in a short while I'll tell you that they have been carried through the streets of Paris in triumph."

Founded on purely military considerations, as it was, Axel's optimism might at first glance seem warranted. In the months of July and August the Allied armies could have walked into Paris without the slightest opposition. The French themselves were the first to recognize this and in July they made secret proposals for an armistice. The Republican General Dampierre wrote Vienna that it might be to the interest of both sides to suspend hostilities, after which it would be possible to release "certain persons" whom the French executive power had caused to be imprisoned. Someone could then come to Paris and arrange for the exchange of the four commissioners and the Minister Beurnonville for those "persons."

The "persons" in question were, of course, the French royal family. Certain men in the National Convention recalled the famous words of Joseph II about his *métier* being that of royalist and they supposed naïvely that the blood of the Habsburgs might have some value to Joseph's heirs. But the Convention itself had stripped Marie Antoinette of the only importance she had ever had in Habsburg eyes. She was now no more than a widow with two children, a possible charge on the family budget should she suddenly appear in Vienna. Orders were issued from the Hofburg: "Should General Dampierre bring up the idea of exchanging the French royal family for Beurnonville and the four commissioners you may let him feel that the possibility might be considered, but under no circumstance would it be considered if the condition attached were an armistice."

Now that they had the French on the run the Austrians had no intention of making peace with France. Ahead lay the prospect of important conquests and rich indemnities. The balls and supper parties in Brussels were renewed as though they had never been interrupted.

Why, then, one well might ask, did they not continue their triumphant march through France, enter Paris, crush the Convention, seize the territory they coveted, and, just incidentally, release the prisoners at the Temple? The answer to this question, as it is to many another about the inexplicable behavior of the Allies throughout the French Revolution, is Poland. Fersen, with the naïveté of most men of arms, saw only the military part of the picture, or, as it were, the surface of the iceberg; he was blind to the depths. "I thought that the desire of the Powers was to re-establish the monarchy in France," sighed General Dumouriez, another deluded man of arms, "and to restore order and peace in Europe. I soon found that I was mistaken. I saw that each only thought of himself and that they were far less concerned with the general situation than they were with their private interests."

The "private interests" of which he speaks was Prussia's determination to share Russia's spoils in Poland and at the same time to prevent Austria from putting her fingers into the Polish pie. On the day after the news of Louis XVI's execution Prussia and Russia signed a secret agreement for the Second Partition of Poland. It had only been with the greatest reluctance that Catherine, plunged in deep mourning for the King of France, bowed before necessity and allowed Prussia to join the robbery. In their shameful pact both parties were agreed that Austria should be excluded from any share in the approaching partition. Vienna would have to content herself with the hope of swapping Bavaria against the Lowlands once the French had been evicted.

When Francis II learned of the agreement between Prussia and Russia he was enraged. The duplicity, the secrecy, above all the shame of finding himself a dupe, threw him into a towering anger. He dismissed his Chancellor Cobentzl and in his place appointed a man named Thugut. Small, ugly, and as squat of soul as he was of body, this man, as the anagram of his name suggests, was little more than a thug, without scruples and without honor. Under Maria Theresa he had sold his services to the government of Louis XV at the same time as he was employed by the Empress. Under Francis II the territorial aggrandizement of Austria and the acquisition for himself of supreme power in the Austrian government were his only interests. "The factions in France should be encouraged to fight with one another," he wrote the Emperor at exactly the same time Toulan and Jarjayes were risking their lives in the plot to save Marie Antoinette. "They will thus enfeeble one another so much that we can profit from the situation by taking as much land as we want."

Thugut's first move as Chancellor was to inform Prussia and Russia that Austria would not consider the exchange of Belgium for Bavaria as equivalent to the land those two had acquired for themselves in Poland. He announced that Austria would take its share of Polish land too. Upon hearing this the King of Prussia angrily retorted that he was not going to have the Austrians use his army to make France an Austrian province. He warned Austria that if she made any claim in Poland he would withdraw from the Coalition— no idle threat, as he immediately demobilized half his army fighting with the Austrians on the French frontier.

Indifferent to this menace, Austria submitted a flat claim to the province of Cracow. When told that this would spell the end of Poland, Thugut replied that "It were best now that a total partition be made of that Republic because it can no longer serve as a buffer to adjoining states."

Russia entered the picture and declared that she would not allow Austria to have Cracow. "Take French Flanders," said Catherine's emissary. "Take Alsace, take Lorraine or Bavaria. Even take Turkey. They are all more suitable to your needs than Poland."

"We only want Poland as a last resort," answered Thugut. "We would prefer territorial gains in France, but those gains have not yet materialized. We therefore demand our fair share of Poland."

"But that unhappy country would then be annihilated!"

"What can that possibly mean to Austria compared to not getting a share of land equivalent to Prussia's in Poland?" came the implacable reply.

So, in that summer of 1793 when the Allied armies could have been in Paris in a week's time and with no difficulty delivered Marie Antoinette and her children from their prison, the Allied operation drew to a total standstill. Prussia refused to advance into Alsace and give it to the Austrians until she was assured of her fair share of Poland. Austria, for her part, refused to countenance any Prussian conquest in Poland until she had been indemnified with an equivalent share of land either in Poland or France. Here, in Mercy's words, was "the labyrinth in which the Coalition was lost."

Quarreling was not limited to the Powers. Other dissensions, long latent and equally venomous, came forth in those first warm rays of hope. In the moment when it seemed probable that Marie Antoinette might be rescued and the monarchy restored in France the question of the Regency presented itself to the princes and the émigrés. The comte de Provence and his party had no intention of relinquishing the powers they had given themselves as the representatives of the French Crown abroad should young Louis XVII be proclaimed King. The possibility that the boy's mother might be appointed Regent instead of the comte de Provence caused the émigré court at Hamm to take alarm. All the old calumnies with which they had blackened her name at Versailles were suddenly revived and passed about the courts of Europe. Even those indifferent to the poor woman's fate, such as the Emperor Francis, were shocked by this torrent of abuse and vituperation.

But the Prince's narrow-sighted ambitions were as short-lived as Fersen's hopes. By mid-July it was apparent that the Powers were hopelessly bogged down in the mire of intrigue. Then, also in July, there came a number of disquieting rumors from Paris. These reports would arrive in fragments—vague, undependable bits of news from the Temple Tower, but they were enough to throw Axel into a fresh fever of apprehension. From Madame de Polignac, who was to be seen at the more fashionable dinner parties of Brussels and Vienna, adorned with all her diamonds, he learned that a friend in common had had news of the Queen through a doctor in Paris who had been called to the Temple to examine her daughter. The doctor had found Marie Antoinette in good health, but Madame Élisabeth was changed beyond all recognition and young Marie Thérèse's body was covered with open ulcers. The Queen wore a nightcap and was dressed in plain, worn garments.

Then they learned that the young King's health had failed and that the Commune had brought in doctors, who diagnosed a hernia. On July 12 a report reached Axel that the boy had been separated from his mother. "What an appalling grief for the Queen, unhappy Princess!" he stated in his Journal. A few days later the report was confirmed and for the first time Fersen got wind of the unsuccessful Toulan-Jarjayes plot to rescue her. "I am afraid that they will use it as an excuse for bringing the Queen to trial," Axel declared.

In the first week of August his fear was confirmed. "The rumor is going around that on the 2nd the Queen was taken to the Conciergerie and handed over to the Revolutionary Tribunal . . . but M. de Mercy who came to dinner this evening with Madame Sullivan doesn't believe it." On the following day the newspapers from Paris verified the news. "My soul is torn apart," he wrote. "I am thinking of her grief and suffering and I remember, too, all that I have lost since the arrest at Varennes. Only Éléonore can console me a little but that does not stop me from feeling this terrible blow . . . The uncertainty of what to do makes my situation all the more awful."

"What to do" became his only thought. His first idea was to raise an army of volunteers who would be independent of the forces of the quarreling Coalition stalled at the frontier. They would march directly on Paris with no other purpose but to go to the Conciergerie and rescue the Queen. Mercy threw cold water on that project. The Ambassador indeed threw cold water on every project. He looked on the situation with the dispassionate eye of a political realist, and he saw that there was no further hope. He said as much to Axel. "Mercy believes the whole royal family doomed and nothing can now be done to save them." One day the old diplomat made another observation that chilled Fersen's blood. "It is with regret that I say it," he declared, "but the Queen of France could be on the steps of the scaffold and that atrocity would not deter the Powers in the slightest." Few were better circumstanced than the comte de Mercy to know how accurate was this statement, for he still occupied a position of confidence in the Imperial government.

Austria would not even contribute the money that at one moment Fersen believed might be used to buy Marie Antoinette's freedom. What made this particularly revolting was that the money need not have come from the Habsburg coffers, but could have been taken from the large deposit that Louis XVI had sent abroad just before the flight to Varennes. Mercy had handed this over to the Emperor, whereupon it vanished or in any case became inaccessible.

Fersen's plan to ransom the Queen was not so chimeric as it might seem, for through an intermediary named Ribes, a Belgian banker, he planned to approach Danton. And in July of 1793 Danton had reasons for being extremely hospitable to such an overture. In the first place Danton was a man of human flesh and blood and was accessible to the promptings of compassion. He saw individuals not symbols—a weakness that was to destroy him—and he had no vindictive or vengeful feelings about the Widow Capet. He had just remarried and his young wife was filled with pity for the mother in the Temple Tower. But it was as a man of state or politician that Danton's attitude toward Marie Antoinette offered the most hope for her release. He wanted to stop the war. He had a new balance of European power in mind, a farseeing and audacious design that might have brought peace and perhaps even harmony to what remained of old Europe. The cornerstone of this plan was to be a treaty with England and Prussia and peace with Austria. He saw the liberation of the prisoners of the Temple as an indispensable preliminary to these negotiations. It was Danton who had been behind General Dampierre's overtures, which Thugut had so abruptly cut short.

Undiscouraged by Austria's rejection of his first proposal, Danton soon afterward made another move, again using the Queen as a card in his game. He sent two agents into Italy to secure the neutrality of Naples, Florence, and Venice. His promise for that neutrality was the delivery of Marie Antoinette. These negotiations—and there may well have been others too—are shrouded in mystery. They belong to the back corridors of history, for Danton had dangerous enemies in the Convention and any written word might have been used against him.

What is certain is that the two agents—their names were Maret and Sémonville—were sent into Italy openly and officially as accredited representatives of the French Republic. While on their way to Switzerland they were captured by the Austrians and on Thugut's orders thrown into prison. With their arrest all Danton's political projects crumbled. The secret of their mission soon leaked out and the rumor of it, distilled like poison, became associated with Danton's name. He was expelled from the Committee of Public Safety.

In Brussels, Fersen was unaware of these things and he supposed, as everyone in Europe continued to suppose, that Danton was still a leader of the Revolution. Danton's day was in fact over and less than six months after Marie Antoinette's execution he was to mount the steps of her scaffold. Thus, even had Axel been able to raise the money he thought might purchase Danton's help, his project would have been in vain.

From that moment he could only wait in anguish, as bound and helpless as the Queen of France herself. Of what had taken place at the Temple Tower and of Marie Antoinette's last moments in her cell at the Conciergerie he knew nothing.

During the weeks when Jarjayes and Toulan were planning the royal family's escape from the Temple it had been observed that the guards Lepitre and Toulan always seemed to be together on night duty in the prisoners' rooms. One evening the Tison couple heard loud laughter coming from behind the closed door. Certain rumors began to circulate among the other guards. It was said that the Widow Capet had given Toulan a gold box—Toulan's wife had shown it to a friend who happened to be the friend of another guard's wife. And Lepitre with his pedantic airs, always exhibiting his superior education before his less-educated colleagues, seemed an odd sort of patriot to be entrusted with guarding the family of the guillotined tyrant. At the end of March one of their fellow commissioners made a denunciation. The two men were brought before the Procurer of the Commune. With characteristic boldness Toulan simply laughed in his face at the absurdity of such an accusation while Lepitre's innocence seemed evident in his pompous, schoolmasterish ways. Few rough-and-ready men of the people will ever take a professor very seriously. The charges were dismissed.

But a few weeks later, when another guard denounced them, the authorities of the Commune listened with more attention. This time, instead of calling Toulan and Lepitre on the carpet, they decided to squeeze the Tisons for information. Inaccessible though this hard-hearted pair might seem to the warm emotions that are the weakness of most people, they happened to have one chink in their armor. They had a daughter, a pretty child of fourteen who was the light of their lives, and on this girl they lavished all that was in them of human affection. Because of their position at the Temple Tower the girl was not allowed to live with them, but the Commune had always been generous about permitting her a daily visit to her parents. Now, without any explanation, the Commune ordered these visits stopped. The Tisons were enraged. Time and again they had seen unauthorized people come and go from the Temple with the complicity of the guards. And they weren't even allowed to see their own daughter! A few days later the Mayor of Paris happened, as though by accident, to be at the Temple. Tison asked to see him. There was a stenographer in the room and as Tison unburdened himself his words were transcribed.

"Of what do you complain?" asked the Mayor.

"Of not being able to see my daughter," replied Tison. "And I would also like to report certain municipal guards who have not been behaving properly."

"What do these guards do?"

"They are always speaking in a low voice to the prisoners and they help them communicate with the outside."

"Who are they? Name them!"

"Toulan and Lepitre."

And then he told of one day seeing Marie Antoinette with a pencil in her hand and of finding a pen and sealing wax in a box belonging to Madame Élisabeth. He repeated his assertion that Toulan and Lepitre were agents who carried the prisoners' notes outside the prison. Madame Tison was sent for and she confirmed all that her husband said and added some more. She said that the two guards were incessantly in conversation with the prisoners and that sometimes they sat down and talked with them in a familiar way that was unsuitable to the dignity of a true Republican. She told them what she had seen

277

and she told them what she suspected. She and her husband then signed the *procès-verbal*. The next day they saw their daughter.

But Madame Tison suffered another human weakness: buried deep in her nature, well out of her own sight, she had a conscience. Having won her way by denunciation, she began to feel misgivings. They were gentle at first. She couldn't sleep at night. Then the nightmares began. When Toulan and Lepitre were suddenly removed from duty at the Temple her agitation increased and her behavior became very strange. "She was always sad," recalled Turgy, "and sighed deeply like a person suffering from remorse." One day in the first week of July she burst into the prisoners' room and in front of two guards, whose presence she ignored, flung herself at Marie Antoinette's feet. "Madame," she cried, "I implore Your Majesty to forgive me!" Turgy, who was present at the scene, asserts that these were exactly the words she used. "I am a miserable, unhappy woman," she continued, "for I have caused your death and that, too, of Madame Élisabeth. Forgive me, I beg you!"

Marie Antoinette raised the woman to her feet and tried to calm her. But Madame Tison was beyond human help. She began to scream and rave like a creature demented and then fell to the floor in convulsions. It took eight men to remove her. Two days later she was taken to the hospital of the Hôtel Dieu, where she was pronounced insane. She never returned to the Temple.

Marie Antoinette's first concern after this scene was for Madame Tison rather than herself. At the first opportunity she wrote Turgy a little note when she heard that Madame Tison had been removed to the Hôtel Dieu. "Is Tison's wife as mad as they say? Do they mean to replace her here? Are they taking good care of her?" Turgy records that Tison was very touched by the Queen's concern for his wife and henceforth tried to make amends.

In her raving and self-recrimination to Marie Antoinette, Madame Tison omitted mention of what was the real source of the remorse that drove her mad. It was because of her denunciations that the Commune decided to separate the young King from his mother. Madame Tison, when she flung herself at the Queen's feet, had already heard of this decision about which Marie Antoinette was still happily ignorant. Madame Tison, who so passionately loved her own child, now suffered in her mind something of what Marie Antoinette was about to endure.

The dauphin—and despite his father's death he was still known by that title—was a particularly bright and engaging child. In the deluge of disasters that she and her family had suffered for four years and which might have overwhelmed most people, Marie Antoinette had retained her own sanity largely because of her son. Her letters to Fersen, her statements to other "contacts" in the outside world, and the testimony of a number of eyewitnesses all confirm this fact. To her strong maternal love was added another element that made her relationship with the boy more complex. She saw him as heir to the vanished throne and to the end she retained the illusion that one day he would reign as King of France. She was both his mother and, as it were, trustee. In these two roles she tried to protect him on one hand from shocks and blows such as very few eight-year-old children are called upon to experience and on the other to instil in him the strength of character and self-discipline that by bitter experience she knew to be necessary to a king. It is not least among the credits that must be given her at this period of her life that she performed both roles admirably. The very natural instinct that might have prompted her to overindulge a boy who had suffered so cruelly and for so little fault of his own was restrained by parental good sense. The deplorable deficiencies of her own childhood were enough to guide her. For herself she had learned too late life's great lesson: that it is through suffering, not through what appears to be happiness, that we acquire wisdom. Like many parents who have not themselves been good children she hoped to impart the painful knowledge of experience to her son.

She continued the daily lessons that his father had begun. Two or three hours of the morning were devoted to supervising his studies. She insisted that he show respect to the guards and others who were responsible for their care and more than once she obliged him to say, "*Bonjour, Monsieur,*" to men whom he had heard address his mother in the coarsest terms. The boy's good manners and Marie Antoinette's sound maternal instincts were inevitably noted by many of their guards. It was this among other things that had brought Toulan over to Marie Antoinette's side. The effects of so careful an education were reflected in the boy's personality. By every report he was an unusually attractive and interesting child whose good nature had been unbruised by the sorrow and fear that had been his portion almost since his birth. He became the central fact of his mother's life and although she had failed as Queen she took comfort in the fact that she might one day give France a good king. The decision of the Commune to take the boy away from her was the worst blow to befall her in the long road that led her from Versailles to the scaffold. Bearing their orders, the commissioners arrived at night, after the evening meal. The boy was asleep but the other members of the family were peaceably employed. Madame Élisabeth and Marie Antoinette were mending their clothes. Marie Thérèse was reading.

"We have come to execute a decree of the Commune which orders that the son of Capet shall be separated from his mother."

Not immediately comprehending, Marie Antoinette looked at the man without speech. Then with a cry she rose from her chair. "Never! Take my son from me? Never! You cannot do it. I won't let you do it."

Two of the commissioners started toward the boy's bed. Marie Antoinette flung herself in front of them. "You cannot do it!" she declared. "I will not let you do it."

The boy, who had been wakened by the uproar, soon realized what was afoot and ran to his mother. "Don't let them take me," he implored her. Marie Antoinette clutched him to her side and tried to calm him, but his cries were now added to all the others.

"What's the use of all this wailing?" asked one of the commissioners. "Nobody is going to kill the child. Now hand him over, because if you don't we will know how to take him."

Marie Thérèse, the only witness who lived to describe the scene, says in her memoirs that "the municipals threatened to call up the guard and use force. An hour then passed in discussions, in menaces, in tears and pleading. Finally my mother consented to give up her son and, bathing him with her tears as though she foresaw she would never see him again, she handed him over to the commissioners. The poor boy kissed us all tenderly and left in sobs with the guards."

When, on the following day, Marie Antoinette learned that his keeper and "tutor" was the illiterate Simon, one of the rougher of the Temple warders, she was prostrated. This man was appointed by the Commune to "turn the Capet boy into a good *sans-culotte*" and he accepted the assignment with confidence. "It is true that the wolf's cub is insolent, Citizens," he announced, "but I'll know how to curb him."

For three days Marie Antoinette heard her son weeping in Simon's rooms on the floor below her—they occupied Louis' old quarters. Sometimes Simon would take him up to a platform on the top of the tower and his mother would wait hours on end by a small opening in the wall near the stairs out of which she could catch a glimpse of him when the pair went up to the tower.

The boy's sobs gradually abated but Marie Antoinette's anguish in no way diminished. One day she turned to Madame Élisabeth with a cry of despair and said, "I know that he is suffering at this moment. Yes, I would know if he suffered even though he were a hundred miles away and my heart would tell me if he were ill. For the last two days the tears of my child have been falling on my heart. God himself has now forsaken me! Oh, Sister, I dare no longer pray."

In the immeasurable abyss of her suffering Marie Antoinette was mercifully spared the knowledge of what would have been a still worse sorrow. A child's attachment to his memories is of short span and it is in the nature of things that children of seven or eight should soon adapt themselves to new circumstances. In a week or two after his tears had dried the young Capet looked around and began to brighten. Things were not so bad as they had first seemed in his new surroundings. They were better, in fact, than they had been when he was cooped upstairs with three women fluttering over him. Dressed in the clothes of a patriot and wearing a red bonnet, he was allowed out in the courtyard where the guards would roughhouse with him. He soon discovered that a good Republican remark couched in scatological or blasphemous language would make the men laugh and he wasn't long in picking up the age-old vocabulary of the guardroom. The irksome restraints imposed on him by his mother and aunt were soon forgotten. He was introduced to the pleasures of wine and then —this was later admitted by Simon—to stronger stimulants such as brandy. Simon's promise to turn him into a good *sans-culotte* was all too quickly realized. One day a guard named Danjon was playing a game of checkers with him in the room below his mother's. "We could hear the sound of thumping or of chairs being moved over our heads," Danjon relates. "All at once the child turned to me and said with an impatient gesture, 'Haven't they guillotined those two whores yet?'"

Danjon left the room sickened.

So susceptible was the boy to his education as a patriot that certain officials of the Commune began to regard him as a good source of evidence that could be used against his mother in her approaching trial. They pumped him about what he knew about her, Toulan, and Lepitre. But Marie Antoinette and Toulan had taken care that their conversations should never be overheard by the boy, for his mother was well familiar with his propensity to chatter. Some years earlier she had touched on this very matter in a letter to Madame de Tourzel: "He keeps his word faithfully once he has given it, but he is very indiscreet and easily repeats what he has heard and often without meaning to lie, he adds things suggested by his own imagination. It is his greatest fault and it must be firmly corrected."

Dropping the path that might have led them to evidence against Toulan and Jarjayes, the Commune, led by Hébert, was soon hot on another more promising trail. They remembered the boy's hernia for which doctors had been summoned a few weeks earlier and using this as a foundation on which to fabricate their story they coaxed and forced the boy into the telling of terrible lies. Of this ultimate blow which, like the blow that is given cattle led to the slaughter, was to precede her execution by only a few hours, Marie Antoinette had no premonitory hint. It was conceived in darkness and silence in the downstairs room of the Temple after she had been taken to the Conciergerie and it was delivered in the courtroom where she sat on trial for her life.

After her son was taken from her Marie Antoinette relinquished her last grip on life. She sank into a stupor from which neither Madame Élisabeth nor her daughter could rouse her. Like all those whose central being has been injured by some profound shock she was no longer able to react to external circumstance. When, therefore, four police administrators entered her room in the early hours of the morning of August 2 and informed her that they had come to remove her to the Conciergerie, she seemed indifferent. She listened to the reading of the Convention's decree without emotion. Then she rose and, helped by her sister-in-law and daughter, prepared a little parcel of clothes. She was forced to dress in the presence of the men and then at their request to empty her pockets. They left her only a handkerchief and a bottle of smelling salts. They did not see a small gold watch that she wore on a chain around her neck. It had been a present from her mother that she brought to France with her from Vienna twenty-three years before. Nor did they notice a yellow glove belonging to the dauphin that she managed to conceal on her person. They urged her to make haste. She embraced her daughter and told her to be brave and take care of her health. She turned to Madame Élisabeth and entrusted the children to her care. Then, without looking back, she left the room and, escorted by the police, descended the Tower stairs. At the end of the last flight there was a low lintel over the door. Either she did not see it in the dark or she forgot to stoop. She hit her forehead. One of the guards was concerned. "Did you hurt yourself?" he asked.

"No," she murmured. "Nothing more can hurt me now."

Two carriages accompanied by twenty gendarmes took the little group across the deserted city to the Conciergerie. They did not arrive there until nearly three. The turnkey on duty that night, a man named Larivière, was dozing when the soldiers of the guard beat on the door with the butts of their muskets. Still full of sleep and through the gloom he discerned a "tall and beautiful woman" standing among the group of gendarmes. She bent down to pass through the wicket gate and then when she entered the hall he saw with astonishment that the new prisoner was the Queen of France. He knew her features well, for he had once been a pastry cook at Versailles.

Marie Antoinette was taken directly to her cell without the clerical formalities in the director's office that usually preceded an incarceration in the Conciergerie. The prison director or "concierge," a man named Richard, was sent for and he brought his register to her cell, where he enrolled her among the inmates with the note that she was accused of "having conspired against France." Madame Richard and her servant, a girl named Rosalie Lamorlière, joined the group that had gathered in the small stone room. The night was hot and the air very close. Marie Antoinette submitted to the clerical routine standing. She made no complaint but Rosalie noticed that her face was drenched with sweat and that she had to wipe her forehead three or four times with the handkerchief they had allowed her to keep.

At last it was over. The men departed, leaving only two guards, who were to be in the same cell with her night and day for the next two and a half months. Madame Richard, a kindly woman, and the serving girl Rosalie remained. Rosalie stepped forward and offered to help her undress.

"No, thank you, child," answered the prisoner. "Now that I have no one I do everything for myself."

Day was breaking and the two women retired, taking their candles with them. The daughter of Maria Theresa looked about her and saw to what shore the tides of life had finally brought her. The cell was less than twelve feet square. No rug covered the rough stone floor, no cloth or paper covered the thick walls that dripped with the slime and damp of centuries. The only light came from a narrow and barred window that looked out onto the so-called Women's Court of the jail where the female prisoners of the Conciergerie were permitted to take the air during certain hours of the day. A camp bed and mattress, two cane chairs, a stool, and a small table were the only furniture in this cell that was no different and indeed worse than those allocated to common thieves and prostitutes. Its only "luxury" was a small screen thoughtfully provided by the concierge's wife behind which Marie Antoinette could undress out of sight of the guards. This, in time, was to be taken from her.

During the month of August the little cell was insufferably hot. As the autumn wore on it grew unbearably cold. It was always wet. Her shoes were soon covered with mold and her few clothes reduced to rags. She was allowed no needles and no thread so she was unable to mend her worn black dress. But the kindly Madame Richard arranged to have some of this work done and to have her big widow's cap reduced in size and made into two simple caps. One of the police commissioners, a man named Michonis, a former vendor of lemonade, had some of her linen sent from the Temple. It was packed by Madame Élisabeth and it contained two pairs of black silk stockings, two pieces of ribbon, a white wrapper "to wear in the morning," and a pair of shoes. There was no cupboard in her cell, but Rosalie lent her a cardboard box in which to put these treasures. She received the box, as Rosalie later recalled, "with as much satisfaction as if it were the most beautiful treasure in the world."

Her worse privation proved to be lack of work or occupation. Forbidden pen and paper or needles and thread, she had nothing to do all through the day. Sometimes she would lean over the guards' shoulders when they were playing backgammon and follow the progress of their game, but they were forbidden to talk to her except in the most perfunctory way, so there was no conversation. Rosalie noticed that she had managed to pull a few strands of canvas out of the screen by her bed and these she polished with her hands and braided together.

The prison officials discovered her watch and confiscated it. Madame Richard was present when this happened and she told Rosalie that the Queen wept like a child when this last link with Vienna was taken from her. No one had yet noticed two solitaire rings she still wore on her fingers. Rosalie wrote that "although she was unconscious of the fact, these rings became a sort of toy for her. As she sat dreaming she would take them off and put them on again, slipping them from one hand to the other several times a minute."

She would sit thus for hours on end, staring into space as she moved the rings about her thin fingers. In these long periods of musing she seemed haunted by memories, but she never spoke of what she thought, not even to Rosalie, whose gentle manners and unobtrusive respect had become the last ray of brightness in days that were now engulfed by the dark. Despite Marie Antoinette's isolation and the Convention's extreme vigilance there were people from the outer world who managed to penetrate the walls of the Conciergerie and enter the Queen's cell. Many of these people were men and women of royalist conviction and a curious number of them were English. Their visit was usually arranged through heavy bribes and the complicity of the police administrator, Michonis. They would arrive in disguise and be taken to the threshold of the Queen's cell where they would look at her for a moment or two and then pass on. No word was ever exchanged between the prisoner and her clandestine visitors. Marie Antoinette in any case would not have known or recognized most of them. She sat unseeing as they came and went. A description of one of these visits reached Fersen in Brussels in early September and filled him with horror. "An Englishman who has just arrived in Switzerland claims to have paid 25 louis to enter the Queen's prison. He carried a pitcher of water with him. He found the Queen seated with her head lowered and covered by her hands and extremely poorly dressed. She didn't look up and he said nothing to her. That was agreed upon in advance. The last detail is horrible . . ."

One day toward the end of August, Michonis entered her cell on his usual rounds. This time he was accompanied by a short, round-featured man of about thirty-six who wore a suit of dark material. In his buttonhole there were two carnations. Marie Antoinette saw him and started. She recognized him at once, for he was none other than the chevalier de Rougeville, the man who had saved her life on the day of the invasion of the Tuileries in June of the previous year. She was unable to hide her emotion at the sight of this visitor whom she knew to be a friend. Suddenly she began to tremble.

Rougeville was better able to contain himself. As he later recalled, he was shocked by the sight of the emaciated old woman who had once been the Queen of France. Betraying no emotion and giving no sign of recognition he took the two carnations from his buttonhole and threw them behind the screen. Marie Antoinette stared at him uncomprehendingly. In a low voice the chevalier told her they contained notes. There was time only to say this. Michonis was already out of the room and Rougeville was obliged to follow. Marie Antoinette thought quickly. When she saw that Michonis and the chevalier were in the women's courtyard she approached the guard, a man named Gilbert, and asked him to send Michonis back, that she had something to say to him about the food. The gendarme went to the window and called the administrator. The moment his back was turned she retrieved the carnations and took out the notes, which she was able to read rapidly behind the screen. The first of these notes read: "I shall never forget you. I shall always seek to show my devotion. If you need three or four hundred louis for those about you I shall bring them next Friday." The other, which has long vanished, was a plan of escape.

The "Plot of the Carnation," as it became known in official records, is an obscure and mysterious affair. In the course of the investigations that followed its failure, everyone was to lie, some to save their own skins, others to protect their fellow conspirators. The Convention itself hurried to draw a veil over it. In its details the true story will probably never be known, but its general outline is enough to show how tenacious were those who hoped to rescue Marie Antoinette from her executioners. One wonders how many more such plots there may have been whose whisper has not come down to us through the back corridors of history. The extraordinary fact about the Carnation Plot is that, like Toulan's plot at the Temple, it might have succeeded.

The essential fact in the business was the complicity of the police administrator Michonis. For Michonis was another of the Queen's remarkable "conquests." It is not known at what point he revealed his sympathies to her. It is certain, however, that he was deeply involved in another obscure plot led by a man named Batz to rescue the Queen from the Temple Tower after the failure of Toulan's two projects. Unlike Toulan, Michonis moved in the dark, with caution and less *brio*. It is doubtful whether Toulan ever knew of Michonis' attempts to save the Queen, or Michonis of Toulan's. Marie Antoinette's last concern in life was to protect these men who without thought of personal reward risked everything to help her. It probably seemed to her that their best protection was a mutual ignorance of each other's complicity in these plots. During the exhaustive interrogations that followed the Carnation affair she managed to protect Michonis with dexterity. But not enough to save him. Like Toulan he was to follow her to the guillotine.

His scheme was bold and simple. It all depended on his reputation as a good patriot and his position of responsibility and rank in the police. He planned to enter the Conciergerie late in the evening of September 2, wave some official-looking papers at Richard, the concierge, and announce that on the orders of the Convention he had come to escort Marie Antoinette back to the Temple. The two guards would accompany them out the door of the prison to the carriage in which Rougeville would be waiting. From there she would be taken to the seclusion of a château in the country and then, a few days later, to Germany.

The difficulty in this plan was winning the complicity of two guards, Gilbert and Dufresne. In his position of police administrator Michonis may have secured the appointment of these two men with the possibility of rescue in mind. In any case, neither appears to have been a political fanatic and both seem to have been the kind who would be amenable to a good bribe. That was why Rougeville promised to come back with the money.

Marie Antoinette wasted no time in approaching Gilbert. It was an enormous gamble and all that remained of hope depended on its outcome. It must have been with a pounding heart that she informed Gilbert that the man who had come to her cell with Michonis was a Chevalier of Saint Louis who wanted to help her. And as she proffered the promise of an immediate reward in cold cash she no doubt spoke of more substantial indemnities, when after her escape it would be in her power to command large sums. She then showed him a note that she had written with pinpricks on a piece of paper that was to be given to Rougeville. This note was later mutilated by Michonis and no one will ever know what it really said. It is supposed to have read as follows: "I am closely watched. I can speak to no one. I trust you. I shall come." It may be that she asked Gilbert to deliver this note to Rougeville. He later claimed that he took it and gave it at once to Madame Richard. But this was probably a lie. According to Madame Richard, also probably a lie, she found it accidentally in his pocket. In any case the note did end up in the Richards' hands a few days before the attempt at rescue was made. Madame Richard showed it to Michonis, who took it from her and told her to pay no attention to it. And Madame Richard, either averting her eyes from her suspicions or else herself an open accomplice in the plot, said nothing more.

What is certain beyond doubt in this murky business is that

Gilbert and the other guard, Dufresne, agreed to lend themselves to the conspiracy and that shortly before eleven o'clock on the night of September 2–3 Michonis in official capacity appeared at the Conciergerie and announced that he had orders to conduct the Widow Capet back to the Temple. The door of the Queen's cell was unlocked and, flanked by her two guards, she stepped into the long corridor that led to the main exit from the prison and the street. To arrive there they had to pass through a number of small gates or wickets. They managed to go through all of these without obstruction or hindrance. They had just passed the last of them and were about to go through the street door when one of the guards, probably Gilbert, moved forward threateningly and prevented the prisoner from advancing any farther. With this the fragile threads that held the plan together, the silent complicity of the Richard couple, the ignorance of the other sentinels, were snapped and Marie Antoinette was returned to her cell. Rougeville fled, but Michonis audaciously returned the next day in the midst of the Convention's investigation of the business and denied any complicity. He was arrested.

The Carnation Plot had immediate consequences. Marie Antoinette was moved to an even smaller and darker cell—it is this which is shown to today's visitor to the Conciergerie. She was permitted no screen behind which to dress and undress and was subjected to a far closer vigilance. The Richard couple were removed and replaced by a stern pair named Bault who were warned that they would pay with their heads should the Queen attempt another escape. No one, neither the guards nor the Bault couple, was allowed to speak to her, except in exceptional circumstances. Surrounded by her jailers she was more alone than if she had been condemned to solitary confinement. The devoted Rosalie did what she could to mitigate her loneliness. After dark the Queen was allowed no candle or lamp, but Rosalie devised a way to lessen that hardship. "I prolonged as much as possible the various little preparations for the night so that my mistress might not be left in solitude and darkness until the last possible moment." Although Rosalie was not allowed to talk to the Queen, the girl's presence in the room seems to have brought some comfort to the prisoner for "She noticed these little attentions which were the natural outcome of my loyalty and respect and she thanked me for them with a glance full of friendliness as if I had done more than my simple duty."

Another consequence of the Carnation affair was the settling of opinion in the Committee of Public Safety about bringing her to trial. That a trial was sooner or later inevitable cannot be doubted, but until this moment there were a few rational men in the Committee who still hoped to use Marie Antoinette as some kind of barter with the Austrians or the other Allies. Cambon was the most conspicuous of these and for weeks he and his party tried to defer the moment when the Queen would be brought to trial, after which step everyone realized that there could be no further hope. As time passed and no encouraging sign or word came from Vienna it grew more and more difficult to forestall the demands of the *enragés*. The most bloodthirsty of these was Hébert, one of the worst of the psychopathic personalities to emerge during the Reign of Terror. Along with being a leader of the Commune he was editor of a newssheet of the gutter called *le Père Duchesne* in which he represented himself as a pipe-smoking sage, a folksy, rough-speaking man of the people. In reality he was a dandified overscented little man with a tendency to scream. His hatred of Marie Antoinette was pathological in its intensity and partook of blood lust. In a secret session of the Committee of Public Safety held at the time of the Carnation Plot he rose and again demanded that Marie Antoinette be brought to trial.

"I have promised the head of Antoinette to my readers. I shall go and cut it off myself if there is any further delay in giving it to me!" he declared. And this time he had his way. Those who hoped to use Marie Antoinette and her children in some negotiation with Austria could hold out no longer. The Public Prosecutor Fouquier-Tinville was sent for. He then informed the Committee that to be sure of their case they should allow him to replace the jurors and judges of the Tribunal with men of his choice. The Committee used the Carnation Plot to bludgeon the Convention into granting Fouquier-Tinville and his Tribunal this dangerous favor. By September 29 the new machinery was well oiled and ready for business. On October 3, Fouquier was formally informed by the Convention that he was to prepare a case against the widow of Louis Capet.

Back at the Temple Tower, Hébert was busy gathering evidence of his own against the woman he called "the salacious whore." The boy talked freely. Given a little brandy, he admitted to anything they suggested. And in the end he signed his name to the appalling confession they had prepared for him. His cramped and broken signature on that document is among the most terrible souvenirs of the Revolution. First his sister and then Madame Élisabeth were sent for and confronted with the boy and his words. Marie Thérèse looked at him in horror, left the room and turned her back on him forever. Madame Élisabeth, hearing things she did not know existed, averted her head.

It was to be Marie Antoinette's final grief to discover during her trial that they knew what her son had said against her.

No one in Europe had any illusion about the fate that awaited the former Queen of France when it was learned that the Convention had decreed her trial. Axel learned of that decision four days after it had been made in Paris. "Should this trial take place," he wrote in his Journal, "all will be lost. The Convention will never acquit her." The rumor that the Public Prosecutor had complained to the Convention that he had no documentary evidence to use against her gave him no cheer. "Despite the fact that they have no proofs against her," he wrote Taube, "we can hope for nothing with these scoundrels who invent evidence when they don't have it and condemn people on vague accusations and suspicions. No, my friend, let us hope for nothing. Let us resign ourselves to the Divine Will. Her death is already decided upon and we must now prepare ourselves for it and gather enough strength to endure this terrible blow. I have been trying to do so for some time and I think that I will feel little when the news comes. God alone can save her now. Let us pray for His mercy and submit to His decree . . ."

Marie Antoinette's friends in Brussels followed the progress of her trial with horror. Prompted by Fersen and perhaps too by his conscience Mercy took up his pen and made a private appeal to the Powers. As a polished and experienced diplomat he did this through proper channels and he couched his words in phrases that might in no way give offense to his superiors. "So long as the Queen of France has not been directly threatened," he wrote Coburg, "we have been able to keep our silence for fear of arousing the rage of the savages around her. But now that she has been handed over to a bloody tribunal any step that gives hope of saving her should be taken as a duty. Posterity will hardly believe that so enormous a crime took place only a few steps away from the victorious armies of Austria . . . and that those armies did nothing to prevent it."

Mercy knew as well as every other diplomat in the service of the Emperor that all that was needed to secure Marie Antoinette's rescue was the exchange of the five commissioners held prisoner by his government. But he made no mention of that either in his letter to Coburg or in another he wrote Thugut: "Is the Emperor going to allow the Queen to perish without even trying to snatch her from her executioners? I know the impossibility of taking any *political* step in common with the other Powers in this matter, but are there not *private* attentions, separate from political considerations, owed by the head of the House of Austria to the daughter of Maria Theresa who is about to mount the scaffold of her husband? Is it either to the dignity or the interest of His Majesty the Emperor to see the fate with which his august aunt is menaced and do nothing to try to deliver her from the hands of her executioners?"

To these appeals Mercy received no reply nor was he ever to have a reply. Marie Antoinette's execution happened to coincide with the condemnation of the Girondins and the beginning of the Terror. By October 14 the frenzy was well underway and heads, to use Fouquier-Tinville's descriptive words, were starting to fall "like slates." The Austrians examined the scene and decided to let France bleed herself to death. Why waste an army on them when they would destroy themselves? If Marie Antoinette's execution added a little blood to the bath so much the better. In words that prefigure exactly those of Robespierre and St. Just a spokesman for this policy translated Thugut's political program into philosophy: "A great purge should be effected in France. When the human soul has lost its strength through softness, incredulity, and the gangrenous vices that follow too much civilization it can only be strengthened through bloodshed. The human species must be looked on as a tree that is pruned without cease by an invisible hand—blood is the fertilizer of the plant that is called genius."

Mercy accepted Thugut's rebuff philosophically. He went off to the country to spend a fortnight with his mistress. Fersen was disgusted by his behavior and from that moment lost what little regard he had ever had for him. "Mercy talks a great deal about his devotion to the unfortunate Queen," wrote Axel, "and he expresses grief at her fate, but these feelings spring from his respect for the memory of Maria Theresa. He has always made it clear that he was only devoted to the Queen because of her mother while he should have been because of her generosity to him and her trust in him."

So in the end nothing was done by those who at so little cost to themselves might have saved Marie Antoinette. In the end as at the beginning she was the victim of the political projects of her house and a sacrifice to the implacable device of the Habsburgs: *Tu Felix Austria Nube.* Seventeen years later the same Emperor who viewed the execution of his aunt with equanimity was with equal equanimity to send another archduchess, his own daughter, to France to marry the autocrat who had established his throne upon the ashes of that once occupied by Louis XVI.

The Queen of France had no more partisans in Europe. A widow and prisoner, she was no longer useful to anyone and so the politicians abandoned her to her fate. But Marie Antoinette the woman still had friends and this little band now drew together in anguish to await the news they knew to be inevitable.

The rumor heard by Fersen that Fouquier-Tinville complained of insufficient evidence to concoct a case against Marie Antoinette was true. Three or four times the Public Prosecutor had sent an urgent appeal to the Convention asking them for documents and particularly for the papers that had been found in the Queen's rooms at the Tuileries after the Flight to Varennes. In the end they sent him the transcripts of the interrogation that had followed the Carnation Plot. That was all. The Convention's reticence seems inexplicable, but they had in fact very little evidence to give their prosecutor. There were no papers that could be used against the accused. Fouquier was obliged to root through the inquiry into the Carnation affair to gather his evidence. Night after night he pored over these transcripts, taking notes and adding marginal comments in red ink.

The purpose behind the interrogations that followed the Carnation Plot seems to have been to trap Marie Antoinette into an admission of unpatriotic thoughts. Her inquisitors probed relentlessly into her political views but, debilitated though she was by long imprisonment and psychologically shattered though she must have been by the failure of the plot to rescue her, she answered the questions with skill.

"Are you pleased with the success of our enemies' forces?"

"I sympathize with the success of those of my son's country."

"What is your son's country?"

"Surely there can be no doubt. Is he not French?"

They turned to Varennes. "Why were you so eager to use any means to be united with your family that was at war with the French nation?"

Marie Antoinette might have reminded them that France and Austria were not at war in June of 1791, but the old insinuation that she was Austrian rather than French appears to have stung and distracted her.

"My children are my family," she replied. "And I can only be happy with them."

All in all, there wasn't much Fouquier could glean from these pages. He therefore decided to subject the accused to what was called a Preliminary Examination. Her trial was to take place two days later, after the Prosecutor's office had had an opportunity to sort and organize what had been harvested at this "preliminary examination."

Marie Antoinette was given no hint that her trial was at hand. She was in bed and asleep when on the night of October 12 four guards and an usher came to her cell to bring her up to the Tribunal for questioning. All during that day she had suffered greatly from the cold and, uncomplaining though she usually was, she spoke of her acute discomfort to Rosalie. Through the concierge Bault she asked the authorities if she might have an extra blanket. Fouquier angrily rejected the request and threatened Bault with the guillotine should he dare ask for such a thing again. Worse than the cold, she had suffered a severe menstrual hemorrhage that morning and was badly weakened by loss of blood. She had been asleep for nearly two hours when the door of her cell was suddenly thrown open and she was ordered to get dressed to appear before the examining magistrate of the Revolutionary Tribunal.

Preceded by a turnkey carrying a torch, she was escorted through the stone corridors of the Conciergerie, up a pair of winding stairs and down another to the vast, bare rooms that had once been the Grand Chamber of the Parlement of Paris, one of the architectural glories of the *ancien régime*. Gone were the tapestries that once adorned its walls, gone the Crucifixion by Dürer and Coustou's bas-relief. Stripped of its former finery and lighted on this night by only two candles placed on the desk of the examining magistrate, the cavernous room, now the seat of the Revolutionary Tribunal, seemed to swallow all life. Since this was not a trial, the hearing was closed to the public, but far away in the deeper shadows of the spectators' gallery Marie Antoinette may have discerned a few motionless figures, as dim as ghosts, who came as observers sent by the Convention or as guests of Fouquier. She was given a bench in front of the magistrate's desk and the inquiry began.

The questions put to her that night forecast the charges that would be brought against her at her trial. Over and again they returned to four points: that she had squandered French money on intrigues and pleasures; that as Queen she had always favored Austrian interests over French and had sent carloads of French gold to her brother, the Emperor ("the King of Hungary and Bohemia," as the President of the Tribunal described him); that during the Revolution she had intrigued with foreign powers against France while at home she intrigued against Liberty; that she had been responsible for her husband's decision to leave Paris that had ended with the arrest at Varennes. There was no hint during this preliminary examination of the charge of lascivious and immoral living that was to be brought against her at her trial.

To each of these accusations there was, of course, a grain of truth. From the vantage point of our more liberal time one might wonder if the squandering of the government's money might justify a death sentence, but the other two charges, that she had "intrigued with foreign Powers against France and against Liberty at home," were not without foundation. All the same, the Prosecutor had not a shred of evidence with which to substantiate the accusation that she had been in correspondence with foreign Powers. Her letters to Fersen were not to be discovered until many years later, while her open appeal for help from her brother was somewhere behind locked drawers in Vienna—unanswered. The charge that she had intrigued against Liberty at home was one of those loose and convenient accusations that could be interpreted in any way the court chose. A few weeks after Marie Antoinette's execution twenty-two Girondins, the flower of Revolutionary idealism, were to perish under the knife on the same charge. Indeed, nearly all of Marie Antoinette's accusers were themselves to be condemned on those grounds. Robespierre was to secure Hébert's head with that accusation and the Convention in its turn was to secure Robespierre's by declaring that he, too, had conspired against Liberty. Like Love and Truth, Liberty is a word that may lend itself to a variety of definitions.

Marie Antoinette answered their questions with composure. When she was accused of "opening the doors of the Tuileries" at the time of the King's trip to Varennes she replied, "I do not think that opening a door for someone proves that you are dominating him." When at one point she made the reply—a reply she was to give to several questions and one that was as meaningless as her accusers' use of the word Liberty—that "all she and Louis had ever wished was the happiness of France" the examining magistrate turned on her and said that if this had been true she would have kept her brother from making war on France. Marie Antoinette reminded him that it was France, not Austria, who had declared war and that Louis XVI had been ordered by his ministers to read a declaration already prepared for him. The magistrate admitted that he had lost that round. "All the same," he retorted lamely, "you cannot be unaware that the declaration of war came through the intrigues of a liberticide faction."

But on many points she was vulnerable and she knew it. The accusation of extravagance and squandering could have had a deadly effect if the Prosecutor were to read off some of the pension lists and private account books in front of a jury. He did not, in fact, do this. They were probably too certain of their case to send for that damning and irrefutable evidence. At no point during her interrogation did the accused know how much evidence they might have accumulated against her, so every answer had to be hedged against the possibility of being exposed as a liar. Although she appeared outwardly calm, her mind at all times had to be vigilant and wary. She made no misstep during that long and exhausting session.

At the end they asked her if she had any counsel.

"No, I do not know anyone."

"Would you like the Tribunal to appoint one or two for you?"

"I am willing."

They then named Citizens Chauveau-Lagarde and du Coudray as her counsel. She signed the transcript of the hearing to which Fouquier, the magistrate Herman, and the court stenographer added their initials and she was immediately conducted back to her cell where, exhausted, she fell into bed.

There was no sleep that night for the industrious Public Prosecutor. As soon as the hearing was finished he retired with a copy of it to his office in one of the towers of the Conciergerie and here he prepared the indictment that was to be used at her trial. "Like Messalina, Brunehaut, Frédégonde, and the Médicis, once called Queens of France, whose names are forever odious, Marie Antoinette, the widow of Louis Capet, since her arrival in France has been the curse and the leech of the French people . . ." The opening words set the tone of what was to follow. Comparing Marie Antoinette to a vampire who had slaked her thirst on the blood of the French, he touched on her "criminal intrigues," her "abnormal pleasures" and "perfidious thoughts" as he introduced the charges with which he planned to secure her head. He did not introduce Hébert's accusation until the end, but it was there, timed to explode like a mine when the woman's uncertain footing had been well weakened by the earlier charges. "Finally," it read, "the Widow Capet, immoral in every way and a new Agrippina, is so perverted and so familiar with every crime that, forgetting her position as mother and the line drawn by the laws of nature, she did not recoil from indulging with Louis-Charles Capet, her son, as confessed by the latter, in indecencies the mere idea and mention of which arouse a shudder of horror."

Of this she had no hint when two days later she appeared in the courtroom. Either Fouquier omitted it from her copy of the indictment or Chauveau-Lagarde, impelled by pity, thrust it from her sight for it is certain that, as Fouquier intended, this final infamy took her by surprise.

Chauveau-Lagarde was a brave lawyer who had defended Charlotte Corday in July of that year. He was in the country when the news reached him that he had been appointed to defend the Widow Capet. He did not arrive at the Conciergerie until two in the afternoon. Since the trial was to begin at eight o'clock on the following morning he had very little time to prepare a defense. He begged the Queen to solicit a delay of three days from the Convention. Marie Antoinette was at first reluctant to beg any favor from the men who had condemned her husband, but when her lawyer told her that she owed it to her children "to omit nothing necessary for her defense" she acceded to his request. Chauveau took her letter to Fouquier, who promised to deliver it to the Convention. In fact, he did no such thing. He kept it and after Marie Antoinette's death he gave it to Robespierre, who hid it along with some other papers under his mattress, where it was found after his execution.

Delay or no delay, Marie Antoinette's death certificate had virtually been signed and only she seems to have entertained the faintest illusion about the outcome of her trial. Both Chauveau-Lagarde and Rosalie received the impression that somewhere in the back of her mind she did indeed still retain some flickering spark of hope.

If this was the case it can only have been part of a larger hope that one day she might be reunited with her children. The thought of being separated from them forever was, as she herself declared when all was over, "unendurable." For them she was prepared to fight for a life that was hardly worth the struggle.

Another element, founded more on a certainty of death than on any hope for life, entered into her attitude toward her trial. She was determined that her comportment before the Tribunal should be worthy of the Empress, her mother. All during her imprisonment she had been polite and submissive to her jailers and many of them at the Conciergerie like their colleagues at the Temple had been surprised to discover that the former Queen was a woman like any other. Now something else made its appearance. Chauveau, when he met her for the first time in her cell, was immediately struck by her air of immense majesty. From that moment she held herself in the posture of a queen. Her dignity did indeed impress that court as it has come to impress posterity. But it was a dignity that had little to do with the manner once prized at the court of Versailles, where the ability to place one foot in front of the other with elegance constituted an important attribute of nobility. Rather, Marie Antoinette's stance before her judges is one that may be admired by the common portion of humanity, for it belongs to the realm of the unbroken spirit. Her case, though hardly unique, remains an impressive instance of the victory of the individual over one of those tribunals to which the political and religious fanatics of history will always be partial.

All through the night of October 13–14 the spectators had been gathering to secure themselves a choice seat in the gallery. Since places were limited, admission was given to well-known *sans-culottes*, friends or relatives of those in some way associated with the Commune of the revolutionary Sections. There were a great many women present and conspicuous among these was a large representation of the *tricoteuses*, the famous harridans who carried their knitting with them from the courtroom to the foot of the guillotine and who with their incessant shrieking recalled to mind a chorus of harpies out of some drama of antiquity. It was thus not merely Fouquier's jury, hand-picked and paid for by him, who was determined to have the Widow Capet's head. It was most of the spectators too.

The accused was escorted into the courtroom promptly at eight o'clock. She had taken considerable pains over her appearance, and after adding a piece of black crepe to her widow's bonnet, she dressed her hair with care. But a gasp that was audible passed through the court at the sight of this woman whom many had seen when she had been Queen of France. Her legs were so thin they could hardly support her, her hair was snow-white and she had nearly lost the sight of one eye. She was thirty-seven years old. She looked seventy. But she crossed the room without help, holding her head high and in apparent command of her footing. She was taken to a small armchair elevated on a platform where she would be visible to everyone in the court and as soon as she was seated the indictment was read. She seemed to listen with indifference, drumming her fingers lightly over the arm of her chair, "as though she were at the keyboard of her clavecin." Her attitude irritated the President of the Tribunal, for when the witnesses were summoned he ordered her "to pay close attention."

There were forty-one witnesses. Fouquier had managed to assemble them in the brief time between the drawing up of the indictment and the trial. Of these witnesses nineteen declared they had nothing to say since they were ignorant of the business in question. Some of this group went so far as to state openly that they had nothing to depose against the Widow Capet. The number of witnesses who finally did offer evidence came to twenty-two and few of these had anything concrete to say against the accused. One or two even spoke in her defense.

But it is not the paucity of evidence that distinguishes Marie Antoinette's trial from so many that were to follow before that Tribunal. The day was at hand when all witnesses were to be eliminated and not even the accused permitted to speak in his defense. In a few months an accusation would be enough to send a man to the guillotine and the whole time-consuming procedure of a trial would be done away with. What lends Marie Antoinette's trial its unusual character, apart from the rank of the accused, is that almost every charge against her may be traced back to the slander and calumny of Versailles. It was not "the people" who handed Fouquier-Tinville the material with which he was to send her to her death. It was the highborn noblemen of the vanished court. It was Mesdames, the aunts, who first dubbed her "the Austrian" and in doing so branded her ineffaceably as a foreigner among her husband's subjects. It was the duc d'Aiguillon and his party who lent substance to the aunts' malicious chatter, for it was d'Aiguillon who first mouthed the story that she was her brother's agent at the French court and sent French gold to Austria. It was Artois, her brother-in-law, who in a spirit of light mischief began the gossip that she was a Lesbian. It was left to other factions of the court to embroider Artois' gossip into imputations that were monstrous. It was the comte de Provence, her other brother-in-law, who, casting doubt on the legitimacy of her children, attributed male lovers to her. And it was with the comtesse de Provence and others not invited to the intimate supper parties of Trianon that the whispers began of orgies and debaucheries. From the hired scribblers of the duc d'Orléans came the flood of lewd lampoons that were to provide Hébert with most of the epithets in *le Père Duchesne*: "bloodsucker," "Messalina," "vampire," "whore" . . . they had all been used at Versailles.

Indeed, at a very early moment in the trial the connection between the malicious gossip of the vanished court and the accusations of the Revolutionary Tribunal became apparent. A witness declared that he had it from a "good citizen" who was once employed at Versailles that Marie Antoinette sent huge shipments of gold to her brother during his campaign in Turkey. Fouquier asked the name of this person and the "good citizen" was sent for. She turned out to be a former maid and she deposed that one day at Versailles the comte de Coigny had told her that the Queen had already sent more than two hundred millions in gold to her brother during his campaign in Turkey and that she planned to send a great deal more. It is generally stated that the maid must have invented this story since there was no "comte" de Coigny then at Versailles and it was most unlikely that the duc of that name would make such confidences to a lowly servant. But in fact there was a branch of the Coigny family at Versailles who were among Marie Antoinette's bitterest enemies. The marquise de Coigny was the mistress of that duc de Lauzun whom the Queen had once mortally offended. This woman, who joined the extremist party of the Jacobin Club in order, as she said, to "put that insolent Marie Antoinette in her place," would in fact have been perfectly capable of spreading slander about the Queen among the palace servants. In her eyes the servants at least were French, Marie Antoinette was not.

As she sat there on trial for her life one wonders if the Queen herself saw how direct and clear was the line that connected the gossip of the court nobility—which with all the ill-placed pride of youth and innocence she had once disdained—and the indictment of

Fouquier-Tinville. Under the prosecution's questioning her mind must have returned more than once to the pastoral follies of Trianon and the gilded artifice of Versailles where the road that had brought her to this end had begun.

"Why were the Polignacs and other families gorged with gold from you?"

"They had places at court that procured riches for them."

"Where did you get the money to have the Petit Trianon built and furnished where you gave parties at which you were always the goddess . . . ? The Petit Trianon must have cost enormous sums."

"Perhaps it cost more than I might have wished. We became engulfed in more and more expense."

By the time Marie Antoinette was brought before the Revolutionary Tribunal most of these bluebloods—including Madame de Coigny—had left the sinking ship and made their way to Austria, England, or the Netherlands. It was among the French "people" that Marie Antoinette, like Louis XVI before her, was finally to find disinterested compassion. It was a pantry boy, a concierge and his wife, a poor serving girl, a Gascon peasant, a schoolmaster, and a former lemonade vendor who at great peril to themselves offered her kindnesses that were beyond the possibility of reward.

The trial meandered through the morning of the first day without much interest. At one point the *tricoteuses* in the spectators' gallery demanded that the prisoner should stand when answering. "Will they never grow tired of my sufferings?" she sighed to her counsel.

At last a sensational witness, Hébert, was called. He began by voicing suspicions about the guard Toulan, whom he claimed had been too sympathetic to the Widow Capet, and he spoke of finding counter-Revolutionary articles among her personal effects. Then, without warning, he announced that "Simon had surprised the young Capet in self-pollutions that were bad for his constitution. When Simon asked him who had taught him to do such things he replied that it was his mother and aunt whom he had to thank for the habit. From the declaration which the young Capet had made in the presence of the Mayor of Paris and the Procuror of the Commune it appeared that the two women often made him lie between them and so he committed the most disgusting acts of debauchery. After what the young Capet had confessed there was no reason to doubt that there was an incestuous relationship between mother and son."

One is left to imagine Marie Antoinette's feeling as she heard these words. She said nothing and the stenographic report records no gesture or movement of shock. She sat as though transfixed.

Hébert continued: "There is reason to believe that this criminal intercourse was not dictated by pleasure but in the calculated hope of enervating the boy, whom they still thought was destined to occupy a throne and whom they wished to dominate morally as a result of their scheme. As a result of the efforts he was forced to make he suffered a hernia. But since he has been taken from his mother his constitution has become robust."

The President turned to the accused. "What reply do you have to this desposition?" he enquired.

"I have no knowledge of the incidents Hébert speaks of," she replied quietly. The President himself seems to have been troubled by Hébert's testimony, for he tried to turn to other issues. But one of the jurors rose. "Citizen President," he declared, "would you draw attention to the accused that she has not answered the charge made by Citizen Hébert on the subject of what passed between her and her son." Unwillingly perhaps, the President turned to Marie Antoinette and repeated his question.

The Queen now rose from her chair. The stenographer records that she appeared "very moved." She addressed the President. "If I have not answered," she said, "it is because Nature refuses to answer such a charge made to a mother." Then, with a gesture worthy of a *tragédienne*, she turned from the President to the public gallery where sat the fishwives and women of the street. "I appeal to all mothers in this room!"

The words shot through the spectators like a jolt of electricity. The unexpected appeal of woman to woman, of mother to mother over the heads of men and across the borders of class and political differences was a masterful stroke, entirely characteristic of Marie Antoinette's instinctively correct gestures. Pandemonium broke out in the gallery, accompanied by something like applause. Several of the women fainted and had to be removed from the courtroom. Herman, the President of the Tribunal, rang his bell and called for order. He turned hastily to another subject, this time Varennes. After a few questions he introduced a name that must have filled the prisoner with another wave of emotion.

"Who furnished you with the famous carriage in which you left with your family?"

"It was a foreigner."

"Of what nationality?"

"Swedish."

"Was it not Fersen who was living in the rue de Bac?"

"Yes." Another murmur went through the court.

When at three o'clock the sitting was adjourned for a two-hour recess it was observed that the judges wore worried expressions as they left the courtroom.

Robespierre was to dine with one of the jurors that night in a private room at Venua's restaurant. When he heard of Hébert's charges and of Marie Antoinette's reply he hurled his fork against the plate in a rage. "The fool!" he cried. "It is not enough that the Capet woman should be a Messalina but that fool must turn her into an Agrippina, too!" Like the judges Robespierre feared that Hébert might have lost them their case.

At the Tribunal the sitting resumed soon after four. The former maid at Versailles gave her testimony, adding that someone at the palace had once told her that Marie Antoinette had tried to murder the duc d'Orléans. The King had found two pistols hidden on her and had ordered her confined to her apartments for a fortnight.

"It may be that my husband once ordered me to remain in my rooms for a fortnight, but it was for no such reason as that," replied Marie Antoinette.

The editor of a revolutionary gazette then deposed that Marie Antoinette had once ordered three men to murder him. The prisoner didn't trouble to answer that charge. The interrogation moved on to the Carnation Plot and Marie Antoinette was again obliged to keep her wits about her in order not to compromise those who had tried to help her. The first day's sitting came to an end at eleven o'clock and the prisoner was taken back to her cell by the officer of the guard, de Busne.

On the following day, her last, Marie Antoinette was brought before the Tribunal at nine in the morning. It was raining when she crossed the courtyard and there was a high wind. The first witness was the former Admiral d'Estaing, who stated that her intrigues at court had once caused him to lose a promotion. There was a minor sensation when the former marquis de La Tour du Pin, who had been a Minister of War under Louis XVI, was called as a witness. Asked whether he recognized the accused he turned to her and with a low, court bow he replied, "I have indeed the honor to know Madame."

For that reason and because of the bow, he was to lose his own head when in the following April he appeared before Fouquier-Tinville as a prisoner.

Through La Tour du Pin the Prosecutor had hoped to secure evidence that Marie Antoinette had meddled in affairs of state. This was a particularly dangerous area of inquiry for the Queen. But she bluntly denied the charges that rained down on her.

"Was it not you who appointed the ministers and filled other civil and military posts?"

"No."

"Did you not have a list of persons whom you wanted places for?"

"No."

"Did you not compel the Ministers of Finance to send you money . . . and did you not threaten those who refused?"

"Never."

The questioning seemed interminable but Marie Antoinette gave no sign of fatigue. The sitting was not suspended until four thirty. It had been going for seven and a half hours and during that time the accused had been without food and drink. Below in the Conciergerie it was announced that she would not be coming down during the recess. Rosalie was asked to bring up some soup. "I went up to find the Queen," Rosalie recalled, "and was just on the point of entering the room when a police superintendent named Labuzire snatched the bowl from me and gave it to his mistress. 'She wants to see the Widow Capet,' he said to me, 'and this is a perfect opportunity for her to do so,' whereupon the woman went off carrying the soup, half of which was spilt."

Darkness had fallen when the hearings were resumed. A few candles had been placed about the vast sepulchral hall. The trial had entered its final phase when Marie Antoinette was escorted back to her chair. During the recess a rumor had reached the Conciergerie that she would be acquitted and sentenced to banishment. "Marie Antoinette will get out of it," one of the spectators declared. "She has been answering like an angel." Some of this optimism may have communicated itself to the Queen. The questioning went on for another seven hours, but at no time did she falter or seem to weaken. It was after midnight when Fouquier finally turned to her and asked if she had anything to add to her defense before the hearing was pronounced closed. She rose and stated that, "Yesterday I did not know the witnesses and I did not know what they would testify. Well, no one has uttered anything positive against me. I conclude by observing that I was only the wife of Louis XVI and I was bound to conform to his will."

Chauveau-Lagarde then stepped forward and for two hours gave his defense, which was based on the nullity of the evidence. When he returned to his seat Marie Antoinette turned to him and in a low voice said, "How tired you must be, Monsieur Chauveau-Lagarde! I am very appreciative of all the trouble you have taken."

But Chauveau's spirited defense infuriated Fouquier-Tinville, who summoned a gendarme and ordered the advocate arrested on the spot. Undismayed by Chauveau's fate the Queen's second defense attorney, Tronson du Coudray, stepped forward and made his plea, which touched on Marie Antoinette's domestic intrigues. When he returned to his seat he too was placed under arrest. At the end of the trial the two lawyers, like their doomed client, were taken down to the prison of the Conciergerie. It is one of the minor mysteries of the Revolution that they should have lived to tell the tale, for a denunciation of them that was as good as a death sentence appeared in Hébert's *Père Duchesne* on the following day: "Is it possible that there should exist scoundrels bold enough to defend her? And yet two babblers from the law courts have had that audacity . . . I myself saw those two devil's advocates not only dance like cats on hot bricks to prove the slut's innocence, but actually dare to weep for the traitor Capet and say to the judges that it was enough to have punished the fat hog and that his whore of a wife should be pardoned."

When the defense was finished the President of the Tribunal stepped forward and addressed the jury. "Today a great example is given to the universe. Nature and reason, so long outraged, are at last to be satisfied . . ." He admitted what was obvious to everyone, that there were no material proofs against the accused, but he used a clever evasion. He simply tossed the Queen's case in with that of the King and declared her to be guilty of instigating Louis to most of the crimes of which he had been proven guilty before the bar of the Convention. At three in the morning the jury finally retired. Marie Antoinette had been in the courtroom for eighteen hours and except for the cup of soup sent up by Rosalie she had taken neither food nor drink. As she was being conducted into a small side room to await the jury's verdict she murmured, "I am thirsty." There was no usher near and no one moved to help her. Her guard, Lieutenant de Busne, finally went in search of a glass of water.

Despite the lateness of the hour and the cold—during the night the thermometer had dropped to near freezing—the spectators' gallery was still thronged. During the jury's absence groups of them gathered in the dark halls to discuss the trial and its probable outcome. Outside in the street a small crowd had gathered in front of the gates of the Palais de Justice.

At four the President's bell informed the prisoner of the return of the jury. She could hear a hubbub in the courtroom that Herman had to quiet in a stern voice. The accused was then sent for. She crossed the room and took her place in an ominous silence that should have informed her of the jury's verdict. Apparently it did not. The announcement that she had been found guilty on every count seemed to reach her as though from afar, but when she heard Fouquier-Tinville's demand that "in accordance with Article One of the first Section of the first Chapter of the penal code she be condemned to death" there was a fleeting expression in her eyes that Chauveau-Lagarde interpreted as astonishment. "All one could see," he later declared, "was that at that moment there took place within her soul a kind of revulsion of feeling that struck me as remarkable. She did not give the least sign of fear or indignation or weakness, but she seemed as it were stunned by surprise."

Before pronouncing formal sentence the President asked her if she had any objection to the application of the law invoked by the Public Prosecutor. She shook her head without answering. The President then declared that her property and possessions within the territory of France were to be confiscated for the benefit of the Republic and he ordered that the judgment of death be executed that day in the Place de la Révolution.

She rose and stepped down from the platform without a word or gesture, crossing the long hall of the Tribunal as though she neither heard nor saw. According to Chauveau-Lagarde she raised her head with "very great dignity" when she passed in front of the spectators' gallery. The ever-present de Busne was at her side to take her back to her cell. As they descended the narrow stone stairway of the Bonbec Tower she suddenly faltered and groped helplessly in the dark. "I can no longer see," she whispered. "I can go . . . no farther." The gendarme offered her his arm and so with halting steps, leaning on her last bodyguard, the former Queen of France returned to her cell to prepare for her execution. Because he had offered her his arm and because he had brought her a glass of water in the courtroom, de Busne was denounced by a fellow guard and arrested that same morning.

Weakened by serious hemorrhaging, racked by cold and damp, exhausted by two days of trial, the second of which had lasted for more than twenty hours without interruption, Marie Antoinette must have reached the outer limits of moral and physical suffering. Death at that moment can only have seemed a merciful release. But she was not yet through with life and there remained a final obligation to herself and to those whom she loved. She asked for pen and paper and when they were brought her she sat down and by the light of two candles wrote her last letter. It was addressed to Madame Élisabeth, but its every sentence suggests she hoped that one day it would be read by her children and that it would be through these last words written at such terrible cost of spirit that they would one day recall her. This alone explains the tone of exaltation that informs it. It is an altogether remarkable document and no account of Marie Antoinette's life could be considered complete without quotation from it, for it is here that one can finally measure the distance that suffering had brought her. That the semiliterate dauphine, that the light-headed and careless Queen could pen these words of dignity and wisdom may be considered the most significant fact in her life. It was written without erasure and apparently without pause. On the original document one can still see the stain of her tears that fell on the paper as she wrote.

> The 16th October at four thirty
> in the morning
>
> It is to you, my dear sister, that I write for the last time. I have just been condemned not to a shameful death, that is only for criminals, but to join your brother. Like him innocent, I hope to show the same firmness as he in his last moments. I am at peace as one is when one's conscience holds no reproach. I regret deeply having to leave my poor children; you know that I lived only for them. And you, my good, kind sister, you who in the goodness of your heart have sacrificed everything to be with us, in what a position I am leaving you! I learned during the trial that my daughter has been separated from you. Alas, poor child, I dare not

write her. She would not receive my letter. I do not even know if this will reach you. Receive my blessing on them both. I hope that one day when they are older they will be able to be with you again and enjoy your tender care and that they will both remember the lesson I have always tried to instill in them that principles and the exact execution of obligations should be the first foundation of life and that friendship and mutual trust should be its greatest happiness. May my daughter remember that in view of her age she should always help her brother with advice born of her wider experience and let them both remember that they will never be truly happy unless united. Let them both learn from our example how much comfort our affection brought us in the midst of our unhappiness. My son must not forget his father's last words which I expressly repeat to him here: he must never seek to avenge our deaths. I have to mention something that hurts me greatly. I know how much distress the child must have caused you. Forgive him, dearest sister. Remember his age and remember how easy it is to make a child say anything you wish even if he does not understand. The day will come I hope when he will feel even more the worth of your tenderness toward them both. I now have only to confide in you my last thoughts. I would like to have written them at the beginning of the trial, but apart from the fact that I was not allowed to write, everything moved so quickly that I would not have had time.

I die in the Catholic, Apostolic, and Roman religion, that of my fathers in which I was raised and which I have always professed, having no expectation of spiritual solace and not even knowing if there are any priests of that religion here and in any case the place where I am would expose them to too much danger if they should enter. I sincerely beg pardon of God for all the wrong I have done during my lifetime. I hope that in his goodness He will receive my soul in His mercy and goodness. I ask pardon of all whom I know and of you in particular, sister, for all the distress that, without wishing, I may have caused. I forgive my enemies the harm that they have done me. I say farewell here to my aunts and to all my brothers and sisters. I had friends. The idea of being separated from them forever and of their grief is one of my greatest regrets in dying. May they know at least that my thoughts were with them until the last moment.

Farewell, my good and loving sister. May this letter reach you! Think of me always. I embrace you with all my heart, together with those poor, dear children. Oh God, what an anguish it is to leave them forever! *Adieu! Adieu!* From this moment I shall occupy myself only with my spiritual duties . . .

This letter was never to reach Madame Élisabeth. When she had finished it Marie Antoinette gave it to Bault, the concierge, who in turn gave it to Fouquier-Tinville. Fouquier then handed it over to Robespierre along with other papers pertaining to the Queen. Did Robespierre requisition it? Or did Fouquier offer it? We will never know. But both men knew well that it was something more than the last letter of a woman on her way to the scaffold. It was a card that one day might be of high value in the game of politics. To the very end Marie Antoinette the woman was inseparable from Marie Antoinette the symbol.

Yet there is a passage in her letter that was written only by the woman: *"I had friends. The idea of being separated from them forever and of their grief is one of my greatest regrets in dying. May they know at least that my thoughts were with them until the last moment."* So, discreetly, she bade farewell to Axel Fersen. He was no more fated than Madame Elisabeth to recieve her *adieux.* He too was dead when twenty-three years after her execution Marie Antoinette's last letter finally came to light. The day after Robespierre's death it was found under his mattress by a Conventional named Courtois. Courtois quietly pocketed it and hid it himself until the Restoration of the Bourbons, when he brought it forth in the hope of purchasing amnesty from the royalist government.

It was close to five o'clock when Marie Antoinette finished writing. Already the call to arms was sounding all over Paris and the troops, more than thirty thousand, that were to line her way to the scaffold were being assembled. Without undressing, she flung herself on her bed and turned her head away from the guards toward the window. It was thus that Rosalie found her when she entered the cell at daybreak. The two candles had guttered out. Marie Antoinette was awake. Her head was resting on her arm for support and she was weeping. She had moved her pillow to the foot of her bed to warm her feet.

"Madame," said Rosalie, "you ate nothing yesterday. What would you like this morning? I have kept some broth and vermicelli on the range."

"I need nothing, my child. Everything is now over for me." But when Rosalie turned to leave Marie Antoinette saw that the girl too was weeping. "Very well, then, Rosalie," she said. "I would like some of your broth."

She was able to swallow only a mouthful of Rosalie's soup, but before the maid left Marie Antoinette asked her to return at eight to help her dress. The last of her ceremonial appearances lay ahead and with sound historical intuition she knew that it was to be more important than any of the glittering *levées* and *couchers* of the past, for it was not Marie Antoinette the woman who was taken to the scaffold. Stripped of all the regalia of her rank, reduced to rags, lurching on a plain board seat in the back of a manure cart, it was once again the Queen. "Marie Antoinette on Her Way to the Guillotine," like "Marat Stabbed in His Bathtub," is one of the celebrated vignettes of the French Revolution. It is certain that the victim herself knew that it was destined to be so. When she asked Rosalie to help her dress it was with this final sacrifice in mind.

Her courage on that trip through the streets of Paris has been described many times. Even the revolutionary journals were to make note of it. In truth, however, everything that occurred in the prison that morning indicates that the poor woman was terrified. Her courage before the public stare resembled the expression of life that is painted upon a corpse by an undertaker. When the executioner Sanson entered her cell and told her to put out her hands so that they could be bound she was aghast and, feeble though she was, made a gesture of resistance. "But Louis XVI did not have his hands tied!" she cried.

On the order of the President of the Tribunal, who was in her cell at that moment, Sanson forced her hands behind her back and bound them with considerable brutality. He then tore off the bonnet that she and Rosalie had arranged so carefully and with a pair of scissors cut the hair about the nape of her neck. When she felt the scissors on her neck she thought that they had decided to execute her on the spot with a knife and she turned around with an expression of terror in her eyes. Sanson, not Rosalie, replaced the cap. Her hair now fell from it in jagged locks.

When toward eleven o'clock they led her through a double row of gendarmes into the courtyard of the Palais de Justice she was overcome by another wave of horror. Ahead she saw the cart in which she was to be taken through the streets of Paris. She had expected the protection of a closed carriage such as had been accorded Louis XVI, for the possibility of being torn to pieces by the Paris populace was much on her mind. Before leaving her cell she had asked one of the guard if he thought she might be murdered by the mob before she reached the scaffold. The sight of the open tumbrel drawn by two plowhorses was too much for her and nature suddenly overcame her resolution. She had to ask Sanson to unbind her hands and she relieved herself in a corner of the wall of the prison. Then she herself offered her hands to the executioner, who bound them again. He helped her up a little ladder into the tumbrel. They made her sit with her back to the horses. The Tribunal had sent a priest to accompany her and he sat beside her on the board, but she barely acknowledged his presence, for he had abjured.

Such eyewitness accounts as remain of her trip to the Place de la Révolution confirm the supposition that it was little more than a figure of wax, an effigy, that was conducted to the scaffold that morning. She was already half-dead. After many long months of imprisonment her face was ashen. Two burning spots of red high on her cheekbones were the only sign that life still flowed in her veins. Her eyes were bloodshot from weeping and fatigue. She rarely raised them and when she did they appeared sightless. The artist David was on the rue St. Honoré when she passed that morning and with rapid and terrible strokes he made his famous sketch, which communicates the woman's appearance more forcefully than any words.

It was nearly noon when the cart finally turned from the rue St. Honoré into the place of execution. The square was filled with a crowd that had been waiting there since early morning. If we are to believe contemporary engravings of the event, a triple line of mounted troops formed a wide circle about the foot of the scaffold. The tumbrel came to a halt in front of the steps leading up to the platform. An assistant of the executioner stood there waiting to help her mount. But the waxen effigy suddenly came to life. With a gesture of her head she declined the man's arm. Many who were present at the scene were later to recall that she ascended the wooden stairs unassisted, with that lilting, hurried step that had once enchanted the vanished civilization of which she was henceforth to be the symbol. She stood for a moment on the platform while they made their last preparations and she was seen to gaze over the heads of the men at her feet in the direction of the palace of the Tuileries, where four years earlier her death had begun.

When they were ready for her she flung herself onto the plank with an embrace that seemed to be of joy. A moment later Sanson, in the tradition of the time, lifted her bleeding head from the basket and showed it to the spectators on all sides of the scaffold. A great cry arose and then another, but the crowd did not linger long. For them life's business went on and the lunch hour was at hand. During the weeks and months to come there were to be many more such sights in that square. In batches of ten and twenty they were to be brought there, statesmen thrown in with poets, politicians with prostitutes and beggars, until the ground was so soaked with blood that cattle refused to cross it. Marie Antoinette's execution was but the beginning, although it was, and still remains today, the most spectacular.

PART IV

Conclusion

THE NEWS OF THE QUEEN'S DEATH DID NOT REACH BRUSSELS UNTIL October 20, four days afterward. Fersen's first response was of stupefaction. There are blows so violent that the human spirit cannot immediately respond to them. The blow itself contains its own anaesthetic. So it was with Axel Fersen when in a newspaper he learned the details of Marie Antoinette's execution.

"I am surprised that I wasn't more upset," he wrote in his Journal that evening. "It seemed to me that I felt nothing. Yet I have been thinking of her all day without cease and of the terrible circumstances of her suffering, of her children, of her poor son and the ill treatment to which he is probably subjected, of the Queen's unhappiness at not seeing him in her last moments, of the doubts she may have had about my devotion to her . . . in short, I thought of everything and nothing."

But the anaesthetic that numbed his senses wore off. Three days later he noted in his Journal that "My grief rather than diminishing grows worse as the shock leaves me."

He would ride for hours in the autumnal drizzle of the Lowlands and everywhere he would see her face. "It follows me wherever I go. Her suffering and death and all my feelings never leave me for a moment. I can think of nothing else . . . That she was alone in her last moments with no one to comfort her or talk to her, with no one to whom she could give her last wishes, fills me with horror."

To his grief was added indignation at the behavior of many of the French émigrés in Brussels. "The French are mourning in a scandalous manner a Queen whose feet they should have kissed and whose ashes they should adore. Several are only in half mourning and others, lead by Monsieur de Courban, former page in the Royal Stables, wanted to give a play and concert in honor of the Archduke's birthday. What frivolity and insensitivity! Miserable, detestable nation . . . ! !"

But in Vienna, among the Queen's Austrian relatives, the news was received with equal indifference. Mourning was ordered for the official period prescribed for an archduchess who was an aunt of the Emperor. A memorial Mass was said at the Hofburg and that was the extent of Austria's recognition of the execution of the daughter of Maria Theresa. The Emperor, like Chancellor Thugut, made no mention of her thereafter. In private the round of evening parties and amateur theatricals that constituted the charm of Viennese life continued as before.

Although he had no further reason to remain abroad, Fersen could not bring himself to return to Sweden. His father, old and ailing, begged him to come home, but his consolation, Éléonore Sullivan, was in Brussels and refused to go to Sweden with him. "She is my only comfort," he wrote in his Journal. "We can talk together of the past and because she knows everything that I know we can talk of things freely." In the privacy of his diary he couldn't prevent himself from comparing Éléonore to the woman he mourned. "Oh, how I reproach myself for the wrongs I did Her and how deeply I now realize how much I loved Her. What kindness, what tenderness, what a fine and loving heart! The other isn't like that, although I love her and she is my only comfort and without her I should be very unhappy."

Apart from Éléonore the business of the 1,500,000 livres bequeathed him by Louis and Marie Antoinette kept him abroad. On the eve of the Flight to Varennes, Louis had handed him a note giving him this legacy. It was the money that Fersen had raised to defray the expense of the military movements at the frontier had the King's flight succeeded. Part of it had been contributed by Fersen, part by Crauford, and the remainder by the two women, Baroness de Korff and her mother, Madame Stegelman. For reasons of tact Axel had not mentioned his claim during the Queen's lifetime, but three months after her death he decided that the time had come to seek reimbursement, particularly since Mesdames de Korff and Stegelman were reported to be in dire financial straits.

After the arrest of the King and Queen at Varennes, General de Bouillé had given the money to Mercy. It was to Mercy therefore that Fersen now went with his claim. The old diplomat, after scrutinizing the paper and examining the two signatures that he knew so well, admitted the validity of the instrument and expressed astonishment that Axel had not spoken of the matter when he arrived in Brussels in 1791. Axel replied that decency of feeling had prevented him from doing so during the lifetime of Marie Antoinette and Louis

XVI. Mercy told Fersen that he had given the money to the Arch-duchess Maria Christina, the Regent of the Lowlands, who in turn had passed it on to the Emperor. It was to the court in Vienna there-fore that Fersen would have to present his claim. In September, four months after broaching the matter, he received his first reply from the Hofburg. It was written by Thugut and phrased in a slippery French that should have forewarned him of the hopelessness of his quest. *"Il aurait été à désirer que vous eussiez jugé à propos . . .* It would have been better had you seen fit to make use of the instru-ment that is the basis of your pretension during the lifetime of the late King and Queen of France. This might perhaps have forestalled the difficulties and delays that your petition may now suffer."

At the very moment he received Thugut's note Axel learned of the death of his father. The division of the Senator's property obliged him to return to Sweden. So on October 12 he set out for Stockholm. October 16, the first anniversary of Marie Antoinette's death, found him crossing the Baltic. "Today," he wrote in his Jour-nal, "is a terrible day for me. It is when I lost the person who loved me the most in the world and who loved me truly. I shall mourn her loss until the end of my life and all that I feel for Éléonore can never allow me to forget what I have lost."

The return to his native land of the man who was reputed to have been the lover of Marie Antoinette caused a considerable ripple in the narrow little world of Stockholm society. A tragic past or the rumor of some hidden sorrow has never done a man or woman harm in those circles where the idle gather. "People look at me with cu-riosity," Fersen observed. "I noticed this particularly at the Opera when I entered the theater. Everyone in the boxes and the parterre turned in my direction."

Grief and four years' strain had indeed lent his features an ar-resting appearance. He looked far older than his thirty-nine years. His hair had begun to whiten and those lines, the token of suffering that will arouse the interest of women of a romantic or passionate disposition, had bit deep into his face. It was not long before a num-ber of candidates offered to console him for the loss of Marie An-toinette. Among them was the wife of the Regent, the Duchess of Södermanland, who some years before had granted him all her favors. In 1795 this was a dangerous solace and Axel knew it. The Regent, who may or may not have been implicated in the murder of his brother Gustavus III, knew well that his wife had once been the mistress of Fersen. And he had other reasons to dislike the handsome nobleman who had been his brother's favorite. His wizard, Baron Reuterholm, had for some time been urging him to recognize the government of Revolutionary France. The downfall of Robespierre and the end of the Terror in Paris made the moment propitious and in secret Södermanland was preparing to sign a treaty with the Convention and to send Staël-Holstein, Fersen's old enemy, back to Paris as ambassador. The Regent viewed Fersen and all the party that surrounded him as insubordinate and intriguing noblemen. The Swedish court was divided into two warring cabals: those who hoped for the early succession of Gustavus' son, still a minor, and those who hoped for a continuation of the Regency.

Axel was soon enmeshed in these intrigues. Very prudently he evaded the advances of the Duchess of Södermanland. "Her husband had noticed," he wrote, "and it appears he has put spies on me. I do not go to my friend's house at the hours she might be there. I do not want to get involved with anyone. I only want to live quietly until I can leave Sweden and join Éléonore."

He saw much of his sister Sophie and his friend Taube, who were now living together. Taube's health had begun to fail, so that summer the three went to the little spa of Medevi, on the shores of Lake Vättern, where the sick man took a cure. Axel's spirits were revived by the happiness Taube and his sister enjoyed. "I envy them the perfect life they share. It must be very agreeable."

He was happy, too, at his country property of Steninge, where the brief Swedish summer unfolded in the tranquillity of an age already past. "The strawberries are just fruiting but the peas haven't started yet. My overseer is an excellent man and the *basse-cour* is very well maintained. When I look at all this I can understand the pleasure of having a country estate and I can see how deeply one could become attached to one's land. Then I regret ever having traveled and of having needs that call me away."

At Steninge he received a piece of news from France that greatly upset him. It was here he learned of the death of the dauphin, the little boy Marie Antoinette had so much loved and who, as Louis XVII, was never to reign. "He was the last and only interest remaining to me in France . . . The news is too painful to bear and it brings back memories that are heart-rending."

But the dauphin's death as it was reported in the French and Swedish gazettes was not quite the cut-and-dried affair that rent Fersen's heart. It opened doors then as it does today onto one of the most perplexing mysteries in history, for the body that was buried by the prison officials of the Temple under the marker that bore the name Louis Charles Capet was almost certainly not the body of Marie Antoinette's son. In later years the skeleton was subjected to an examination by medical experts, all of whom pronounced it to be that of a young man at least seventeen years of age. More than this, the hair taken from the grave in no way corresponded with the hair of the dauphin. These medical examinations only lent substance to rumors that began immediately after the Convention's announcement of the boy's death.

A few months after Marie Antoinette's execution the dauphin's "tutor" Simon had been abruptly removed from the Temple on order of the Committee of General Security. The boy was then taken to a room on the second floor that had been converted into a prison cell where, behind bolted doors, he was placed in a solitary confinement that was to last for a year and five months—until, in fact, the day of his death. Without fresh air, with little light, with no human contact, he gradually fell into a condition of physical and moral degradation from which it appeared there could be no recovery.

"He slept in a bed that had not been made for six months. It was covered with lice and fleas, as were the boy's clothes and body. His filth stayed in the cell with him. Since the window was never opened the room was filled with a noxious stench. They rarely gave him a light, but he asked for nothing although he was terrified of the dark . . . Even had he lived it is to be feared that he would have been an imbecile."

The description is that of his sister and one would like to believe that it is exaggerated, but it is, alas, confirmed by all who saw him after the 9th Thermidor when Robespierre's Committee of Public Safety was overthrown and a number of "official"—but always clandestine—visits were made to the Temple Tower. The men who saw the dauphin on these visits were all struck by the fact that he could not or would not speak. He appeared to be mute. Some were later to attribute this silence to the boy's remorse over the terrible words he had uttered against his mother and to a vow he then made never to speak again. Others use it as additional evidence in support of their contention that the rachitic half-witted boy seen by these officials at the Temple Tower was not the son of Marie Antoinette but a substitute who had been placed there at the time Simon had been removed from duty. They claimed that the substitution had been made either because the real dauphin had died or because the real dauphin, Louis XVII, had been smuggled out of the Tower and taken abroad, where he awaited the hour when he could lay claim to the throne that was his heritage.

Many books have been written about this mystery and the arguments used by the author of one book are convincingly refuted by the author of the next. One or two of the forty "pretenders" to the throne of Louis XVI who were to emerge at the time of the Restoration managed to marshal an impressive body of supporters and it was not the least of Marie Thérèse's ordeals when twenty years later, as the duchesse d'Angoulême, she returned to France in the household of her uncle Louis XVIII, that her conscience called her to examine the credentials of some of these claimants. Although to the world she always insisted that her brother had died in the Temple, she in fact seems to have been troubled by a faint but persistent doubt that was to cast a shadow over her life until its end. The infamies she had heard her brother pronounce against her mother and aunt made her confusion the more painful because it is probable that even though she knew her brother to be alive she could not have greeted him with the love that her mother had enjoined upon her in her last letter.

Marie Thérèse—or "Madame" as she was henceforth called in royalist circles—was released from her captivity seven months after her brother's death. Like the dauphin she too had lived in solitude for many months. Her aunt and only companion Madame Élisabeth had been guillotined in May of 1794. But before being taken to the scaffold Élisabeth, whose character was more that of a housewife than princess, had instructed her in the rudiments of cleanliness and housekeeping. The girl, who was then fifteen, was well able to take care of herself. Every morning she would briskly pace her room for an hour. She made her bed, kept her quarters tidy, and twice a day would say her prayers. Thus, when she was released from the Temple, she was in relatively good health.

The Convention had no further need of her by June 1795. Indeed, she had become something of an embarrassment to them. The political climate of France abruptly changed after the downfall of Robespierre and the end of the Terror. The Paris populace, like all humanity *en masse,* could be as sentimental as it was cruel. It now suddenly saw in the girl whom it dubbed "the Orphan of the Temple" a symbol of persecuted youth and innocence. Crowds would gather in the vicinity of the Tower to serenade her with lachrymose songs. Windows of houses along the rue de la Corderie were rented out to those who wanted to catch a glimpse of her as she walked in the garden of the Temple enclosure. The city viewed her with all the proprietary affection it might accord some baby animal at the municipal zoo. The Convention, fearful that she might become a banner about which royalist sentiment would rally, proposed to Vienna that she be exchanged for the Conventionals that Austria still held captive. Negotiations began in June but Madame was not finally released until December. The delay came from Vienna.

Thugut received the Convention's proposal with consternation. "The arrival of the Princess here can only be embarrassing to us," he informed the Emperor's secretary, Colleredo. "What are we going to do with her? Put her in the Archduchess Marie Anne's convent in Prague? Suggest that the Queen of Naples take charge of her? And what about the other Bourbons in France who might also become a charge on His Majesty's budget?"

So far as Thugut was concerned it would have been better if Marie Antoinette's daughter spent the remainder of her days in prison. His first response to the Convention's proposal was silence. Then someone—probably Colleredo—pointed out to him that destitute though Madame might be in France, she would not be a pauper abroad. A balance sheet listing her financial assets was submitted to the Chancellor, who in turn passed it on to the Emperor. There were first of all the diamonds of the Queen and those of Madame Élisabeth, valued at nearly a million livres, that had been taken out of France by Léonard at the time of Varennes. By inheritance these indisputably belonged to Madame. Then there was Marie Antoinette's dowry, still in deposit in Vienna, worth a half million livres, with accumulated interest adding substantially to its capital value. There were the châteaux of Rambouillet and St. Cloud with all their contents, paintings, porcelain, silver, and books that had been the private property of her parents. Although it appeared difficult to realize their value at that moment, they were viewed by the Emperor's financial advisors as sound "long-term" holdings. Sounder still was the sum of one and a half million livres on deposit in the Netherlands and fetching an annual interest of four percent. This was the money that the King and Queen of France had bequeathed to Fersen, but from the instant the Hofburg saw it as part of Madame's inheritance or dowry his chances of ever laying hands on it diminished to nothing.

"Dowry" was in fact the key to all that now followed, for Thugut and the Emperor, having examined the balance sheet, quickly abandoned their plan of sending the threadbare daughter of Marie Antoinette off to a convent in Prague. They decided instead that she should marry the younger brother of the Emperor, the Archduke Charles. Behind this scheme lay considerations more far-reaching than mere cash. Madame was, after all, the only surviving child of the late King of France. Although the Salic Law had always disallowed female children from inheriting the throne of France, the Revolution in that country had forever broken such feudal conventions. To Thugut and Francis II it seemed possible that if Austria played her cards with skill, Madame might someday be installed on the throne of her ancestors as the legitimate and sovereign Queen of France. Palaces more dazzling than Rambouillet and St. Cloud, possessions more important than Alsace and Lorraine now danced before their eyes. There would be Versailles itself, the Tuileries, and the Louvre; there would be all of France. *Tu Felix Austria Nube* . . .

So, when in December of 1795 Madame left her prison at the Temple Tower and was taken under armed escort and in obscurity to the Austrian frontier, she found that she was only being transferred from one prison to another. The bars fell around her the moment she entered her uncle's realm. They were bars covered with velvet, it is true, but they were as firm as any in the Temple. The Habsburgs were determined that until she married the Archduke Charles she should have no private contact with the outer world and most particularly no contact with her Bourbon relatives, whose plan it was she should marry the son of the comte d'Artois, her first cousin, the duc d'Angoulême.

When Axel Fersen learned of the impending release of Madame he decided to go to Vienna and see her. His reasons were both sentimental and practical. To see the daughter of the woman he mourned, the only living witness to her imprisonment, was foremost in his mind, but there was the matter of the legacy, too. Although his own finances were now on a sounder foundation, the desperate plight of the two old women was much on his mind. In a phrase that satisfactorily reconciled business with sentiment he wrote in his Journal that he hoped "to receive from Madame's own hands the legacy given me by her parents." So he set out for Vienna.

He arrived there in mid-January of 1796. He found the city

full of French refugees, including the duc de Guiche, Madame de Polignac's son-in-law, who told him of the impenetrable curtain that had been drawn about the young Princess. All her French suite had been dismissed and they were replaced by Austrians, countesses and princesses perhaps, but spies all the same and informers. All correspondence with her uncle Louis XVIII was intercepted, while the prince de Condé whom Louis XVIII had sent to greet his niece was rudely forbidden her presence. The French were only allowed to glimpse her from afar, in the corridors of the Hofburg as she went to and from Mass.

It was at the Hofburg on her way back from the chapel that Fersen, accompanied by the duc de Guiche, first saw her. His knees were shaking and he was nearly overcome with emotion when she passed before the crowd of courtiers that had assembled to salute her. He had not seen her since 1791 when on the night of June 20 he carried her in his arms to the coach in which they made their escape from the Tuileries. She had been crying then.

"She is large," he wrote in his Journal, "and well built, but she is more like Madame Élisabeth than the Queen. Her features are now more natural, but unchanged. Her feet are small and she has grace and nobility, but she does not walk well. When she passed us she blushed and just before going into her apartments she turned around to look at us again . . . I think she would have liked to have shown us some politeness or let us know that she recognized us."

He saw her again a few weeks later when she gave a reception for the city of Vienna, and this time she spoke to him. "She looked about the crowd the way her mother used to do to find people she knew and when she saw me she went up to me and in a most agreeable tone greeted me. 'I am so glad to see that you are in safety.' Her words gave me the greatest pleasure, but tears of sorrow sprang to my eyes at least twenty times."

But when the weeks had become months and he still had had no answer to his petition, Axel's attitude toward Madame underwent a change. The Emperor told him that the money he solicited belonged to her and that it was from her, when she had reached her majority, that he would have to receive it. But he was never allowed to see her alone to discuss the business and she never answered his letters. Evasive verbal replies were sent through her lady-in-waiting. On one occasion she gave him an appointment in her private apartments but when he arrived there he found eighteen other guests. "She looked at me often but her lady-in-waiting kept an eye on all her movements. I don't think she is happy. They say here that when she is alone she weeps a great deal."

After four months of these prevarications Fersen grew angry. "I am disgusted," he wrote Taube. "I can now understand why people become democrats. I have been unable to see Madame in private and I doubt if I ever will. It is one more disillusionment and one more regret, but I'm used to those by now. I'm not really surprised because everything that has to do with those unfortunate sovereigns is forgotten here. It is only to be expected that my devotion to them should be forgotten too . . ."

Madame never invited him again to one of her private receptions and ceased even to recognize him among the courtiers that surrounded her in public. Axel was first hurt, then angry. "The lack of sensitivity, of nobility, generosity, or justice in their behavior has outraged me," he wrote, "and Madame's conduct has particularly shocked and upset me. It would have been a great comfort to have been able to see her and talk to her. The opposite has hurt me badly."

In June, realizing the hopelessness of his quest, Axel left Vienna. He was never to see Marie Antoinette's daughter again. The attitude of the Princess toward her mother's old friend was more understandable than Fersen perhaps realized. Had she known—and almost certainly she did know—what the courts and chancelleries of Europe said about her mother and the man who now came to her for her parents' money, she can only have viewed him with embarrassment if not open distaste. Marie Thérèse had none of her mother's charm, neither did she inherit her father's kindly nature. Everything she was ever to write or say indicated that the central figure in her memory was not her mother but her aunt Madame Élisabeth. And Élisabeth, "saint" though she may have been in royalist eyes and saint though indeed she may have been, had very Presbyterian views about the fleeting pleasures of this sinful world. She looked on the *fêtes champêtres* of Trianon with a disapproval equal to that of some of today's historians. She disliked the Polignacs, their *entourage,* and everyone whom she finally came to believe had led her poor sister-in-law astray. Fersen was certainly among those and almost certainly, too, Élisabeth communicated her disapproval, albeit discreetly and with saintly forbearance, to young Marie Thérèse. He should not have been surprised that the young woman gave him the cold shoulder.

A future almost as unhappy as her past lay ahead for this only survivor of the Bourbons' imprisonment at the Temple Tower. Her confinement at the Hofburg seems to have embittered her far more than her experiences at the Temple. She arrived in Vienna expecting love and kindness. She found instead that she was no more than a pawn in political maneuverings, to which her parents had already been sacrificed. The Emperor finally realized that she would never consent to a marriage with the Archduke Charles and he handed her over to her uncle, Louis XVIII, who married her at once to Artois' younger son, the duc d'Angoulême. She then became the prisoner of another *politique* and the token in another game. She must have known surely that the former comte de Provence had betrayed her parents, but she kept her silence. During the Restoration she wandered about her uncle's court like some unhappy specter. Her eyes were always red, it was said, from secret weeping, and she dressed in mourning. She lived to witness two more revolutions in France and twice more was sent into exile. She died in 1851, fifty-eight years after the execution of her parents. On her tombstone are inscribed the words: "Ask yourselves, all ye who pause here, if your sorrows are equal unto mine."

After leaving Vienna, Fersen went to Frankfurt, where he stayed with Éléonore and Crauford. One day when Crauford was absent he asked Éléonore to marry him, but Éléonore, who three years earlier had begged Axel to marry her, now hesitated. Time and habit had lent her liaison with Crauford the respectability and security of marriage. The thought of uprooting herself at this late date to run off with another man, perhaps to end her days in the snows of Sweden, did not appeal to her. She gave Axel a few evasive promises. Their situation continued as it had been.

At the end of 1796 the political situation in Sweden suddenly changed. The Duke of Södermanland resigned the Regency and the young son of Gustavus III ascended the throne of Sweden as Gustavus IV Adolphus. The new King, still a boy, broke off all negotiations with the revolutionary government of France. Gustavus IV Adolphus was both an enemy of the French Revolution and a loyal supporter of his father's old friend, Axel Fersen. His accession meant that Fersen and his party were now in power at the Swedish court. The new King's first favor was to appoint Fersen his representative to the Congress of Rastatt, where he was commissioned to treat with General Bonaparte over Sweden's fiefs within the Holy Roman Empire. But Bonaparte refused to recognize Fersen's credentials. There was a brief, unsatisfactory meeting between the two men. Bonaparte disliked him on sight and announced to the representative of the Margrave of Baden that he would have nothing to do with a man who was listed in France as an *émigré*, who had been at the head of an anti-revolutionary party, and who was known, furthermore, "to have slept with the late Queen." Fersen's first diplomatic mission for his new sovereign thus ended in failure. He was given other missions of no particular importance but they kept him on the continent and near Éléonore, with whom he continued to press his suit.

In the spring of 1799 Taube and Sophie came to Germany, where Taube took a cure at Karlsbad. Fersen was always happiest in their company and he spent June and July with them. Unfortunately, while he was at Karlsbad, a letter from Éléonore addressed to him was delivered to Crauford by mistake. There was a terrible scene when the old Scotsman discovered that for ten years his mistress had secretly been the mistress of Fersen, too. He forced her to make a choice between himself or Fersen. Éléonore chose Crauford, and so the last foundations of Axel's life on the continent fell into dust. Wounded and bitter, he drew still closer to Taube and Sophie. But sorrow was not done with him yet. In August, while he was trying to recover from the blow dealt him by Éléonore, Taube died suddenly at Karlsbad. Five days later Axel and his sister, henceforth inseparable, returned to Sweden. Apart from a few brief trips abroad, he was never to leave his homeland again. In 1804 he learned that Éléonore and Crauford had returned to Paris. Through their friend Talleyrand they had become great favorites at the new court. The Emperor did not countenance loose living among his acquaintances, so they were finally married. Éléonore was to survive her husband by some years and under the Empire and Restoration to become one of the most brilliant hostesses in Paris. From time to time news of her would reach Sweden, but Fersen heard it with indifference. His life in Europe was over and he had closed the doors on it forever.

The years went by. They were years that brought Count Fersen all the honors that could be won at a pompous, provincial court. The King showered him with emoluments and dignities. He was created a Knight of the Order of the Seraphim, he was appointed Chancellor of the University of Uppsala and made Grand Marshal of the Court of Sweden. In 1800, 1803, 1808, and 1809 he was Lieutenant Governor of the Kingdom. Loaded with medals and resplendent in his many uniforms, he appeared to have reached the summit of worldly ambition.

In reality these prizes left him unmoved. Taciturn, always melancholy and withdrawn from the social life of the court, he went through the ritual of his various offices with mechanical competence. His real life lay elsewhere—with his sister Sophie and his memories. He was haunted by memories. In his Journal one catches a glimpse of this secret life, a life preoccupied with anniversaries and devoted almost entirely to the *volupté* of mourning and regret.

October 16, 1796 (the anniversary of Marie Antoinette's death): "A thousand heartrending memories have been with me all day. Her suffering torments me without cease . . ."

October 16, 1798: "Today is a day of prayer for me. I cannot forget all that I have lost. My grief will last as long as my life."

January 21, 1799: "I have been sad all day. I cannot forget that today is the anniversary of the death of Louis XVI and all my life I shall be devoted to the memory of that prince."

November 1, 1800: "They gave *Oedipe* at the Opera this evening. Although it was badly done it brought back many memories that filled me with grief."

But of these anniversaries it was Varennes that most tormented him. Over and again, year in, year out, on June 20 his mind would return to the year 1791. With the insight of a dramatist he seems to have seen that Varennes was the pivotal episode of his life to which all roads had led and from which the road that followed was fixed with the immutability of classical tragedy.

June 20, 1794: "I can only think of this same day in 1791 . . ."

1797: "Today is an anniversary that I shall remember forever. I was happy then . . ."

1798: "I have been thinking all day of this same day seven years ago."

1800: "I have not stopped thinking of this day nine years ago and of how busy I was then with their departure."

His preoccupation with Varennes had morbid undertones. "It would have been better for me," he wrote a friend, "if I had died on the 20th of June." And to himself he repeated the thought, "Why didn't I die for them on June 20th? I would have been happier."

Seven years ago, nine years ago, twelve years . . . Time passed. When, in 1810, the nineteenth anniversary of Varennes came round, Sweden was in the throes of another political upheaval. Despite outward appearances the party of the King to which the Fersen family was attached had never made peace with the party of the Duke of Södermanland. Violence lay just below the polished surface of the royal palace where the minuet was still danced and the etiquette of the eighteenth century still observed. The King's position in this fratricidal struggle was considerably weakened when it became apparent to everyone, including his own supporters, that he was insane. For some generations madness had been a scourge of the House of Vasa. It was madness indeed that had lent to Gustavus III's reign much of its charm, for among princes megalomania may sometimes be the parent of audacious landscaping and interesting architecture. But during Gustavus IV Adolphus' reign, alas, the times were not favorable for kings who had lost their minds. To survive in 1806 when the armies of Napoleon were overrunning Europe, absolute monarchs were required to have some contact with reality.

In the twilight world of Nordic myth, of witchcraft and mystical revelation to which his sick mind had retreated Gustavus IV Adolphus was informed by discarnate voices that the Emperor of France was the Beast of the Apocalypse and that it was God's will that he should destroy him. Incited by the prophecies of a German seer named Stilling Jung, he entered into a series of rash military engagements that brought Sweden to the brink of ruin. In Pomerania his armies were engulfed by the French. Russia seized his Finnish possessions, and at Erfurt Napoleon gave Denmark and Russia his permission to divide Sweden between them. To save their homeland from extinction two generals named Adlerkreutz and Adlersparre assembled an army of patriots and marched on the palace, where they seized the King and forced him to abdicate. He was then sent into exile and his descendancy barred from inheriting the Swedish throne. A few weeks later the Riksdag recalled the Duke of Södermanland and elected him King of Sweden under the name of Charles XIII. Södermanland was old and childless. The Riksdag therefore appointed its own heir to the Swedish throne, a man named Charles Augustus of Holstein-Augustenburg. This prince, who was the puppet of Generals Adlersparre and Adlerkreutz, was a nondescript man of forty-four. The power of the Fersen family thus came to an end. Adlersparre and the officers surrounding him, the Duke of Södermanland and the new Heir Apparent were all sworn enemies of Axel and his faction.

Fersen viewed this revolution impassively. He and his sister retired from court and henceforth he only went to the palace to perform the duties that the position of Grand Marshal required of him. Nothing in his manner betrayed the slightest disaffection or hostility and perhaps he felt none. But his adversaries were convinced that he dreamed of vengeance and was secretly plotting a counterrevolution.

It was in this atmosphere of suspicion that on May 18 of 1810, while reviewing troops in the province of Skåne, the Heir Apparent to the throne had an apoplectic stroke, fell from his horse and died. The Prince was the cornerstone on which Adlersparre and the generals had constructed their hopes and his unexpected death had the effect of a match thrown into a room filled with some explosive gas. The generals accused Fersen of having poisoned the heir and they spread this accusation through the streets of Stockholm. With malice they now fanned into flame the latent fury of a populace that nursed many grievances against the court. Fersen had never been popular in the streets. Among the crowd he maintained the same cold reserve as among his peers. He was the fit representative of all that an irritated mob might consider haughty and aristocratic.

When the day of the heir's funeral came round Stockholm was a caldron. The police sent a number of reports to the military governor of the city warning of violence should Count Fersen attend the services. Unfortunately the governor, a man named Silfersparre, was one of the Duke of Södermanland's colleagues and an old enemy of Fersen. General Silfersparre blandly informed the city fathers that there was no danger and assured them that in any case Fersen would have adequate protection should he attend the funeral. Even as he gave these assurances General Silfersparre knew that inflammatory pamphlets urging the populace to take vengeance on "the traitor Ferson" were being distributed throughout Stockholm and its outlying provinces. When the King was told of the danger in which the Grand Marshal found himself he merely said, "It wouldn't be so bad if that puffed-up aristocrat were taught a good lesson."

Among Fersen's remaining friends at court was an *émigré* of Burgundian origin named General de Suremain. He had breakfast with Axel on the morning of the heir's funeral and he implored him not to attend the ceremony. Suremain had connections in very high places in the government and he had a good idea of what was afoot. But Fersen listened to his warnings with what Suremain describes in his memoirs as "the calm of a man whose conscience is pure and who is troubled by no fear."

General de Suremain cannot have known that for nineteen years on this same day, June 20, Fersen had longed for death. Here, undoubtedly, is the explanation of the *sang-froid* with which he faced the possibility of a death that was terrible. Did he embrace that end with open arms as Marie Antoinette had embraced the plank of the guillotine? Or did he allow himself to be carried passively toward a fate that a most curious coincidence of date seemed to designate as inevitable?

Nothing in Count Fersen's demeanor gave an answer to these questions when toward noon he entered the great gilded coach of the Grand Marshal of the Swedish Court. He sat alone in the back seat and it was observed as he passed that his features were expressionless and his posture rigid. His carriage, preceded by a squadron of cavalry, led the procession. This arrangement was unfortunate because the Grand Marshal's beplumed coach with its six white horses and its powdered footmen in red livery "contrasted shockingly with the simplicity of the funeral cart and gave the impression of a triumphant conqueror dragging some vanquished enemy behind him." As the parade entered the narrow heart of the city the crowd began to thicken and with menacing gestures to surge toward the Grand Marshal's coach. All at once someone cried, "Traitor!" And that cry was followed by another more sinister epithet, "Murderer!" The squadron of cavalry pranced forward, apparently oblivious to the rumblings that surrounded the coach only a few paces ahead.

But in the instant that followed those cries of "Traitor!" and "Murderer!" the barrier that separates threatening words or gestures from overt violence was suddenly crossed. Someone hurled a stone and shattered the window of the carriage. And with that first stone the dam was broken. A shower of stones followed. When the cortège turned into the open square of the Grain Market the exasperated populace began to tear up pieces of the pavement and hurl them. A battalion of the royal guard was stationed in the square but no one lifted a finger to try to stop the attack that was taking place only a few feet away from them. In the investigations that followed, the troops claimed they had received no orders to do so.

Advancing on its appointed course as though nothing were happening, the procession moved into a street called Stora Nygatan, where the rage of the crowd seemed to have reached its pitch. The place was so choked with humanity that the carriage could proceed no further. When it lurched to a halt a group of men tried to cut the harnessing. Fersen was by now so covered with blood that he was obliged to lie down on the back seat of the coach. An officer named Ulfsparre, accompanied by six guardsmen, suddenly appeared. Opening the door of the besieged carriage, he urged the Grand Marshal to descend and take shelter in a house that stood directly opposite to where the vehicle had stopped. Protected momentarily by the six guards, Axel made his way into the house. Colonel Ulfsparre ordered his men to protect the entrance while he went off to seek reinforcements.

The second floor of the house where Fersen sought refuge was a restaurant where a number of people had gathered that day to watch the funeral procession. Someone conducted the wounded man upstairs to a small room above this establishment and brought him water and a towel to staunch his bleeding. Unfortunately the clients of the restaurant who had been hanging out the windows watching the scene on the street below learned of Fersen's presence among them and the little room was soon filled with another mob quite as hostile as the one from which he had just escaped. They came to jeer, but it was not long before they too moved from abusive language to assault. Someone accused Fersen of "having caused the French Revolution." Someone else then stepped forward and ordered him to take off the ribbon of the Order of the Seraphim that hung about his neck. With courage the Grand Marshal refused to do so, saying that the decoration had been given him by the King and that only the King could remove it. It was torn from his neck, passed about the room, and finally thrown out the window to the crowd below.

"Throw him out too!" they cried. "We'll kill him!" The mob surging in Stora Nygatan had now reached such alarming proportions that the city officials could no longer affect to be ignorant of it. The military governor of Stockholm, Fersen's enemy General Silfersparre, now arrived on the scene. Silfersparre's role in events that followed was, to put it mildly, equivocal. He first hurried upstairs to Fersen's room, where he found the unhappy man lying on the floor covered with blood and surrounded by a circle of men who were beating him across the head with their walking sticks. The General made no attempt to clear the room or place it under guard. Instead he assured Fersen that there was nothing to worry about and that order would soon be re-established. With these words he went down to the street, mounted his horse, and asked the populace to return quietly to their homes. Although he was surrounded by a battalion of troops, Silfersparre gave them no order to draw arms. Instead, as he later explained to the court of inquiry, he counted on his ability to placate passions by more peaceable means—a sentiment that might have been admirable from someone other than General Silfersparre, who had never before hesitated to quell public disturbance by the most brutal means.

Far from extinguishing the flames, his words seemed instead to fan them higher. When it became evident that the mob was not going to disperse, but on the contrary had become even more determined to have its victim, Silfersparre returned to Fersen's room and told him that his only hope now lay in putting himself under arrest and being taken to the security of the prison at the City Hall. It was but a short distance away and Silfersparre told him that he would be conducted there in safety. Realizing that this indeed was his only hope, Fersen agreed to Silfersparre's proposal and, leaning on the General's arm, for he could hardly walk, he slowly descended the staircase. He had not reached the bottom step before someone seized him and hurled him to the foot of the stairs, where he lay unable to move. A group of men rushed forward, took him by the legs and dragged him into the street, where the populace fell on him. Before the impassive stare of Silfersparre's militia his clothes were ripped from his body and his hair torn from his head.

Half dead though he was and beaten down four times, he managed to crawl to a guard post near the City Hall, where he found a moment's shelter. But the crowd came after him and dragged him back into the street. Crying, "Murderer," they finally kicked him to death.

Although the life of Marie Antoinette the Queen had come to its end in 1793 on a public square in Paris, it was not until June 20 of 1811 in Stockholm that the tragedy of the woman was finally brought to its close. For whether friend or lover Count Axel Fersen was a figure that carries her story out of the fixed frame of history or the chronology of conventional biography and places it against its proper perspective of a fatality that was Classic in its design.

The French Revolution has been examined in many lights and studied in many facets; too rarely has it been appreciated as a theatrical piece in the tradition of antiquity. Yet in most of its essentials it was a drama that might have been written by Euripides. An inordinate confidence in the superiority of humankind characterized the age of Voltaire. In the age of Rousseau the gods were no longer mocked, they were forgotten. The stage was set for one of those periodic corrections of human pride at which the gods have always excelled. The Enlightenment came to its end with the *noyades* of Nantes, the massacres of Lyon, and the Reign of Terror.

It is against this background, metaphysical in its essence, that Marie Antoinette's story is best viewed. Her doom was forecast with the certainty of astrology, but it is probable that at no time did she glimpse the moving hand. Uncomprehendingly the human being acted out the symbol's role, for the gods with admirable artistry chose an ordinary woman of commonplace intelligence to play the principal part in their drama.

The Revolution destroyed her but it was the Revolution that lent to the life of this essentially uninteresting woman an interest that is spectacular. The symbol of an insouciant and profligate society called to account, she was tortured and put to death. But through affliction the woman grew strong and out of physical destitution she carried that element of individual triumph which is inseparable from great tragedy.

It is through the life of Axel Fersen, whose fortunes were so fatally interbound with her own, that one is accorded the clearest glimpse into the hidden drama of the woman. And it is with those words of tenderness she sent him from the depths of her suffering—words which like some Italian aria sung to the accompaniment of the harpsichord still evoke the flavor of that vanished age—that their story is most fittingly concluded. *Tutto a te mi guida*: "Everything leads me to thee."

Appendix

Not long before *The Fatal Friendship* went to press a book called *Marie Antoinette: l'Impossible Bonheur* by Philippe Huisman and Marguerite Jallut was published in Paris. It is a study of Marie Antoinette, the woman of fashion who lent her name to the light and lovely style of the expiring eighteenth century, rather than of Marie Antoinette, the Queen or political figure. This facet of Marie Antoinette's personality has too often been slighted by students of history. A visit to the golden rooms at Fontainebleau that were furnished by Riesener and decorated by the Rousseau brothers would alter the judgment of all but the most Puritan of them. Indeed, a broader acquaintance with the works of Rousseau the woodcarver rather than Rousseau the philosopher—whose *oeuvre*, incidentally, found its most perfect architectural expression in the *hameau* at Trianon—might make for a more balanced understanding of the eighteenth-century spirit.

It is not to lecture my readers on aesthetics, however, that I mention this book. It is because its authors have come up with a new and arresting piece of information about Fersen's friendship with Marie Antoinette. To appreciate it, one must go back to the Correspondence Book in which the meticulous Swede made note of all the letters he either wrote or received. It will be remembered that in 1784 there appears mention of a correspondence between himself and a certain "Joséphine" over the purchase of a dog. There can be no doubt that this Joséphine was in fact Marie Antoinette. Fersen states so himself at the conclusion of the correspondence. In 1787 there is another rash of letters again written to a certain "Joséphine" in which reference is made to a "stove" (*poêle*) and a "fringe for the stove" (*ruche de poêle*). This has thrown confusion into the ranks of those who believe that Fersen and Marie Antoinette were lovers, for it hardly seems possible that the Commanding Officer of the Royal Suédois Regiment would be writing the Queen of France about so humble an article as a stove fringe. Alma Söderhjelm, editor of Fersen's papers, offers an explanation. She suggests that there were two—and even perhaps three—"Joséphines," the second of whom was none other than Mrs. Sullivan's maid. It is true that Madame Sullivan had a maid named Joséphine and despite a certain strain on one's credulity one might accept Professor Söderhjelm's theory except for one fact: *Fersen did not know Éléonore Sullivan in 1787*. In his Journal he states that he first met her in 1789. Thus the Joséphine with whom he corresponded about a "stove fringe" in 1787 must be another Joséphine or else, despite the lowliness of the article under consideration, the Queen. For several years my personal supposition was that *ruche de poêle* was a code word and that Joséphine was indeed Marie Antoinette. Philippe Huisman has another theory, supported in his case by a very interesting discovery.

Instead of *ruche de poêle* can it not be that Fersen wrote *niche de poêle*? With a small handwriting such as Fersen's it would be easy for an editor to confuse an *n* with an *r* and Alma Söderhjelm seems to have done precisely that. A *niche de poêle* was a niche in the wall, common in the eighteenth century, in which a heating stove was placed. With this reading the passages in Fersen's Correspondence Book begin to take on a different meaning: "*April 7:* Project to live upstairs; that she write me about it at the regiment. That I'll be there May 15. *April 20:* The things she must find in order that I live upstairs. *October 8:* Through M. de Valois wrote that she should have a niche for a stove built . . ."

The papers of the Directeur Général des Bâtiments at Versailles show that all through the month of October of 1787 there was a great deal of work being done in the small apartments of the Queen. Specifically on October 18, at precisely the date Fersen was corresponding with "Joséphine" about a niche for a stove, a set of marble slabs were delivered to those apartments to be used as a hearth for a stove. More than this, however, M. Huisman has published a heretofore unknown letter proving conclusively that in October of 1787 Marie Antoinette was concerning herself with stoves. It is dated October 14 of 1787 and is addressed to the Directeur Général des Bâtiments and signed by a man named Loiseleur.

"I have the honor," writes Loiseleur, "to inform M. le Directeur Général that the Queen has sent for the Swedish stove man who made the stoves for the apartment of Madame and that Her Majesty has ordered him to make one in one of her interior rooms with heating pipes to warm the little room beside it. The Queen also ordered me to arrange the installation of the stove which consists of the removal of two pieces of paneling, the replacing of the bottom of the wooden partition with brick, and the removal of some of the floor to replace it with a brick hearth."

With this in hand, one may be permitted to wonder if Fersen's project to "live upstairs" did not refer, in fact, to a project to move into Marie Antoinette's private apartments upstairs in the palace and that he had persuaded the Queen that her rooms should be properly heated.

Bibliography

The following are among the more interesting or helpful books consulted:

Mémoires de la comtesse de Boigne
Mémoires de Madame de Tourzel
Mémoires du Marquis de Bouillé
Mémoires du comte de Saint Priest
Mémoires du comte de Tilly
Mémoires relatifs à la Révolution française: Choiseul, Goguelat, Bouillé
    Damas, Valory (Paris 1822)
Mémoires de Madame Campan
Mémoires de Madame de La Tour du Pin
Mémoires du duc de Lauzun
Aimond, Charles, *L'enigme de Varennes* (Verdun, 1957)
Almeras, Henri de: *Marie-Antoinette et les pamphlets royalistes et
    révolutionnaires*
——: *Les amoureux de la Reine*
Angoulême, Duchesse d': *Journal* (Paris 1893)
Archives Nationales c. 170 (689); 171 (699); Dxxix b, 36-37-38
d'Arneth and Geoffroy: *Correspondance secrète entre Marie-Thérèse et
    Marie-Antoinette*
Belloc, Hillaire: *Marie Antoinette*
Bimbenet, E.: *Fuite de Louis XVI à Varennes*
Birkenhead, Earl of: *More Famous Trials*
Bord, Gaston: *Autour du Temple*
Bouillé, Marquis de: *Varennes* (Paris, 1969)
Bourgeois, A.: *La Vérité sur l'arrestation de Louis XVI*
Campardon, E.: *Marie-Antoinette à la Conciergerie*
Castelot, André: *Marie-Antoinette*

———: *Le drâme de Varennes*

———: *Le Rendez-vous de Varennes*

Castries, duc de: *Louis XVIII, Portrait d'un roi*

———: *Les émigrés*

Christophe, Robert: *Danton*

Cléry, valet de chambre du Roi: *Journal de ce qui s'est passé à la tour du Temple*

Dard, Émil: *Un rival de Fersen; Quentin Crauford*

Daudet, Ernest: *Histoire de l'émigration pendant la Révolution française*

Fay, Bernard: *Louis XVI*

Flammermont, J.: *Negotiations secrètes de Louis XVI et du Baron de Breteuil avec la cour de Berlin, décembre 1791 à juillet 1792*

Gabriel, Abbé: *Louis XVI, le marquis de Bouillé et Varennes*

Gaulot, Paul: *Un ami de la Reine*

———: *Un complôt sous la Terreur*

Geoffroy, M. A.: *Gustave III et la cour de France*

Gramont, Sanche de: *Epitaph for Kings*

Heidenstamm, O. G. de: *The Letters of Marie Antoinette, Fersen and Barnave*

———: *Marie-Antoinette*

Huisman, Philippe and Jallut, Marguerite: *Marie-Antoinette; l'impossible bonheur*

Klinckowström, R. M. de: *Le comte de Fersen et la cour de France*

Kunstler, Charles: *Fersen et son secret*

———: *La douceur d'aimer*

Lenôtre, G.: *Le drâme de Varennes*

———: *La captivité et la mort de Marie-Antoinette*

———: *La fille de Louis XVI*

Lescure, M. de: *Correspondance secrète inédite sur Louis XVI et Marie Antoinette*

Mathiez, A.: *La révolution et les étrangers*

Morris, Gouveneur: *Diary of the French Revolution*

Morton, J. B.: *Camille Desmoulins and Other Studies of the French Revolution*

Nolhac, Pierre de: *La Reine Marie-Antoinette*

———: *Autour de la Reine*

———: *Marie-Antoinette, Dauphine*

Padover, Saul K.: *Life and Death of Louis Sixteenth*

Ségur, Marquis de: *Marie-Antoinette*

Söderhjelm, Alma: *Correspondance secrète de Marie-Antoinette et de Barnave* (juillet 1791—janvier 1792)

———: *Fersen et Marie-Antoinette; correspondance et journal intime inédits du comte Axel de Fersen*

Sorel, Albert: *L'Europe et la Révolution française*
Suremain, General de: *Mémoires*
Vallotan, Henry: *Marie-Antoinette et Fersen*
Wallon, Henri: *Le Tribunal révolutionnaire*
Wrangel, F. V.: *Lettres d'Axel Fersen à son père*
Young, Arthur: *Travels in France*, ed. by Constantin Maxwell
Zweig, Stefan: *Marie Antoinette*